THE SECRET SERVICE
KINGSMAN

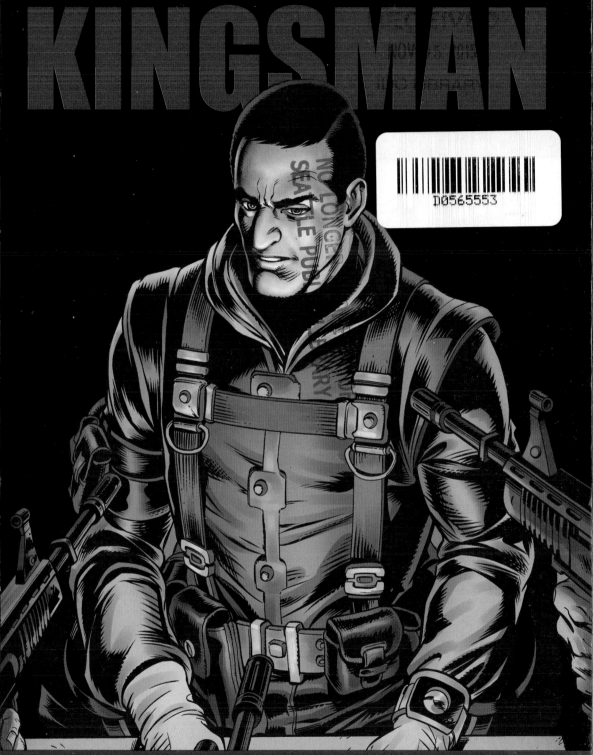

KINGSMAN: THE SECRET SERVICE (MOVIE EDITION). Contains material originally published in magazine form as THE SECRET SERVICE #1-6. First printing 2014. ISBN# 978-0-7851-9277-0. Published by MARVEL WORLDWIDE, INC., a subsidiary of MARVEL ENTERTAINMENT, LLC. OFFICE OF PUBLICATION: 135 West 50th Street, New York, NY 10020. Copyright © 2012, 2013 and 2014 Millarworld Limited, Dave Gibbons Ltd and Marv Films Limited. All rights reserved. THE SECRET SERVICE, the The Secret Service logo, and all characters featured in or on this issue and the distinctive names and likenesses thereof, and all related indicia are trademarks of Millarworld Limited and Dave Gibbons Ltd. MILLARWORLD and the Millarworld logos are trademarks of Millarworld Limited. "Icon" and the Icon logos are trademarks of Marvel Characters, Inc. No similarity between any of the names, characters, persons, and/or institutions in this magazine and those of any person or institution is intended, and any such similarity that may seem to exist is purely coincidental. This work may not be reproduced by any means without written consent from the authors, except in small amounts for journalistic or review purposes. Printed in the U.S.A. ALAN FINE, EVP - Office of the President, Marvel Worldwide, Inc. and EVP & CMO Marvel Characters B.V.; DAN BUCKLEY, Publisher & President - Print, Animation & Digital Divisions; JOE QUESADA, Chief Creative Officer; TOM BREVOORT, SVP of Publishing; DAVID BOGART, SVP of Operations & Procurement, Publishing; C.B. CEBULSKI, SVP of Creator & Content Development; DAVID GABRIEL, SVP Print, Sales & Marketing; JIM O'KEEFE, VP of Operations & Logistics; DAN CARR, Executive Director of Publishing Technology; SUSAN CRESPI, Editorial Operations Manager; ALEX MORALES, Publishing Operations Manager; STAN LEE, Chairman Emeritus. For information regarding advertising in Marvel Comics or on Marvel.com, please contact Niza Disla, Director of Marvel Partnerships, at ndisla@marvel.com. For Marvel subscription inquiries, please call 800-217-9158. Manufactured between 11/21/2014 and 12/28/2014 by R.R. DONNELLEY, INC., SALEM, VA, USA.

10 9 8 7 6 5 4 3 2 1

For my old school friend Eggsy, who cannot believe he's about to become the next James Bond, and for Russ, who helped me with so many wonderful set pieces for this story, most of which were inspired by his military experiences.

—Mark Millar

For the young Mark Millar, whose boyish ambition to work with me led, many years later, to such an enjoyable collaboration, and for Andy and Angus with thanks for all their help.

—Dave Gibbons

THE SECRET SERVICE
KINGSMAN

WRITER
MARK MILLAR

ARTIST
DAVE GIBBONS

CO-PLOTTER
MATTHEW VAUGHN

INKERS
DAVE GIBBONS (ISSUE 1)
ANDY LANNING (ISSUES 2-6)

COLORIST
ANGUS MCKIE

LETTERERS
DAVE GIBBONS
AND ANGUS MCKIE

ISSUE 1 VARIANT COVER
LEINIL FRANCIS YU
AND SUNNY GHO

THE SECRET SERVICE CREATED BY
MARK MILLAR, DAVE GIBBONS AND MATTHEW VAUGHN

Collection Editor: NICOLE BOOSE

Collection Designer: SPRING HOTELING

Production: MAYELA GUTIERREZ & IDETTE WINECOOR

Special Thanks: JENNIFER GRÜNWALD & JENNIFER LEE

SVP Print, Sales & Marketing: DAVID GABRIEL

SVP of Operations & Procurement, Publishing: DAVID BOGART

ONE

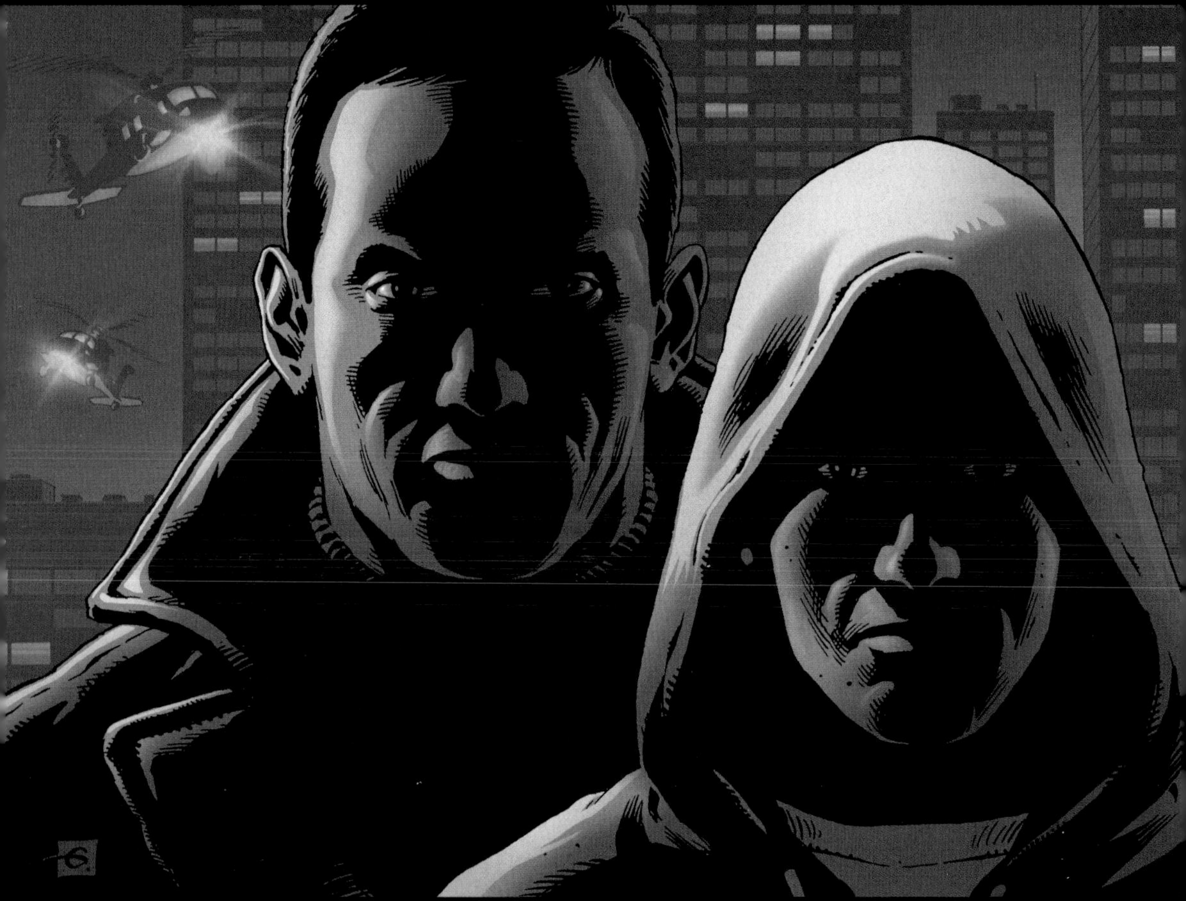

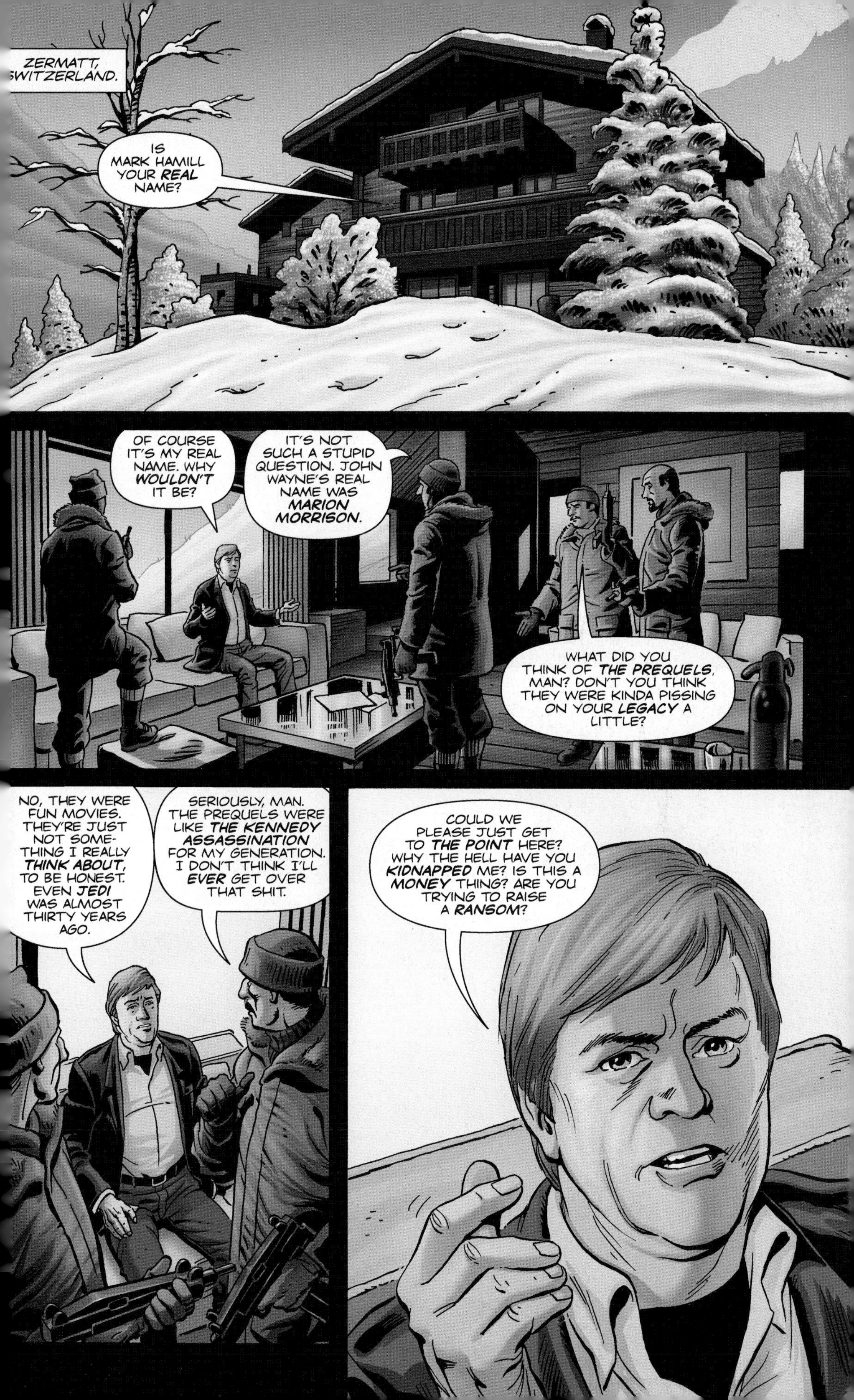
ZERMATT, SWITZERLAND.
IS MARK HAMILL YOUR REAL NAME?
OF COURSE IT'S MY REAL NAME. WHY WOULDN'T IT BE?
IT'S NOT SUCH A STUPID QUESTION. JOHN WAYNE'S REAL NAME WAS MARION MORRISON.
WHAT DID YOU THINK OF THE PREQUELS, MAN? DON'T YOU THINK THEY WERE KINDA PISSING ON YOUR LEGACY A LITTLE?
NO, THEY WERE FUN MOVIES. THEY'RE JUST NOT SOME-THING I REALLY THINK ABOUT, TO BE HONEST. EVEN JEDI WAS ALMOST THIRTY YEARS AGO.
SERIOUSLY, MAN. THE PREQUELS WERE LIKE THE KENNEDY ASSASSINATION FOR MY GENERATION. I DON'T THINK I'LL EVER GET OVER THAT SHIT.
COULD WE PLEASE JUST GET TO THE POINT HERE? WHY THE HELL HAVE YOU KIDNAPPED ME? IS THIS A MONEY THING? ARE YOU TRYING TO RAISE A RANSOM?

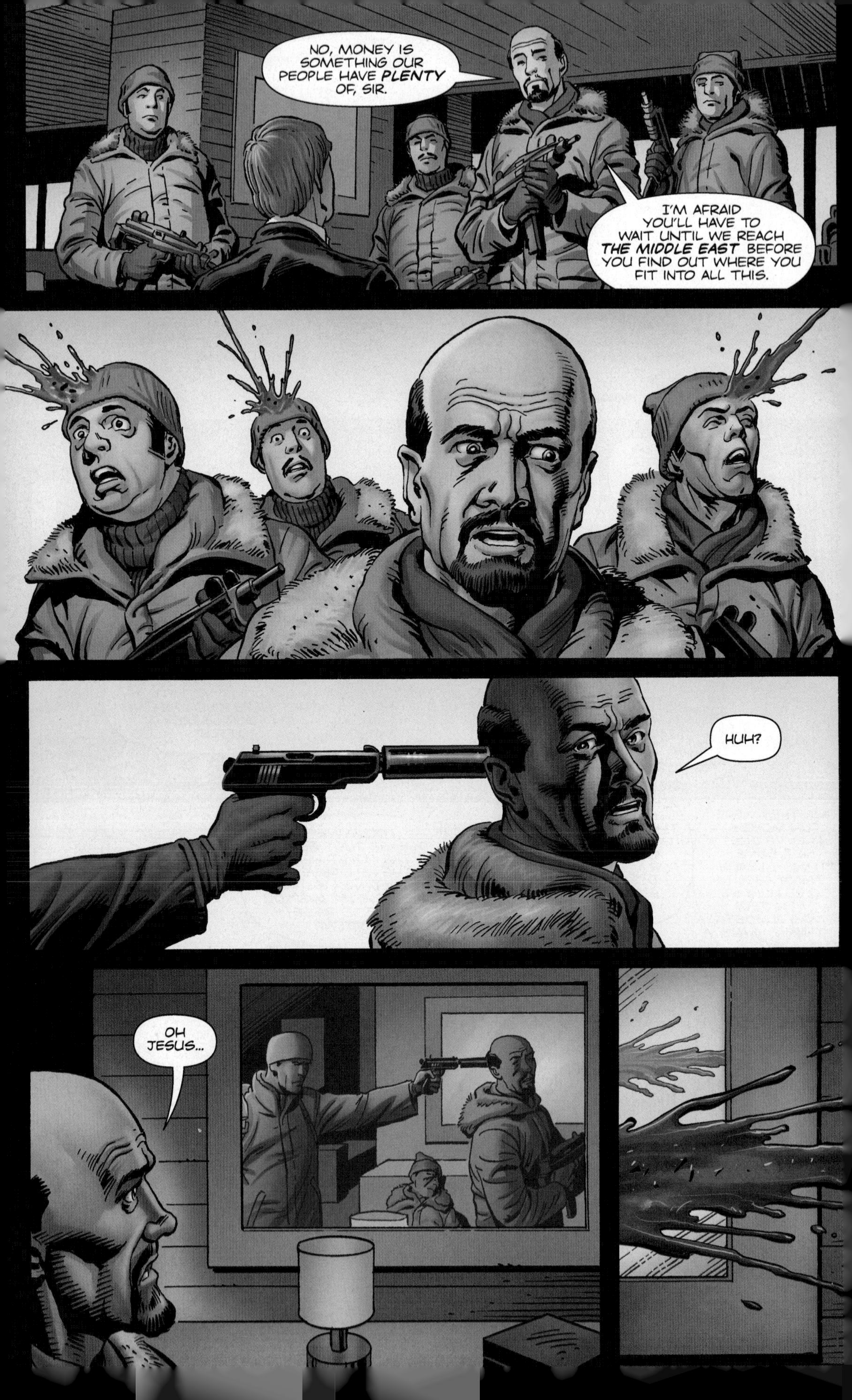
NO, MONEY IS SOMETHING OUR PEOPLE HAVE PLENTY OF, SIR.
I'M AFRAID YOU'LL HAVE TO WAIT UNTIL WE REACH THE MIDDLE EAST BEFORE YOU FIND OUT WHERE YOU FIT INTO ALL THIS.
HUH?
OH JESUS...

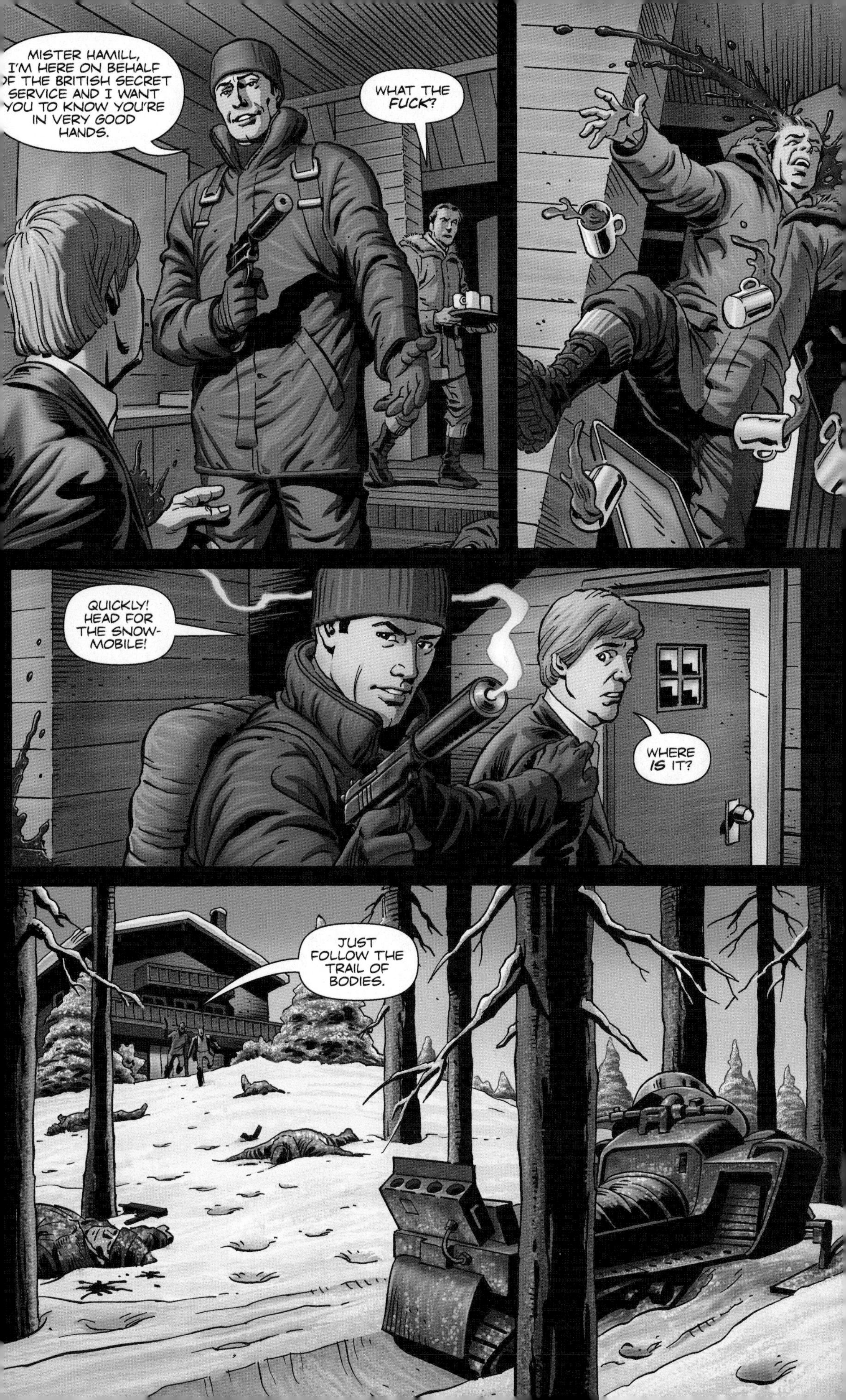
MISTER HAMILL, I'M HERE ON BEHALF OF THE BRITISH SECRET SERVICE AND I WANT YOU TO KNOW YOU'RE IN VERY GOOD HANDS.
WHAT THE FUCK?
QUICKLY! HEAD FOR THE SNOW-MOBILE!
WHERE IS IT?
JUST FOLLOW THE TRAIL OF BODIES.

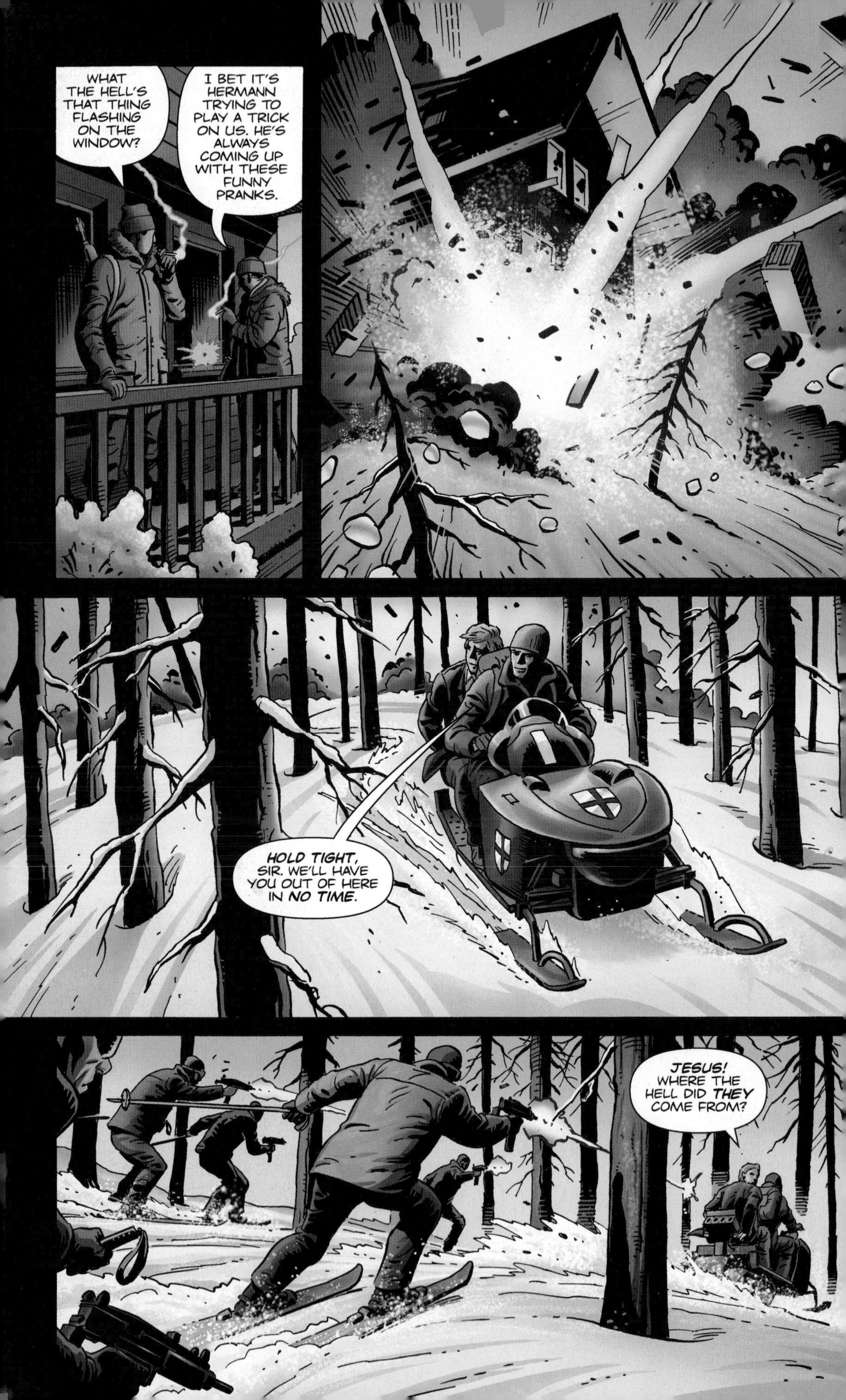
WHAT THE HELL'S THAT THING FLASHING ON THE WINDOW?
I BET IT'S HERMANN TRYING TO PLAY A TRICK ON US. HE'S ALWAYS COMING UP WITH THESE FUNNY PRANKS.
HOLD TIGHT, SIR. WE'LL HAVE YOU OUT OF HERE IN NO TIME.
JESUS! WHERE THE HELL DID THEY COME FROM?

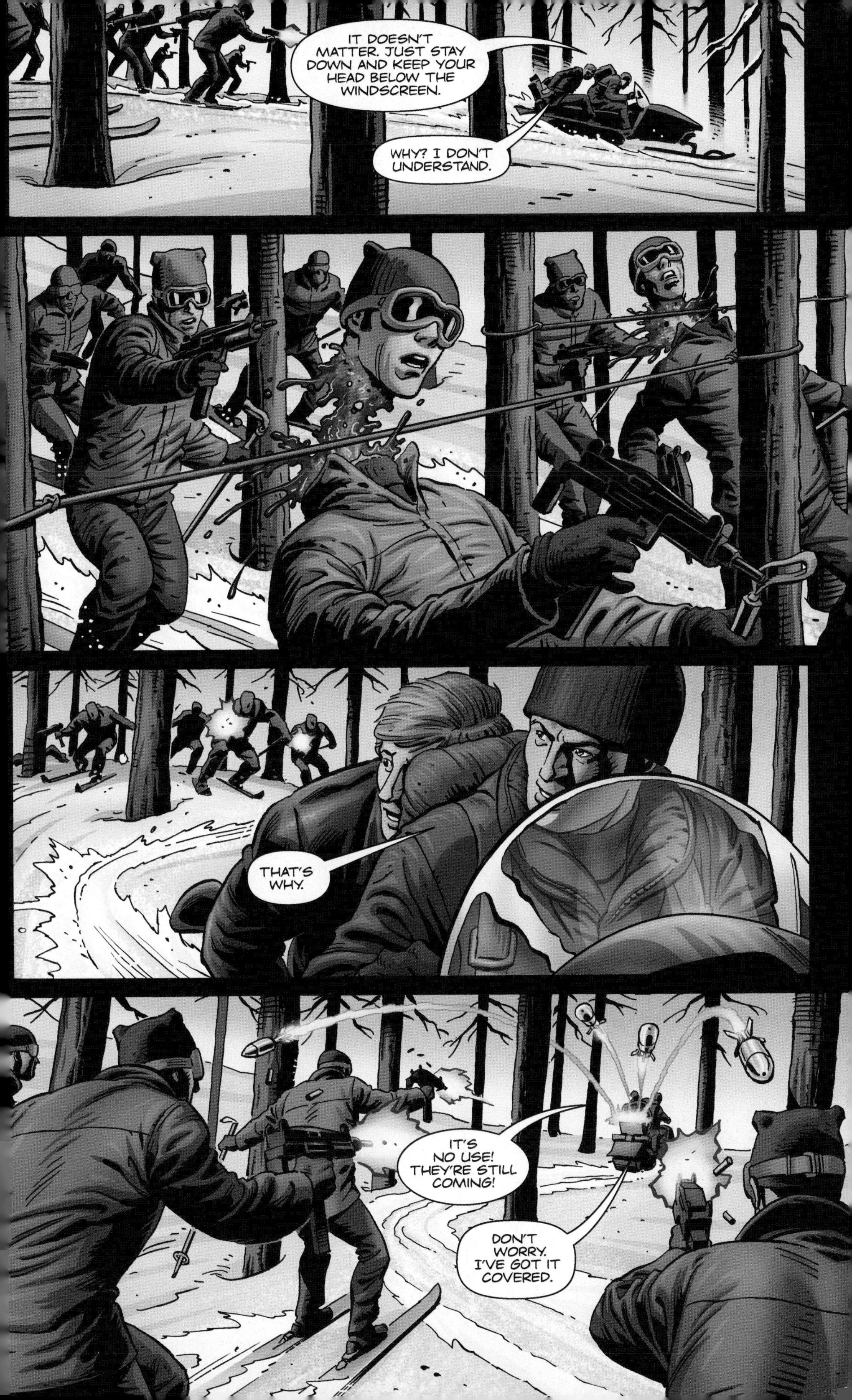
IT DOESN'T MATTER. JUST STAY DOWN AND KEEP YOUR HEAD BELOW THE WINDSCREEN.
WHY? I DON'T UNDERSTAND.
THAT'S WHY.
IT'S NO USE! THEY'RE STILL COMING!
DON'T WORRY. I'VE GOT IT COVERED.

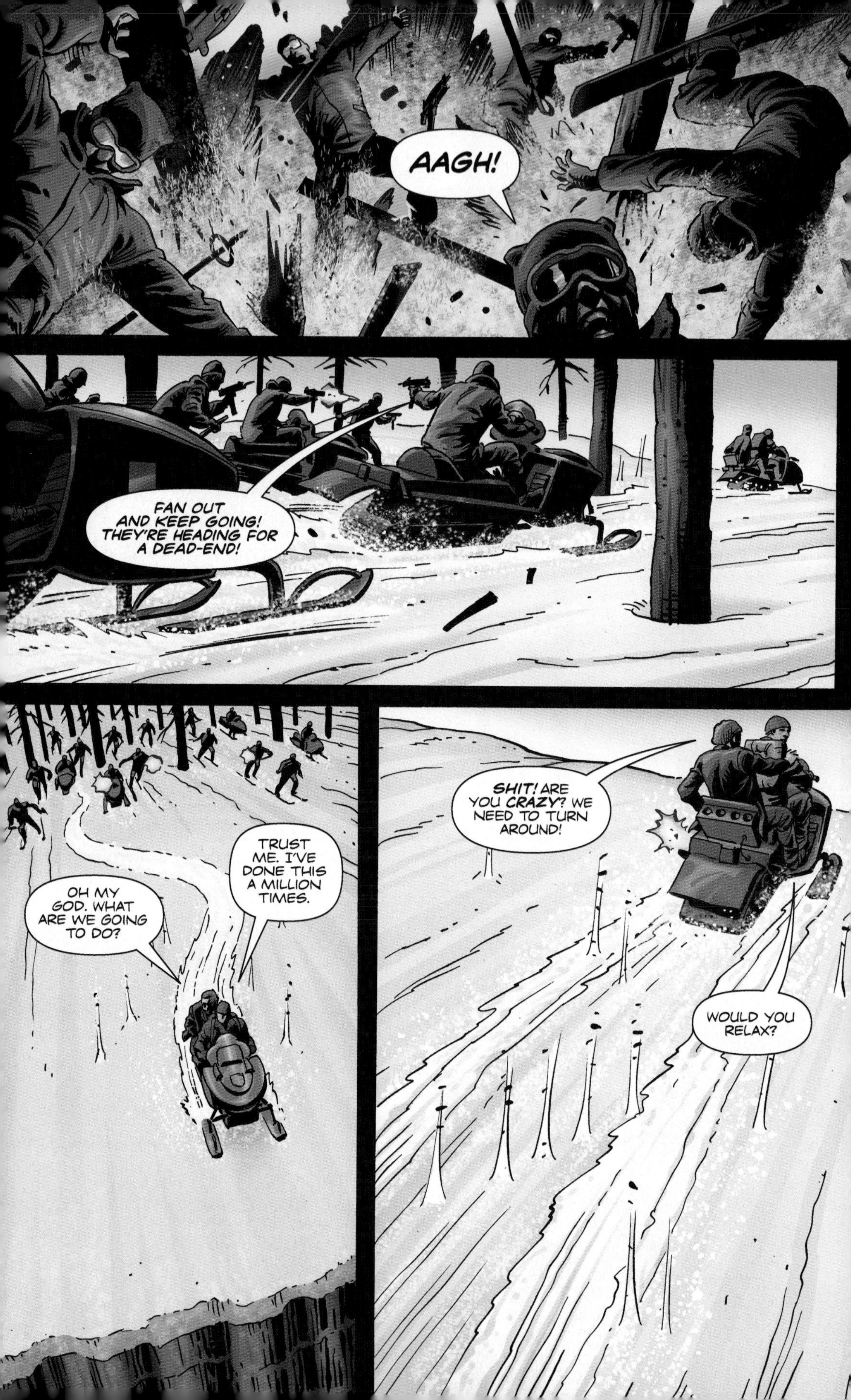
AAGH!
FAN OUT AND KEEP GOING! THEY'RE HEADING FOR A DEAD-END!
OH MY GOD. WHAT ARE WE GOING TO DO?
TRUST ME. I'VE DONE THIS A MILLION TIMES.
SHIT! ARE YOU CRAZY? WE NEED TO TURN AROUND!
WOULD YOU RELAX?

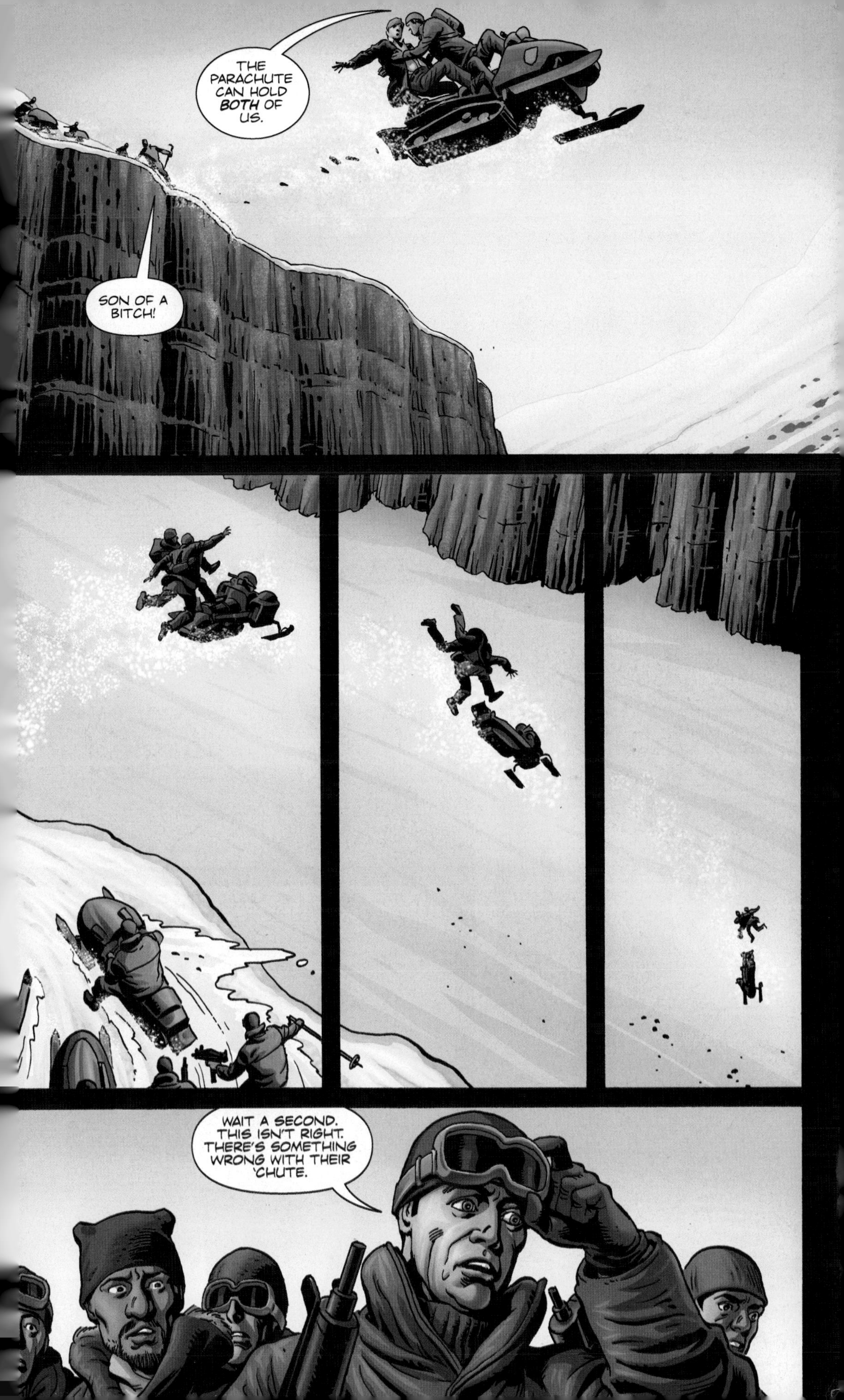
THE PARACHUTE CAN HOLD BOTH OF US.
SON OF A BITCH!
WAIT A SECOND. THIS ISN'T RIGHT. THERE'S SOMETHING WRONG WITH THEIR 'CHUTE.

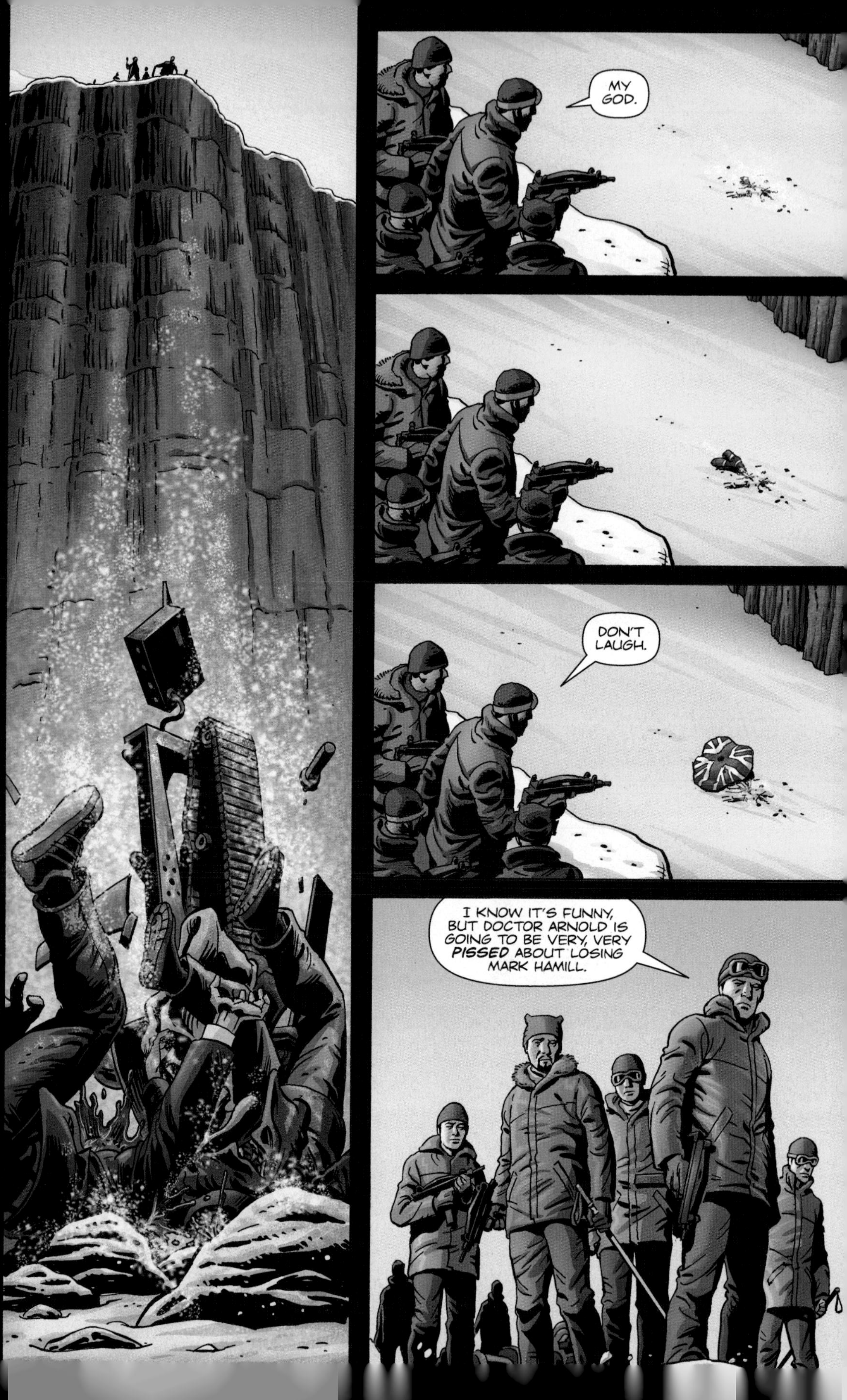
MY GOD.
DON'T LAUGH.
I KNOW IT'S FUNNY, BUT DOCTOR ARNOLD IS GOING TO BE VERY, VERY *PISSED* ABOUT LOSING MARK HAMILL.

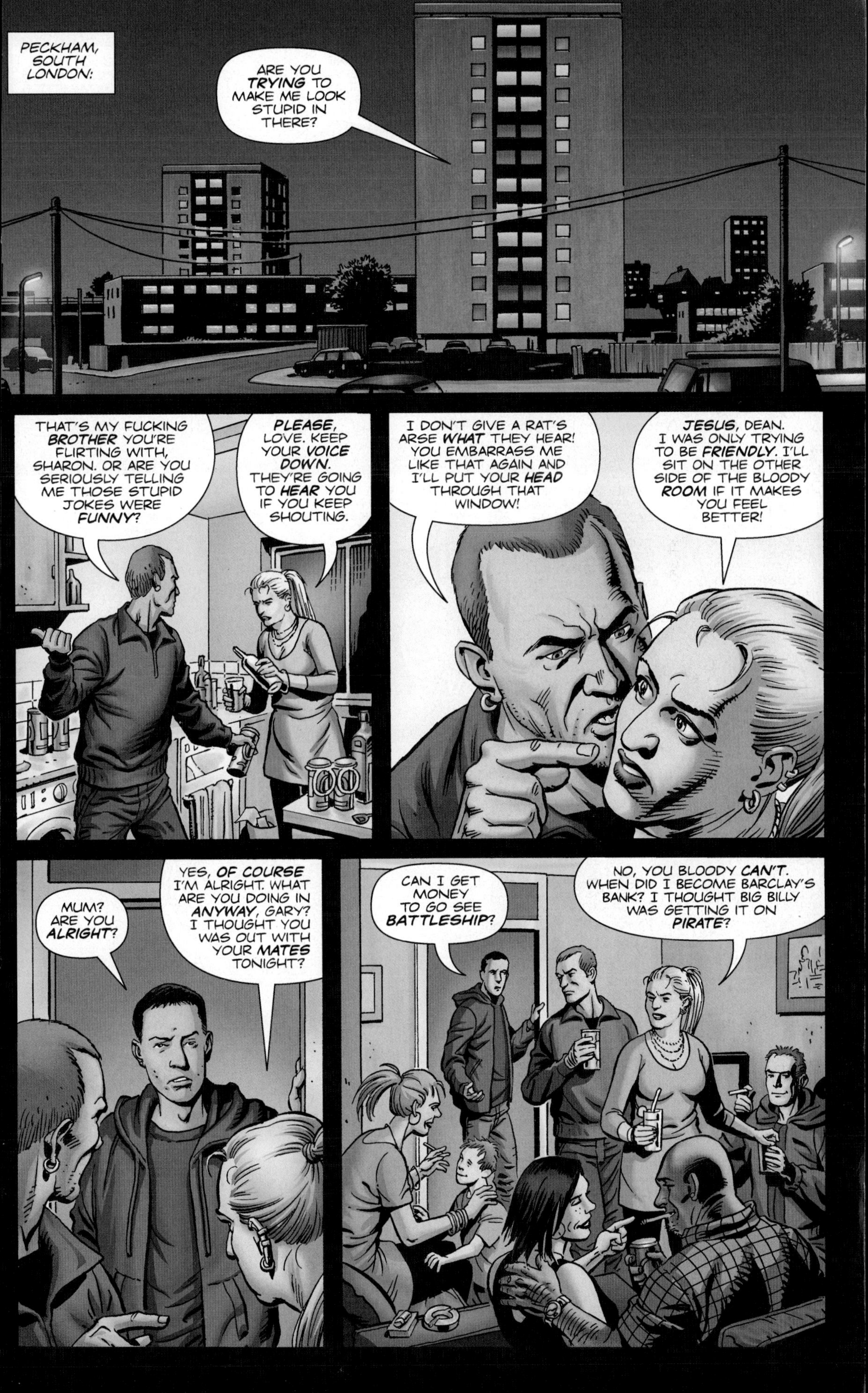
PECKHAM, SOUTH LONDON:
ARE YOU TRYING TO MAKE ME LOOK STUPID IN THERE?
THAT'S MY FUCKING BROTHER YOU'RE FLIRTING WITH, SHARON. OR ARE YOU SERIOUSLY TELLING ME THOSE STUPID JOKES WERE FUNNY?
PLEASE, LOVE. KEEP YOUR VOICE DOWN. THEY'RE GOING TO HEAR YOU IF YOU KEEP SHOUTING.
I DON'T GIVE A RAT'S ARSE WHAT THEY HEAR! YOU EMBARRASS ME LIKE THAT AGAIN AND I'LL PUT YOUR HEAD THROUGH THAT WINDOW!
JESUS, DEAN. I WAS ONLY TRYING TO BE FRIENDLY. I'LL SIT ON THE OTHER SIDE OF THE BLOODY ROOM IF IT MAKES YOU FEEL BETTER!
MUM? ARE YOU ALRIGHT?
YES, OF COURSE I'M ALRIGHT. WHAT ARE YOU DOING IN ANYWAY, GARY? I THOUGHT YOU WAS OUT WITH YOUR MATES TONIGHT?
CAN I GET MONEY TO GO SEE BATTLESHIP?
NO, YOU BLOODY CAN'T. WHEN DID I BECOME BARCLAY'S BANK? I THOUGHT BIG BILLY WAS GETTING IT ON PIRATE?

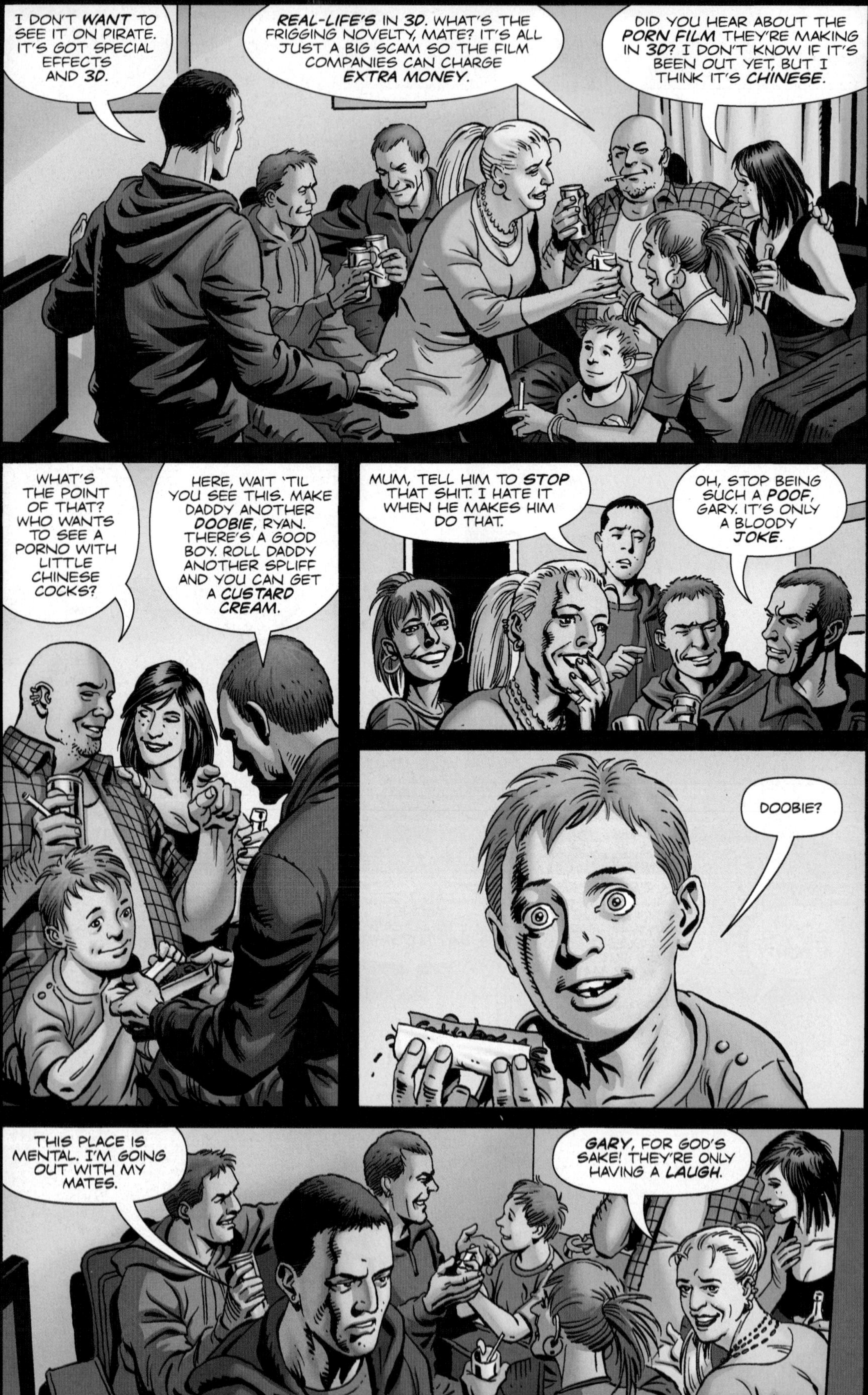
I DON'T WANT TO SEE IT ON PIRATE. IT'S GOT SPECIAL EFFECTS AND 3D.
REAL-LIFE'S IN 3D. WHAT'S THE FRIGGING NOVELTY, MATE? IT'S ALL JUST A BIG SCAM SO THE FILM COMPANIES CAN CHARGE EXTRA MONEY.
DID YOU HEAR ABOUT THE PORN FILM THEY'RE MAKING IN 3D? I DON'T KNOW IF IT'S BEEN OUT YET, BUT I THINK IT'S CHINESE.
WHAT'S THE POINT OF THAT? WHO WANTS TO SEE A PORNO WITH LITTLE CHINESE COCKS?
HERE, WAIT 'TIL YOU SEE THIS. MAKE DADDY ANOTHER DOOBIE, RYAN. THERE'S A GOOD BOY. ROLL DADDY ANOTHER SPLIFF AND YOU CAN GET A CUSTARD CREAM.
MUM, TELL HIM TO STOP THAT SHIT. I HATE IT WHEN HE MAKES HIM DO THAT.
OH, STOP BEING SUCH A POOF, GARY. IT'S ONLY A BLOODY JOKE.
DOOBIE?
THIS PLACE IS MENTAL. I'M GOING OUT WITH MY MATES.
GARY, FOR GOD'S SAKE! THEY'RE ONLY HAVING A LAUGH.

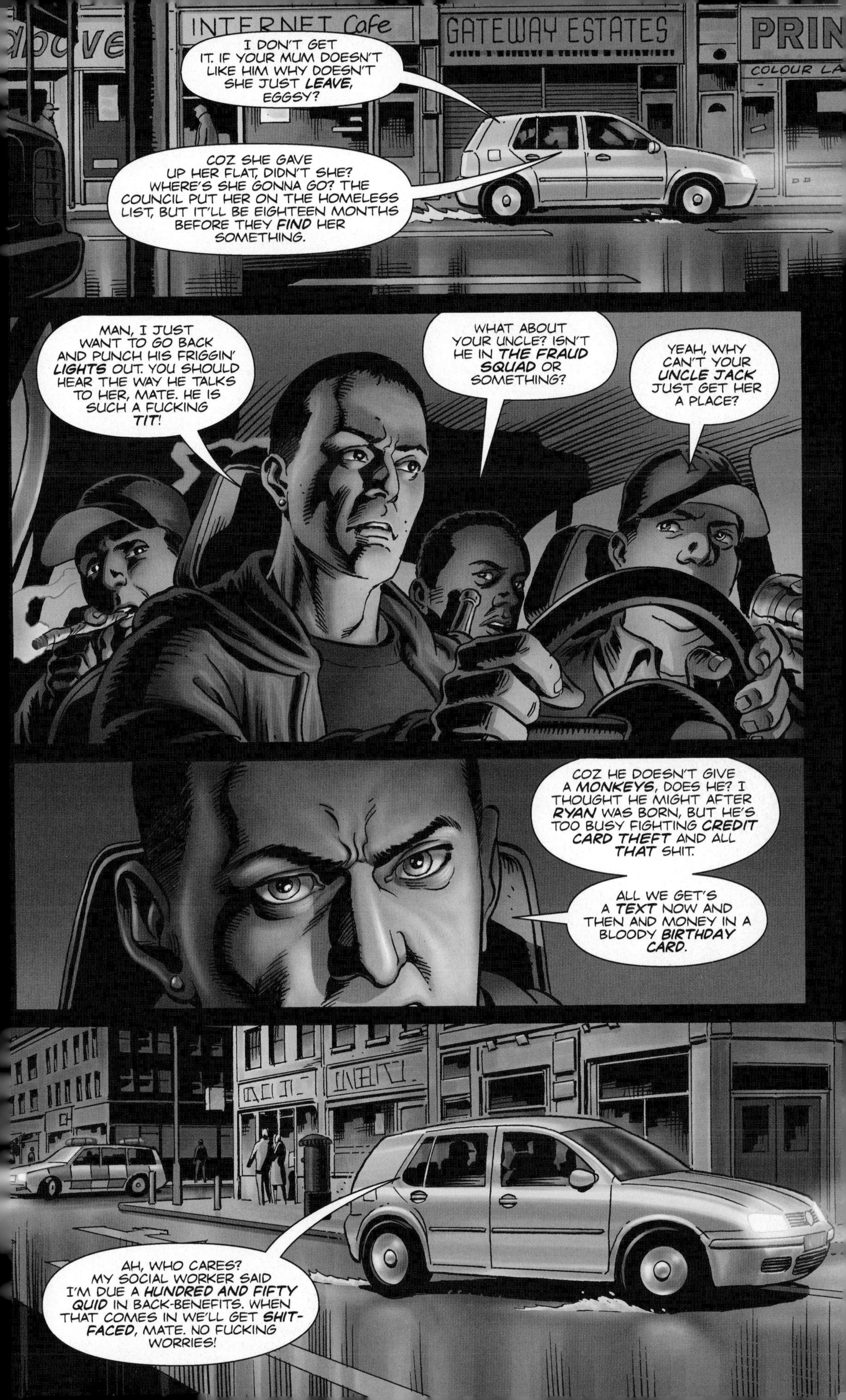
INTERNET Cafe
GATEWAY ESTATES
I DON'T GET IT. IF YOUR MUM DOESN'T LIKE HIM WHY DOESN'T SHE JUST *LEAVE,* EGGSY?
COZ SHE GAVE UP HER FLAT, DIDN'T SHE? WHERE'S SHE GONNA GO? THE COUNCIL PUT HER ON THE HOMELESS LIST, BUT IT'LL BE EIGHTEEN MONTHS BEFORE THEY *FIND* HER SOMETHING.
MAN, I JUST WANT TO GO BACK AND PUNCH HIS FRIGGIN' *LIGHTS* OUT. YOU SHOULD HEAR THE WAY HE TALKS TO HER, MATE. HE IS SUCH A FUCKING *TIT*!
WHAT ABOUT YOUR UNCLE? ISN'T HE IN *THE FRAUD SQUAD* OR SOMETHING?
YEAH, WHY CAN'T YOUR *UNCLE JACK* JUST GET HER A PLACE?
COZ HE DOESN'T GIVE A *MONKEYS*, DOES HE? I THOUGHT HE MIGHT AFTER *RYAN* WAS BORN, BUT HE'S TOO BUSY FIGHTING *CREDIT CARD THEFT* AND ALL *THAT* SHIT.
ALL WE GET'S A *TEXT* NOW AND THEN AND MONEY IN A BLOODY *BIRTHDAY CARD*.
AH, WHO CARES? MY SOCIAL WORKER SAID I'M DUE A *HUNDRED AND FIFTY QUID* IN BACK-BENEFITS. WHEN THAT COMES IN WE'LL GET *SHIT-FACED*, MATE. NO FUCKING WORRIES!

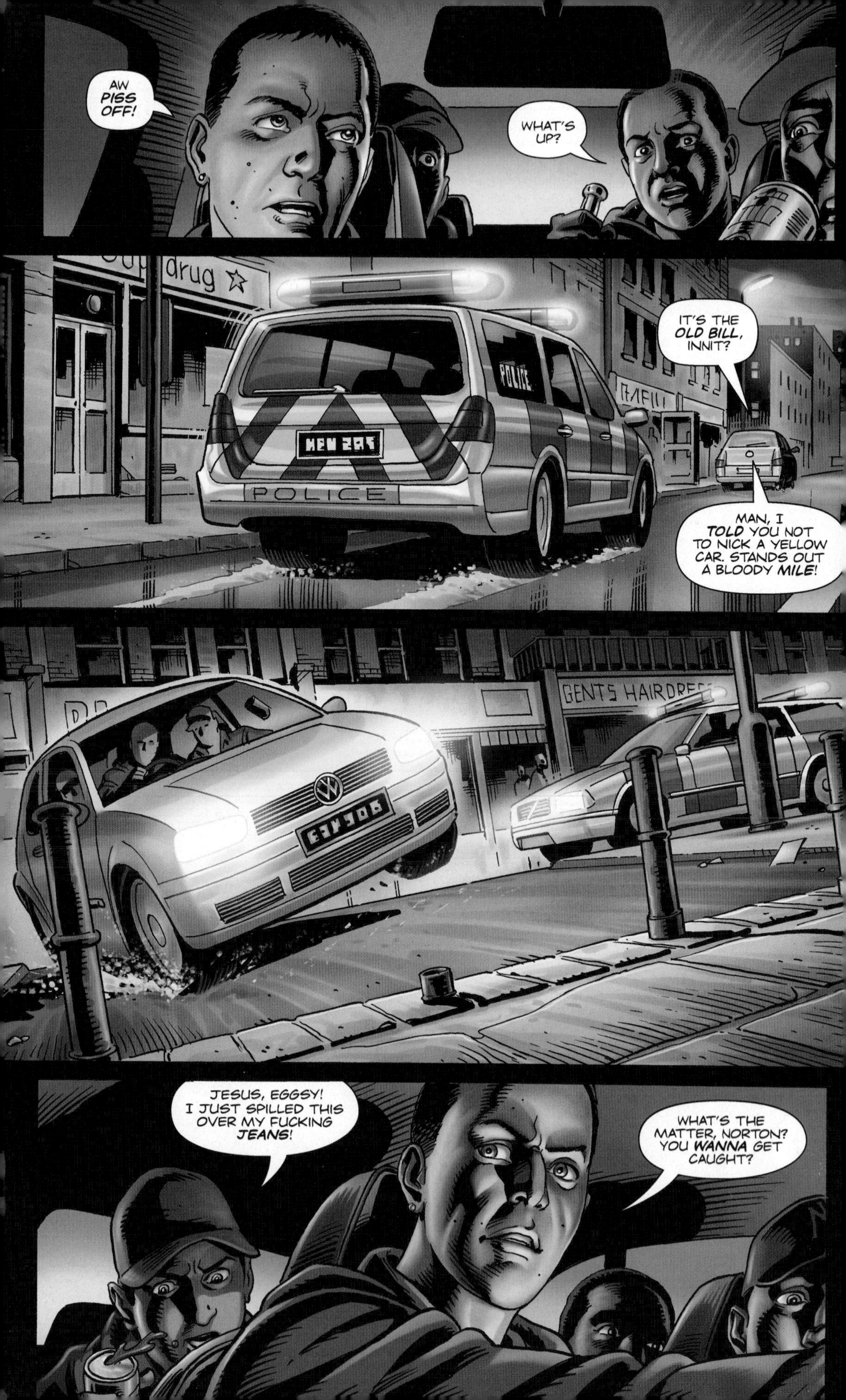
AW PISS OFF!
WHAT'S UP?
POLICE
NEW 285
POLICE
IT'S THE OLD BILL, INNIT?
MAN, I TOLD YOU NOT TO NICK A YELLOW CAR. STANDS OUT A BLOODY MILE!
GENTS HAIRDRE
JESUS, EGGSY! I JUST SPILLED THIS OVER MY FUCKING JEANS!
WHAT'S THE MATTER, NORTON? YOU WANNA GET CAUGHT?

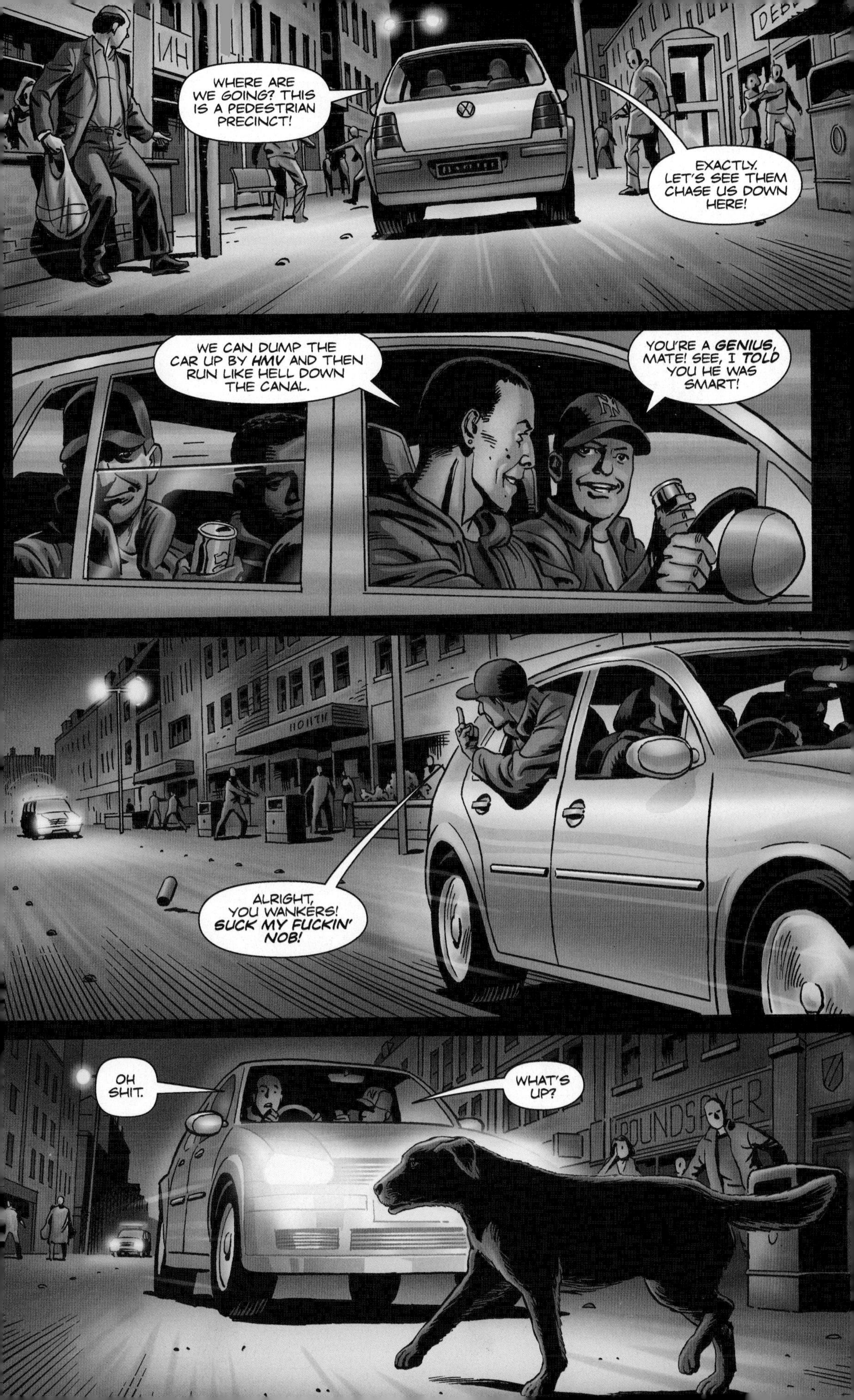
WHERE ARE WE GOING? THIS IS A PEDESTRIAN PRECINCT!
EXACTLY. LET'S SEE THEM CHASE US DOWN HERE!
WE CAN DUMP THE CAR UP BY **HMV** AND THEN RUN LIKE HELL DOWN THE CANAL.
YOU'RE A **GENIUS**, MATE! SEE, I **TOLD** YOU HE WAS SMART!
ALRIGHT, YOU WANKERS! **SUCK MY FUCKIN' NOB!**
OH SHIT.
WHAT'S UP?
POUNDSAVER

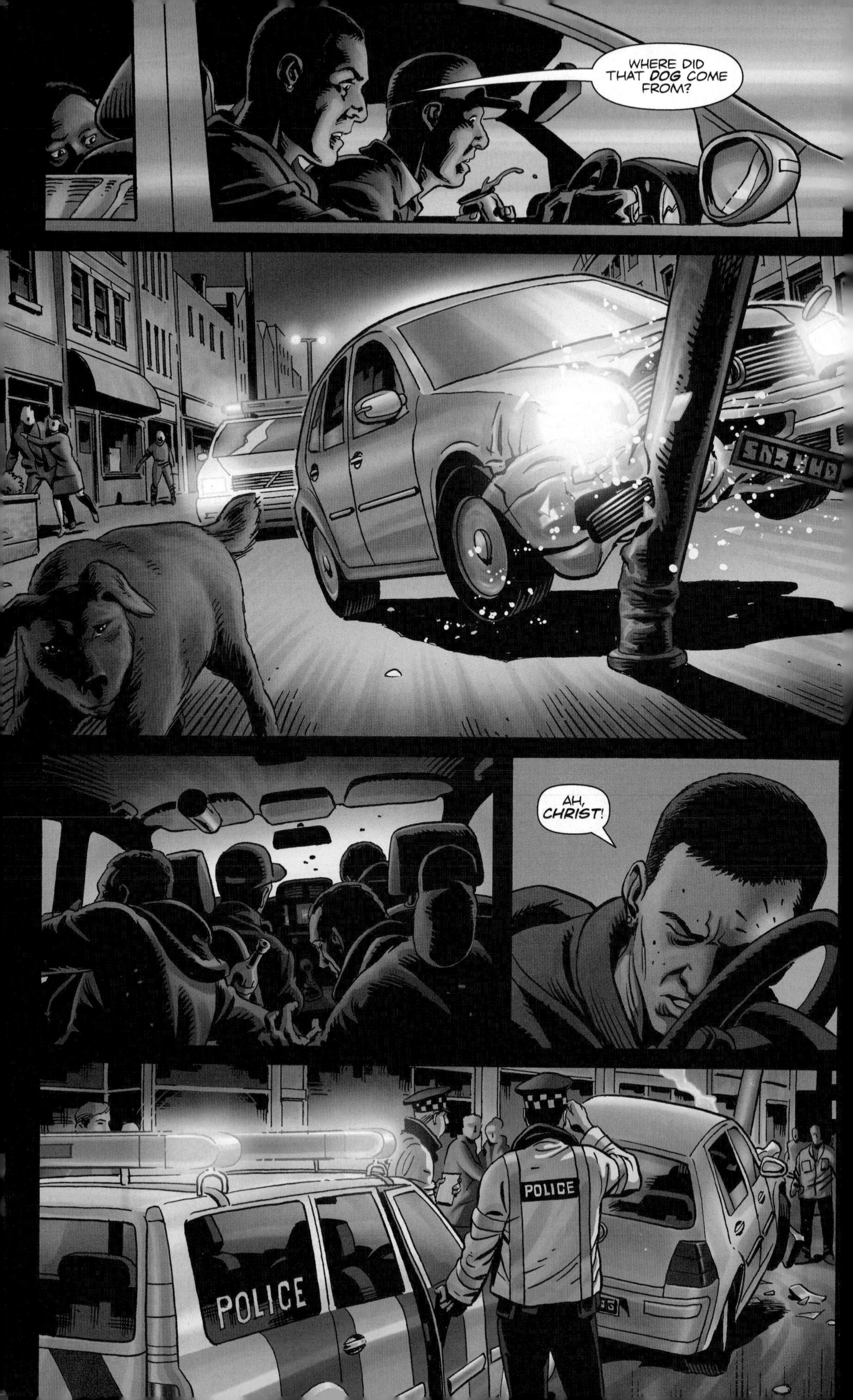
WHERE DID THAT *DOG* COME FROM?
AH, *CHRIST!*
POLICE
POLICE

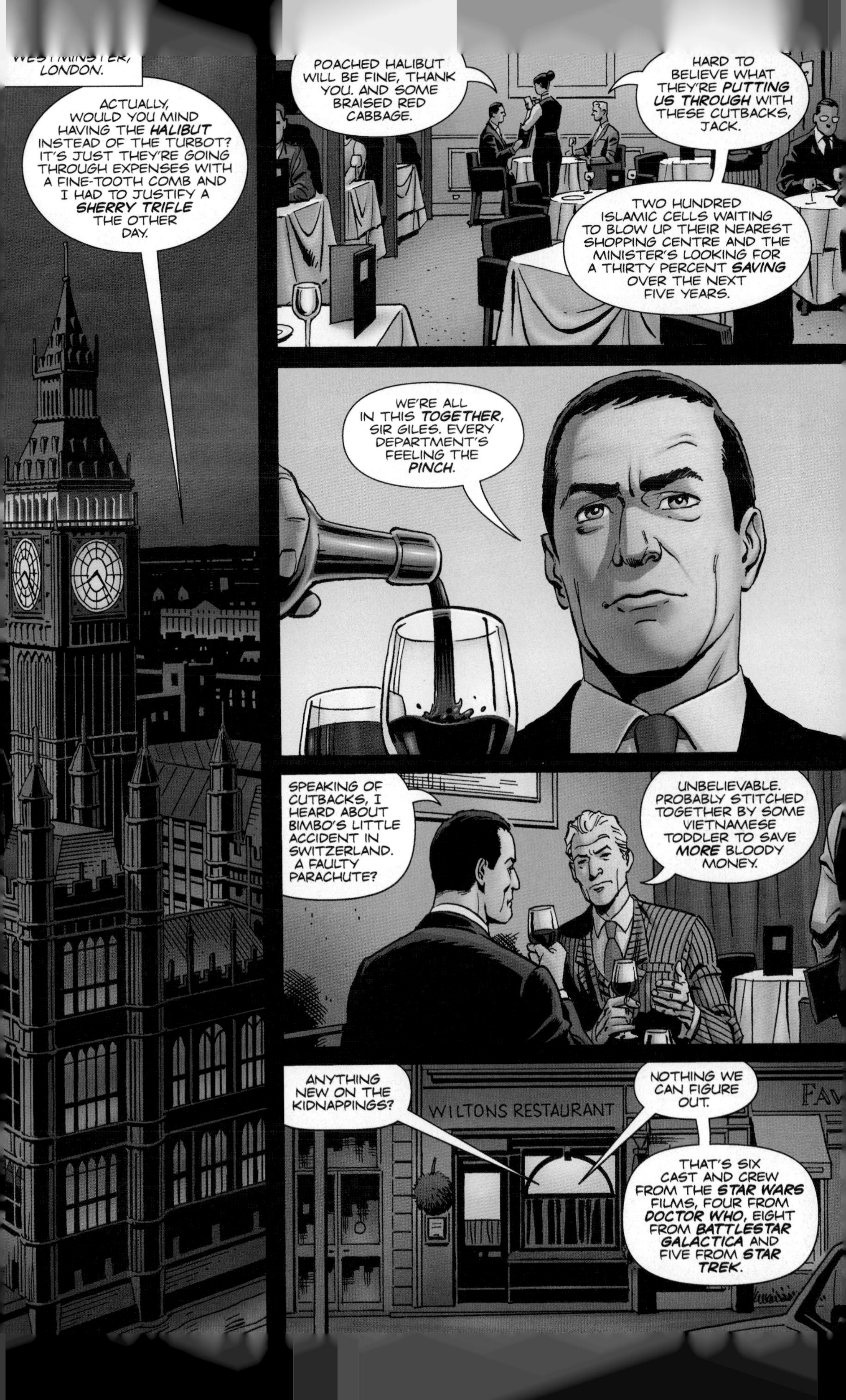
WESTMINSTER, LONDON.
ACTUALLY, WOULD YOU MIND HAVING THE HALIBUT INSTEAD OF THE TURBOT? IT'S JUST THEY'RE GOING THROUGH EXPENSES WITH A FINE-TOOTH COMB AND I HAD TO JUSTIFY A SHERRY TRIFLE THE OTHER DAY.
POACHED HALIBUT WILL BE FINE, THANK YOU. AND SOME BRAISED RED CABBAGE.
HARD TO BELIEVE WHAT THEY'RE PUTTING US THROUGH WITH THESE CUTBACKS, JACK.
TWO HUNDRED ISLAMIC CELLS WAITING TO BLOW UP THEIR NEAREST SHOPPING CENTRE AND THE MINISTER'S LOOKING FOR A THIRTY PERCENT SAVING OVER THE NEXT FIVE YEARS.
WE'RE ALL IN THIS TOGETHER, SIR GILES. EVERY DEPARTMENT'S FEELING THE PINCH.
SPEAKING OF CUTBACKS, I HEARD ABOUT BIMBO'S LITTLE ACCIDENT IN SWITZERLAND. A FAULTY PARACHUTE?
UNBELIEVABLE. PROBABLY STITCHED TOGETHER BY SOME VIETNAMESE TODDLER TO SAVE MORE BLOODY MONEY.
WILTONS RESTAURANT
ANYTHING NEW ON THE KIDNAPPINGS?
NOTHING WE CAN FIGURE OUT.
THAT'S SIX CAST AND CREW FROM THE STAR WARS FILMS, FOUR FROM DOCTOR WHO, EIGHT FROM BATTLESTAR GALACTICA AND FIVE FROM STAR TREK.

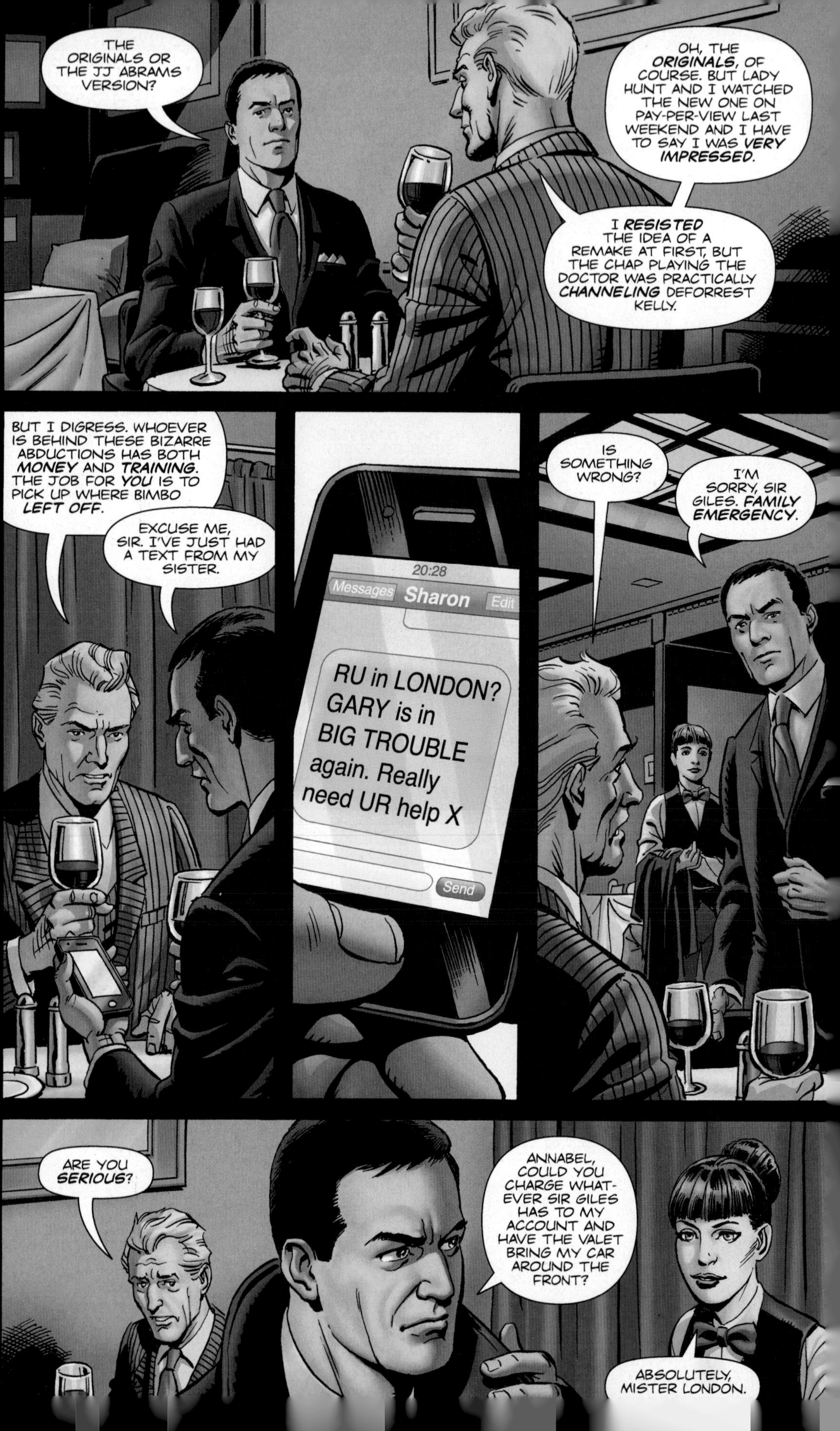
THE ORIGINALS OR THE JJ ABRAMS VERSION?
OH, THE ORIGINALS, OF COURSE. BUT LADY HUNT AND I WATCHED THE NEW ONE ON PAY-PER-VIEW LAST WEEKEND AND I HAVE TO SAY I WAS VERY IMPRESSED.
I RESISTED THE IDEA OF A REMAKE AT FIRST, BUT THE CHAP PLAYING THE DOCTOR WAS PRACTICALLY CHANNELING DEFORREST KELLY.
BUT I DIGRESS. WHOEVER IS BEHIND THESE BIZARRE ABDUCTIONS HAS BOTH MONEY AND TRAINING. THE JOB FOR YOU IS TO PICK UP WHERE BIMBO LEFT OFF.
EXCUSE ME, SIR. I'VE JUST HAD A TEXT FROM MY SISTER.
20:28
Messages
Sharon
Edit
RU in LONDON? GARY is in BIG TROUBLE again. Really need UR help X
Send
IS SOMETHING WRONG?
I'M SORRY, SIR GILES. FAMILY EMERGENCY.
ARE YOU SERIOUS?
ANNABEL, COULD YOU CHARGE WHAT-EVER SIR GILES HAS TO MY ACCOUNT AND HAVE THE VALET BRING MY CAR AROUND THE FRONT?
ABSOLUTELY, MISTER LONDON.

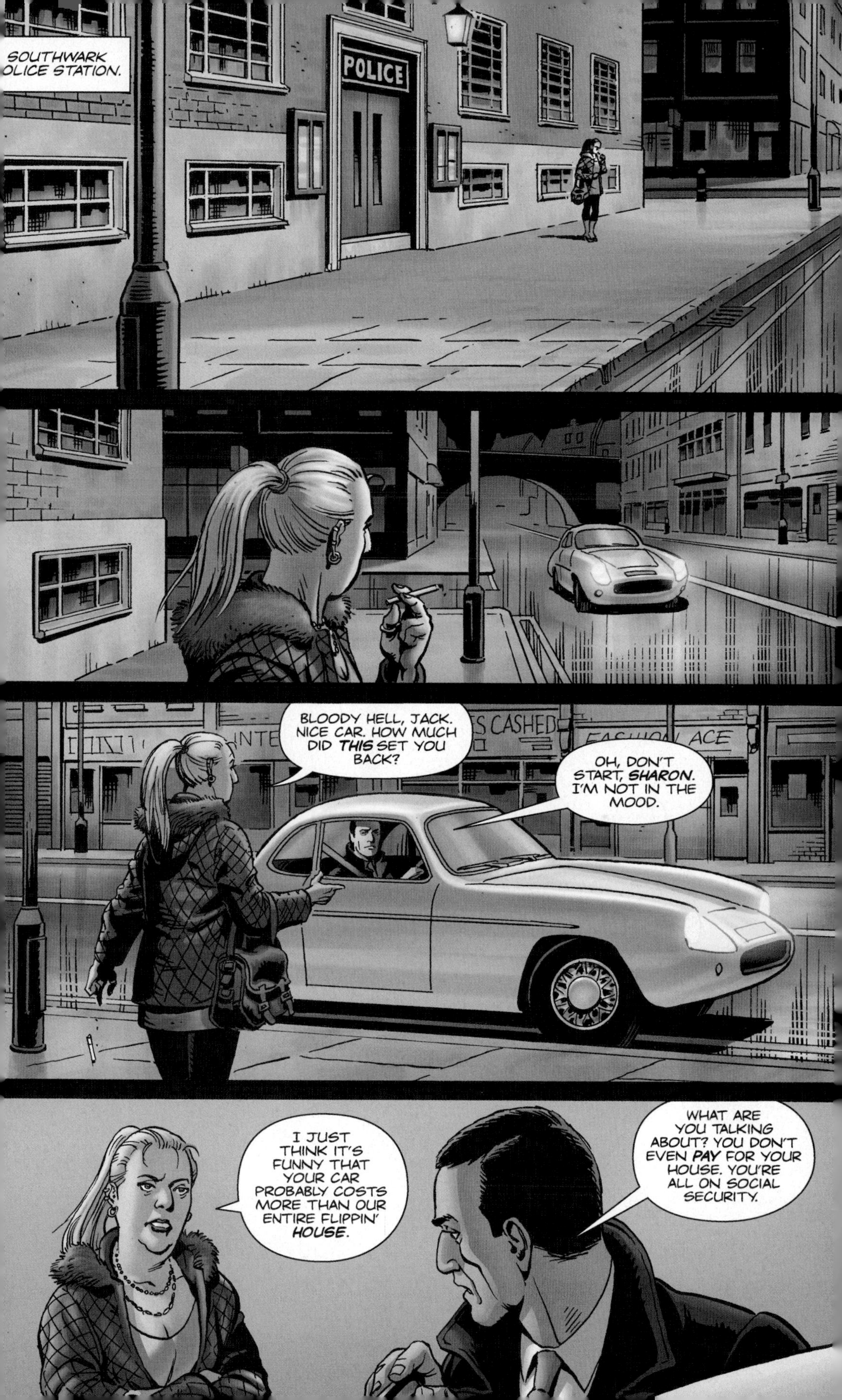
SOUTHWARK
OLICE STATION.
POLICE
BLOODY HELL, JACK. NICE CAR. HOW MUCH DID THIS SET YOU BACK?
OH, DON'T START, SHARON. I'M NOT IN THE MOOD.
I JUST THINK IT'S FUNNY THAT YOUR CAR PROBABLY COSTS MORE THAN OUR ENTIRE FLIPPIN' HOUSE.
WHAT ARE YOU TALKING ABOUT? YOU DON'T EVEN PAY FOR YOUR HOUSE. YOU'RE ALL ON SOCIAL SECURITY.

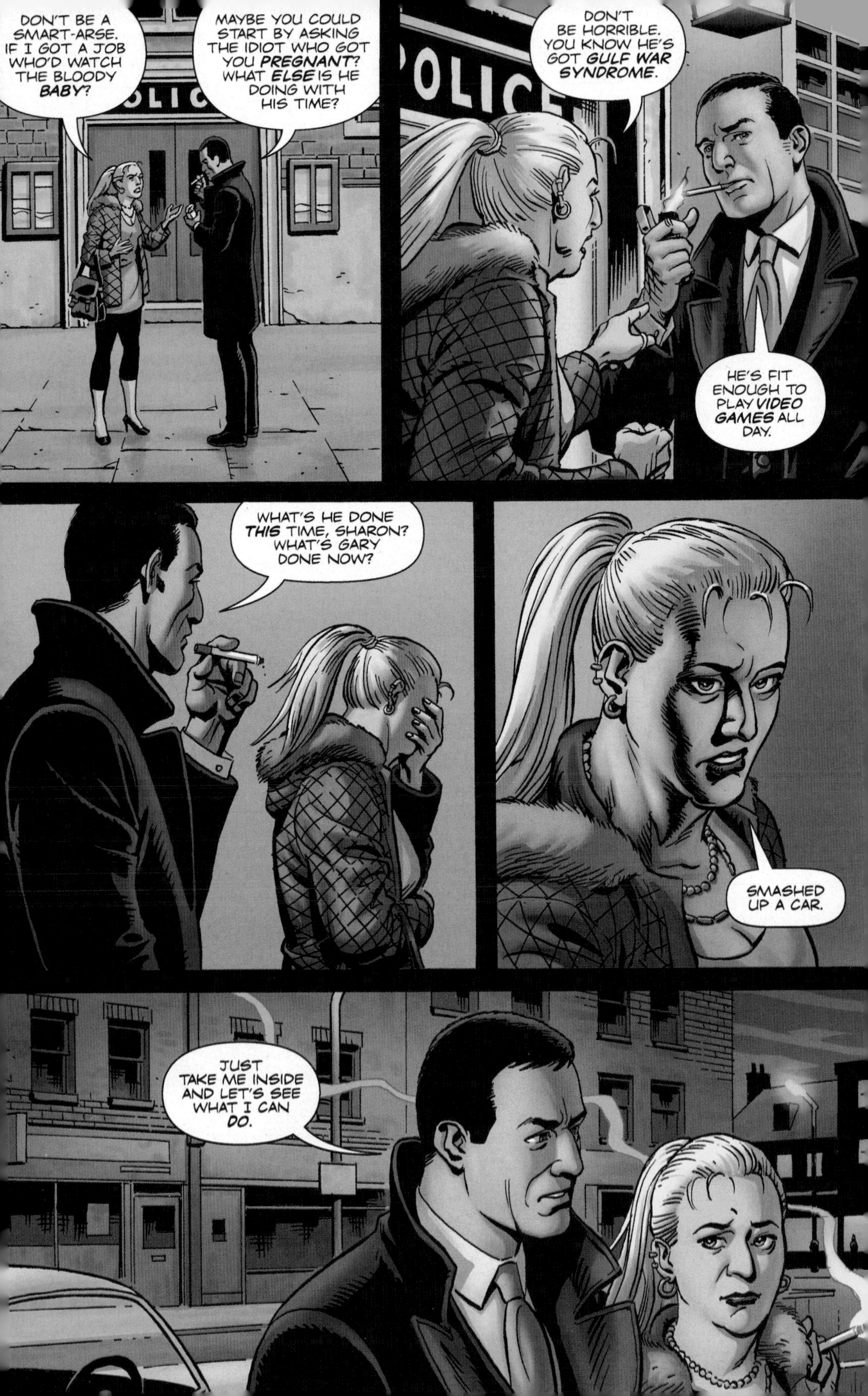

POLICE
DON'T BE A SMART-ARSE. IF I GOT A JOB WHO'D WATCH THE BLOODY **BABY**?
MAYBE YOU COULD START BY ASKING THE IDIOT WHO GOT YOU **PREGNANT**? WHAT **ELSE** IS HE DOING WITH HIS TIME?
DON'T BE HORRIBLE. YOU KNOW HE'S GOT **GULF WAR SYNDROME**.
HE'S FIT ENOUGH TO PLAY **VIDEO GAMES** ALL DAY.
WHAT'S HE DONE **THIS** TIME, SHARON? WHAT'S GARY DONE NOW?
SMASHED UP A CAR.
JUST TAKE ME INSIDE AND LET'S SEE WHAT I CAN **DO**.

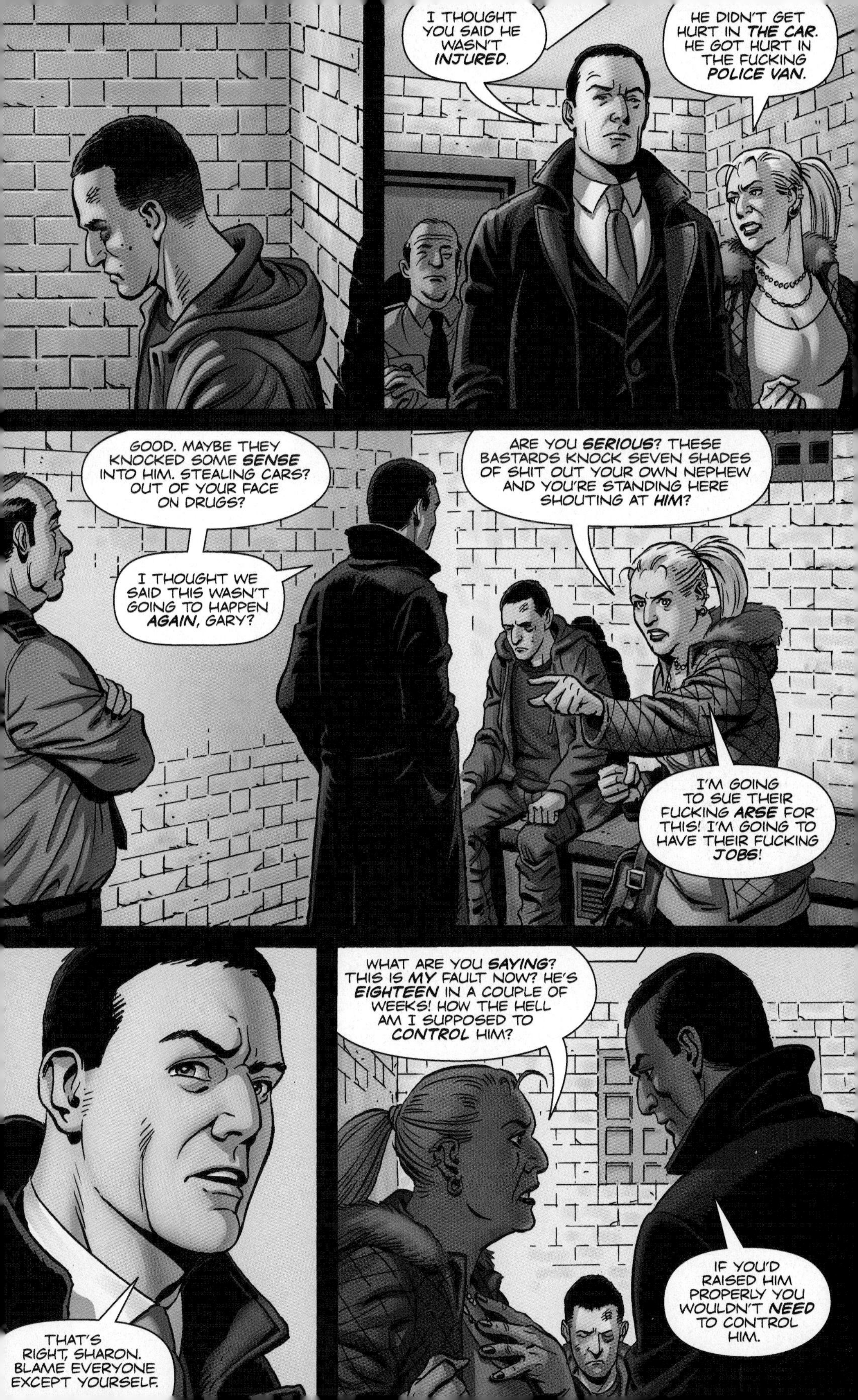

I THOUGHT YOU SAID HE WASN'T INJURED.
HE DIDN'T GET HURT IN THE CAR. HE GOT HURT IN THE FUCKING POLICE VAN.
GOOD. MAYBE THEY KNOCKED SOME SENSE INTO HIM. STEALING CARS? OUT OF YOUR FACE ON DRUGS?
I THOUGHT WE SAID THIS WASN'T GOING TO HAPPEN AGAIN, GARY?
ARE YOU SERIOUS? THESE BASTARDS KNOCK SEVEN SHADES OF SHIT OUT YOUR OWN NEPHEW AND YOU'RE STANDING HERE SHOUTING AT HIM?
I'M GOING TO SUE THEIR FUCKING ARSE FOR THIS! I'M GOING TO HAVE THEIR FUCKING JOBS!
THAT'S RIGHT, SHARON. BLAME EVERYONE EXCEPT YOURSELF.
WHAT ARE YOU SAYING? THIS IS MY FAULT NOW? HE'S EIGHTEEN IN A COUPLE OF WEEKS! HOW THE HELL AM I SUPPOSED TO CONTROL HIM?
IF YOU'D RAISED HIM PROPERLY YOU WOULDN'T NEED TO CONTROL HIM.

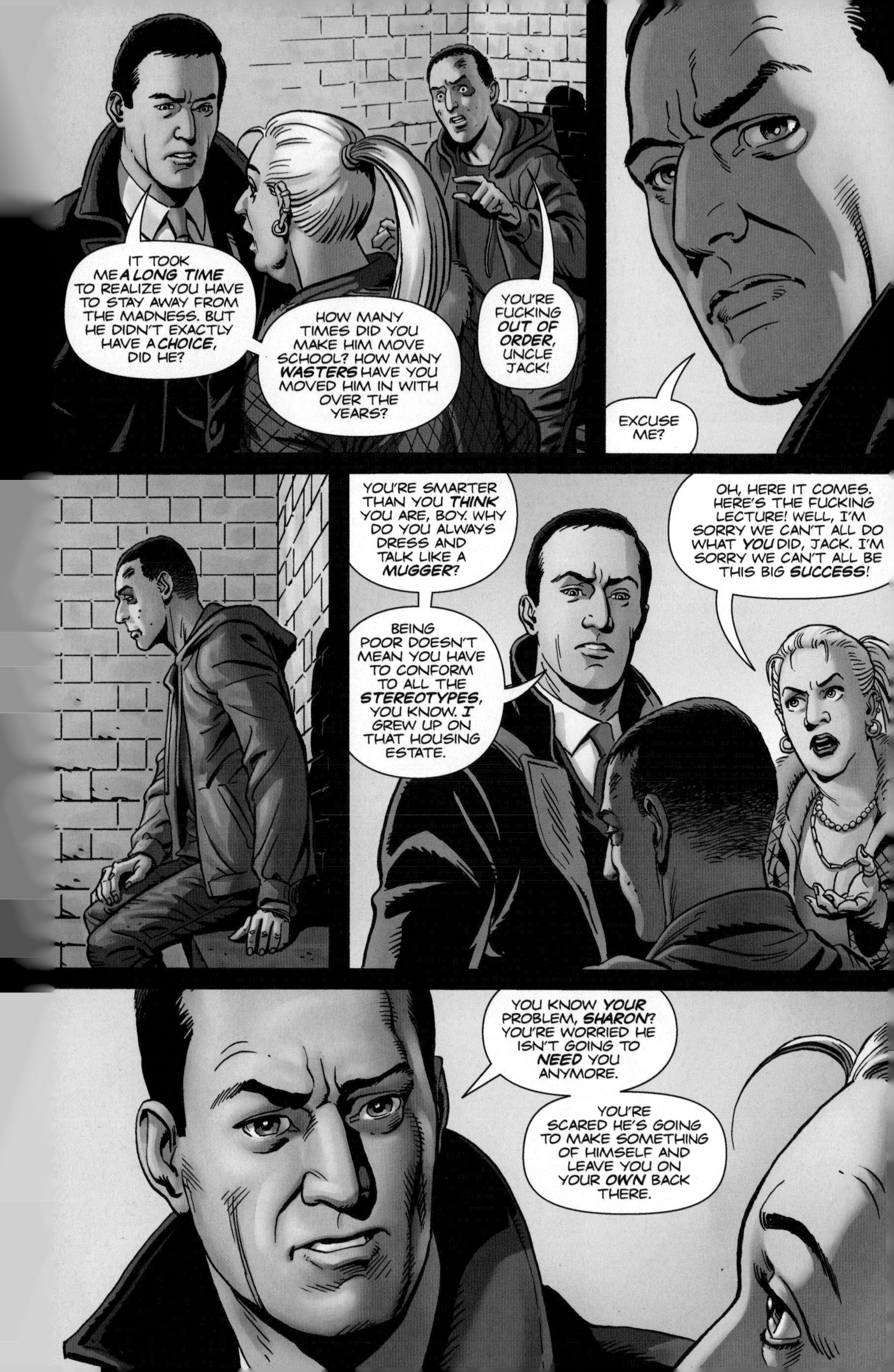
IT TOOK ME A LONG TIME TO REALIZE YOU HAVE TO STAY AWAY FROM THE MADNESS. BUT HE DIDN'T EXACTLY HAVE A CHOICE, DID HE?
HOW MANY TIMES DID YOU MAKE HIM MOVE SCHOOL? HOW MANY WASTERS HAVE YOU MOVED HIM IN WITH OVER THE YEARS?
YOU'RE FUCKING OUT OF ORDER, UNCLE JACK!
EXCUSE ME?
YOU'RE SMARTER THAN YOU THINK YOU ARE, BOY. WHY DO YOU ALWAYS DRESS AND TALK LIKE A MUGGER?
BEING POOR DOESN'T MEAN YOU HAVE TO CONFORM TO ALL THE STEREOTYPES, YOU KNOW. I GREW UP ON THAT HOUSING ESTATE.
OH, HERE IT COMES. HERE'S THE FUCKING LECTURE! WELL, I'M SORRY WE CAN'T ALL DO WHAT YOU DID, JACK. I'M SORRY WE CAN'T ALL BE THIS BIG SUCCESS!
YOU KNOW YOUR PROBLEM, SHARON? YOU'RE WORRIED HE ISN'T GOING TO NEED YOU ANYMORE.
YOU'RE SCARED HE'S GOING TO MAKE SOMETHING OF HIMSELF AND LEAVE YOU ON YOUR OWN BACK THERE.

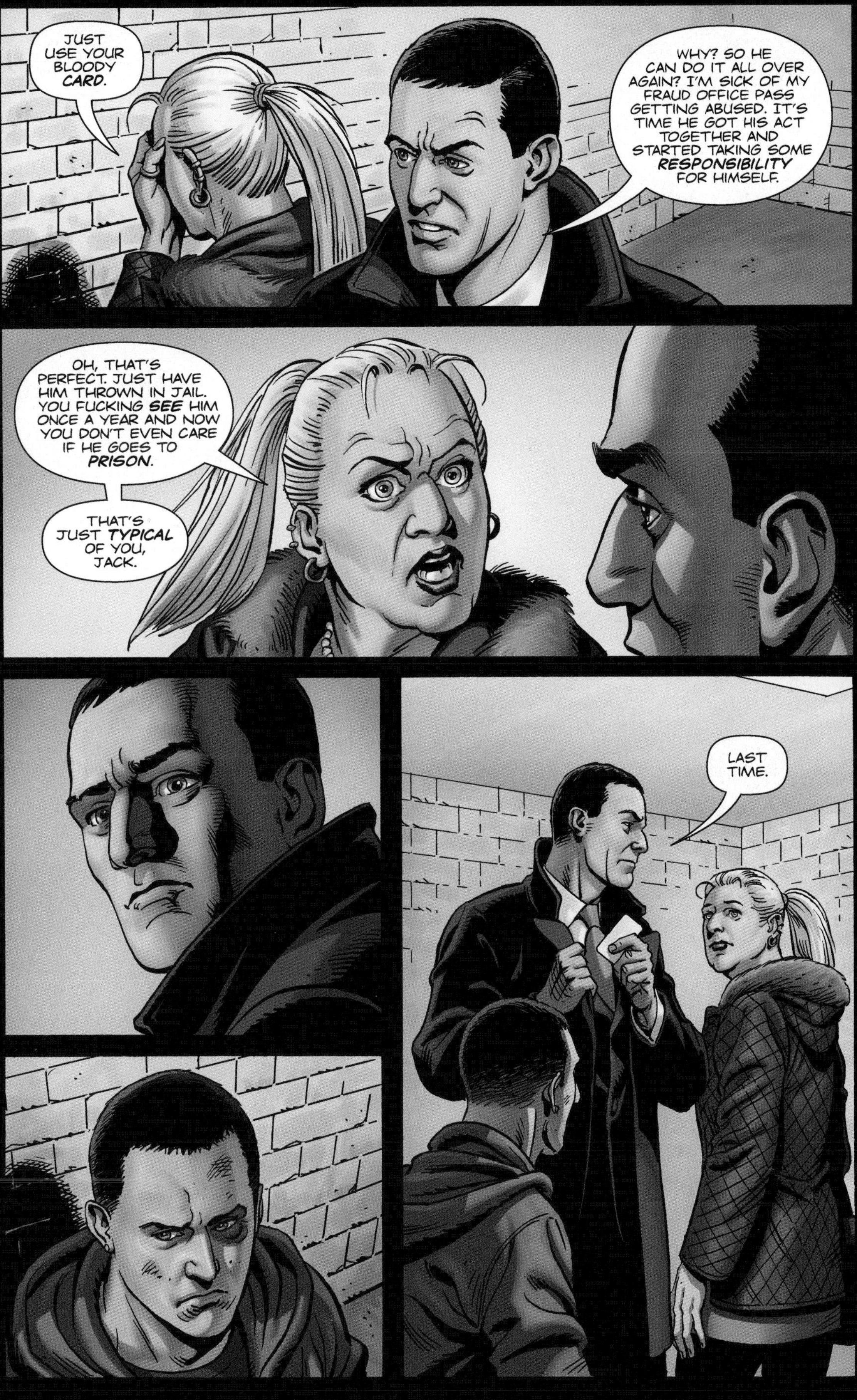
JUST USE YOUR BLOODY CARD.
WHY? SO HE CAN DO IT ALL OVER AGAIN? I'M SICK OF MY FRAUD OFFICE PASS GETTING ABUSED. IT'S TIME HE GOT HIS ACT TOGETHER AND STARTED TAKING SOME RESPONSIBILITY FOR HIMSELF.
OH, THAT'S PERFECT. JUST HAVE HIM THROWN IN JAIL. YOU FUCKING SEE HIM ONCE A YEAR AND NOW YOU DON'T EVEN CARE IF HE GOES TO PRISON.
THAT'S JUST TYPICAL OF YOU, JACK.
LAST TIME.

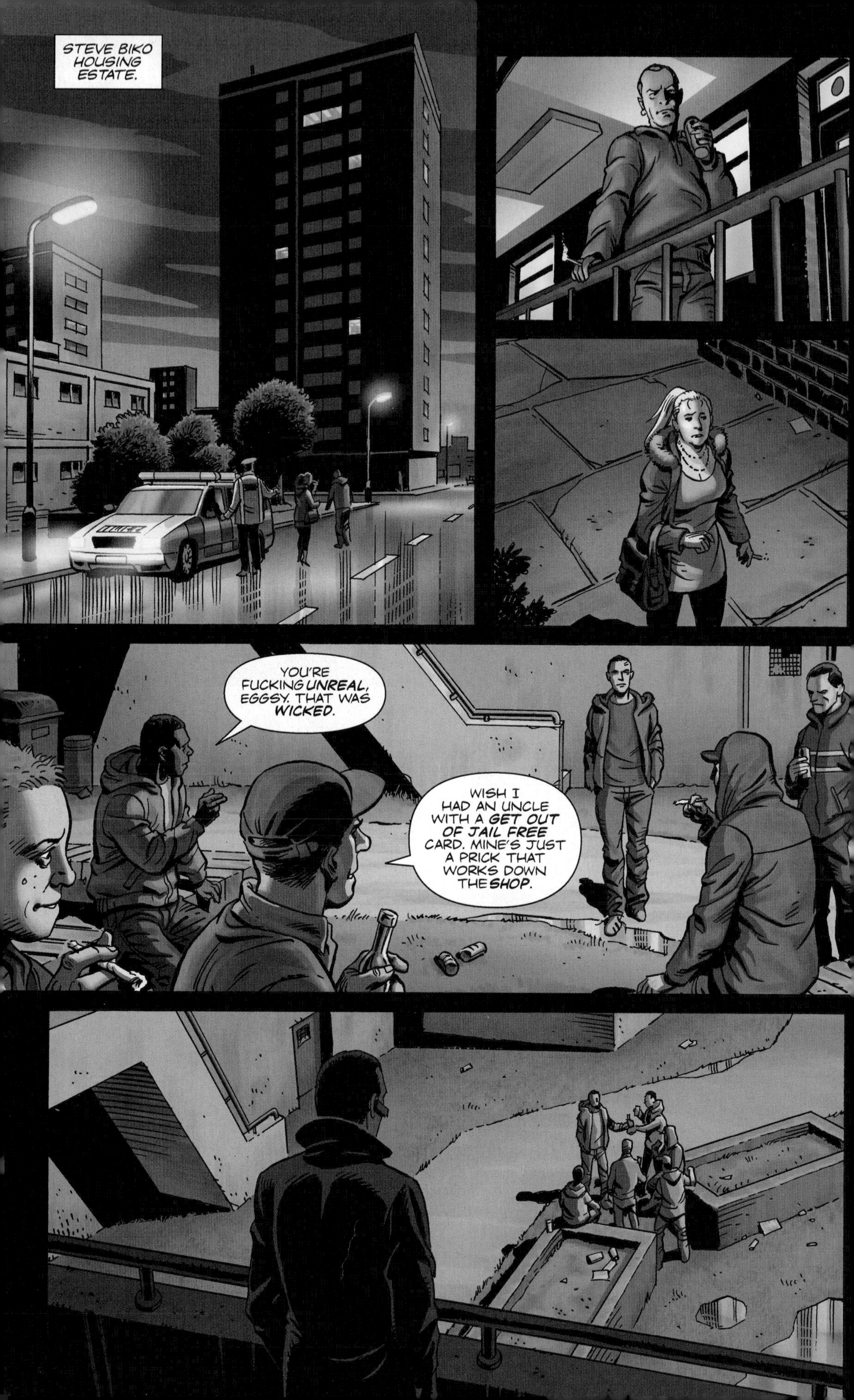
STEVE BIKO HOUSING ESTATE.
YOU'RE FUCKING UNREAL, EGGSY. THAT WAS WICKED.
WISH I HAD AN UNCLE WITH A GET OUT OF JAIL FREE CARD. MINE'S JUST A PRICK THAT WORKS DOWN THE SHOP.

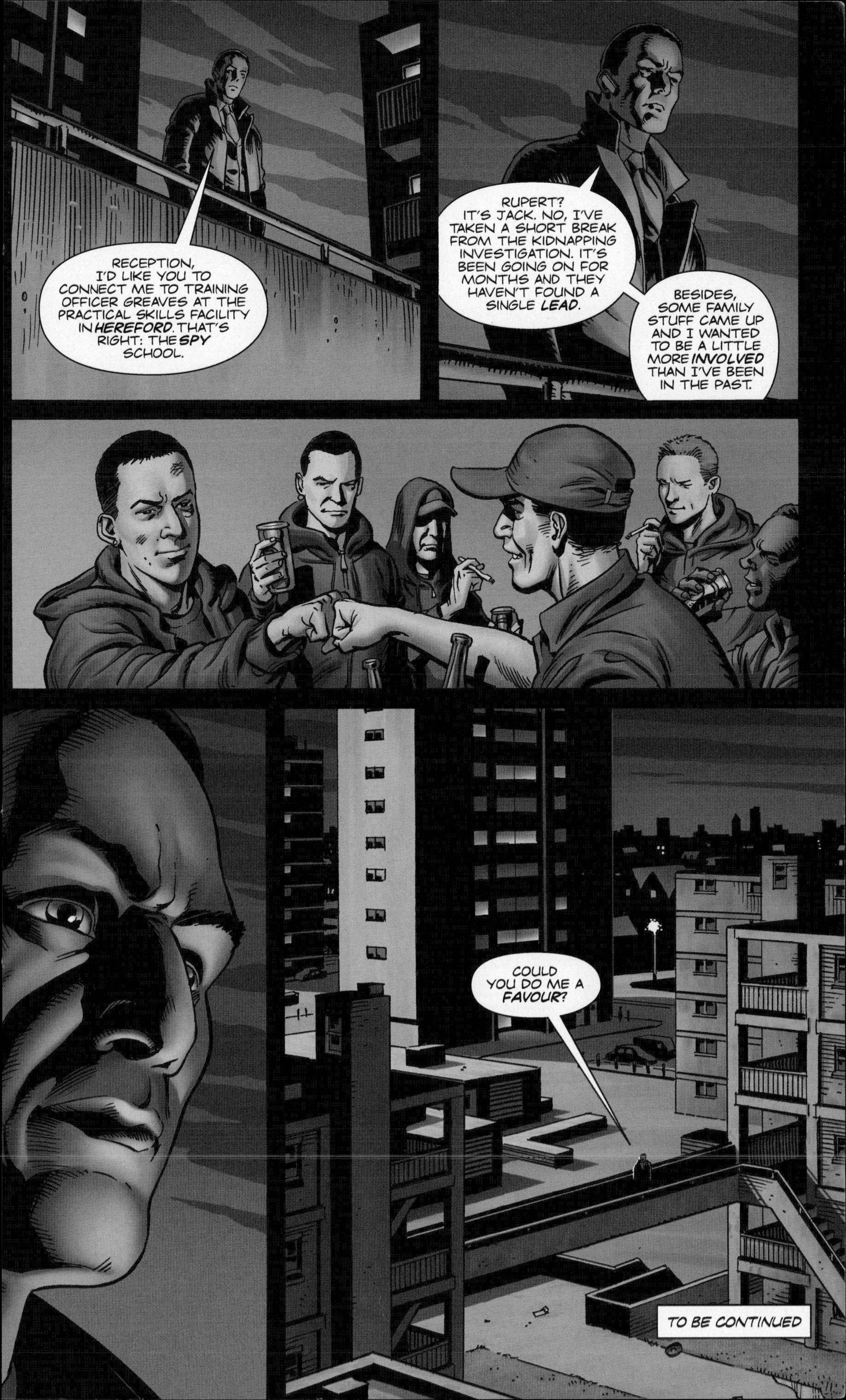
RECEPTION, I'D LIKE YOU TO CONNECT ME TO TRAINING OFFICER GREAVES AT THE PRACTICAL SKILLS FACILITY IN HEREFORD. THAT'S RIGHT: THE SPY SCHOOL.
RUPERT? IT'S JACK. NO, I'VE TAKEN A SHORT BREAK FROM THE KIDNAPPING INVESTIGATION. IT'S BEEN GOING ON FOR MONTHS AND THEY HAVEN'T FOUND A SINGLE LEAD.
BESIDES, SOME FAMILY STUFF CAME UP AND I WANTED TO BE A LITTLE MORE INVOLVED THAN I'VE BEEN IN THE PAST.
COULD YOU DO ME A FAVOUR?
TO BE CONTINUED

TWO

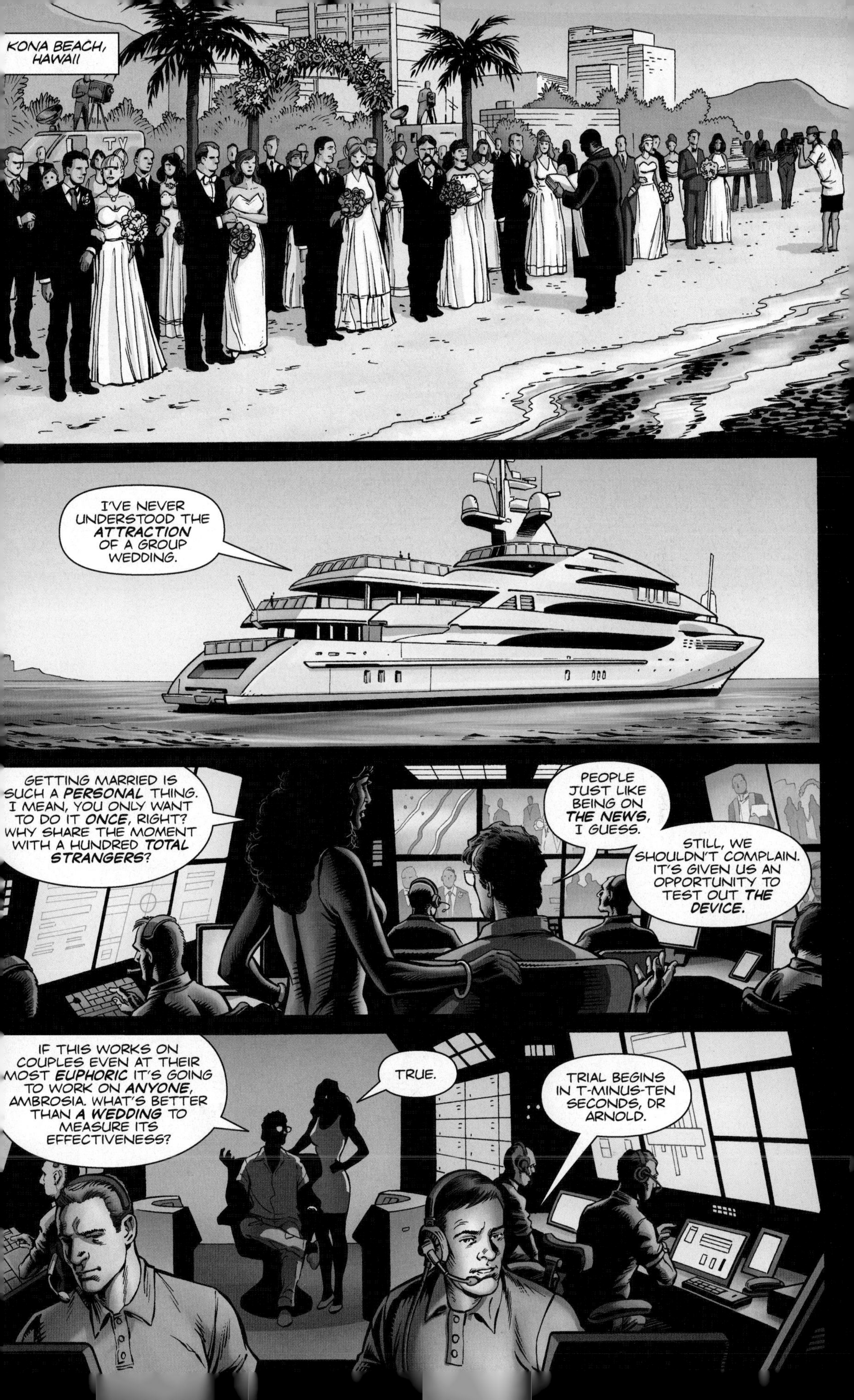
KONA BEACH, HAWAII
I'VE NEVER UNDERSTOOD THE ATTRACTION OF A GROUP WEDDING.
GETTING MARRIED IS SUCH A PERSONAL THING. I MEAN, YOU ONLY WANT TO DO IT ONCE, RIGHT? WHY SHARE THE MOMENT WITH A HUNDRED TOTAL STRANGERS?
PEOPLE JUST LIKE BEING ON THE NEWS, I GUESS.
STILL, WE SHOULDN'T COMPLAIN. IT'S GIVEN US AN OPPORTUNITY TO TEST OUT THE DEVICE.
IF THIS WORKS ON COUPLES EVEN AT THEIR MOST EUPHORIC IT'S GOING TO WORK ON ANYONE, AMBROSIA. WHAT'S BETTER THAN A WEDDING TO MEASURE ITS EFFECTIVENESS?
TRUE.
TRIAL BEGINS IN T-MINUS-TEN SECONDS, DR ARNOLD.

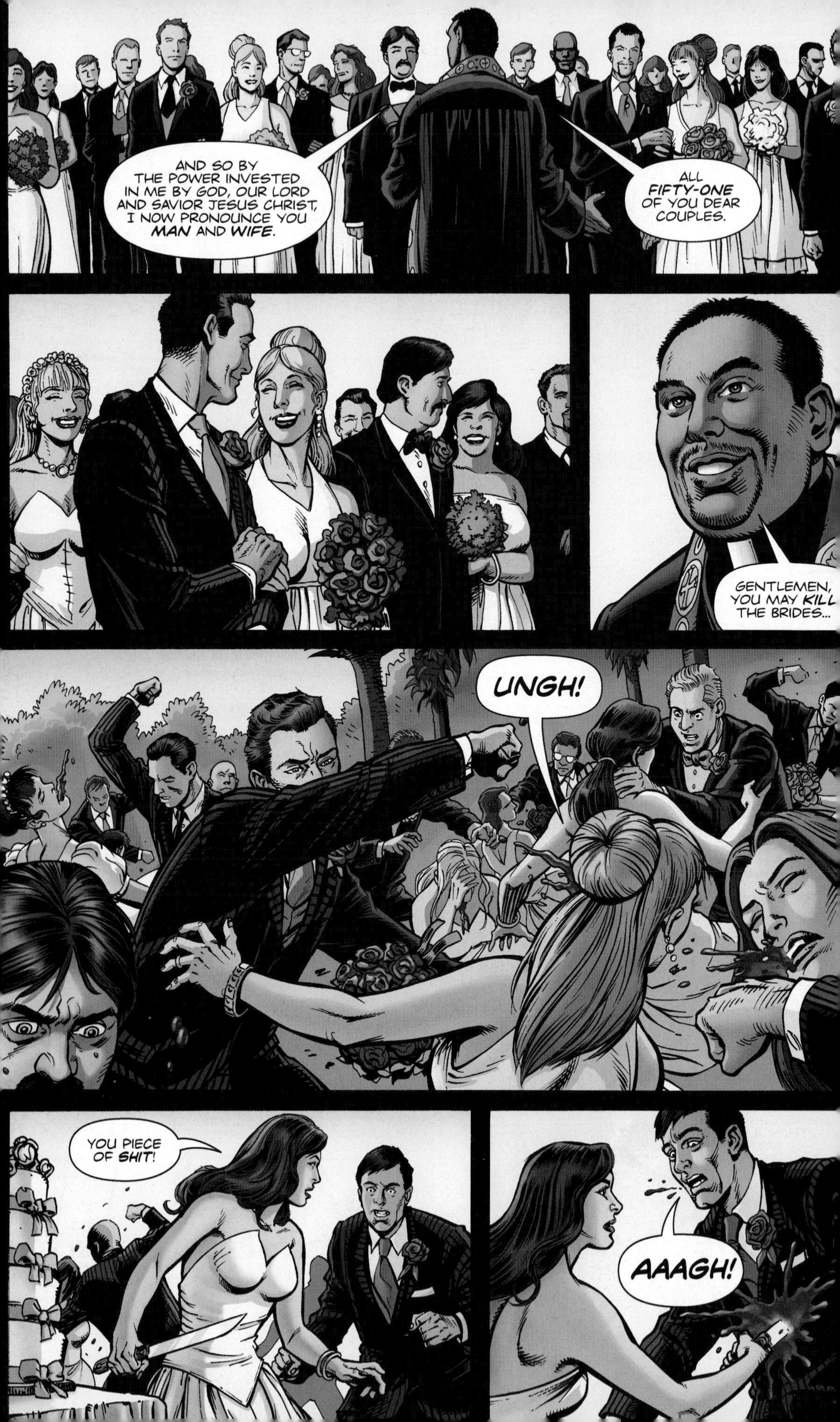
AND SO BY THE POWER INVESTED IN ME BY GOD, OUR LORD AND SAVIOR JESUS CHRIST, I NOW PRONOUNCE YOU MAN AND WIFE.
ALL FIFTY-ONE OF YOU DEAR COUPLES.
GENTLEMEN, YOU MAY KILL THE BRIDES...
UNGH!
YOU PIECE OF SHIT!
AAAGH!

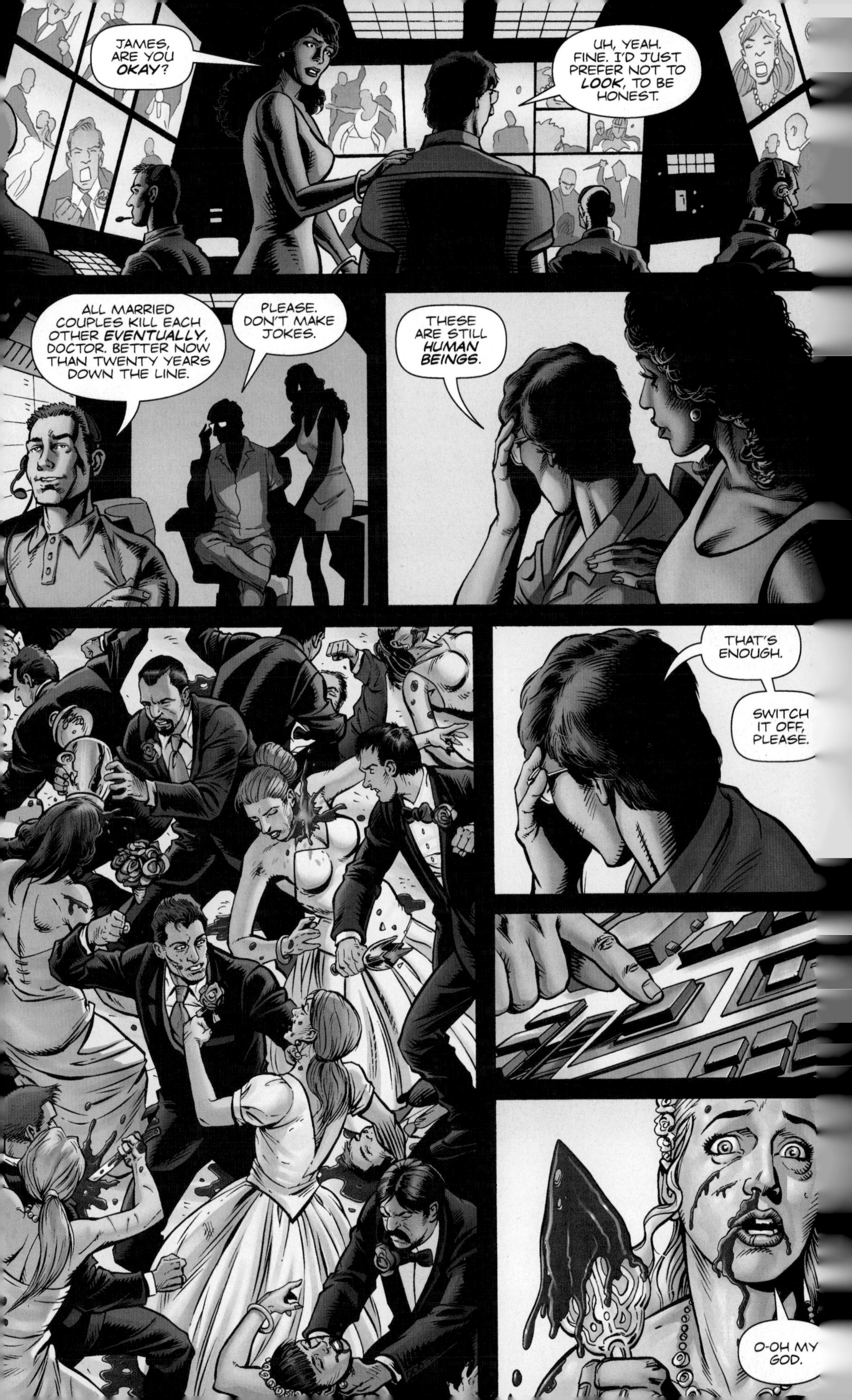
JAMES, ARE YOU OKAY?
UH, YEAH. FINE. I'D JUST PREFER NOT TO LOOK, TO BE HONEST.
ALL MARRIED COUPLES KILL EACH OTHER EVENTUALLY, DOCTOR. BETTER NOW THAN TWENTY YEARS DOWN THE LINE.
PLEASE. DON'T MAKE JOKES.
THESE ARE STILL HUMAN BEINGS.
THAT'S ENOUGH.
SWITCH IT OFF, PLEASE.
O-OH MY GOD.

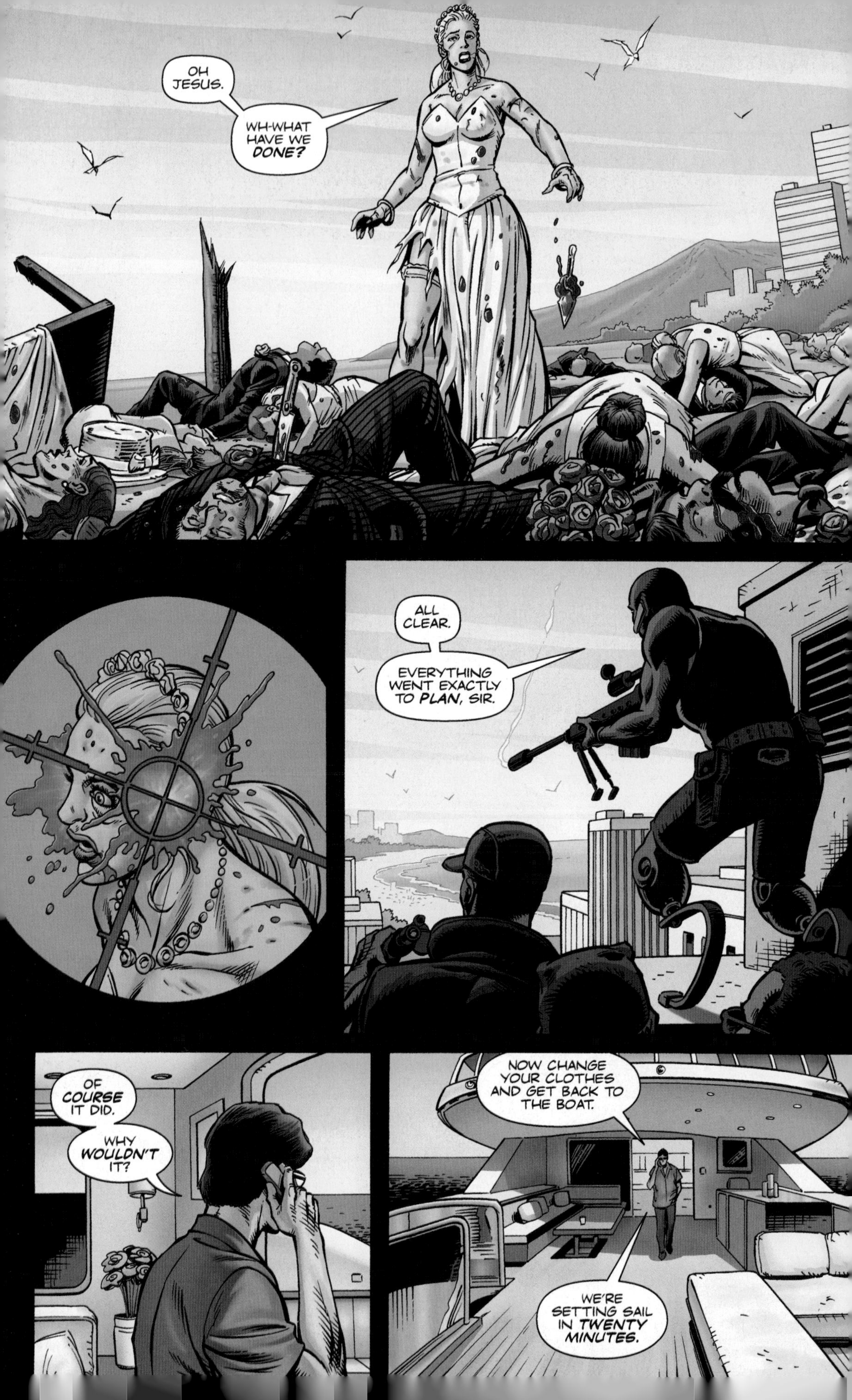

OH JESUS.
WH-WHAT HAVE WE DONE?
ALL CLEAR.
EVERYTHING WENT EXACTLY TO PLAN, SIR.
OF COURSE IT DID.
WHY WOULDN'T IT?
NOW CHANGE YOUR CLOTHES AND GET BACK TO THE BOAT.
WE'RE SETTING SAIL IN TWENTY MINUTES.

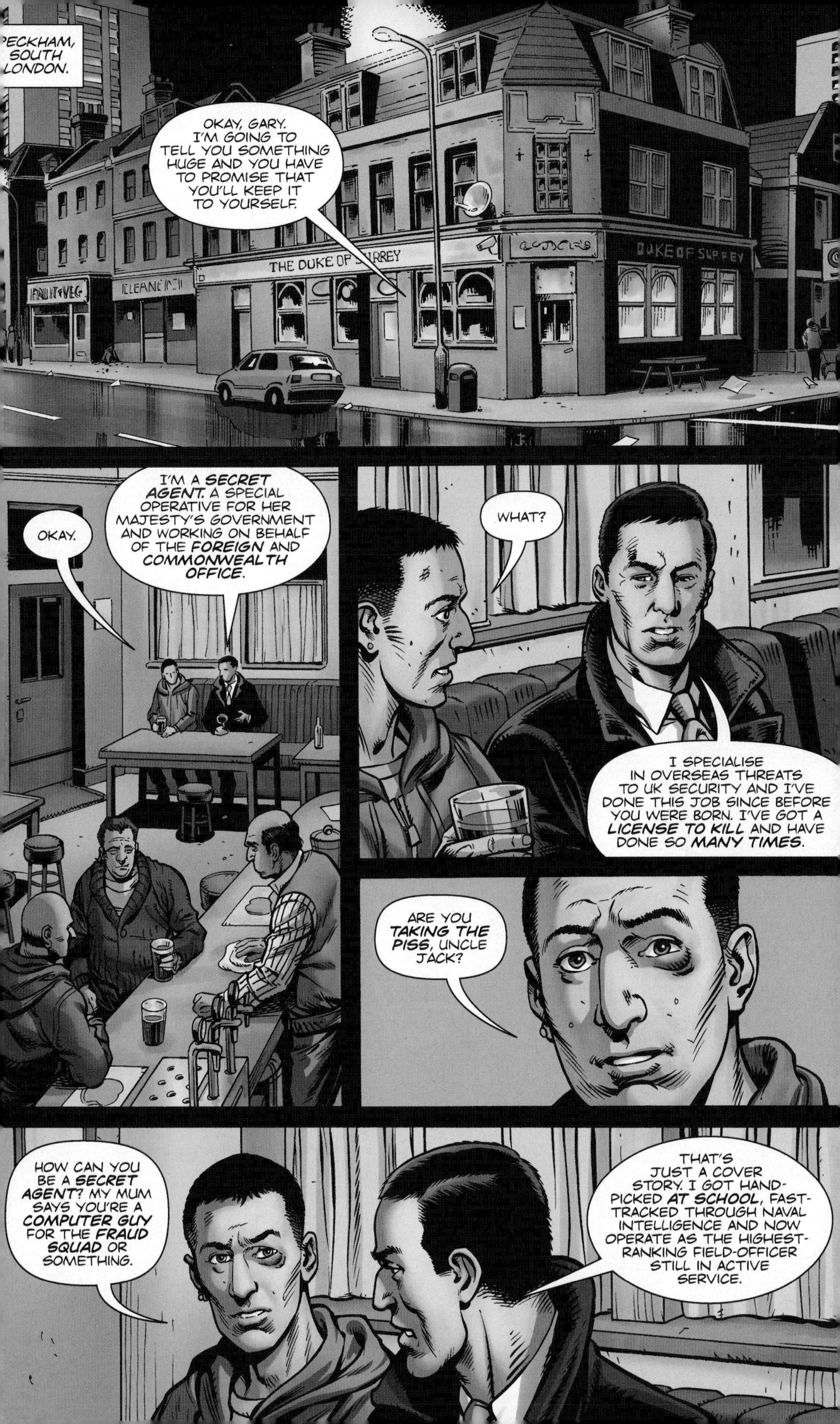
PECKHAM, SOUTH LONDON.
OKAY, GARY. I'M GOING TO TELL YOU SOMETHING HUGE AND YOU HAVE TO PROMISE THAT YOU'LL KEEP IT TO YOURSELF.
THE DUKE OF SURREY
DUKE OF SURREY
I'M A SECRET AGENT. A SPECIAL OPERATIVE FOR HER MAJESTY'S GOVERNMENT AND WORKING ON BEHALF OF THE FOREIGN AND COMMONWEALTH OFFICE.
OKAY.
WHAT?
I SPECIALISE IN OVERSEAS THREATS TO UK SECURITY AND I'VE DONE THIS JOB SINCE BEFORE YOU WERE BORN. I'VE GOT A LICENSE TO KILL AND HAVE DONE SO MANY TIMES.
ARE YOU TAKING THE PISS, UNCLE JACK?
HOW CAN YOU BE A SECRET AGENT? MY MUM SAYS YOU'RE A COMPUTER GUY FOR THE FRAUD SQUAD OR SOMETHING.
THAT'S JUST A COVER STORY. I GOT HAND-PICKED AT SCHOOL, FAST-TRACKED THROUGH NAVAL INTELLIGENCE AND NOW OPERATE AS THE HIGHEST-RANKING FIELD-OFFICER STILL IN ACTIVE SERVICE.

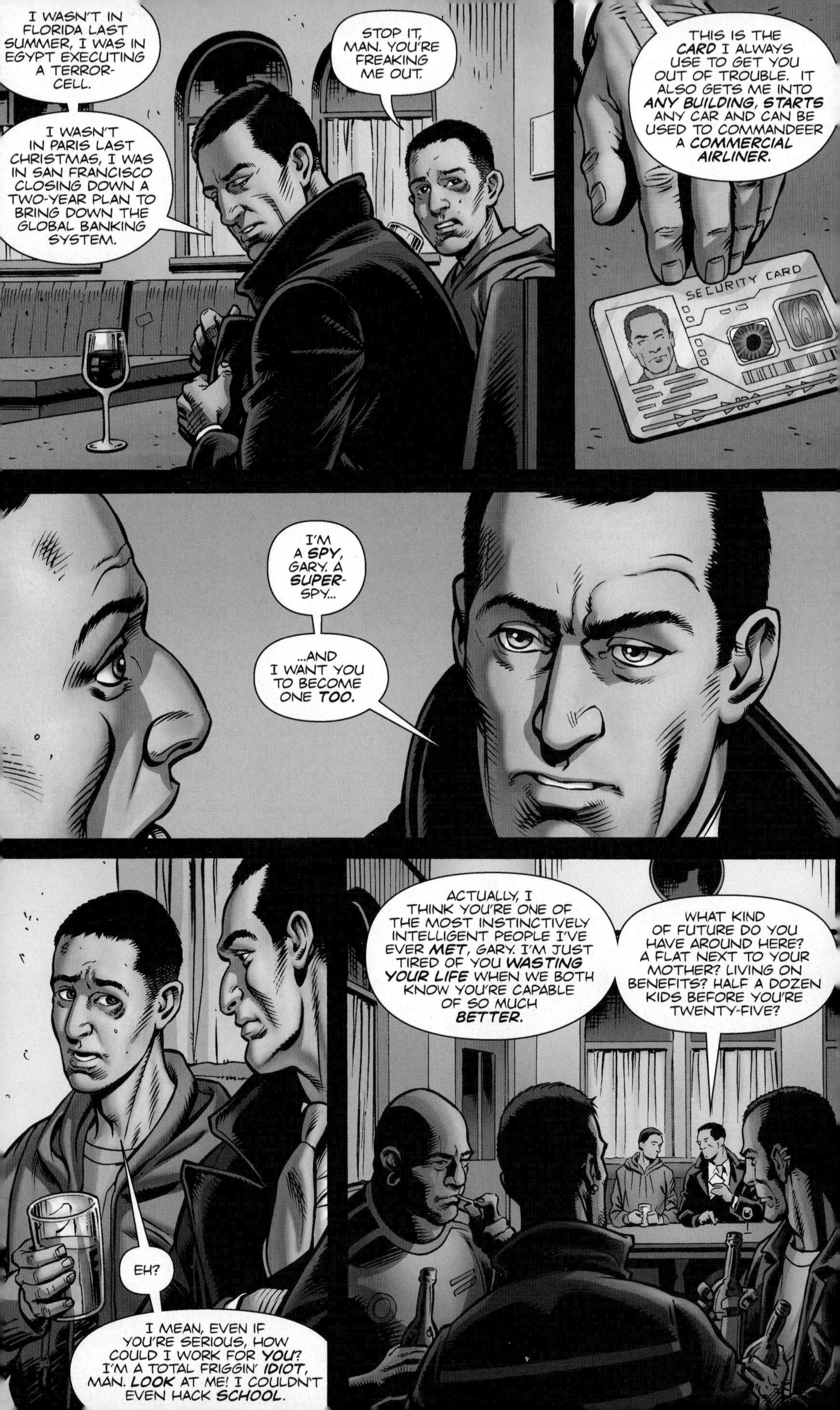
I WASN'T IN FLORIDA LAST SUMMER, I WAS IN EGYPT EXECUTING A TERROR-CELL.
I WASN'T IN PARIS LAST CHRISTMAS, I WAS IN SAN FRANCISCO CLOSING DOWN A TWO-YEAR PLAN TO BRING DOWN THE GLOBAL BANKING SYSTEM.
STOP IT, MAN. YOU'RE FREAKING ME OUT.
THIS IS THE **CARD** I ALWAYS USE TO GET YOU OUT OF TROUBLE. IT ALSO GETS ME INTO **ANY BUILDING, STARTS** ANY CAR AND CAN BE USED TO COMMANDEER A **COMMERCIAL AIRLINER.**
SECURITY CARD
I'M A **SPY**, GARY. A **SUPER**-SPY...
...AND I WANT YOU TO BECOME ONE **TOO.**
EH?
I MEAN, EVEN IF YOU'RE SERIOUS, HOW COULD I WORK FOR **YOU**? I'M A TOTAL FRIGGIN' **IDIOT**, MAN. **LOOK** AT ME! I COULDN'T EVEN HACK **SCHOOL**.
ACTUALLY, I THINK YOU'RE ONE OF THE MOST INSTINCTIVELY INTELLIGENT PEOPLE I'VE EVER **MET**, GARY. I'M JUST TIRED OF YOU **WASTING YOUR LIFE** WHEN WE BOTH KNOW YOU'RE CAPABLE OF SO MUCH **BETTER.**
WHAT KIND OF FUTURE DO YOU HAVE AROUND HERE? A FLAT NEXT TO YOUR MOTHER? LIVING ON BENEFITS? HALF A DOZEN KIDS BEFORE YOU'RE TWENTY-FIVE?

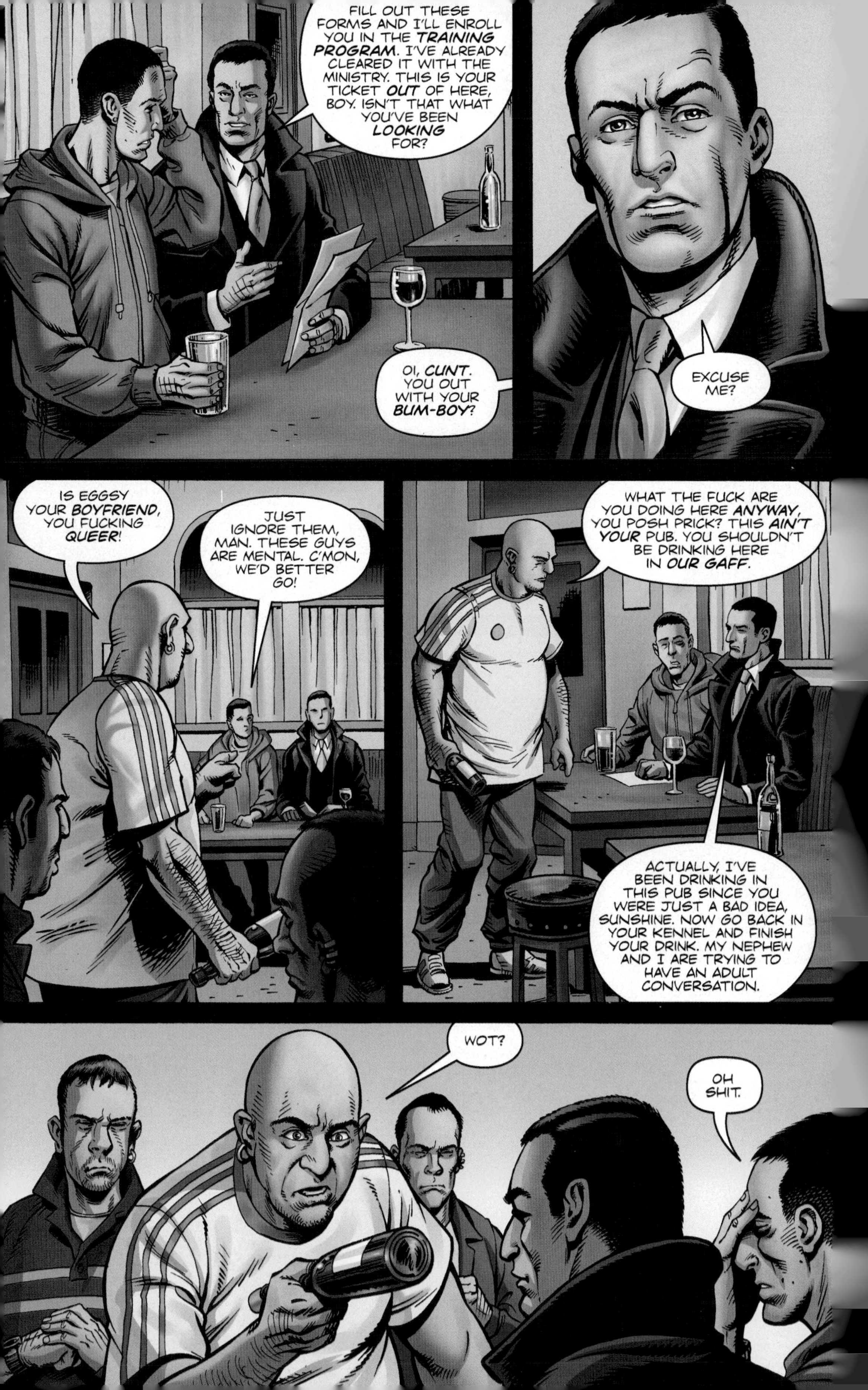
FILL OUT THESE FORMS AND I'LL ENROLL YOU IN THE TRAINING PROGRAM. I'VE ALREADY CLEARED IT WITH THE MINISTRY. THIS IS YOUR TICKET OUT OF HERE, BOY. ISN'T THAT WHAT YOU'VE BEEN LOOKING FOR?
OI, CUNT. YOU OUT WITH YOUR BUM-BOY?
EXCUSE ME?
IS EGGSY YOUR BOYFRIEND, YOU FUCKING QUEER!
JUST IGNORE THEM, MAN. THESE GUYS ARE MENTAL. C'MON, WE'D BETTER GO!
WHAT THE FUCK ARE YOU DOING HERE ANYWAY, YOU POSH PRICK? THIS AIN'T YOUR PUB. YOU SHOULDN'T BE DRINKING HERE IN OUR GAFF.
ACTUALLY, I'VE BEEN DRINKING IN THIS PUB SINCE YOU WERE JUST A BAD IDEA, SUNSHINE. NOW GO BACK IN YOUR KENNEL AND FINISH YOUR DRINK. MY NEPHEW AND I ARE TRYING TO HAVE AN ADULT CONVERSATION.
WOT?
OH SHIT.

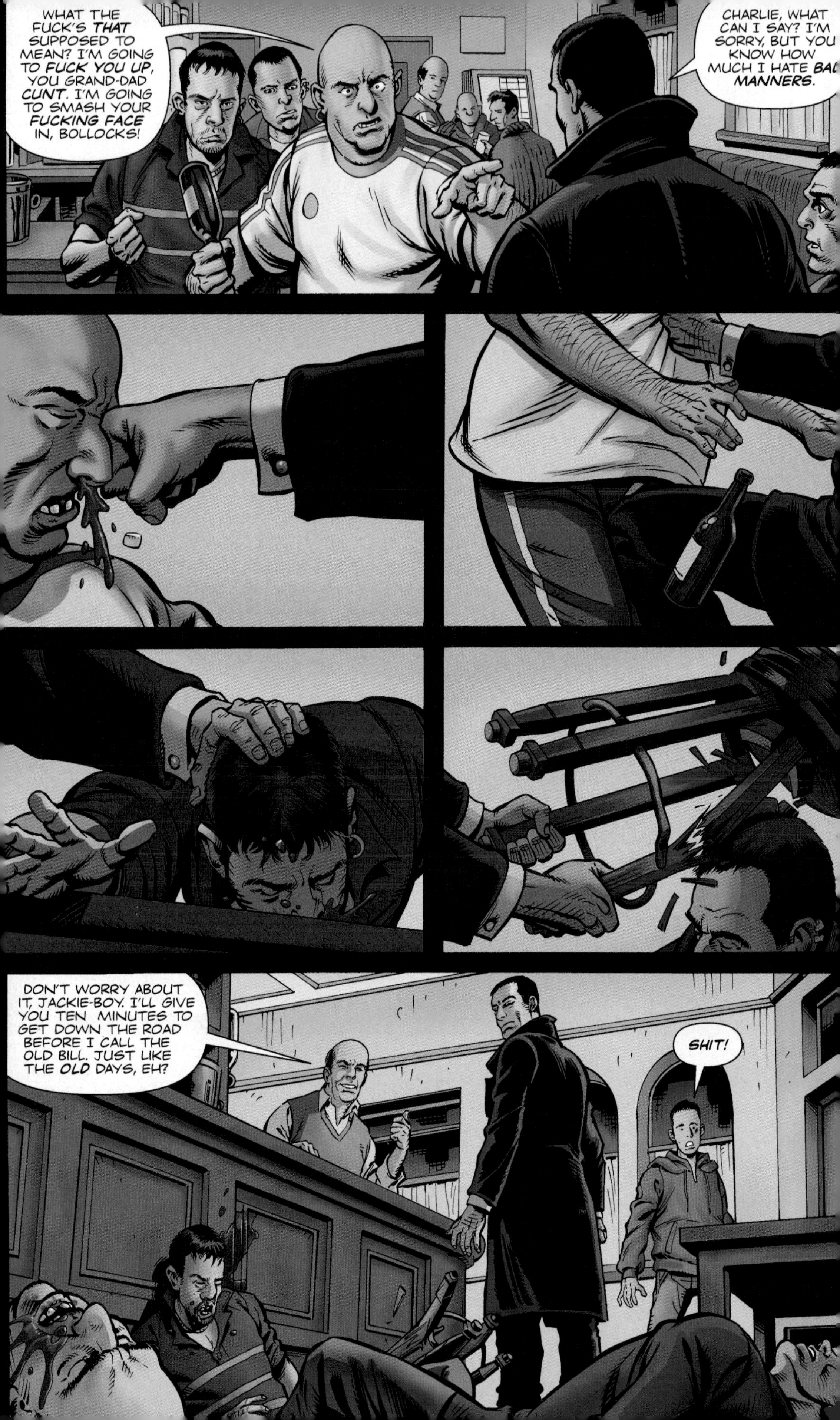
WHAT THE FUCK'S THAT SUPPOSED TO MEAN? I'M GOING TO FUCK YOU UP, YOU GRAND-DAD CUNT. I'M GOING TO SMASH YOUR FUCKING FACE IN, BOLLOCKS!
CHARLIE, WHAT CAN I SAY? I'M SORRY, BUT YOU KNOW HOW MUCH I HATE BAD MANNERS.
DON'T WORRY ABOUT IT, JACKIE-BOY. I'LL GIVE YOU TEN MINUTES TO GET DOWN THE ROAD BEFORE I CALL THE OLD BILL. JUST LIKE THE OLD DAYS, EH?
SHIT!

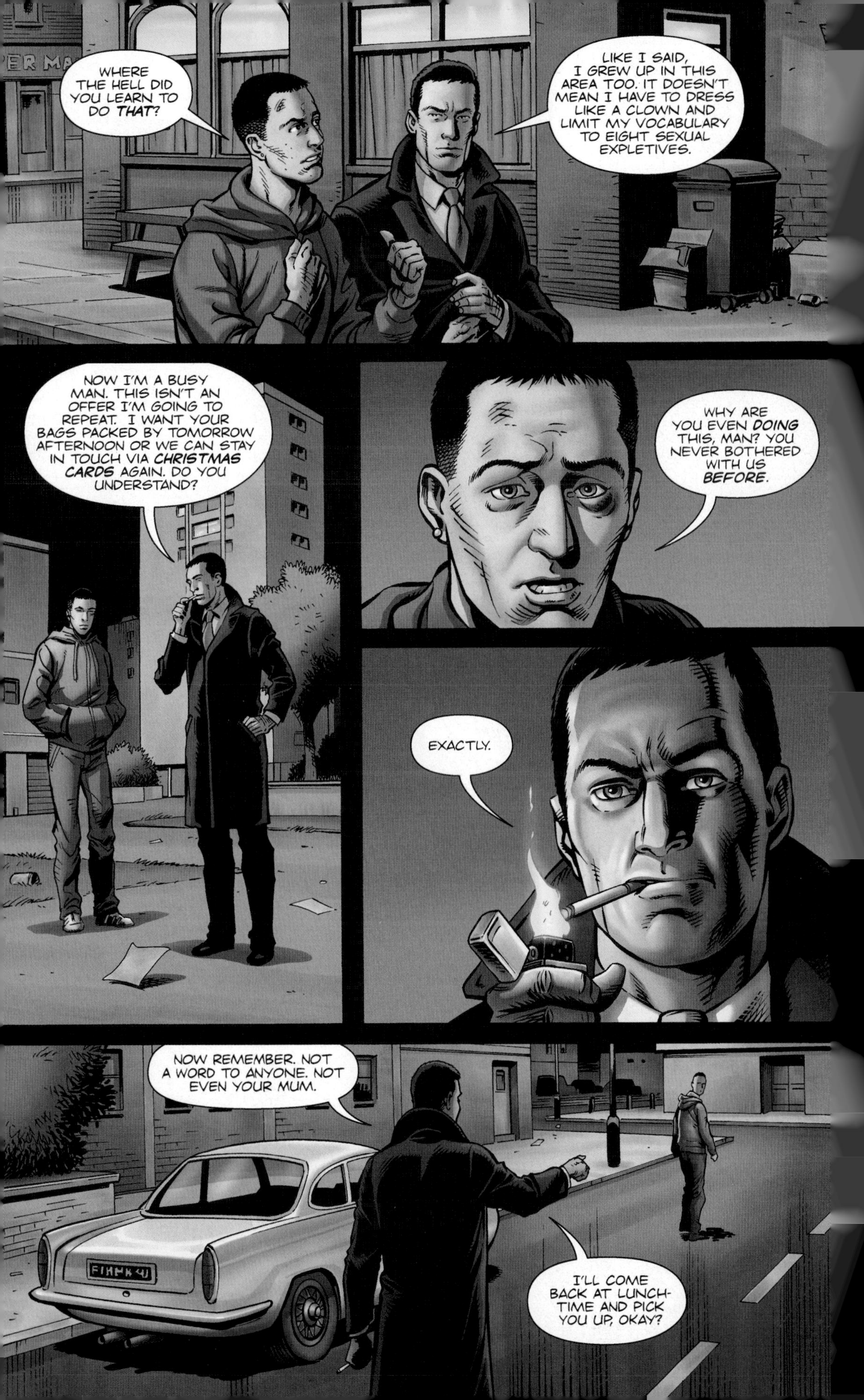
WHERE THE HELL DID YOU LEARN TO DO *THAT*?
LIKE I SAID, I GREW UP IN THIS AREA TOO. IT DOESN'T MEAN I HAVE TO DRESS LIKE A CLOWN AND LIMIT MY VOCABULARY TO EIGHT SEXUAL EXPLETIVES.
NOW I'M A BUSY MAN. THIS ISN'T AN OFFER I'M GOING TO REPEAT. I WANT YOUR BAGS PACKED BY TOMORROW AFTERNOON OR WE CAN STAY IN TOUCH VIA **CHRISTMAS CARDS** AGAIN. DO YOU UNDERSTAND?
WHY ARE YOU EVEN **DOING** THIS, MAN? YOU NEVER BOTHERED WITH US **BEFORE**.
EXACTLY.
NOW REMEMBER. NOT A WORD TO ANYONE. NOT EVEN YOUR MUM.
I'LL COME BACK AT LUNCH-TIME AND PICK YOU UP, OKAY?

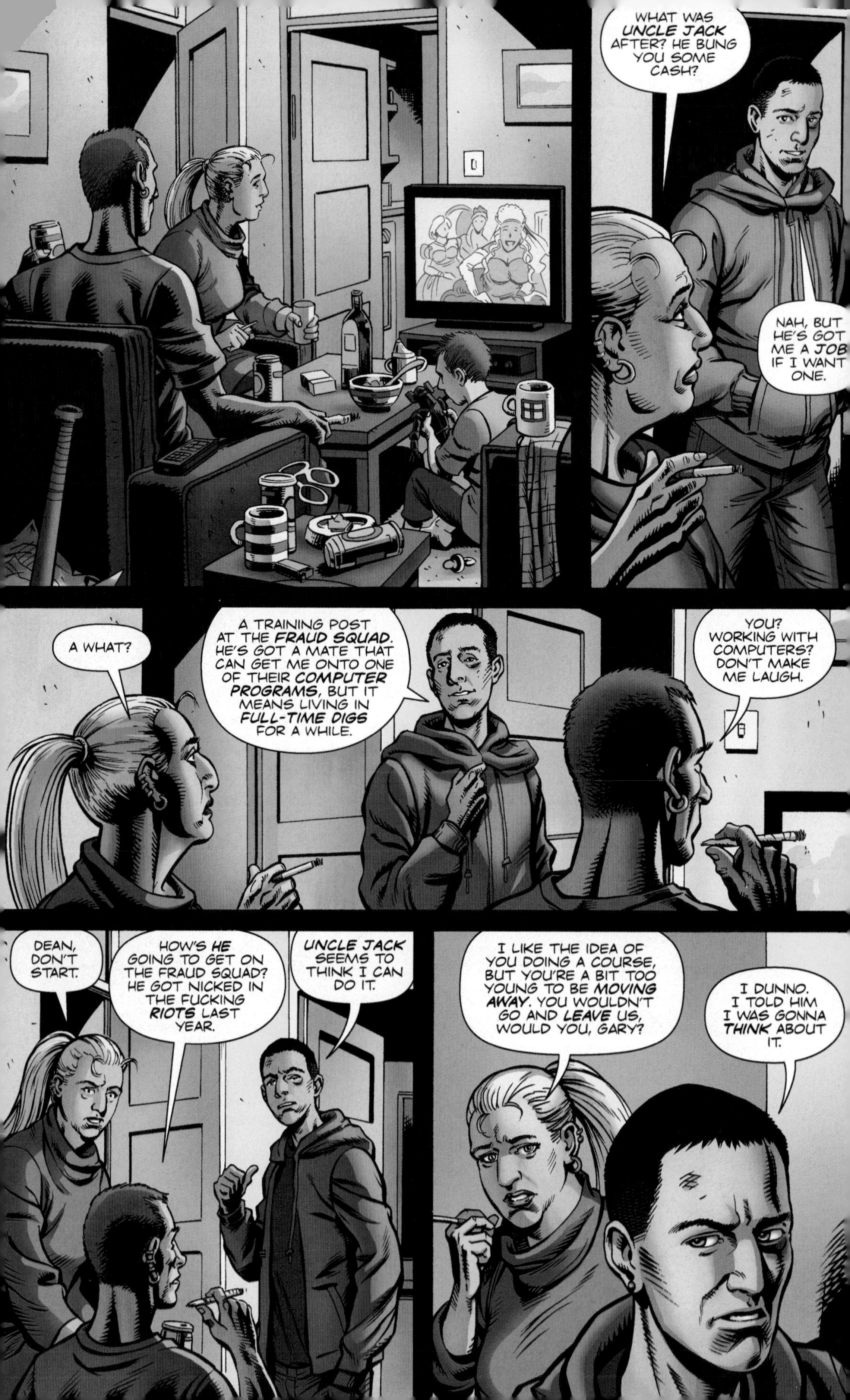
WHAT WAS UNCLE JACK AFTER? HE BUNG YOU SOME CASH?
NAH, BUT HE'S GOT ME A JOB IF I WANT ONE.
A WHAT?
A TRAINING POST AT THE FRAUD SQUAD. HE'S GOT A MATE THAT CAN GET ME ONTO ONE OF THEIR COMPUTER PROGRAMS, BUT IT MEANS LIVING IN FULL-TIME DIGS FOR A WHILE.
YOU? WORKING WITH COMPUTERS? DON'T MAKE ME LAUGH.
DEAN, DON'T START.
HOW'S HE GOING TO GET ON THE FRAUD SQUAD? HE GOT NICKED IN THE FUCKING RIOTS LAST YEAR.
UNCLE JACK SEEMS TO THINK I CAN DO IT.
I LIKE THE IDEA OF YOU DOING A COURSE, BUT YOU'RE A BIT TOO YOUNG TO BE MOVING AWAY. YOU WOULDN'T GO AND LEAVE US, WOULD YOU, GARY?
I DUNNO. I TOLD HIM I WAS GONNA THINK ABOUT IT.

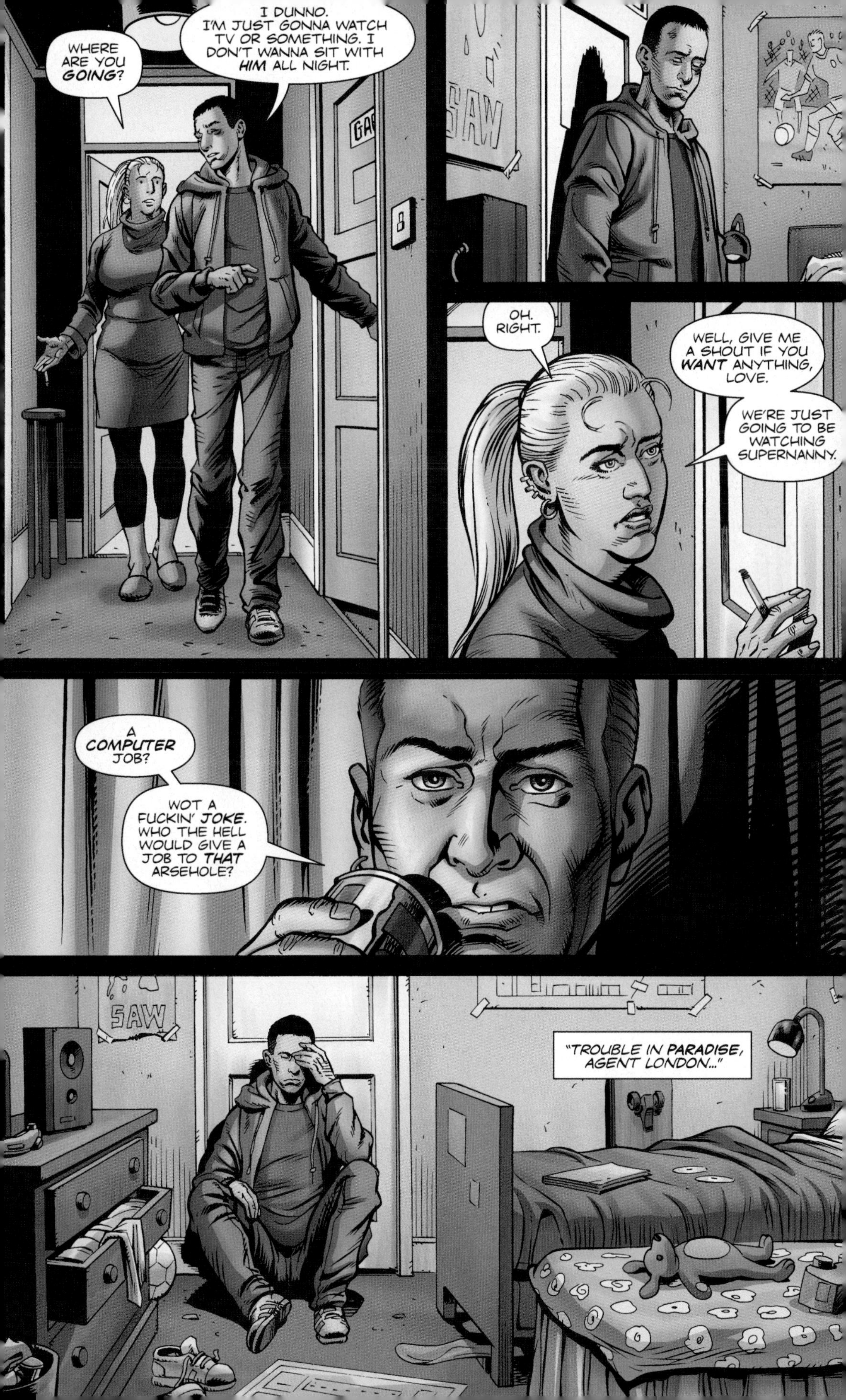
WHERE ARE YOU GOING?
I DUNNO. I'M JUST GONNA WATCH TV OR SOMETHING. I DON'T WANNA SIT WITH HIM ALL NIGHT.
SAW
OH. RIGHT.
WELL, GIVE ME A SHOUT IF YOU WANT ANYTHING, LOVE.
WE'RE JUST GOING TO BE WATCHING SUPERNANNY.
A COMPUTER JOB?
WOT A FUCKIN' JOKE. WHO THE HELL WOULD GIVE A JOB TO THAT ARSEHOLE?
SAW
"TROUBLE IN PARADISE, AGENT LONDON..."

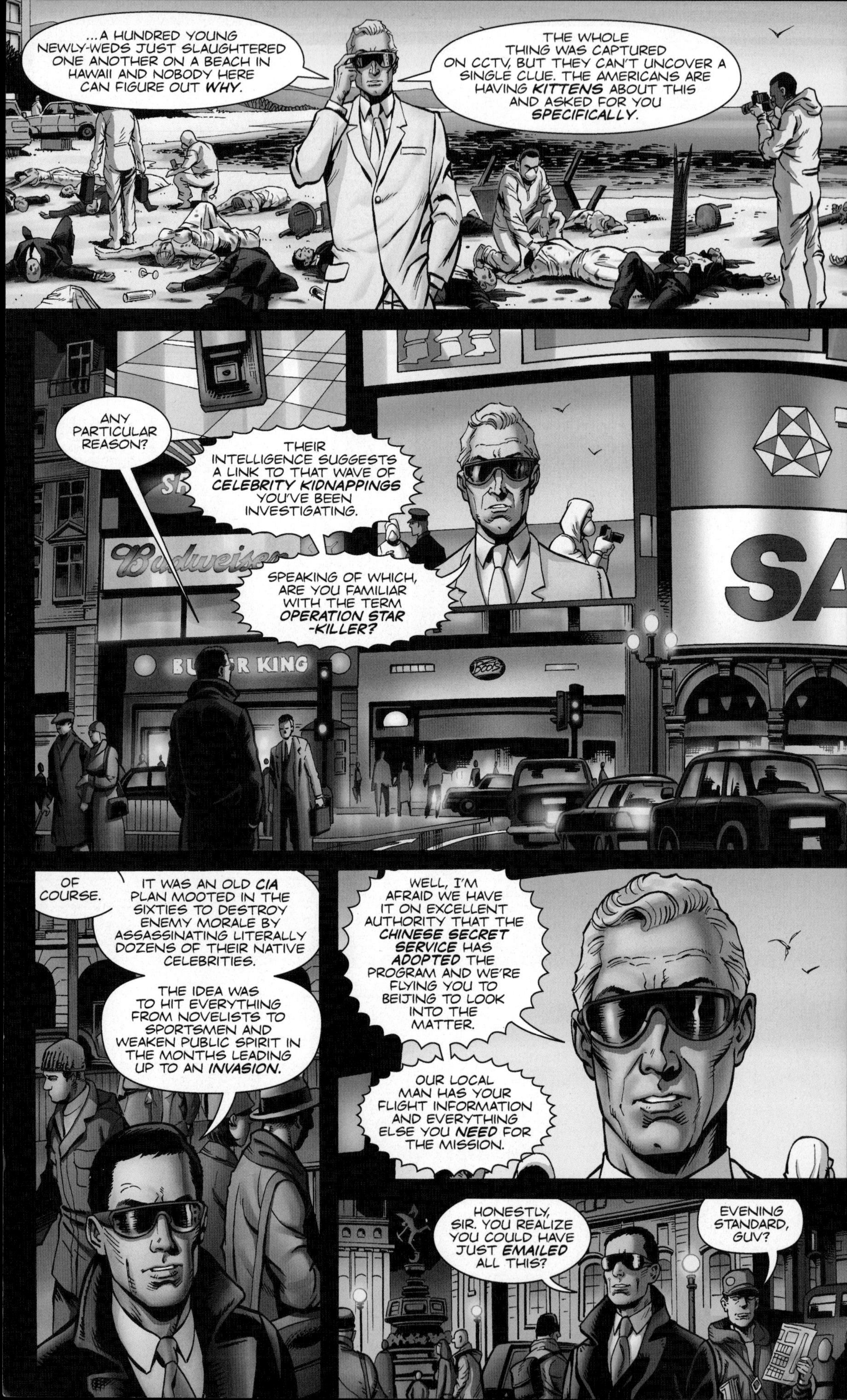
...A HUNDRED YOUNG NEWLY-WEDS JUST SLAUGHTERED ONE ANOTHER ON A BEACH IN HAWAII AND NOBODY HERE CAN FIGURE OUT WHY.
THE WHOLE THING WAS CAPTURED ON CCTV, BUT THEY CAN'T UNCOVER A SINGLE CLUE. THE AMERICANS ARE HAVING KITTENS ABOUT THIS AND ASKED FOR YOU SPECIFICALLY.
ANY PARTICULAR REASON?
THEIR INTELLIGENCE SUGGESTS A LINK TO THAT WAVE OF CELEBRITY KIDNAPPINGS YOU'VE BEEN INVESTIGATING.
SPEAKING OF WHICH, ARE YOU FAMILIAR WITH THE TERM OPERATION STAR-KILLER?
OF COURSE.
IT WAS AN OLD CIA PLAN MOOTED IN THE SIXTIES TO DESTROY ENEMY MORALE BY ASSASSINATING LITERALLY DOZENS OF THEIR NATIVE CELEBRITIES.
THE IDEA WAS TO HIT EVERYTHING FROM NOVELISTS TO SPORTSMEN AND WEAKEN PUBLIC SPIRIT IN THE MONTHS LEADING UP TO AN INVASION.
WELL, I'M AFRAID WE HAVE IT ON EXCELLENT AUTHORITY THAT THE CHINESE SECRET SERVICE HAS ADOPTED THE PROGRAM AND WE'RE FLYING YOU TO BEIJING TO LOOK INTO THE MATTER.
OUR LOCAL MAN HAS YOUR FLIGHT INFORMATION AND EVERYTHING ELSE YOU NEED FOR THE MISSION.
HONESTLY, SIR. YOU REALIZE YOU COULD HAVE JUST EMAILED ALL THIS?
EVENING STANDARD, GUV?

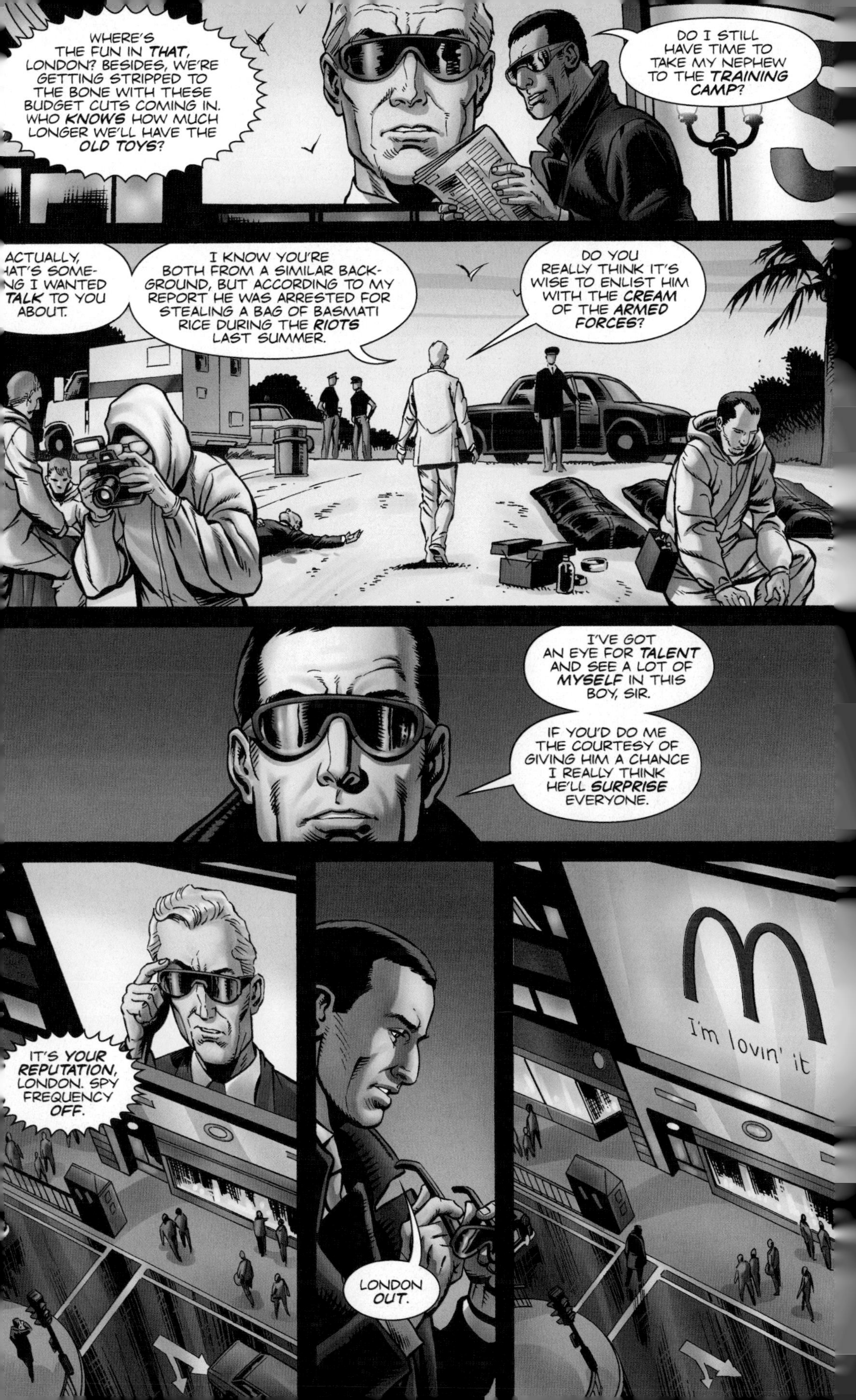

WHERE'S THE FUN IN THAT, LONDON? BESIDES, WE'RE GETTING STRIPPED TO THE BONE WITH THESE BUDGET CUTS COMING IN. WHO KNOWS HOW MUCH LONGER WE'LL HAVE THE OLD TOYS?
DO I STILL HAVE TIME TO TAKE MY NEPHEW TO THE TRAINING CAMP?
ACTUALLY, HAT'S SOME-NG I WANTED TALK TO YOU ABOUT.
I KNOW YOU'RE BOTH FROM A SIMILAR BACK-GROUND, BUT ACCORDING TO MY REPORT HE WAS ARRESTED FOR STEALING A BAG OF BASMATI RICE DURING THE RIOTS LAST SUMMER.
DO YOU REALLY THINK IT'S WISE TO ENLIST HIM WITH THE CREAM OF THE ARMED FORCES?
I'VE GOT AN EYE FOR TALENT AND SEE A LOT OF MYSELF IN THIS BOY, SIR.
IF YOU'D DO ME THE COURTESY OF GIVING HIM A CHANCE I REALLY THINK HE'LL SURPRISE EVERYONE.
IT'S YOUR REPUTATION, LONDON. SPY FREQUENCY OFF.
LONDON OUT.
I'm lovin' it

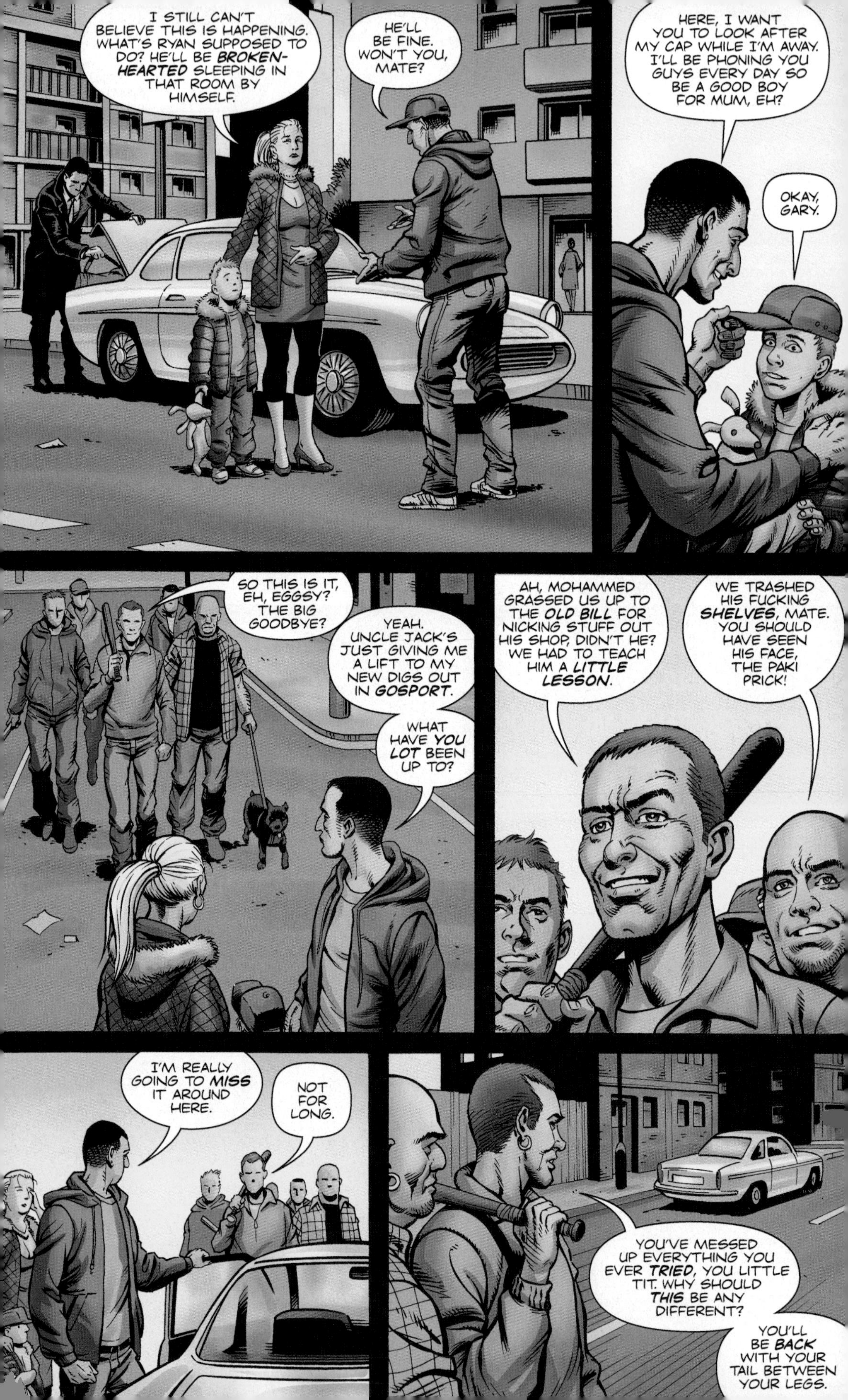
I STILL CAN'T BELIEVE THIS IS HAPPENING. WHAT'S RYAN SUPPOSED TO DO? HE'LL BE BROKEN-HEARTED SLEEPING IN THAT ROOM BY HIMSELF.
HE'LL BE FINE. WON'T YOU, MATE?
HERE, I WANT YOU TO LOOK AFTER MY CAP WHILE I'M AWAY. I'LL BE PHONING YOU GUYS EVERY DAY SO BE A GOOD BOY FOR MUM, EH?
OKAY, GARY.
SO THIS IS IT, EH, EGGSY? THE BIG GOODBYE?
YEAH. UNCLE JACK'S JUST GIVING ME A LIFT TO MY NEW DIGS OUT IN GOSPORT.
WHAT HAVE YOU LOT BEEN UP TO?
AH, MOHAMMED GRASSED US UP TO THE OLD BILL FOR NICKING STUFF OUT HIS SHOP, DIDN'T HE? WE HAD TO TEACH HIM A LITTLE LESSON.
WE TRASHED HIS FUCKING SHELVES, MATE. YOU SHOULD HAVE SEEN HIS FACE, THE PAKI PRICK!
I'M REALLY GOING TO MISS IT AROUND HERE.
NOT FOR LONG.
YOU'VE MESSED UP EVERYTHING YOU EVER TRIED, YOU LITTLE TIT. WHY SHOULD THIS BE ANY DIFFERENT?
YOU'LL BE BACK WITH YOUR TAIL BETWEEN YOUR LEGS.

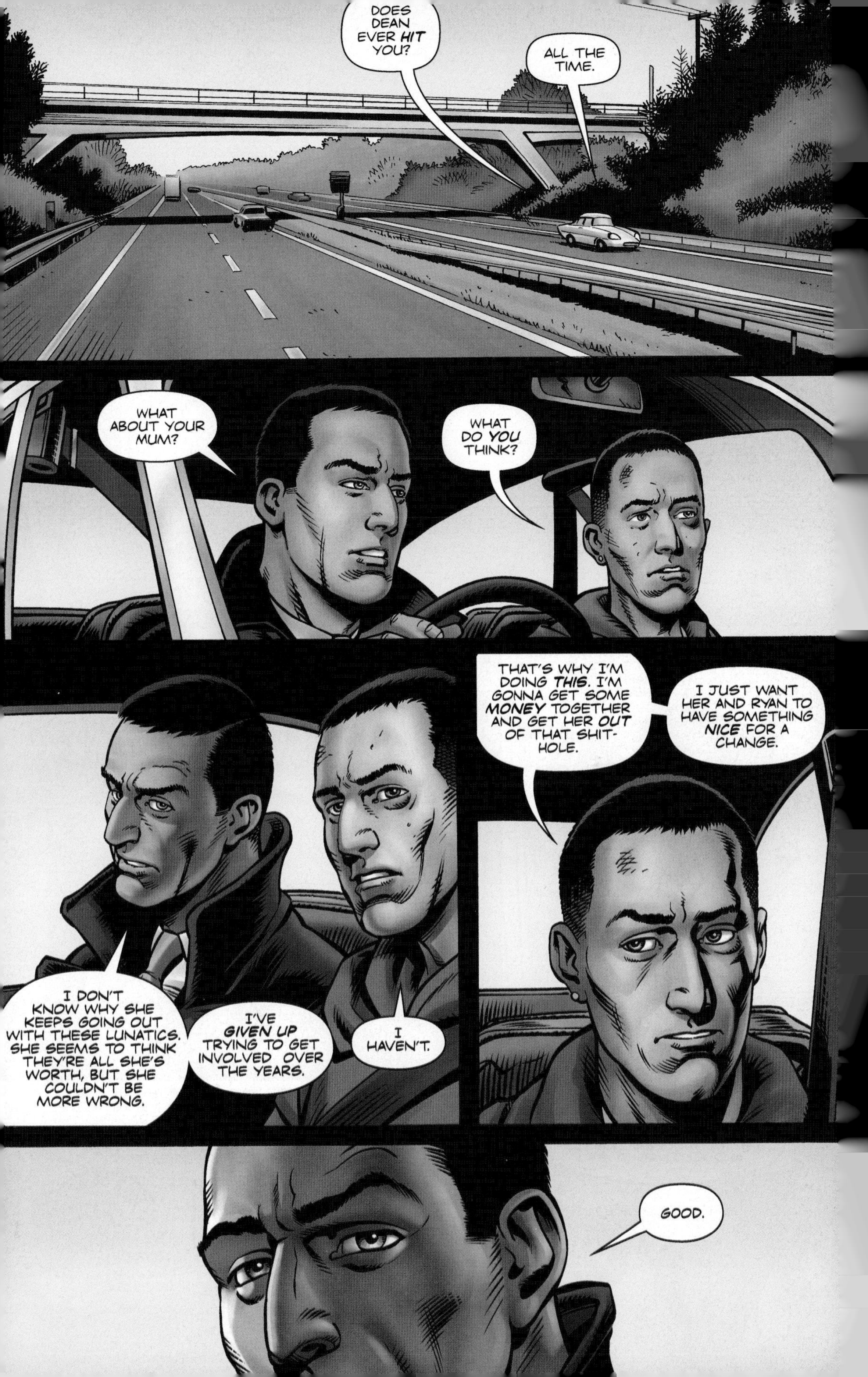
DOES DEAN EVER HIT YOU?
ALL THE TIME.
WHAT ABOUT YOUR MUM?
WHAT DO YOU THINK?
I DON'T KNOW WHY SHE KEEPS GOING OUT WITH THESE LUNATICS. SHE SEEMS TO THINK THEY'RE ALL SHE'S WORTH, BUT SHE COULDN'T BE MORE WRONG.
I'VE GIVEN UP TRYING TO GET INVOLVED OVER THE YEARS.
I HAVEN'T.
THAT'S WHY I'M DOING THIS. I'M GONNA GET SOME MONEY TOGETHER AND GET HER OUT OF THAT SHIT-HOLE.
I JUST WANT HER AND RYAN TO HAVE SOMETHING NICE FOR A CHANGE.
GOOD.

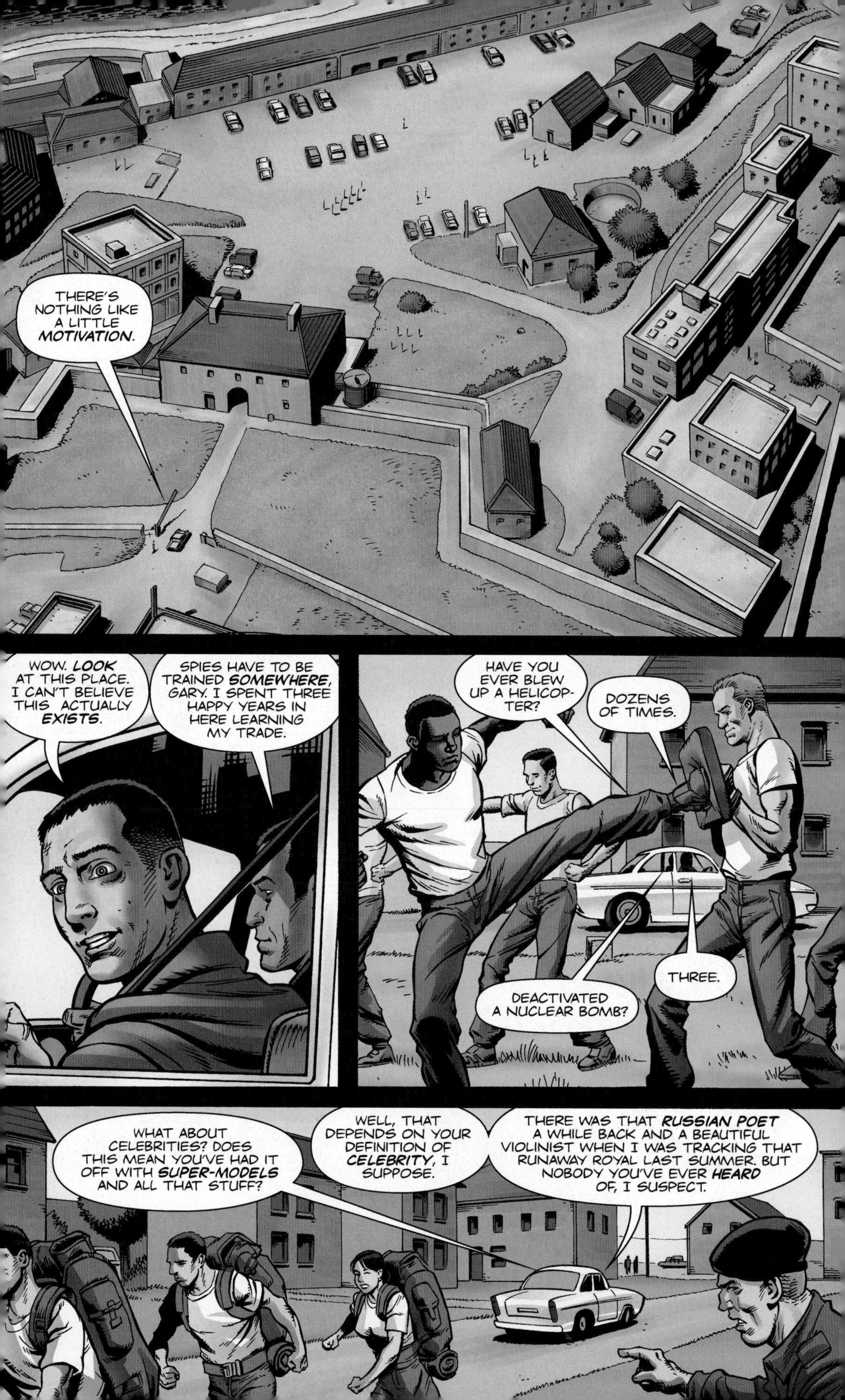
THERE'S NOTHING LIKE A LITTLE MOTIVATION.
WOW. LOOK AT THIS PLACE. I CAN'T BELIEVE THIS ACTUALLY EXISTS.
SPIES HAVE TO BE TRAINED SOMEWHERE, GARY. I SPENT THREE HAPPY YEARS IN HERE LEARNING MY TRADE.
HAVE YOU EVER BLEW UP A HELICOP-TER?
DOZENS OF TIMES.
DEACTIVATED A NUCLEAR BOMB?
THREE.
WHAT ABOUT CELEBRITIES? DOES THIS MEAN YOU'VE HAD IT OFF WITH SUPER-MODELS AND ALL THAT STUFF?
WELL, THAT DEPENDS ON YOUR DEFINITION OF CELEBRITY, I SUPPOSE.
THERE WAS THAT RUSSIAN POET A WHILE BACK AND A BEAUTIFUL VIOLINIST WHEN I WAS TRACKING THAT RUNAWAY ROYAL LAST SUMMER. BUT NOBODY YOU'VE EVER HEARD OF, I SUSPECT.

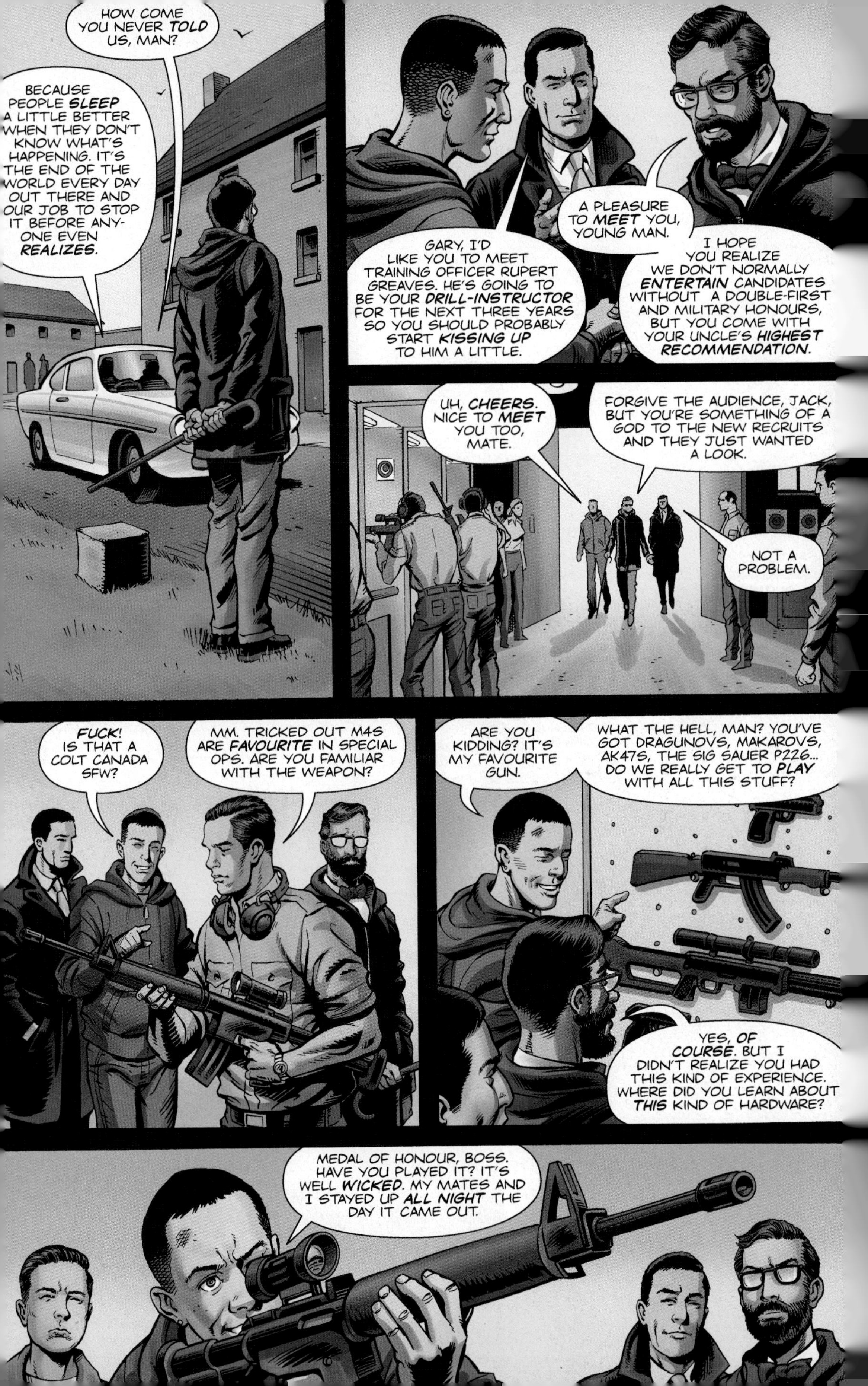
HOW COME YOU NEVER TOLD US, MAN?
BECAUSE PEOPLE SLEEP A LITTLE BETTER WHEN THEY DON'T KNOW WHAT'S HAPPENING. IT'S THE END OF THE WORLD EVERY DAY OUT THERE AND OUR JOB TO STOP IT BEFORE ANY-ONE EVEN REALIZES.
GARY, I'D LIKE YOU TO MEET TRAINING OFFICER RUPERT GREAVES. HE'S GOING TO BE YOUR DRILL-INSTRUCTOR FOR THE NEXT THREE YEARS SO YOU SHOULD PROBABLY START KISSING UP TO HIM A LITTLE.
A PLEASURE TO MEET YOU, YOUNG MAN.
I HOPE YOU REALIZE WE DON'T NORMALLY ENTERTAIN CANDIDATES WITHOUT A DOUBLE-FIRST AND MILITARY HONOURS, BUT YOU COME WITH YOUR UNCLE'S HIGHEST RECOMMENDATION.
UH, CHEERS. NICE TO MEET YOU TOO, MATE.
FORGIVE THE AUDIENCE, JACK, BUT YOU'RE SOMETHING OF A GOD TO THE NEW RECRUITS AND THEY JUST WANTED A LOOK.
NOT A PROBLEM.
FUCK! IS THAT A COLT CANADA SFW?
MM. TRICKED OUT M4S ARE FAVOURITE IN SPECIAL OPS. ARE YOU FAMILIAR WITH THE WEAPON?
ARE YOU KIDDING? IT'S MY FAVOURITE GUN.
WHAT THE HELL, MAN? YOU'VE GOT DRAGUNOVS, MAKAROVS, AK47S, THE SIG SAUER P226... DO WE REALLY GET TO PLAY WITH ALL THIS STUFF?
YES, OF COURSE. BUT I DIDN'T REALIZE YOU HAD THIS KIND OF EXPERIENCE. WHERE DID YOU LEARN ABOUT THIS KIND OF HARDWARE?
MEDAL OF HONOUR, BOSS. HAVE YOU PLAYED IT? IT'S WELL WICKED. MY MATES AND I STAYED UP ALL NIGHT THE DAY IT CAME OUT.

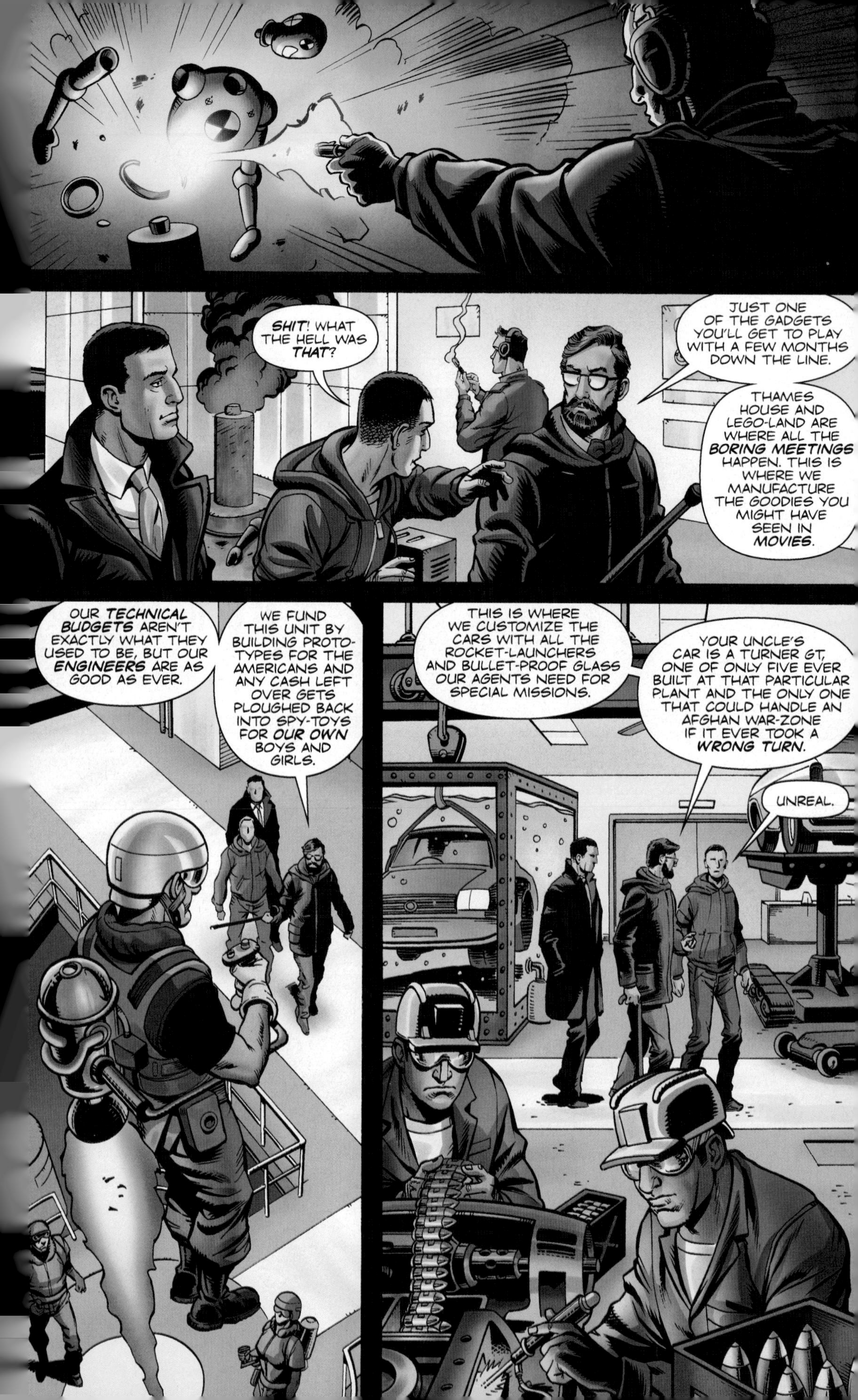
SHIT! WHAT THE HELL WAS THAT?
JUST ONE OF THE GADGETS YOU'LL GET TO PLAY WITH A FEW MONTHS DOWN THE LINE.
THAMES HOUSE AND LEGO-LAND ARE WHERE ALL THE BORING MEETINGS HAPPEN. THIS IS WHERE WE MANUFACTURE THE GOODIES YOU MIGHT HAVE SEEN IN MOVIES.
OUR TECHNICAL BUDGETS AREN'T EXACTLY WHAT THEY USED TO BE, BUT OUR ENGINEERS ARE AS GOOD AS EVER.
WE FUND THIS UNIT BY BUILDING PROTOTYPES FOR THE AMERICANS AND ANY CASH LEFT OVER GETS PLOUGHED BACK INTO SPY-TOYS FOR OUR OWN BOYS AND GIRLS.
THIS IS WHERE WE CUSTOMIZE THE CARS WITH ALL THE ROCKET-LAUNCHERS AND BULLET-PROOF GLASS OUR AGENTS NEED FOR SPECIAL MISSIONS.
YOUR UNCLE'S CAR IS A TURNER GT, ONE OF ONLY FIVE EVER BUILT AT THAT PARTICULAR PLANT AND THE ONLY ONE THAT COULD HANDLE AN AFGHAN WAR-ZONE IF IT EVER TOOK A WRONG TURN.
UNREAL.

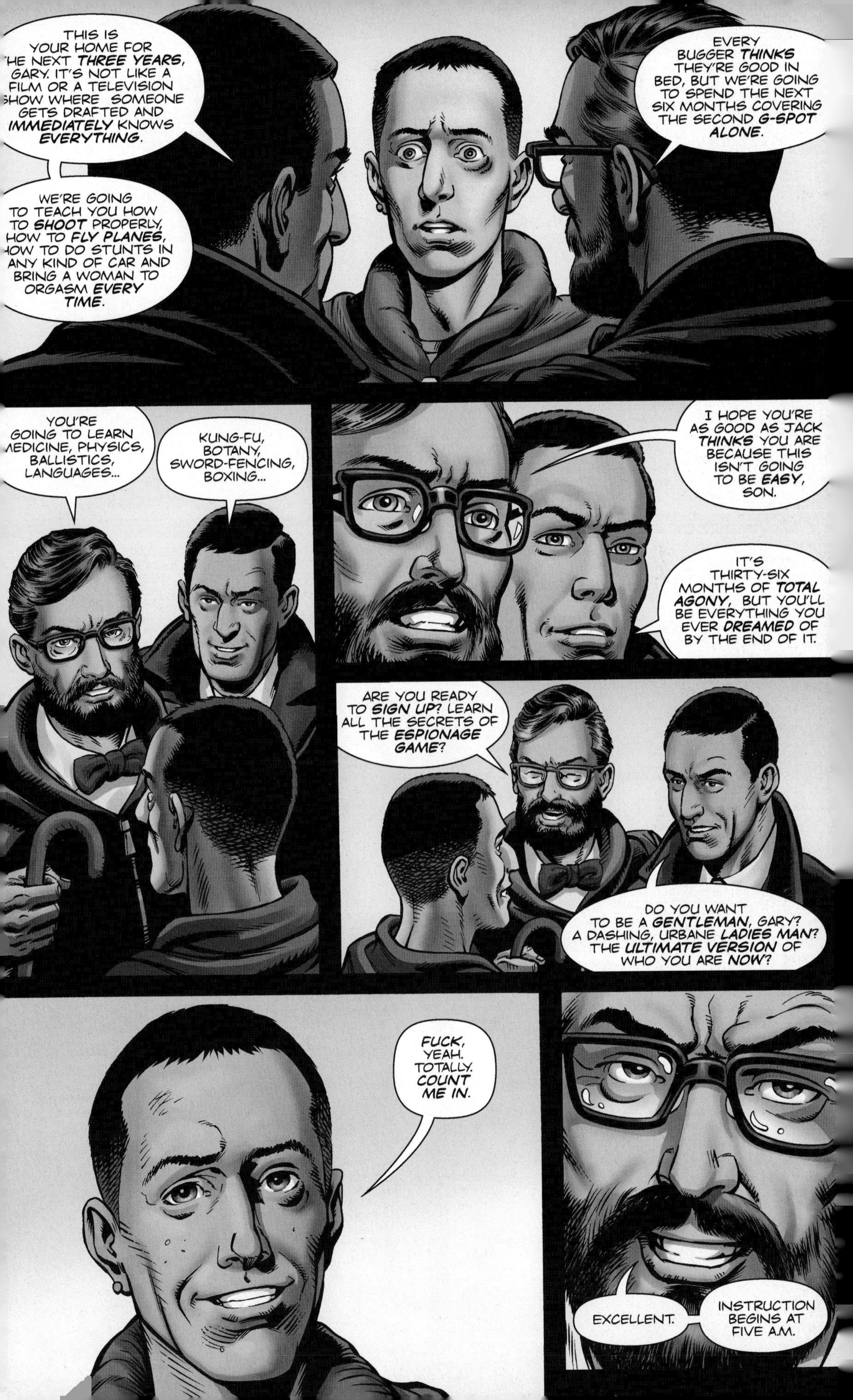
THIS IS YOUR HOME FOR THE NEXT THREE YEARS, GARY. IT'S NOT LIKE A FILM OR A TELEVISION SHOW WHERE SOMEONE GETS DRAFTED AND IMMEDIATELY KNOWS EVERYTHING.
WE'RE GOING TO TEACH YOU HOW TO SHOOT PROPERLY, HOW TO FLY PLANES, HOW TO DO STUNTS IN ANY KIND OF CAR AND BRING A WOMAN TO ORGASM EVERY TIME.
EVERY BUGGER THINKS THEY'RE GOOD IN BED, BUT WE'RE GOING TO SPEND THE NEXT SIX MONTHS COVERING THE SECOND G-SPOT ALONE.
YOU'RE GOING TO LEARN MEDICINE, PHYSICS, BALLISTICS, LANGUAGES...
KUNG-FU, BOTANY, SWORD-FENCING, BOXING...
I HOPE YOU'RE AS GOOD AS JACK THINKS YOU ARE BECAUSE THIS ISN'T GOING TO BE EASY, SON.
IT'S THIRTY-SIX MONTHS OF TOTAL AGONY, BUT YOU'LL BE EVERYTHING YOU EVER DREAMED OF BY THE END OF IT.
ARE YOU READY TO SIGN UP? LEARN ALL THE SECRETS OF THE ESPIONAGE GAME?
DO YOU WANT TO BE A GENTLEMAN, GARY? A DASHING, URBANE LADIES MAN? THE ULTIMATE VERSION OF WHO YOU ARE NOW?
FUCK, YEAH. TOTALLY. COUNT ME IN.
EXCELLENT.
INSTRUCTION BEGINS AT FIVE A.M.

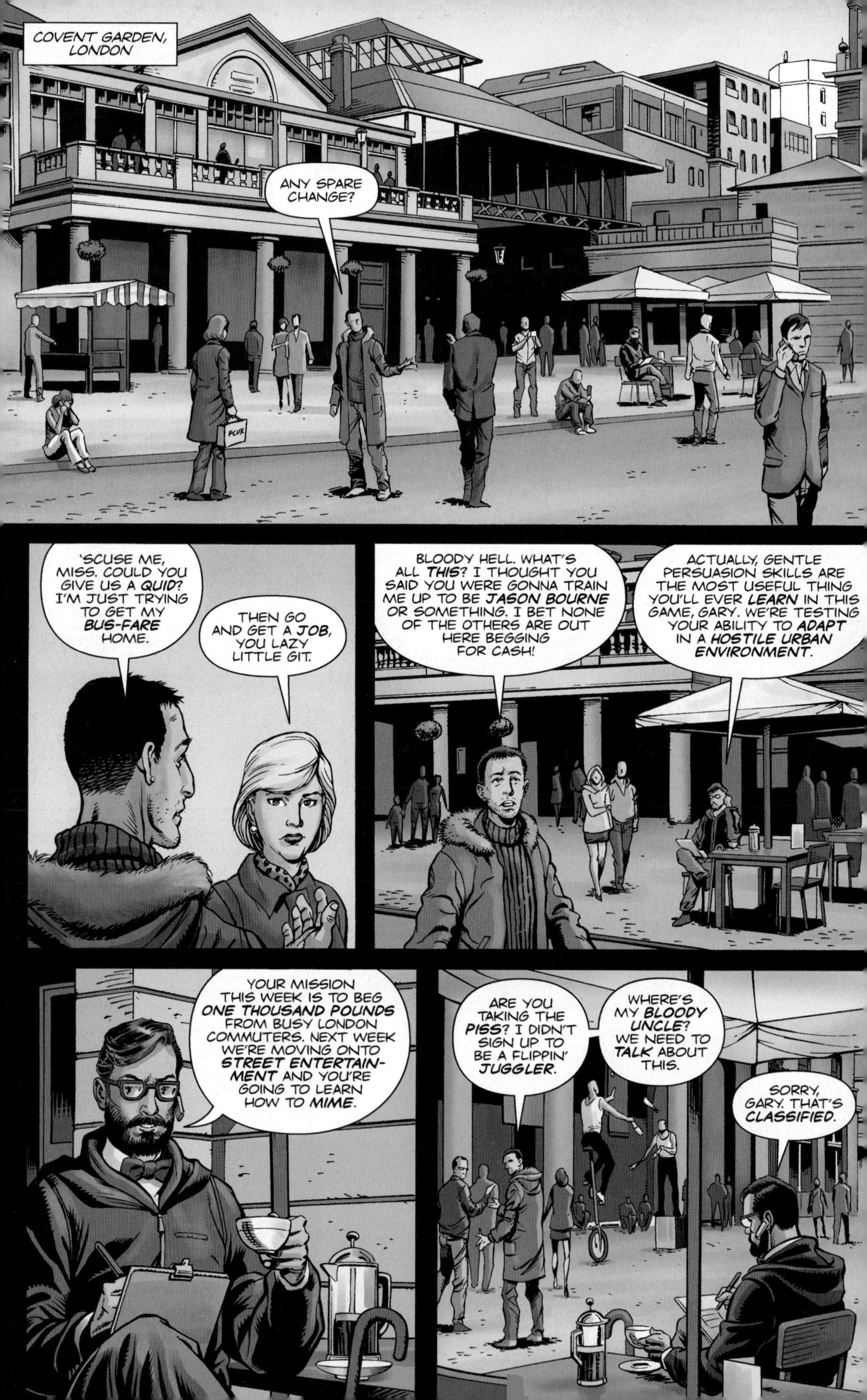
COVENT GARDEN, LONDON
ANY SPARE CHANGE?
FCUK
'SCUSE ME, MISS. COULD YOU GIVE US A QUID? I'M JUST TRYING TO GET MY BUS-FARE HOME.
THEN GO AND GET A JOB, YOU LAZY LITTLE GIT.
BLOODY HELL. WHAT'S ALL THIS? I THOUGHT YOU SAID YOU WERE GONNA TRAIN ME UP TO BE JASON BOURNE OR SOMETHING. I BET NONE OF THE OTHERS ARE OUT HERE BEGGING FOR CASH!
ACTUALLY, GENTLE PERSUASION SKILLS ARE THE MOST USEFUL THING YOU'LL EVER LEARN IN THIS GAME, GARY. WE'RE TESTING YOUR ABILITY TO ADAPT IN A HOSTILE URBAN ENVIRONMENT.
YOUR MISSION THIS WEEK IS TO BEG ONE THOUSAND POUNDS FROM BUSY LONDON COMMUTERS. NEXT WEEK WE'RE MOVING ONTO STREET ENTERTAIN-MENT AND YOU'RE GOING TO LEARN HOW TO MIME.
ARE YOU TAKING THE PISS? I DIDN'T SIGN UP TO BE A FLIPPIN' JUGGLER.
WHERE'S MY BLOODY UNCLE? WE NEED TO TALK ABOUT THIS.
SORRY, GARY. THAT'S CLASSIFIED.

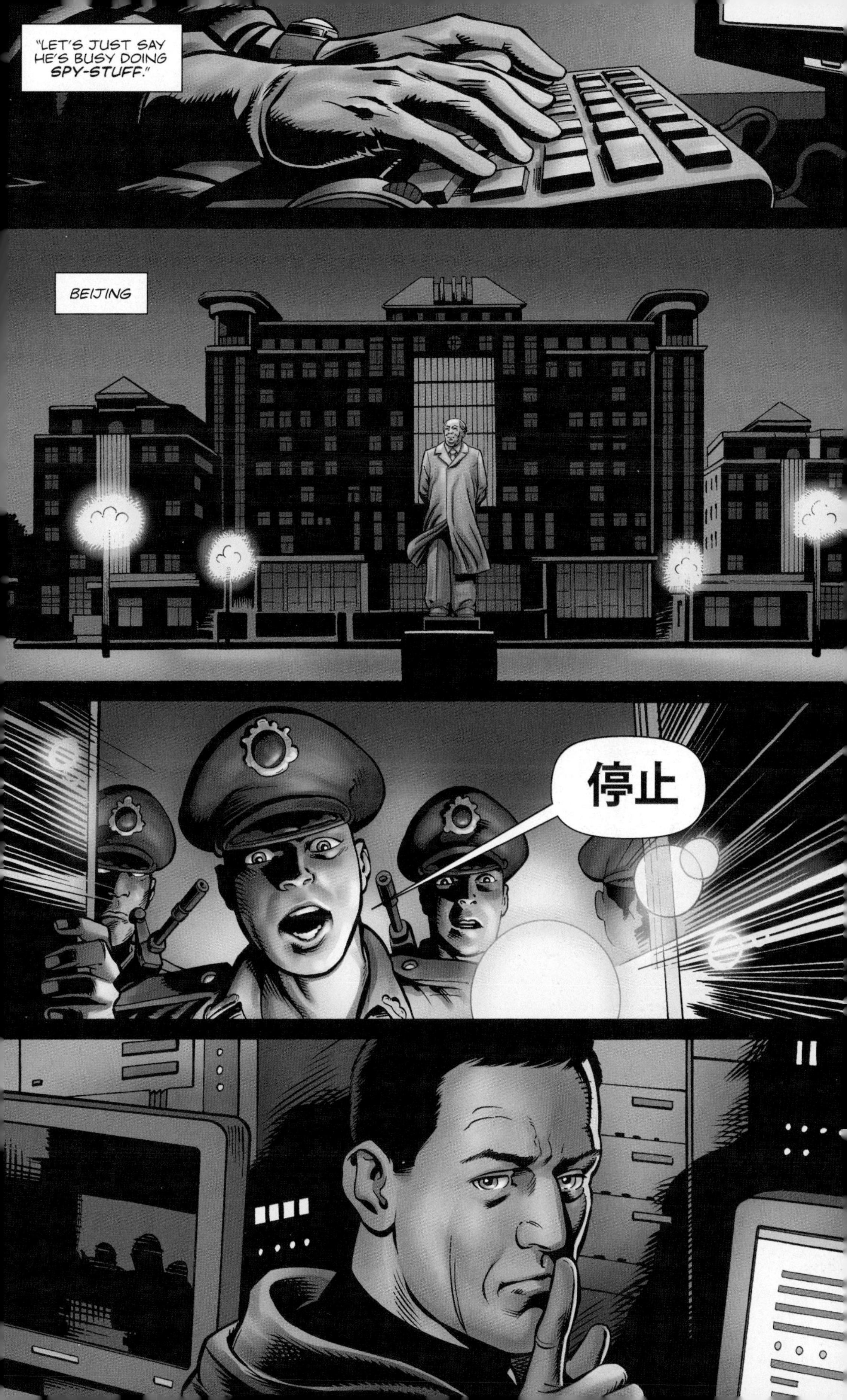
"LET'S JUST SAY HE'S BUSY DOING SPY-STUFF."
BEIJING
停止

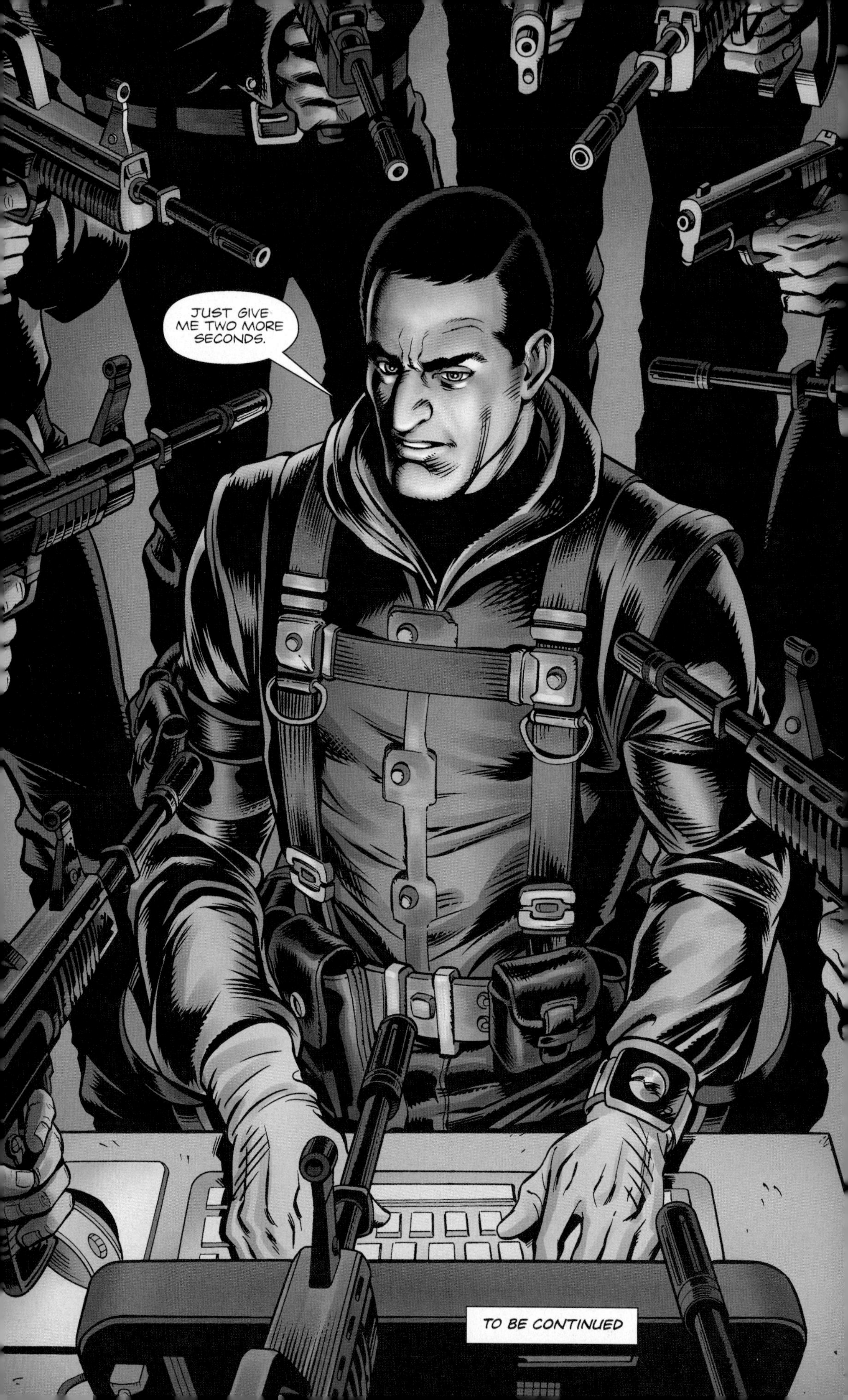
JUST GIVE ME TWO MORE SECONDS.
TO BE CONTINUED

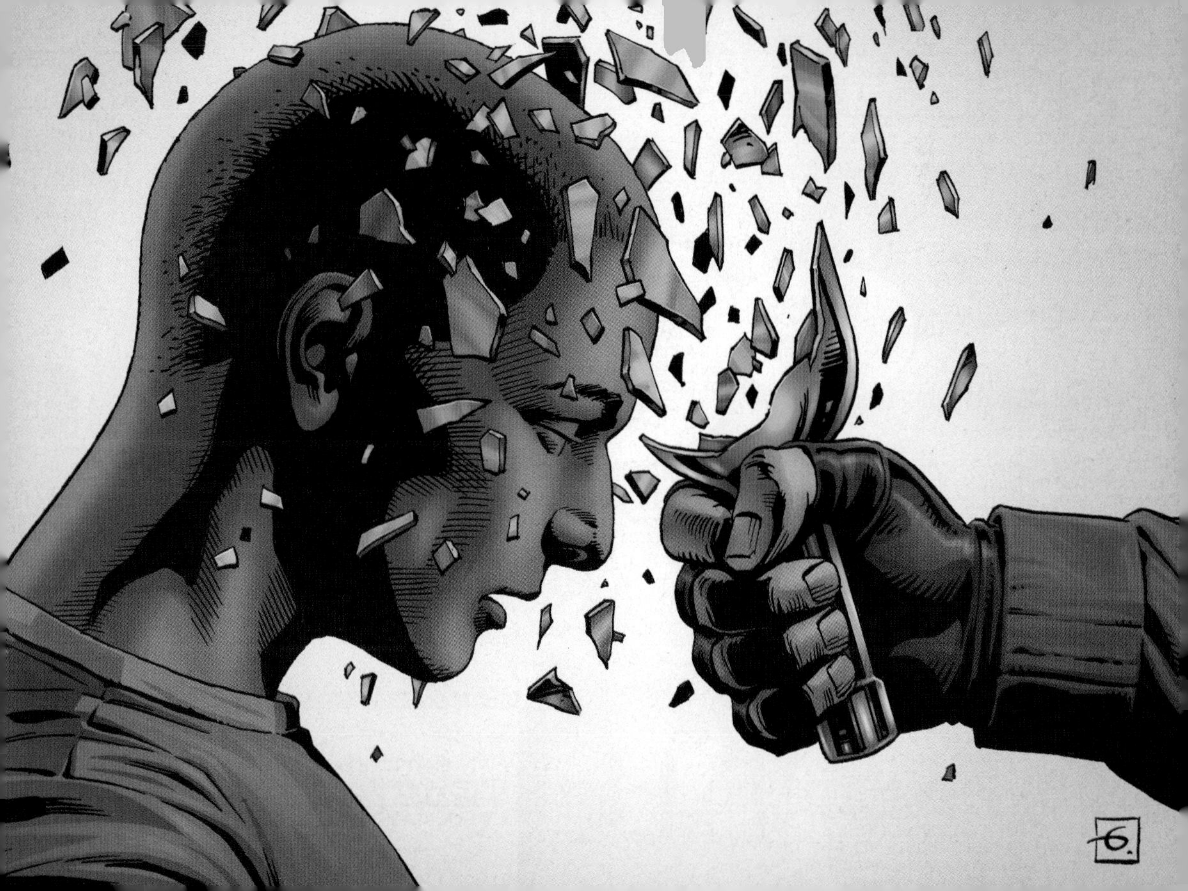

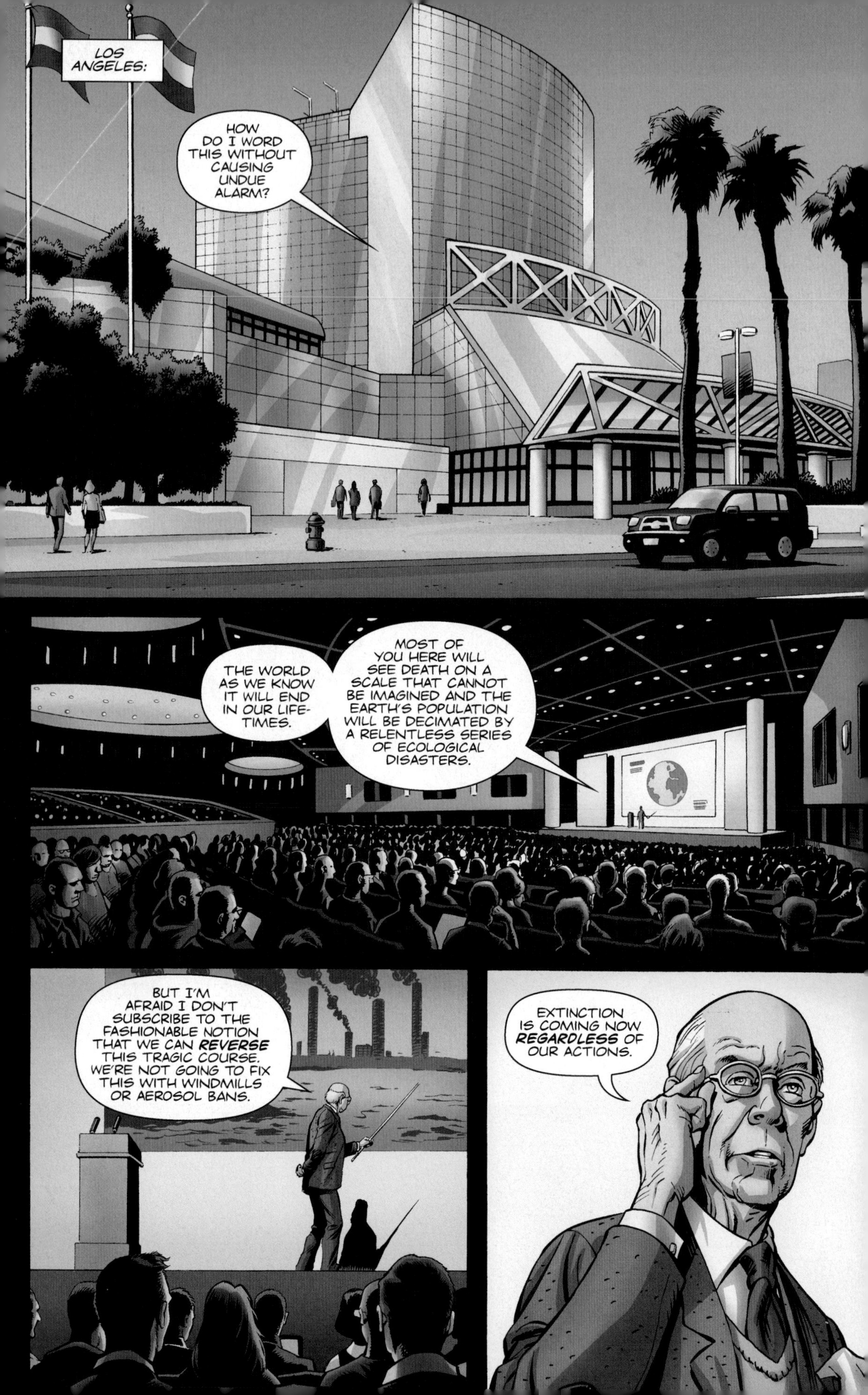
LOS ANGELES:
HOW DO I WORD THIS WITHOUT CAUSING UNDUE ALARM?
THE WORLD AS WE KNOW IT WILL END IN OUR LIFE-TIMES.
MOST OF YOU HERE WILL SEE DEATH ON A SCALE THAT CANNOT BE IMAGINED AND THE EARTH'S POPULATION WILL BE DECIMATED BY A RELENTLESS SERIES OF ECOLOGICAL DISASTERS.
BUT I'M AFRAID I DON'T SUBSCRIBE TO THE FASHIONABLE NOTION THAT WE CAN ***REVERSE*** THIS TRAGIC COURSE. WE'RE NOT GOING TO FIX THIS WITH WINDMILLS OR AEROSOL BANS.
EXTINCTION IS COMING NOW ***REGARDLESS*** OF OUR ACTIONS.

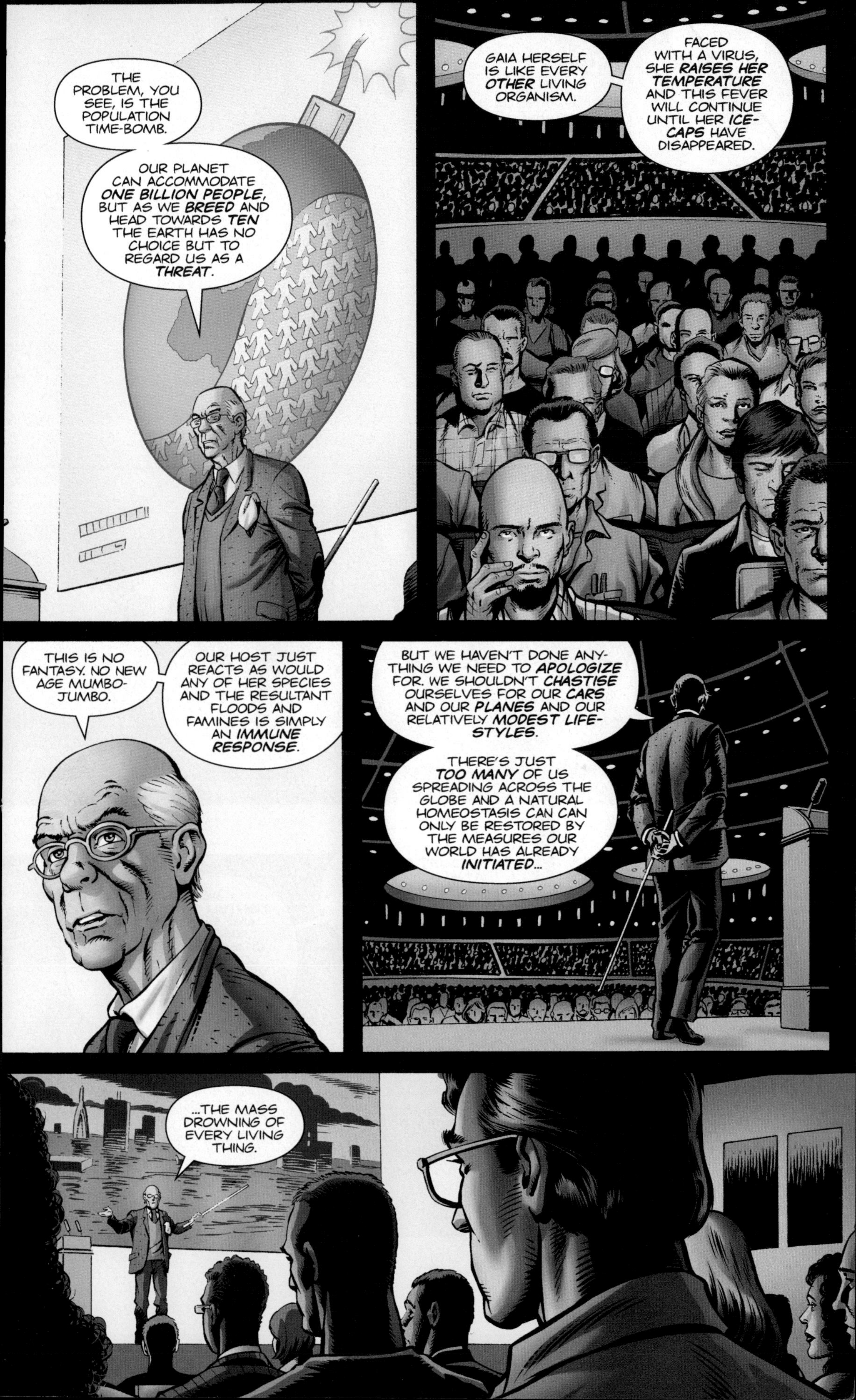
THE PROBLEM, YOU SEE, IS THE POPULATION TIME-BOMB.
OUR PLANET CAN ACCOMMODATE ONE BILLION PEOPLE, BUT AS WE BREED AND HEAD TOWARDS TEN THE EARTH HAS NO CHOICE BUT TO REGARD US AS A THREAT.
GAIA HERSELF IS LIKE EVERY OTHER LIVING ORGANISM.
FACED WITH A VIRUS, SHE RAISES HER TEMPERATURE AND THIS FEVER WILL CONTINUE UNTIL HER ICE-CAPS HAVE DISAPPEARED.
THIS IS NO FANTASY. NO NEW AGE MUMBO-JUMBO.
OUR HOST JUST REACTS AS WOULD ANY OF HER SPECIES AND THE RESULTANT FLOODS AND FAMINES IS SIMPLY AN IMMUNE RESPONSE.
BUT WE HAVEN'T DONE ANYTHING WE NEED TO APOLOGIZE FOR. WE SHOULDN'T CHASTISE OURSELVES FOR OUR CARS AND OUR PLANES AND OUR RELATIVELY MODEST LIFE-STYLES.
THERE'S JUST TOO MANY OF US SPREADING ACROSS THE GLOBE AND A NATURAL HOMEOSTASIS CAN CAN ONLY BE RESTORED BY THE MEASURES OUR WORLD HAS ALREADY INITIATED...
...THE MASS DROWNING OF EVERY LIVING THING.

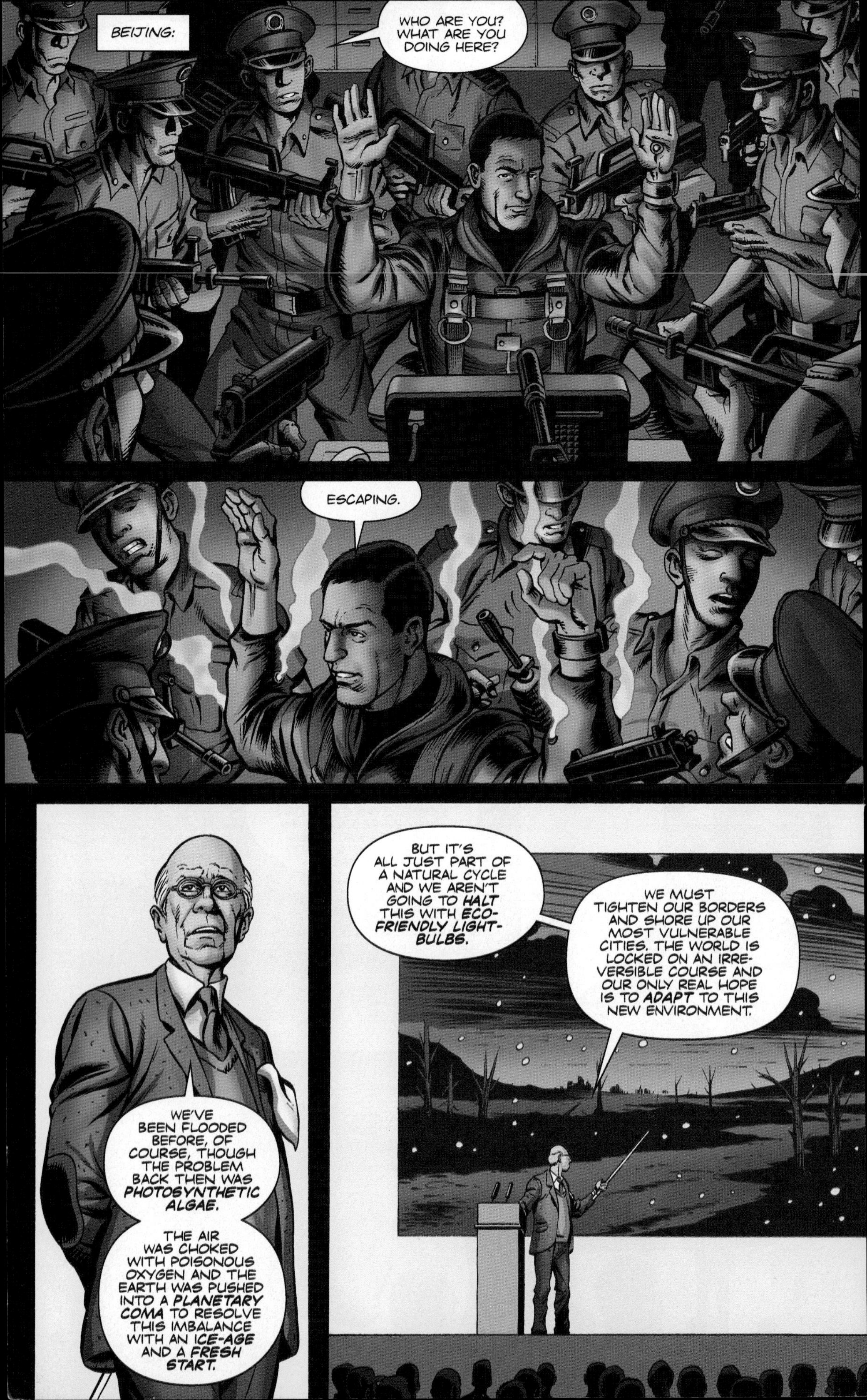
BEIJING:
WHO ARE YOU? WHAT ARE YOU DOING HERE?
ESCAPING.
WE'VE BEEN FLOODED BEFORE, OF COURSE, THOUGH THE PROBLEM BACK THEN WAS PHOTOSYNTHETIC ALGAE.
THE AIR WAS CHOKED WITH POISONOUS OXYGEN AND THE EARTH WAS PUSHED INTO A PLANETARY COMA TO RESOLVE THIS IMBALANCE WITH AN ICE-AGE AND A FRESH START.
BUT IT'S ALL JUST PART OF A NATURAL CYCLE AND WE AREN'T GOING TO HALT THIS WITH ECO-FRIENDLY LIGHT-BULBS.
WE MUST TIGHTEN OUR BORDERS AND SHORE UP OUR MOST VULNERABLE CITIES. THE WORLD IS LOCKED ON AN IRRE-VERSIBLE COURSE AND OUR ONLY REAL HOPE IS TO ADAPT TO THIS NEW ENVIRONMENT.

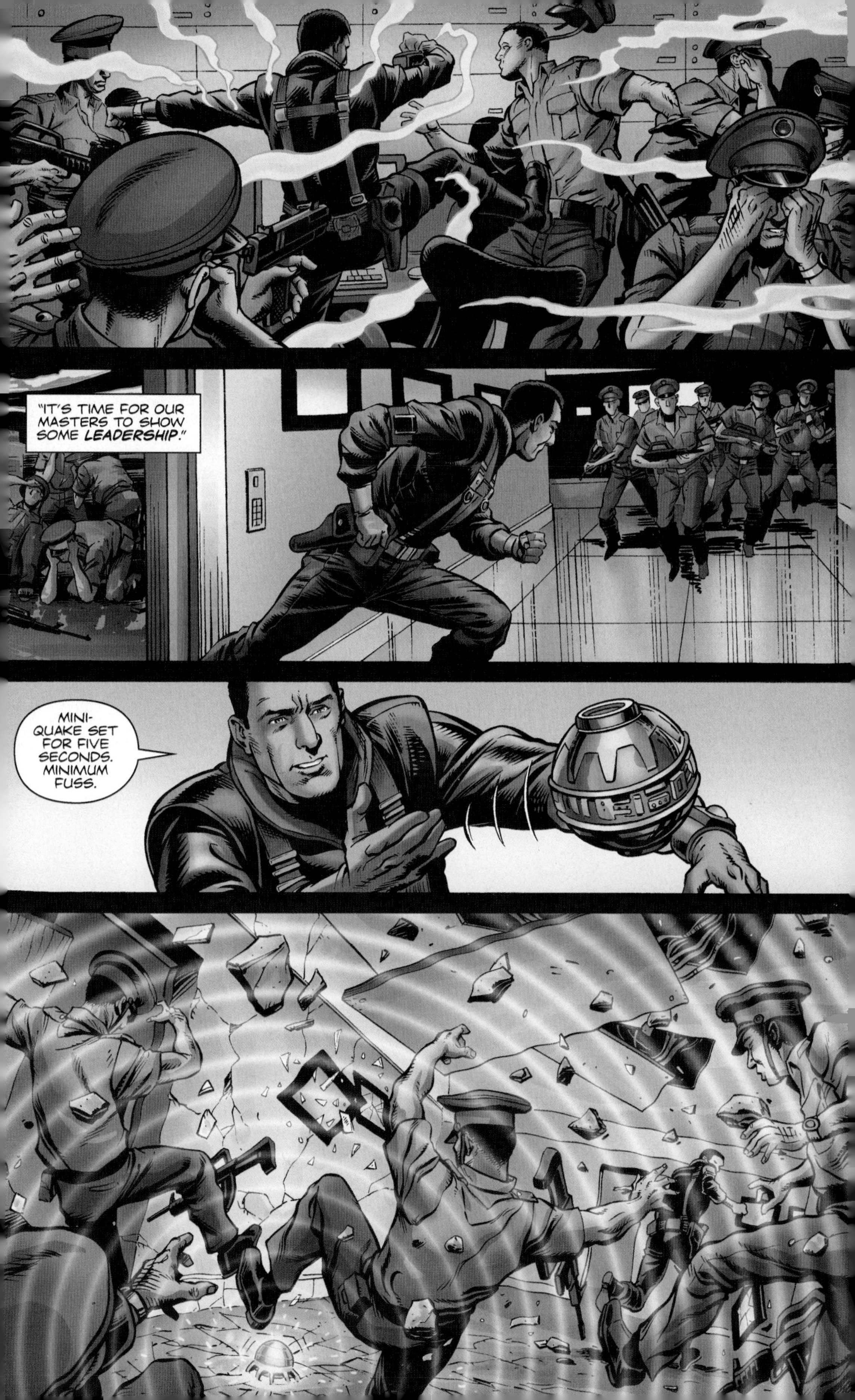
"IT'S TIME FOR OUR MASTERS TO SHOW SOME **LEADERSHIP**."
MINI-QUAKE SET FOR FIVE SECONDS. MINIMUM FUSS.

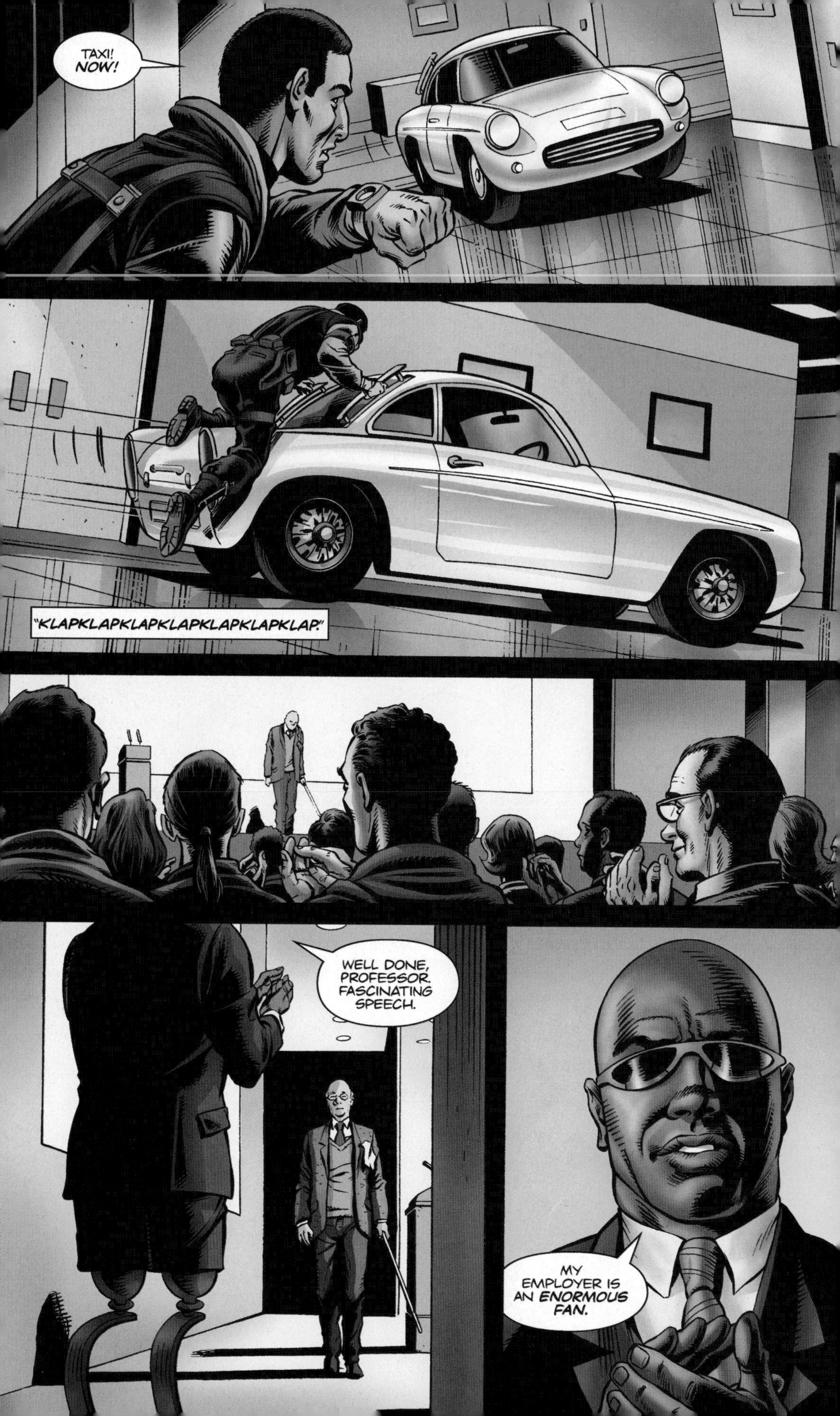
TAXI! NOW!
"KLAPKLAPKLAPKLAPKLAPKLAPKLAP."
WELL DONE, PROFESSOR. FASCINATING SPEECH.
MY EMPLOYER IS AN ENORMOUS FAN.

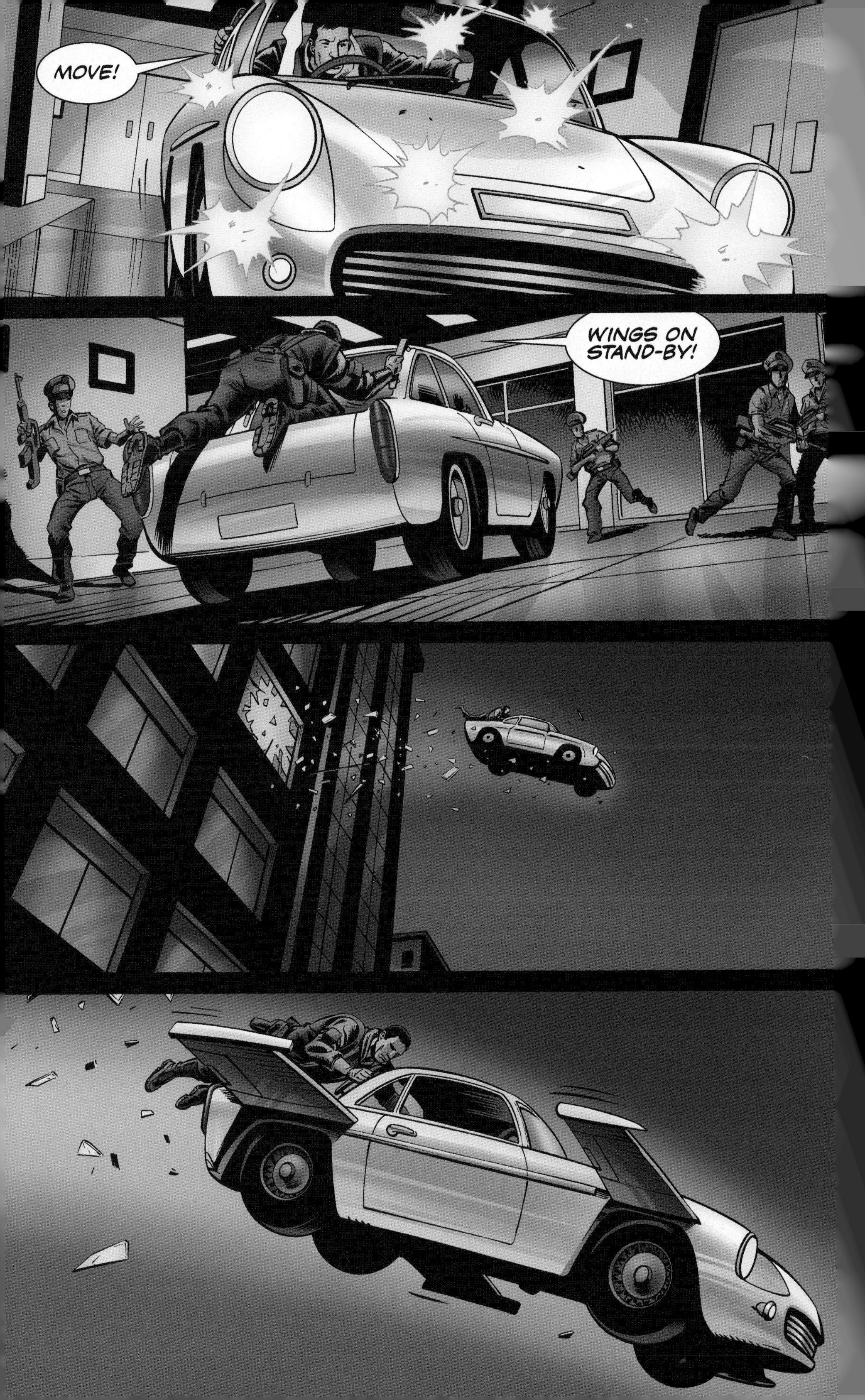
MOVE!
WINGS ON STAND-BY!

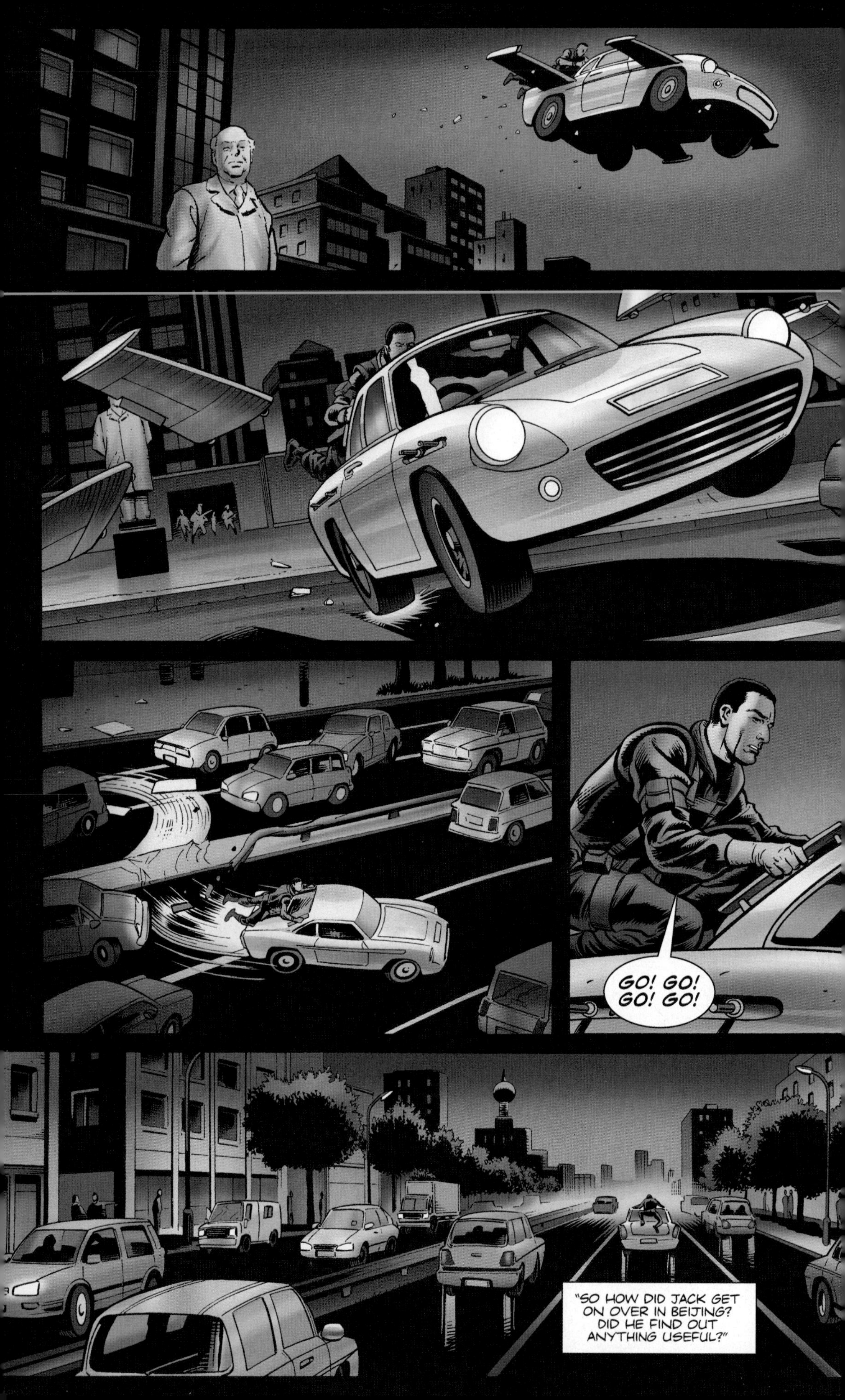
GO! GO! GO! GO!
"SO HOW DID JACK GET ON OVER IN BEIJING? DID HE FIND OUT ANYTHING USEFUL?"

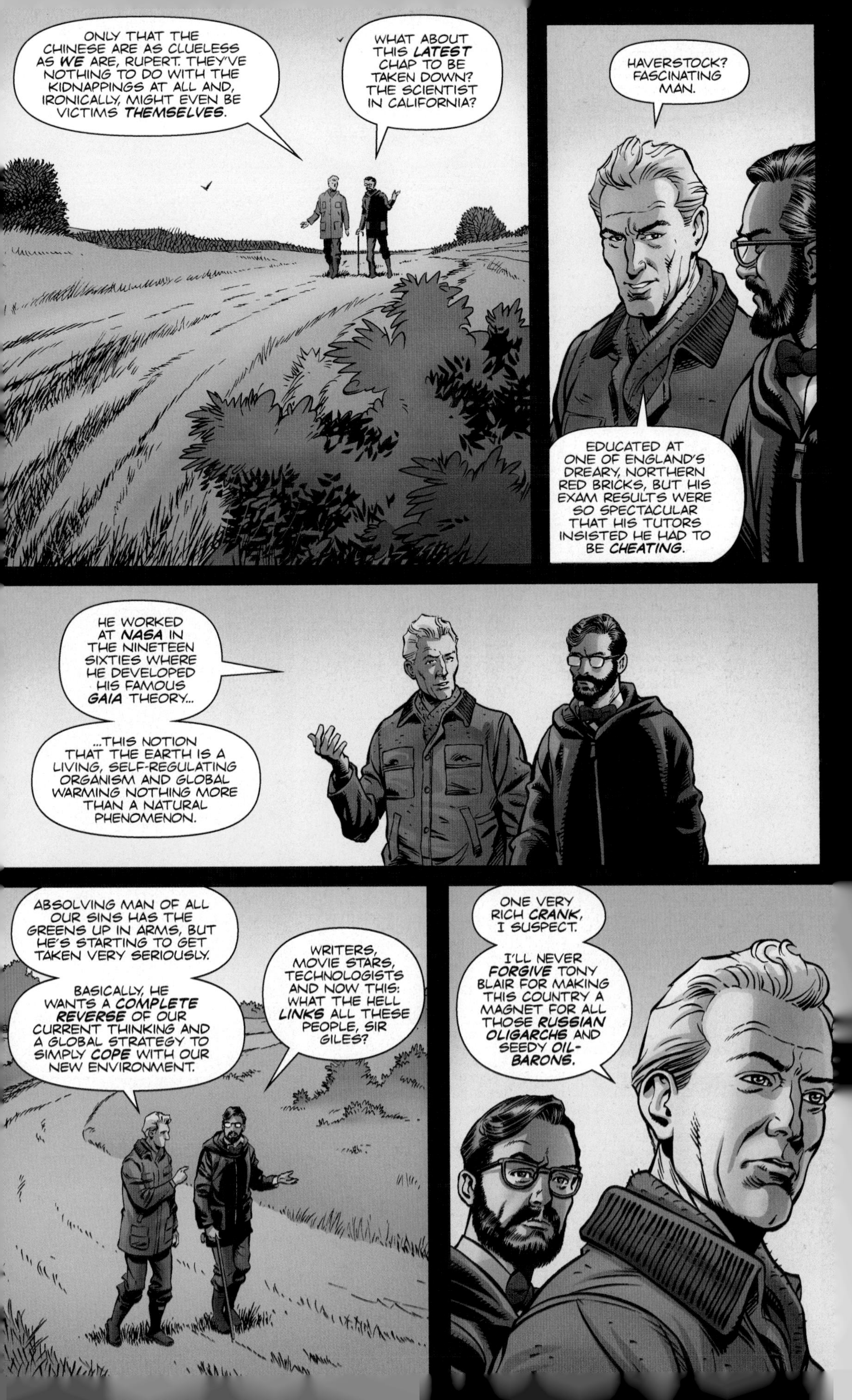
ONLY THAT THE CHINESE ARE AS CLUELESS AS WE ARE, RUPERT. THEY'VE NOTHING TO DO WITH THE KIDNAPPINGS AT ALL AND, IRONICALLY, MIGHT EVEN BE VICTIMS THEMSELVES.
WHAT ABOUT THIS LATEST CHAP TO BE TAKEN DOWN? THE SCIENTIST IN CALIFORNIA?
HAVERSTOCK? FASCINATING MAN.
EDUCATED AT ONE OF ENGLAND'S DREARY, NORTHERN RED BRICKS, BUT HIS EXAM RESULTS WERE SO SPECTACULAR THAT HIS TUTORS INSISTED HE HAD TO BE CHEATING.
HE WORKED AT NASA IN THE NINETEEN SIXTIES WHERE HE DEVELOPED HIS FAMOUS GAIA THEORY...
...THIS NOTION THAT THE EARTH IS A LIVING, SELF-REGULATING ORGANISM AND GLOBAL WARMING NOTHING MORE THAN A NATURAL PHENOMENON.
ABSOLVING MAN OF ALL OUR SINS HAS THE GREENS UP IN ARMS, BUT HE'S STARTING TO GET TAKEN VERY SERIOUSLY.
BASICALLY, HE WANTS A COMPLETE REVERSE OF OUR CURRENT THINKING AND A GLOBAL STRATEGY TO SIMPLY COPE WITH OUR NEW ENVIRONMENT.
WRITERS, MOVIE STARS, TECHNOLOGISTS AND NOW THIS: WHAT THE HELL LINKS ALL THESE PEOPLE, SIR GILES?
ONE VERY RICH CRANK, I SUSPECT.
I'LL NEVER FORGIVE TONY BLAIR FOR MAKING THIS COUNTRY A MAGNET FOR ALL THOSE RUSSIAN OLIGARCHS AND SEEDY OIL-BARONS.

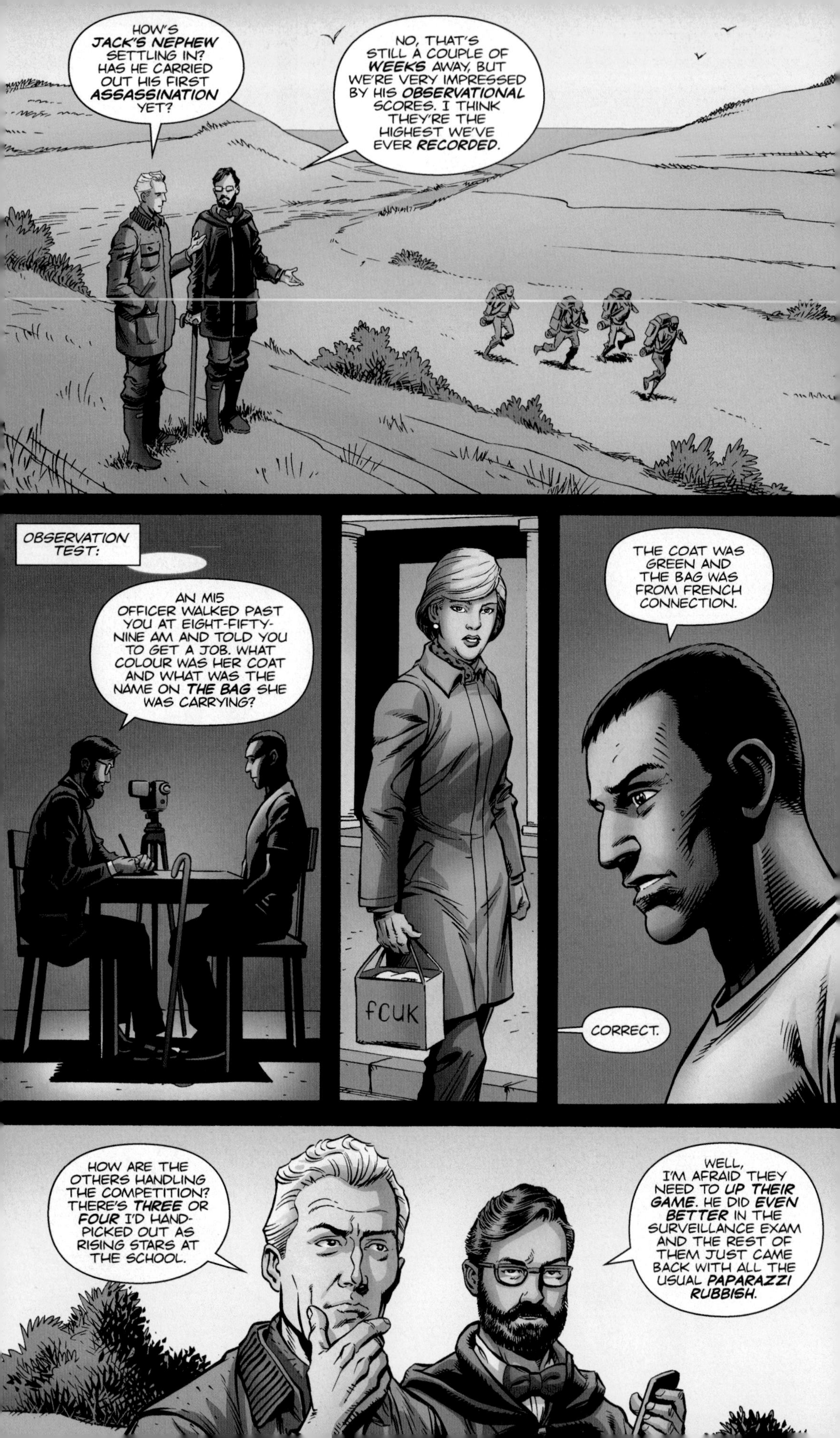
HOW'S JACK'S NEPHEW SETTLING IN? HAS HE CARRIED OUT HIS FIRST ASSASSINATION YET?
NO, THAT'S STILL A COUPLE OF WEEKS AWAY, BUT WE'RE VERY IMPRESSED BY HIS OBSERVATIONAL SCORES. I THINK THEY'RE THE HIGHEST WE'VE EVER RECORDED.
OBSERVATION TEST:
AN MI5 OFFICER WALKED PAST YOU AT EIGHT-FIFTY-NINE AM AND TOLD YOU TO GET A JOB. WHAT COLOUR WAS HER COAT AND WHAT WAS THE NAME ON THE BAG SHE WAS CARRYING?
fcuk
THE COAT WAS GREEN AND THE BAG WAS FROM FRENCH CONNECTION.
CORRECT.
HOW ARE THE OTHERS HANDLING THE COMPETITION? THERE'S THREE OR FOUR I'D HAND-PICKED OUT AS RISING STARS AT THE SCHOOL.
WELL, I'M AFRAID THEY NEED TO UP THEIR GAME. HE DID EVEN BETTER IN THE SURVEILLANCE EXAM AND THE REST OF THEM JUST CAME BACK WITH ALL THE USUAL PAPARAZZI RUBBISH.

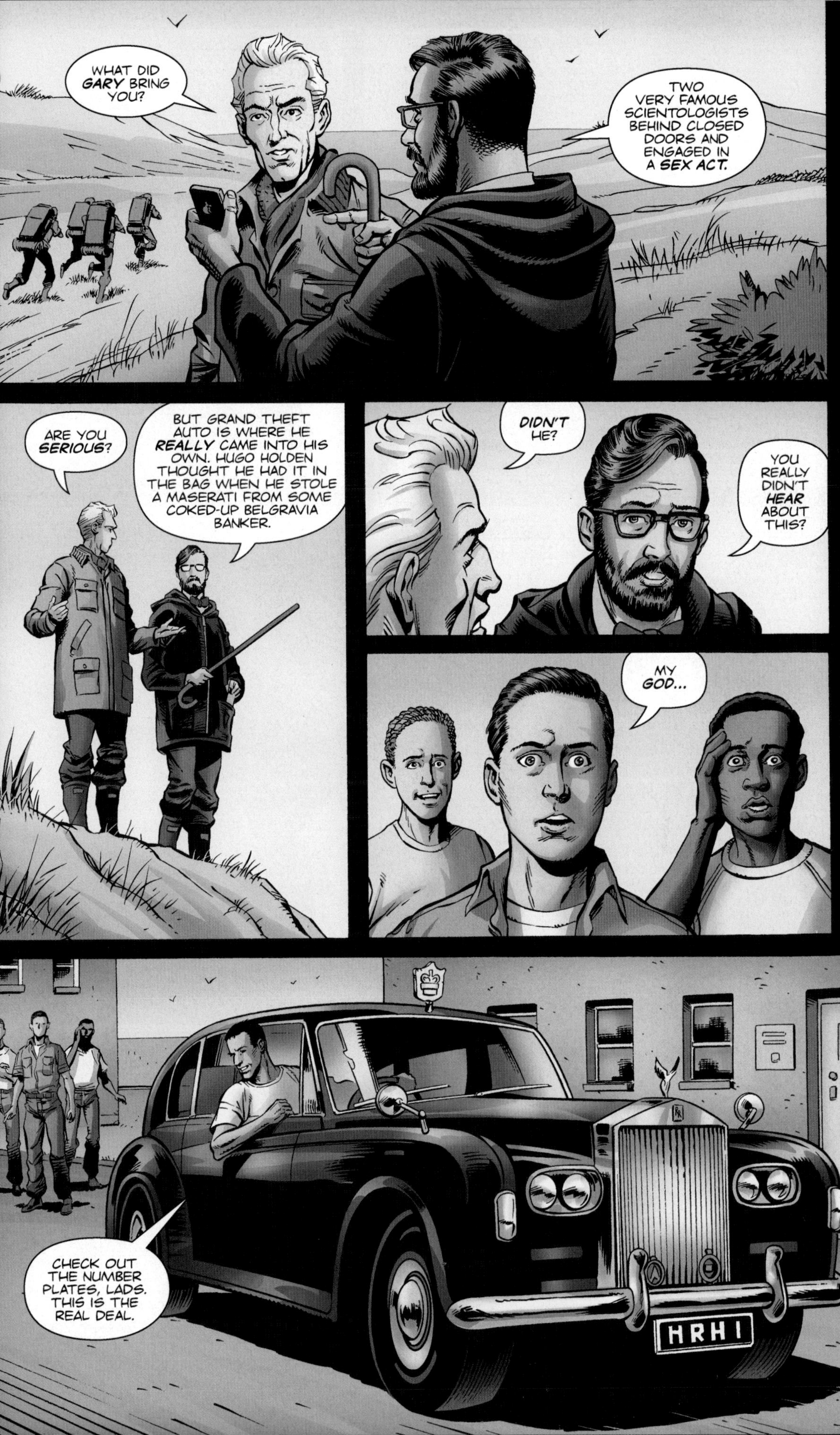
WHAT DID GARY BRING YOU?
TWO VERY FAMOUS SCIENTOLOGISTS BEHIND CLOSED DOORS AND ENGAGED IN A SEX ACT.
ARE YOU SERIOUS?
BUT GRAND THEFT AUTO IS WHERE HE REALLY CAME INTO HIS OWN. HUGO HOLDEN THOUGHT HE HAD IT IN THE BAG WHEN HE STOLE A MASERATI FROM SOME COKED-UP BELGRAVIA BANKER.
DIDN'T HE?
YOU REALLY DIDN'T HEAR ABOUT THIS?
MY GOD...
CHECK OUT THE NUMBER PLATES, LADS. THIS IS THE REAL DEAL.
HRH 1

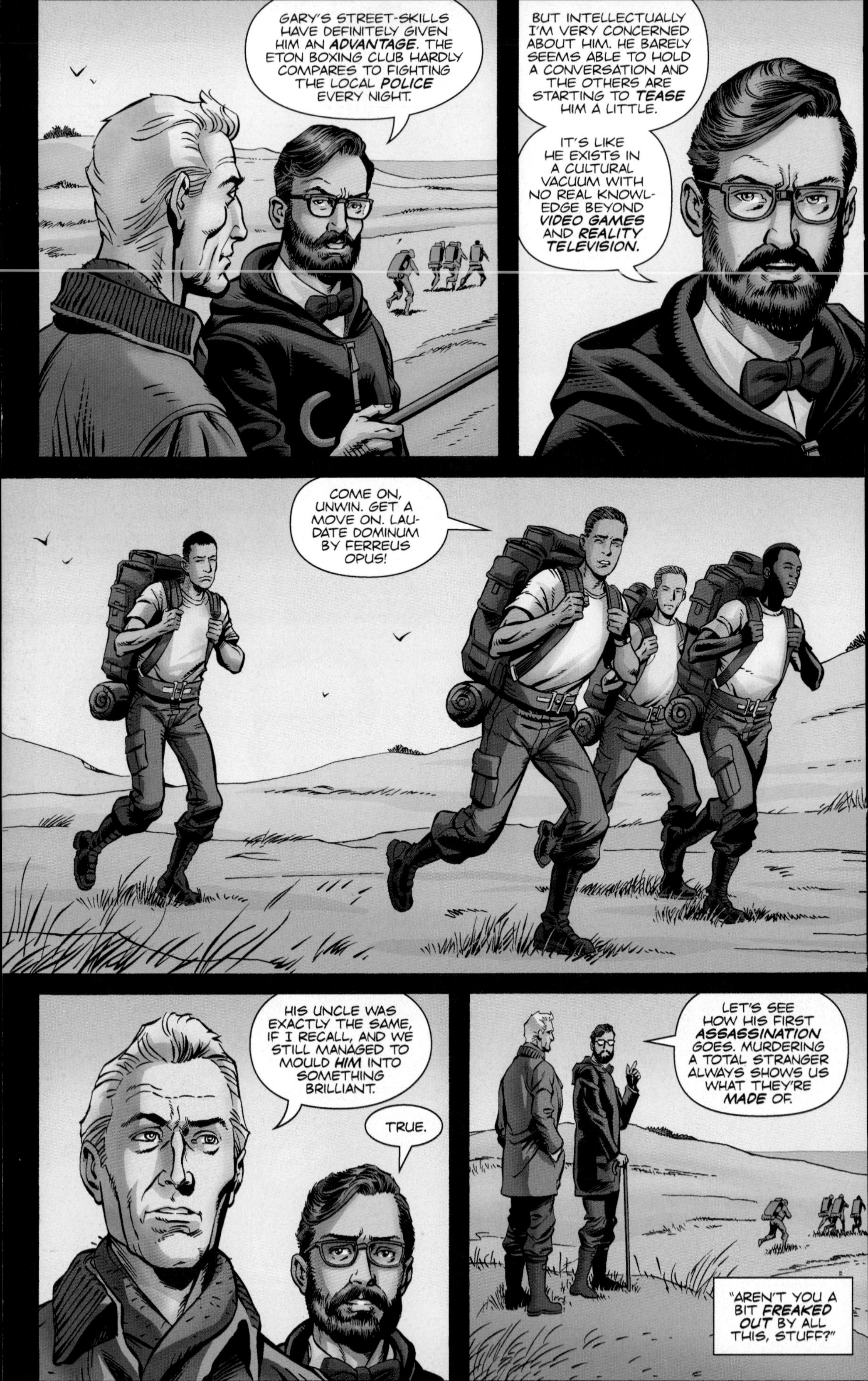
GARY'S STREET-SKILLS HAVE DEFINITELY GIVEN HIM AN ADVANTAGE. THE ETON BOXING CLUB HARDLY COMPARES TO FIGHTING THE LOCAL POLICE EVERY NIGHT.
BUT INTELLECTUALLY I'M VERY CONCERNED ABOUT HIM. HE BARELY SEEMS ABLE TO HOLD A CONVERSATION AND THE OTHERS ARE STARTING TO TEASE HIM A LITTLE.
IT'S LIKE HE EXISTS IN A CULTURAL VACUUM WITH NO REAL KNOWL-EDGE BEYOND VIDEO GAMES AND REALITY TELEVISION.
COME ON, UNWIN. GET A MOVE ON. LAU-DATE DOMINUM BY FERREUS OPUS!
HIS UNCLE WAS EXACTLY THE SAME, IF I RECALL, AND WE STILL MANAGED TO MOULD HIM INTO SOMETHING BRILLIANT.
TRUE.
LET'S SEE HOW HIS FIRST ASSASSINATION GOES. MURDERING A TOTAL STRANGER ALWAYS SHOWS US WHAT THEY'RE MADE OF.
"AREN'T YOU A BIT FREAKED OUT BY ALL THIS, STUFF?"

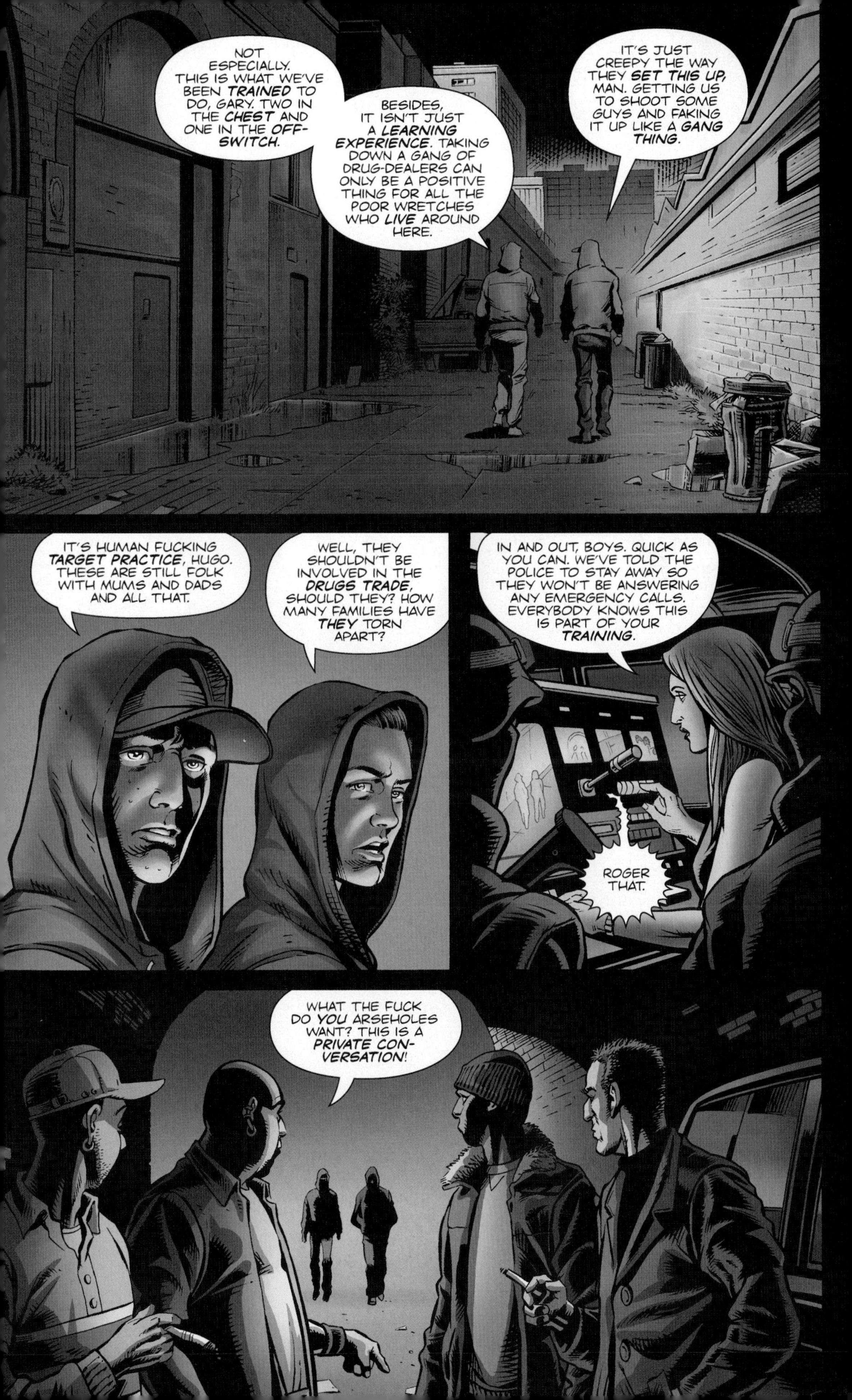
NOT ESPECIALLY. THIS IS WHAT WE'VE BEEN TRAINED TO DO, GARY. TWO IN THE CHEST AND ONE IN THE OFF-SWITCH.
BESIDES, IT ISN'T JUST A LEARNING EXPERIENCE. TAKING DOWN A GANG OF DRUG-DEALERS CAN ONLY BE A POSITIVE THING FOR ALL THE POOR WRETCHES WHO LIVE AROUND HERE.
IT'S JUST CREEPY THE WAY THEY SET THIS UP, MAN. GETTING US TO SHOOT SOME GUYS AND FAKING IT UP LIKE A GANG THING.
IT'S HUMAN FUCKING TARGET PRACTICE, HUGO. THESE ARE STILL FOLK WITH MUMS AND DADS AND ALL THAT.
WELL, THEY SHOULDN'T BE INVOLVED IN THE DRUGS TRADE, SHOULD THEY? HOW MANY FAMILIES HAVE THEY TORN APART?
IN AND OUT, BOYS. QUICK AS YOU CAN. WE'VE TOLD THE POLICE TO STAY AWAY SO THEY WON'T BE ANSWERING ANY EMERGENCY CALLS. EVERYBODY KNOWS THIS IS PART OF YOUR TRAINING.
ROGER THAT.
WHAT THE FUCK DO YOU ARSEHOLES WANT? THIS IS A PRIVATE CON-VERSATION!

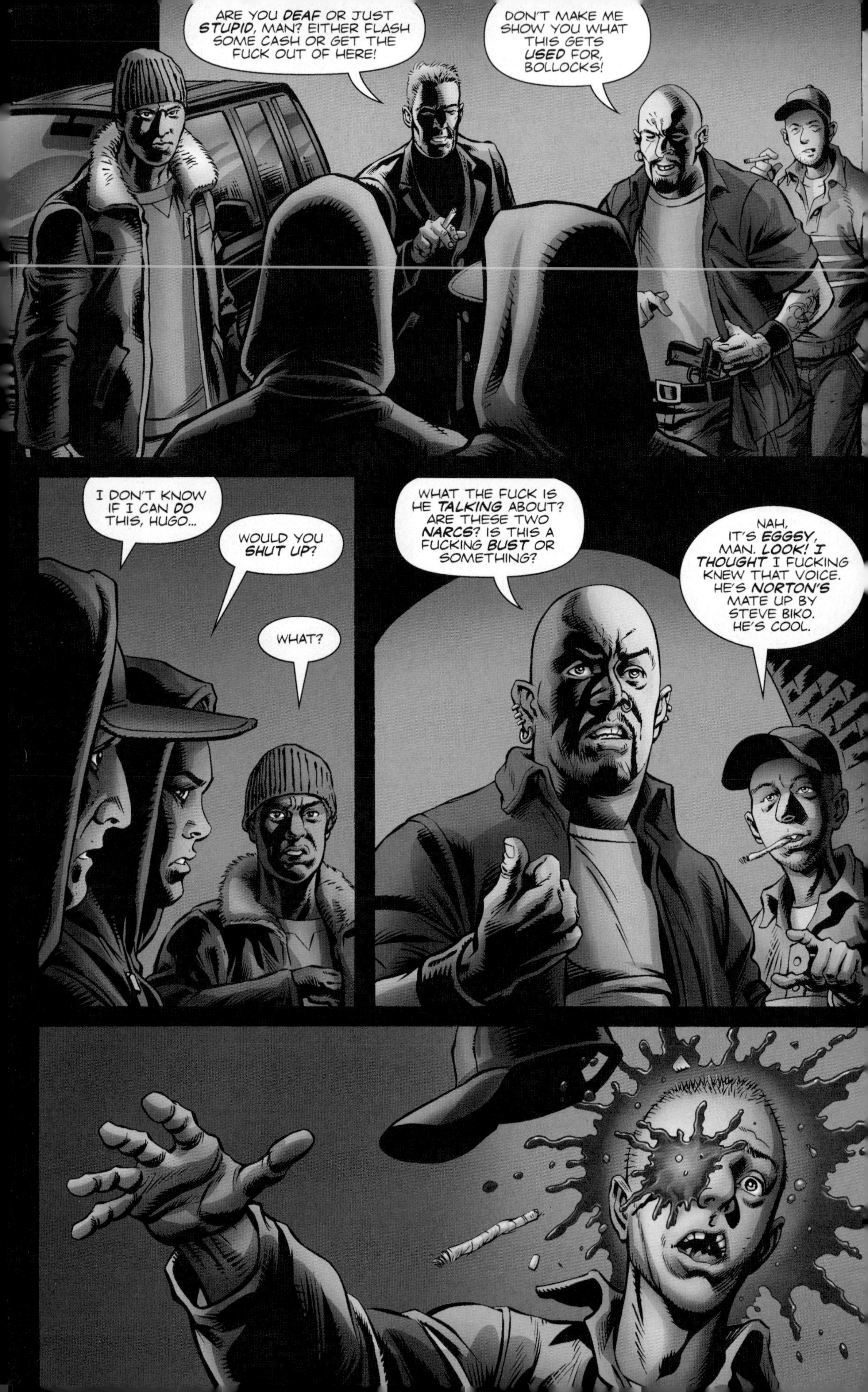

ARE YOU DEAF OR JUST STUPID, MAN? EITHER FLASH SOME CASH OR GET THE FUCK OUT OF HERE!
DON'T MAKE ME SHOW YOU WHAT THIS GETS USED FOR, BOLLOCKS!
I DON'T KNOW IF I CAN DO THIS, HUGO...
WOULD YOU SHUT UP?
WHAT?
WHAT THE FUCK IS HE TALKING ABOUT? ARE THESE TWO NARCS? IS THIS A FUCKING BUST OR SOMETHING?
NAH, IT'S EGGSY, MAN. LOOK! I THOUGHT I FUCKING KNEW THAT VOICE. HE'S NORTON'S MATE UP BY STEVE BIKO. HE'S COOL.

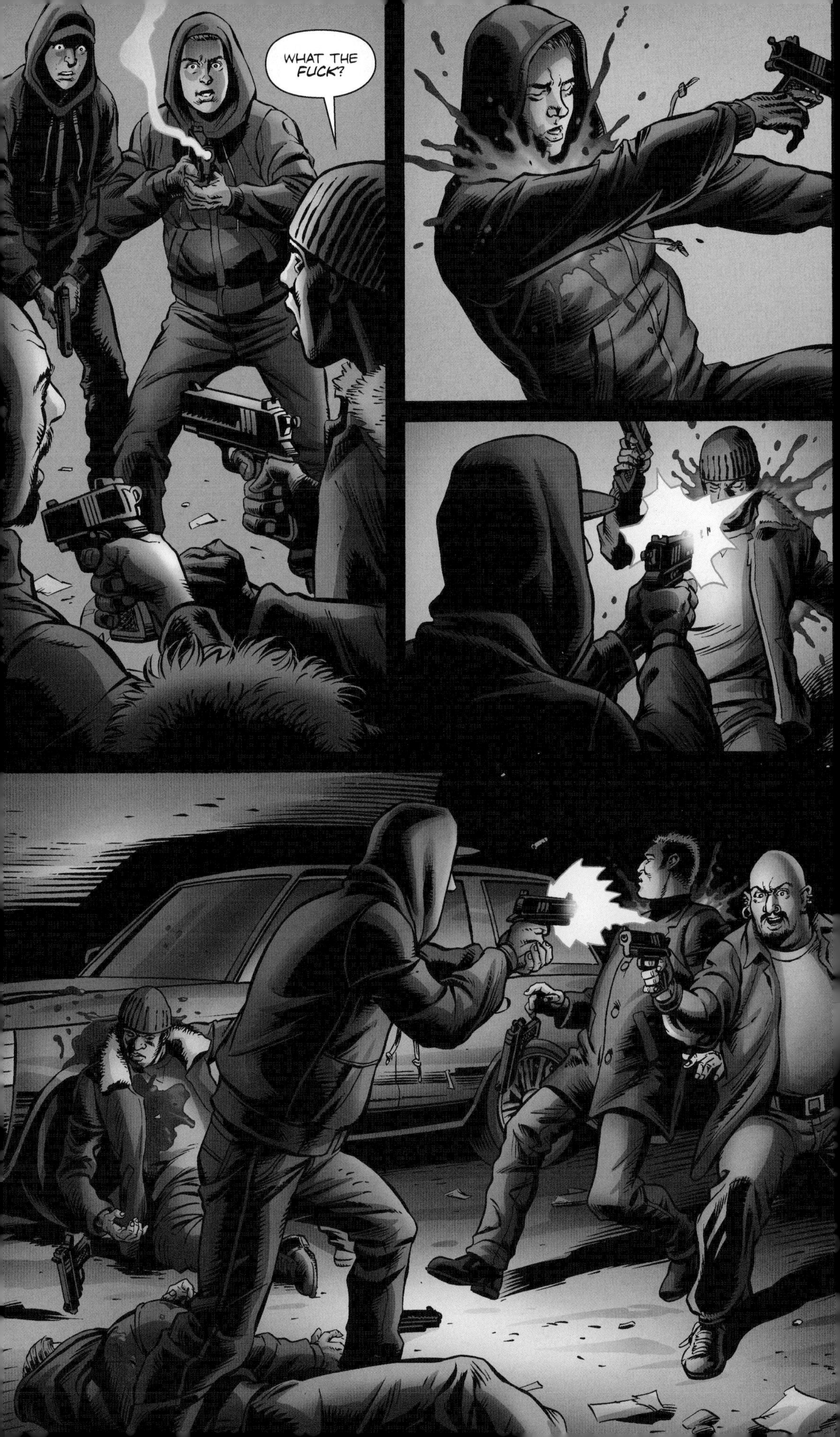
WHAT THE *FUCK*?

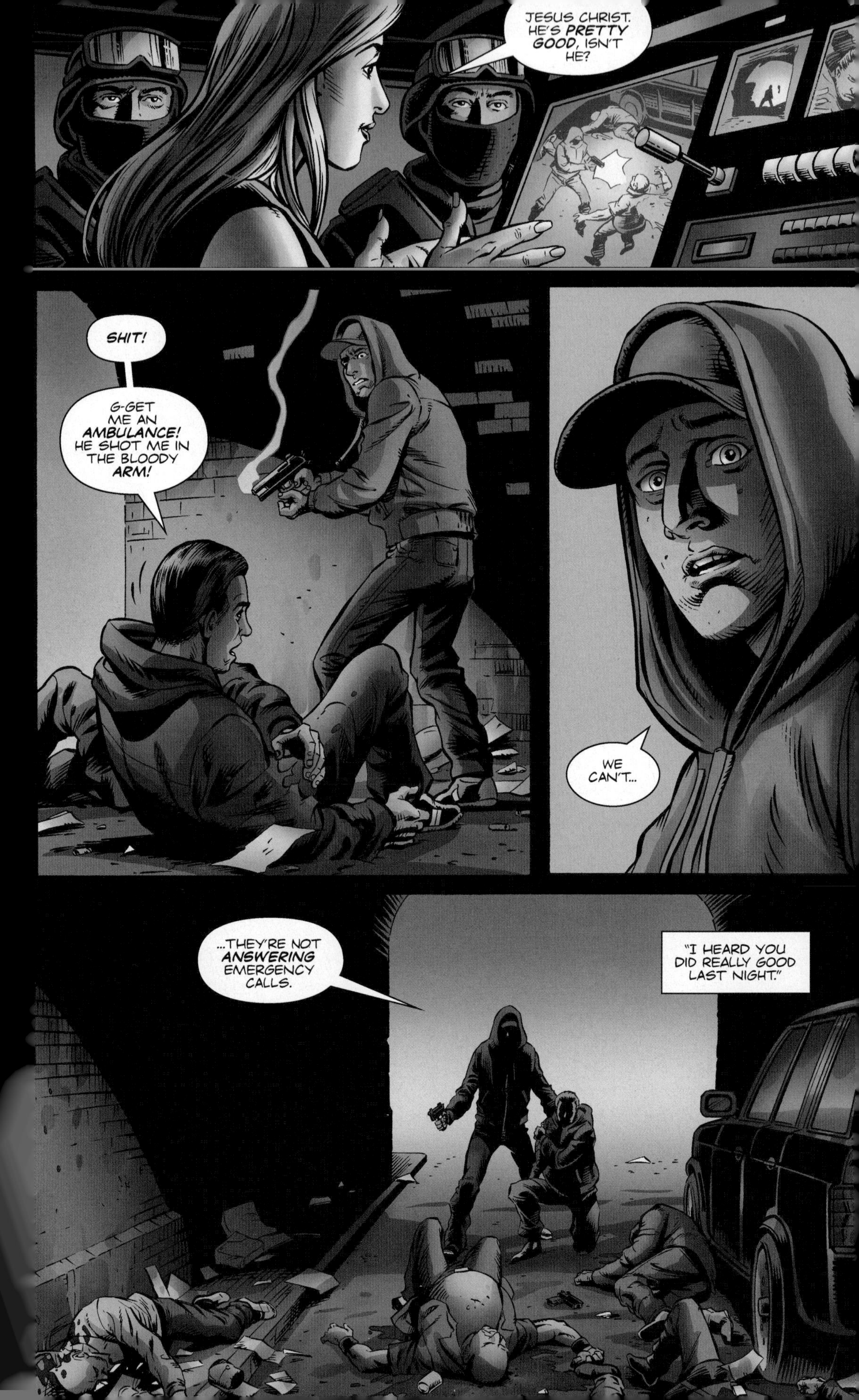
JESUS CHRIST. HE'S PRETTY GOOD, ISN'T HE?
SHIT!
G-GET ME AN AMBULANCE! HE SHOT ME IN THE BLOODY ARM!
WE CAN'T...
...THEY'RE NOT ANSWERING EMERGENCY CALLS.
"I HEARD YOU DID REALLY GOOD LAST NIGHT."

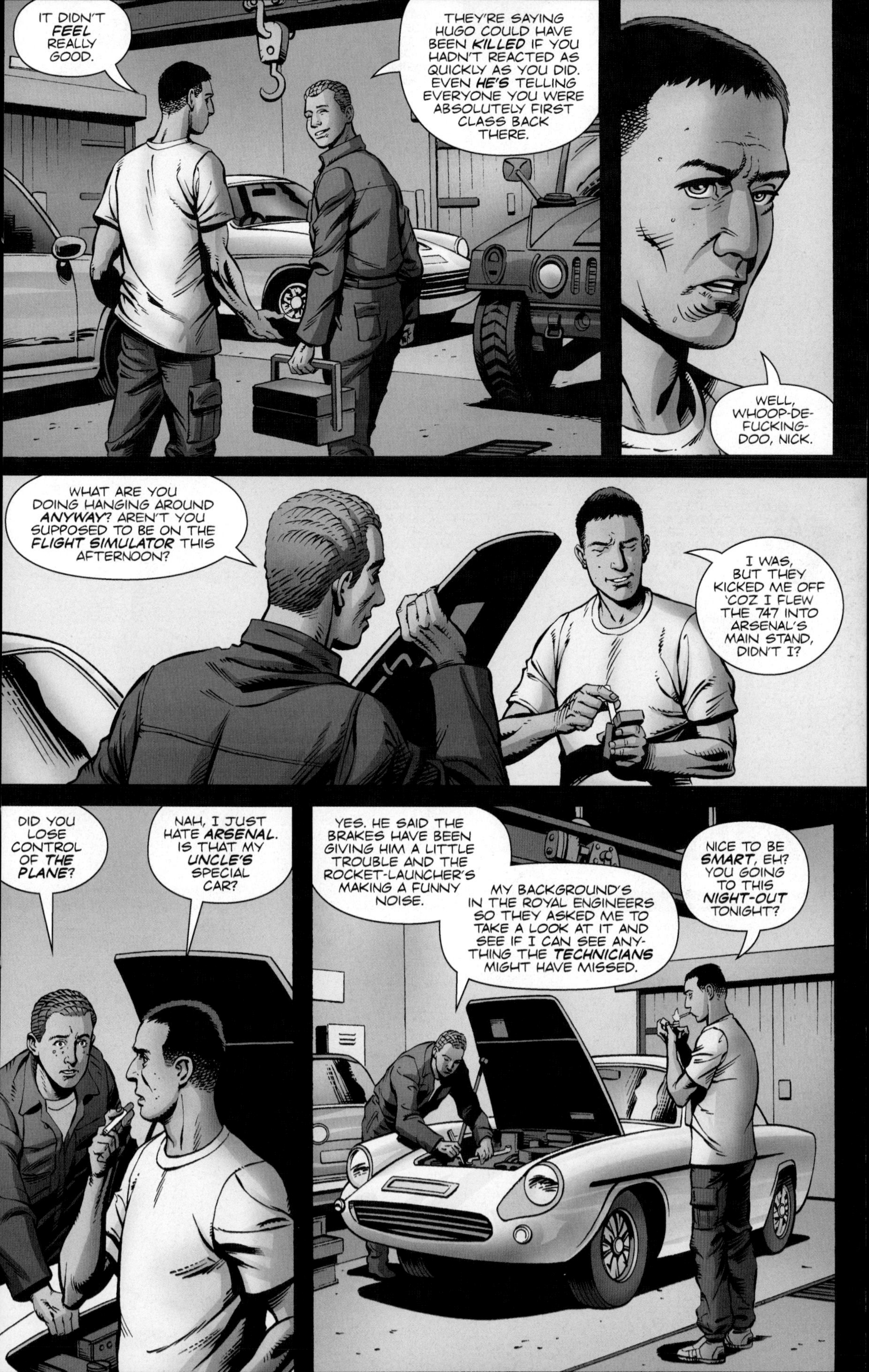
IT DIDN'T FEEL REALLY GOOD.
THEY'RE SAYING HUGO COULD HAVE BEEN KILLED IF YOU HADN'T REACTED AS QUICKLY AS YOU DID. EVEN HE'S TELLING EVERYONE YOU WERE ABSOLUTELY FIRST CLASS BACK THERE.
WELL, WHOOP-DE-FUCKING-DOO, NICK.
WHAT ARE YOU DOING HANGING AROUND ANYWAY? AREN'T YOU SUPPOSED TO BE ON THE FLIGHT SIMULATOR THIS AFTERNOON?
I WAS, BUT THEY KICKED ME OFF 'COZ I FLEW THE 747 INTO ARSENAL'S MAIN STAND, DIDN'T I?
DID YOU LOSE CONTROL OF THE PLANE?
NAH, I JUST HATE ARSENAL. IS THAT MY UNCLE'S SPECIAL CAR?
YES. HE SAID THE BRAKES HAVE BEEN GIVING HIM A LITTLE TROUBLE AND THE ROCKET-LAUNCHER'S MAKING A FUNNY NOISE.
MY BACKGROUND'S IN THE ROYAL ENGINEERS SO THEY ASKED ME TO TAKE A LOOK AT IT AND SEE IF I CAN SEE ANYTHING THE TECHNICIANS MIGHT HAVE MISSED.
NICE TO BE SMART, EH? YOU GOING TO THIS NIGHT-OUT TONIGHT?

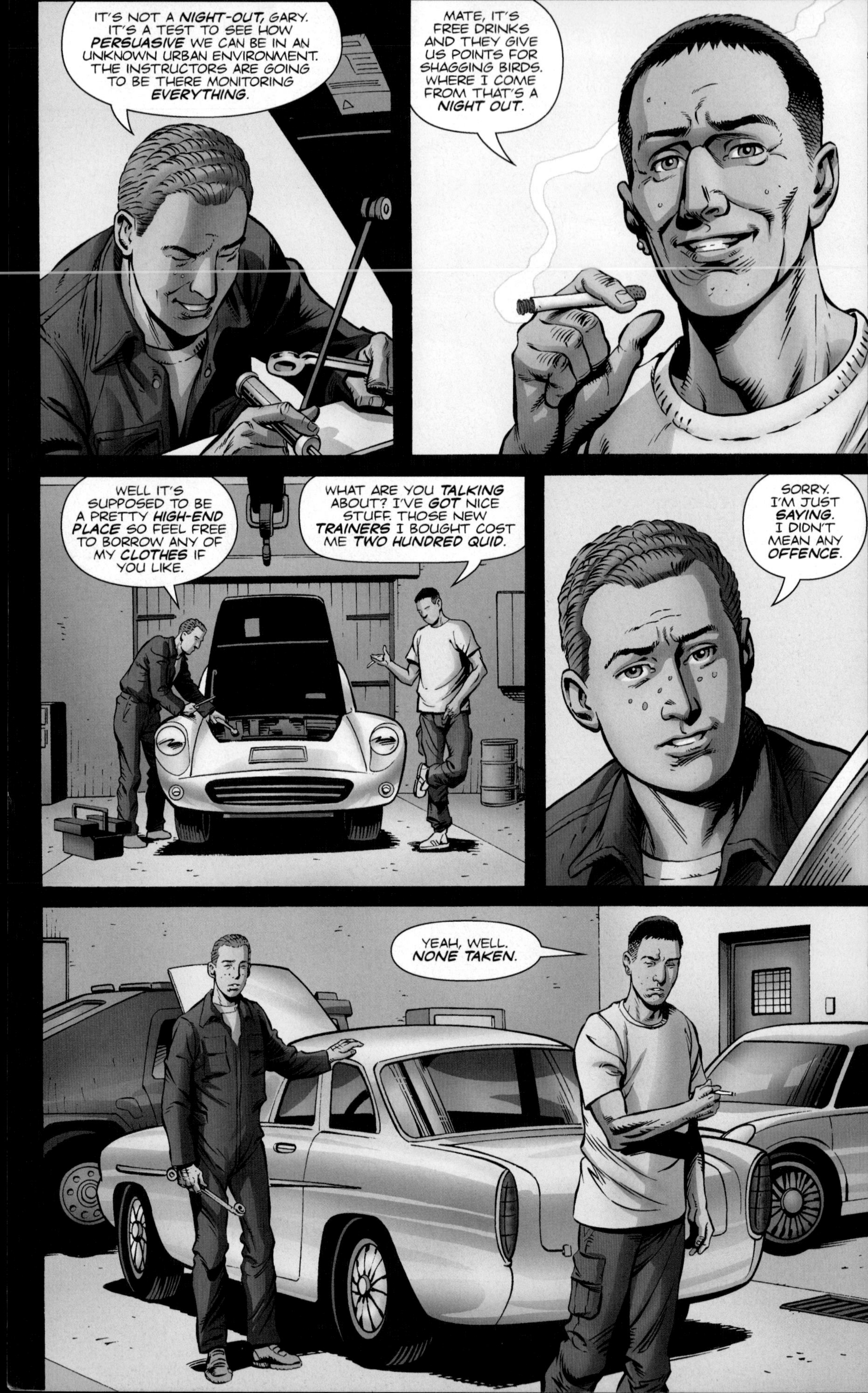
IT'S NOT A NIGHT-OUT, GARY. IT'S A TEST TO SEE HOW PERSUASIVE WE CAN BE IN AN UNKNOWN URBAN ENVIRONMENT. THE INSTRUCTORS ARE GOING TO BE THERE MONITORING EVERYTHING.
MATE, IT'S FREE DRINKS AND THEY GIVE US POINTS FOR SHAGGING BIRDS. WHERE I COME FROM THAT'S A NIGHT OUT.
WELL IT'S SUPPOSED TO BE A PRETTY HIGH-END PLACE SO FEEL FREE TO BORROW ANY OF MY CLOTHES IF YOU LIKE.
WHAT ARE YOU TALKING ABOUT? I'VE GOT NICE STUFF. THOSE NEW TRAINERS I BOUGHT COST ME TWO HUNDRED QUID.
SORRY. I'M JUST SAYING. I DIDN'T MEAN ANY OFFENCE.
YEAH, WELL. NONE TAKEN.

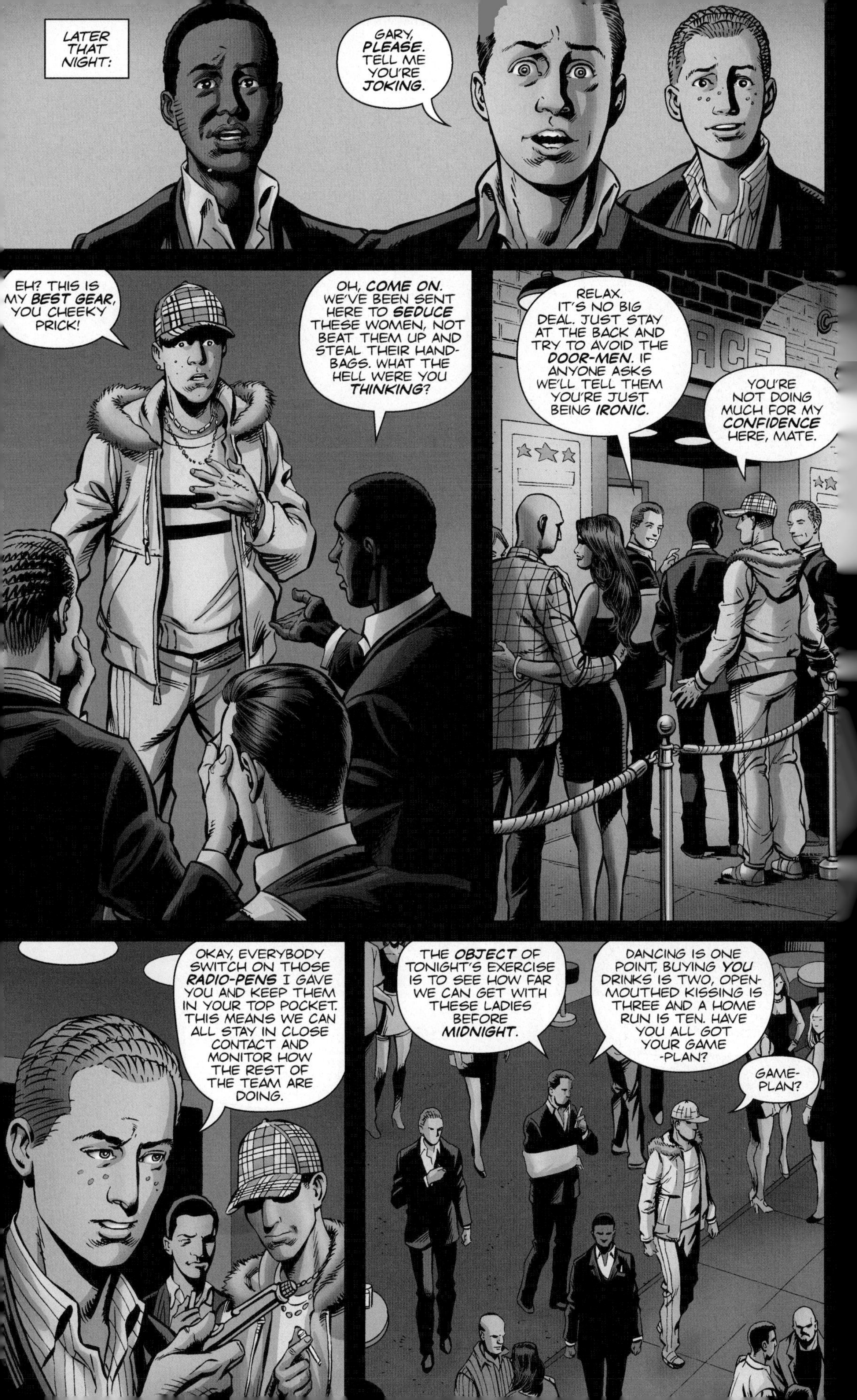
LATER THAT NIGHT:
GARY, PLEASE. TELL ME YOU'RE JOKING.
EH? THIS IS MY BEST GEAR, YOU CHEEKY PRICK!
OH, COME ON. WE'VE BEEN SENT HERE TO SEDUCE THESE WOMEN, NOT BEAT THEM UP AND STEAL THEIR HAND-BAGS. WHAT THE HELL WERE YOU THINKING?
RELAX. IT'S NO BIG DEAL. JUST STAY AT THE BACK AND TRY TO AVOID THE DOOR-MEN. IF ANYONE ASKS WE'LL TELL THEM YOU'RE JUST BEING IRONIC.
YOU'RE NOT DOING MUCH FOR MY CONFIDENCE HERE, MATE.
OKAY, EVERYBODY SWITCH ON THOSE RADIO-PENS I GAVE YOU AND KEEP THEM IN YOUR TOP POCKET. THIS MEANS WE CAN ALL STAY IN CLOSE CONTACT AND MONITOR HOW THE REST OF THE TEAM ARE DOING.
THE OBJECT OF TONIGHT'S EXERCISE IS TO SEE HOW FAR WE CAN GET WITH THESE LADIES BEFORE MIDNIGHT.
DANCING IS ONE POINT, BUYING YOU DRINKS IS TWO, OPEN-MOUTHED KISSING IS THREE AND A HOME RUN IS TEN. HAVE YOU ALL GOT YOUR GAME -PLAN?
GAME-PLAN?

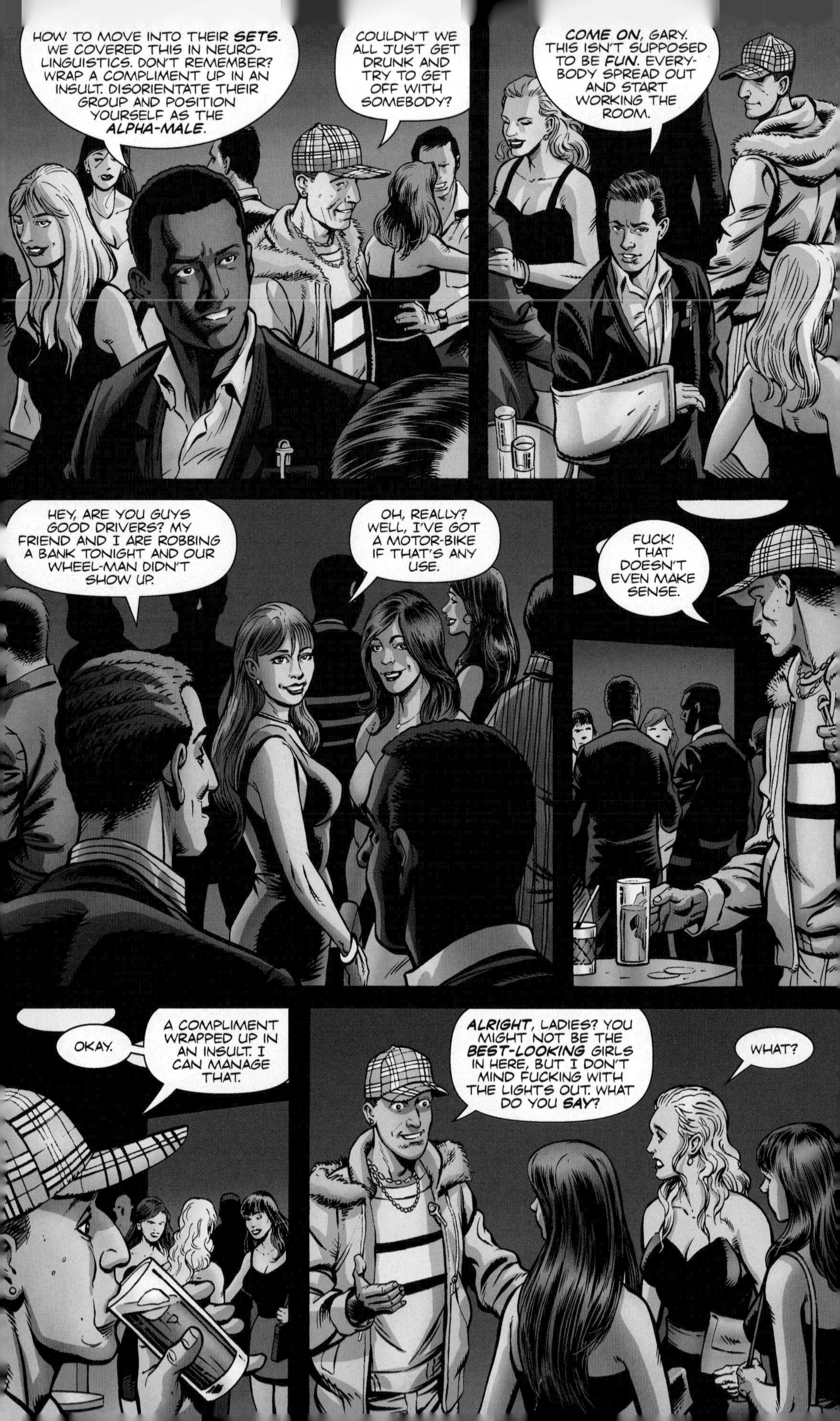
HOW TO MOVE INTO THEIR SETS. WE COVERED THIS IN NEURO-LINGUISTICS. DON'T REMEMBER? WRAP A COMPLIMENT UP IN AN INSULT. DISORIENTATE THEIR GROUP AND POSITION YOURSELF AS THE ALPHA-MALE.
COULDN'T WE ALL JUST GET DRUNK AND TRY TO GET OFF WITH SOMEBODY?
COME ON, GARY. THIS ISN'T SUPPOSED TO BE FUN. EVERY-BODY SPREAD OUT AND START WORKING THE ROOM.
HEY, ARE YOU GUYS GOOD DRIVERS? MY FRIEND AND I ARE ROBBING A BANK TONIGHT AND OUR WHEEL-MAN DIDN'T SHOW UP.
OH, REALLY? WELL, I'VE GOT A MOTOR-BIKE IF THAT'S ANY USE.
FUCK! THAT DOESN'T EVEN MAKE SENSE.
OKAY.
A COMPLIMENT WRAPPED UP IN AN INSULT. I CAN MANAGE THAT.
ALRIGHT, LADIES? YOU MIGHT NOT BE THE BEST-LOOKING GIRLS IN HERE, BUT I DON'T MIND FUCKING WITH THE LIGHTS OUT. WHAT DO YOU SAY?
WHAT?

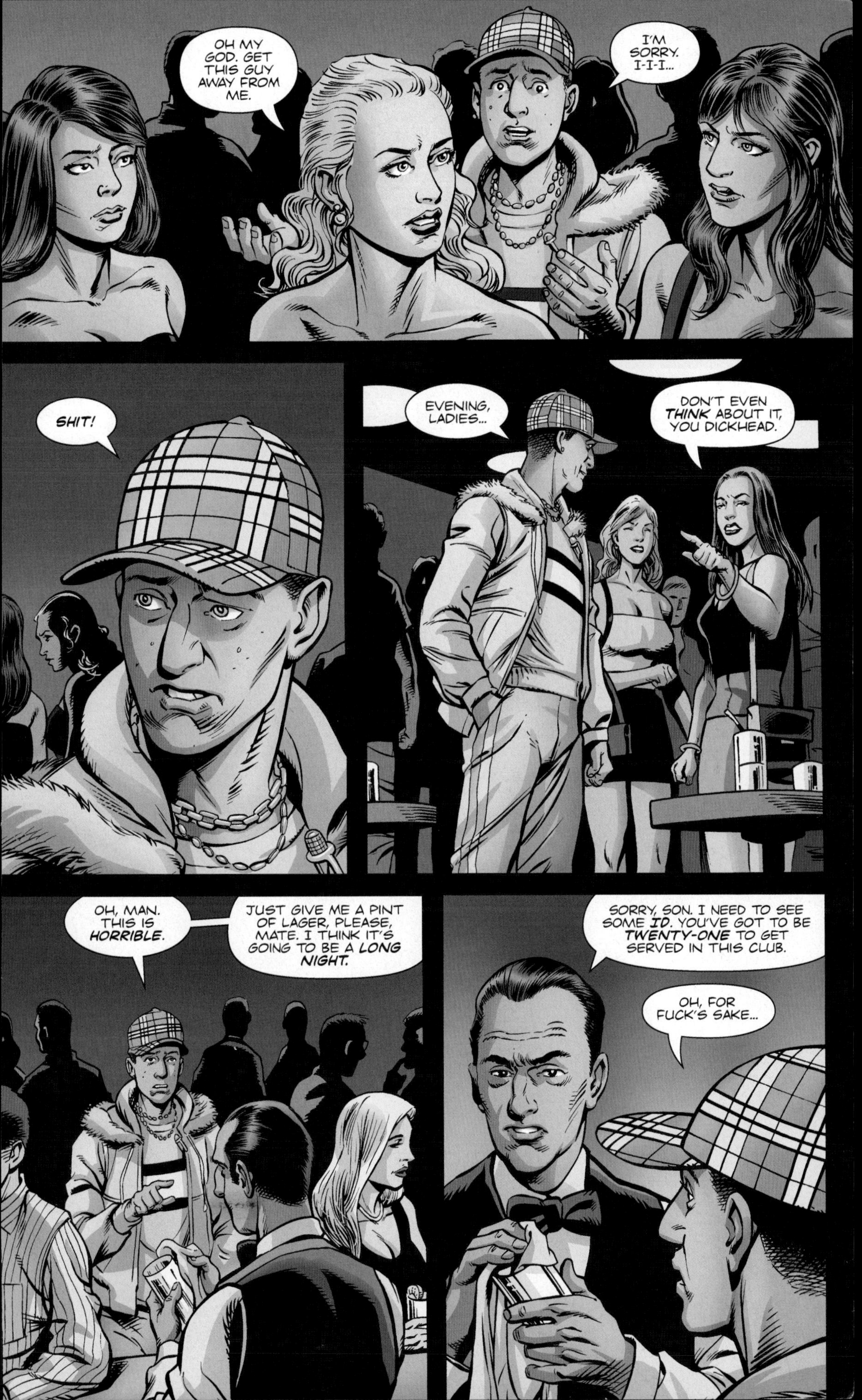
OH MY GOD. GET THIS GUY AWAY FROM ME.
I'M SORRY. I-I-I...
SHIT!
EVENING, LADIES...
DON'T EVEN **THINK** ABOUT IT, YOU DICKHEAD.
OH, MAN. THIS IS **HORRIBLE**.
JUST GIVE ME A PINT OF LAGER, PLEASE, MATE. I THINK IT'S GOING TO BE A **LONG NIGHT**.
SORRY, SON. I NEED TO SEE SOME **ID**. YOU'VE GOT TO BE **TWENTY-ONE** TO GET SERVED IN THIS CLUB.
OH, FOR FUCK'S SAKE...

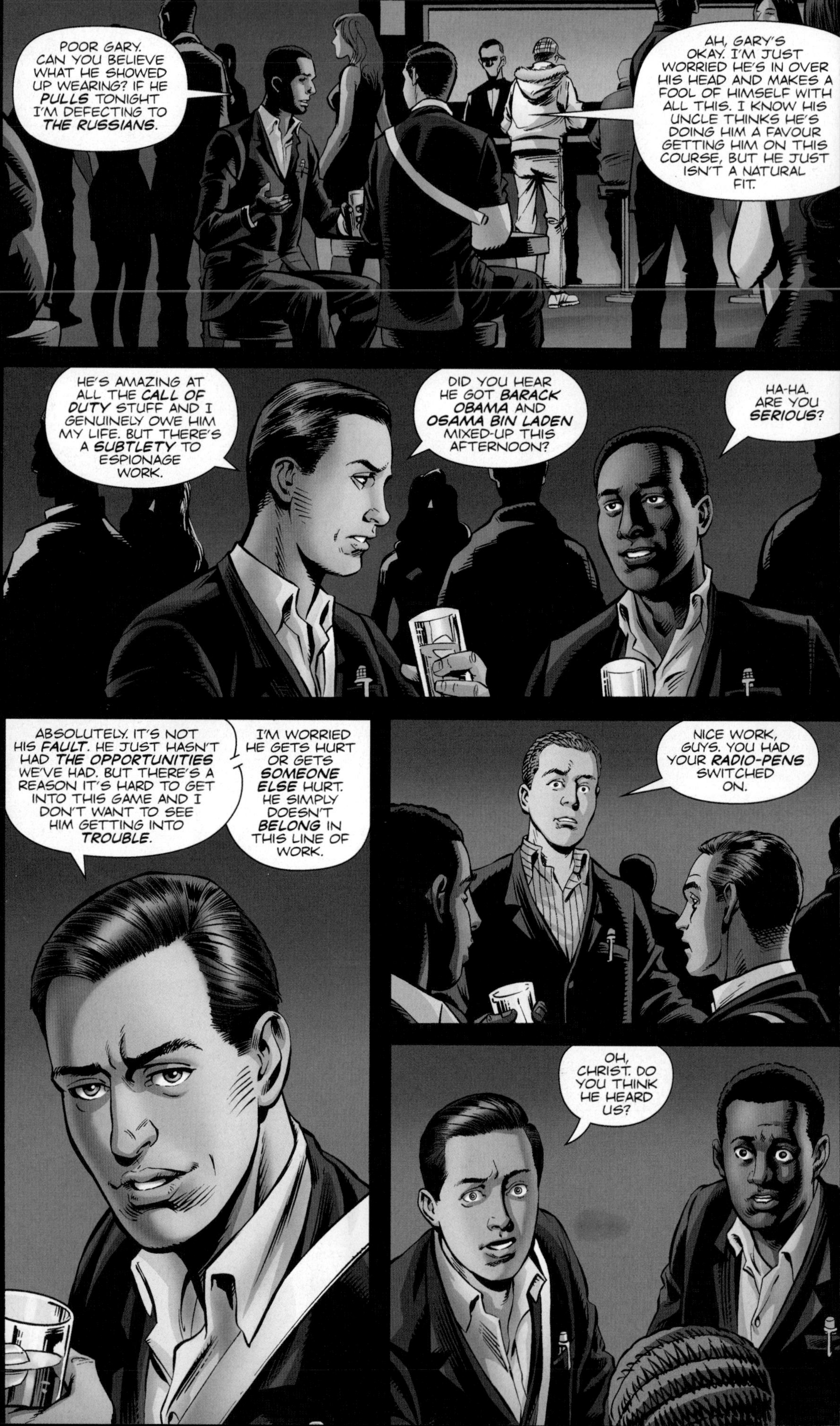
POOR GARY. CAN YOU BELIEVE WHAT HE SHOWED UP WEARING? IF HE PULLS TONIGHT I'M DEFECTING TO THE RUSSIANS.
AH, GARY'S OKAY. I'M JUST WORRIED HE'S IN OVER HIS HEAD AND MAKES A FOOL OF HIMSELF WITH ALL THIS. I KNOW HIS UNCLE THINKS HE'S DOING HIM A FAVOUR GETTING HIM ON THIS COURSE, BUT HE JUST ISN'T A NATURAL FIT.
HE'S AMAZING AT ALL THE CALL OF DUTY STUFF AND I GENUINELY OWE HIM MY LIFE. BUT THERE'S A SUBTLETY TO ESPIONAGE WORK.
DID YOU HEAR HE GOT BARACK OBAMA AND OSAMA BIN LADEN MIXED-UP THIS AFTERNOON?
HA-HA. ARE YOU SERIOUS?
ABSOLUTELY. IT'S NOT HIS FAULT. HE JUST HASN'T HAD THE OPPORTUNITIES WE'VE HAD. BUT THERE'S A REASON IT'S HARD TO GET INTO THIS GAME AND I DON'T WANT TO SEE HIM GETTING INTO TROUBLE.
I'M WORRIED HE GETS HURT OR GETS SOMEONE ELSE HURT. HE SIMPLY DOESN'T BELONG IN THIS LINE OF WORK.
NICE WORK, GUYS. YOU HAD YOUR RADIO-PENS SWITCHED ON.
OH, CHRIST. DO YOU THINK HE HEARD US?

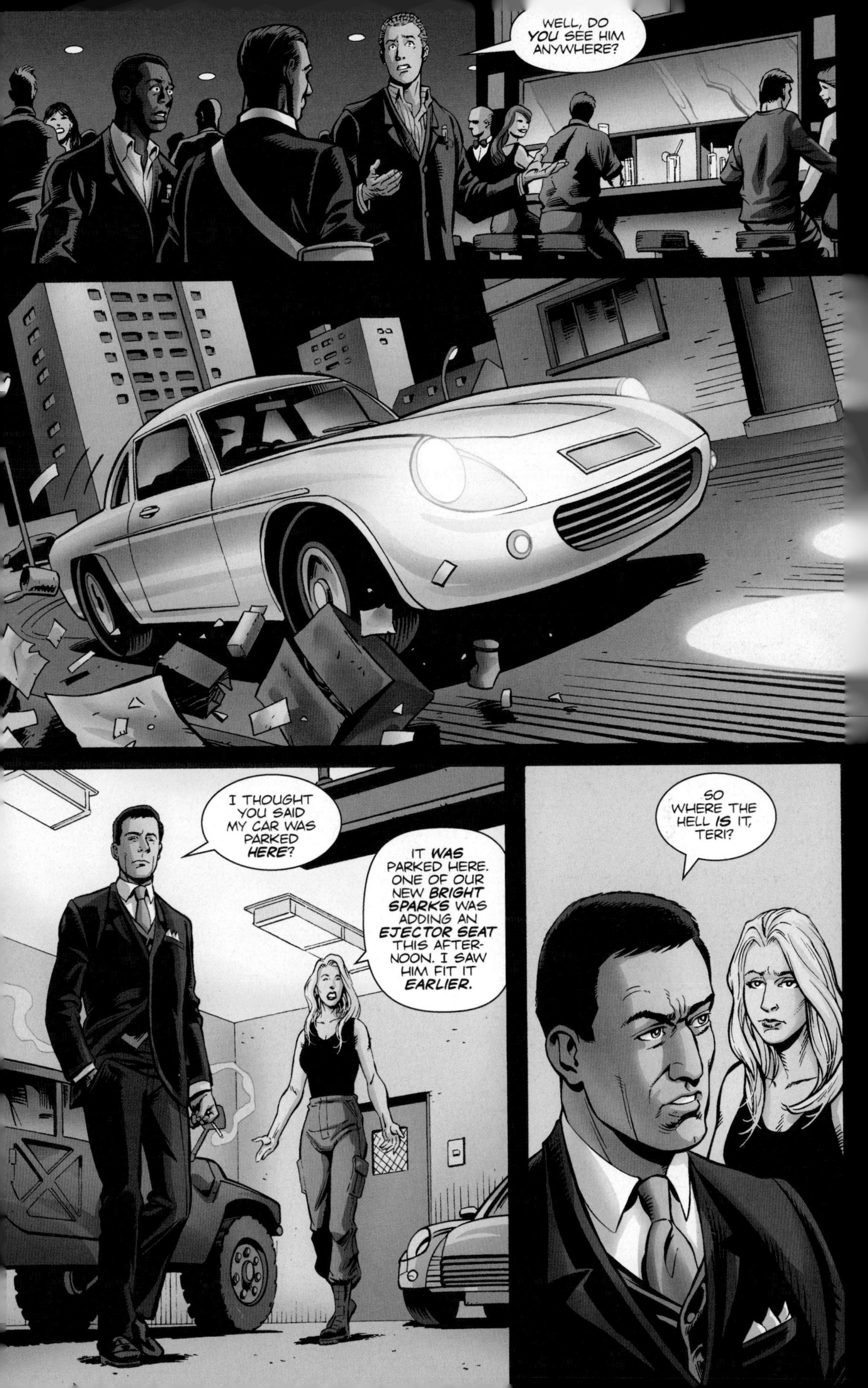
WELL, DO YOU SEE HIM ANYWHERE?
I THOUGHT YOU SAID MY CAR WAS PARKED HERE?
IT WAS PARKED HERE. ONE OF OUR NEW BRIGHT SPARKS WAS ADDING AN EJECTOR SEAT THIS AFTER-NOON. I SAW HIM FIT IT EARLIER.
SO WHERE THE HELL IS IT, TERI?

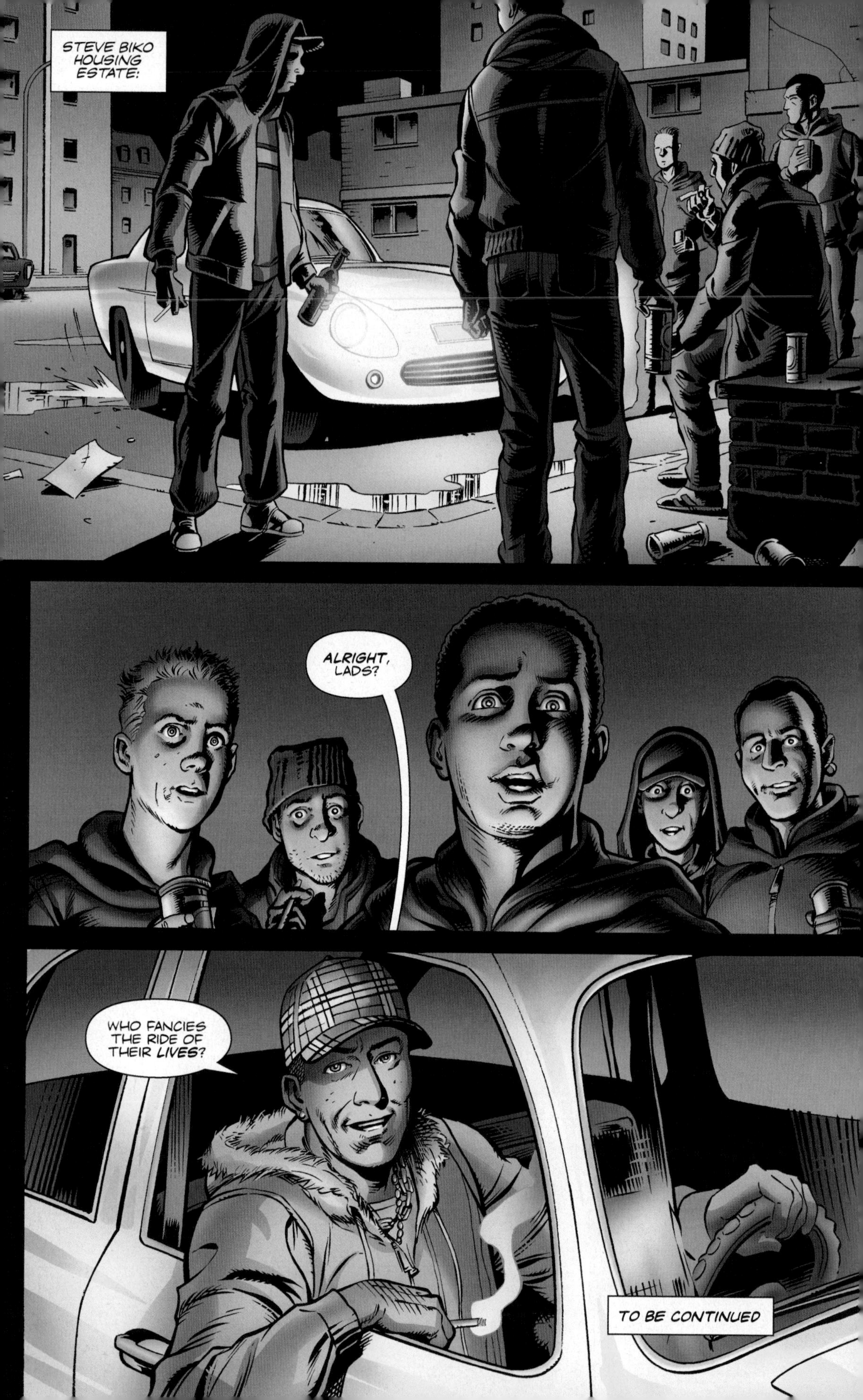
STEVE BIKO HOUSING ESTATE:
ALRIGHT, LADS?
WHO FANCIES THE RIDE OF THEIR LIVES?
TO BE CONTINUED

FOUR

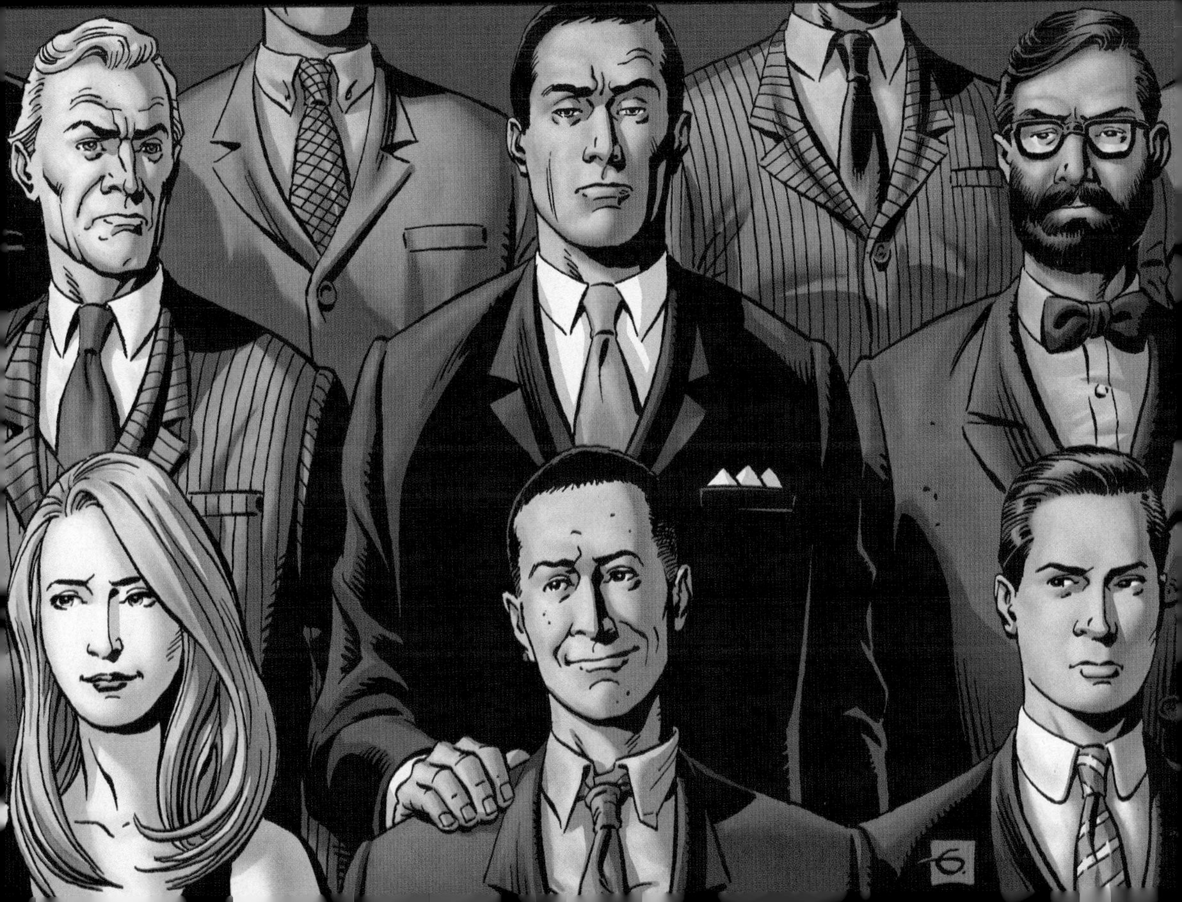

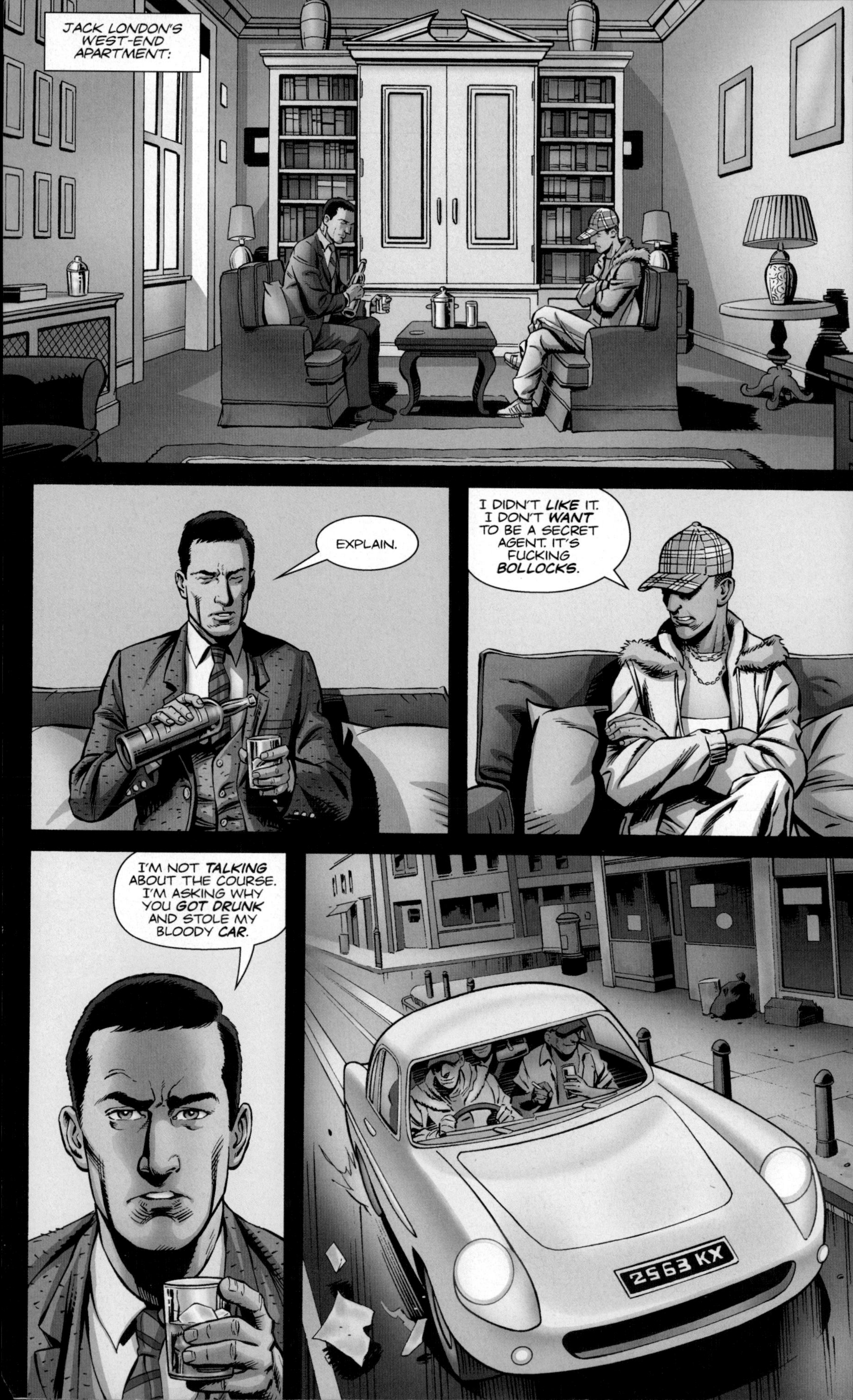
JACK LONDON'S WEST-END APARTMENT:
EXPLAIN.
I DIDN'T LIKE IT. I DON'T WANT TO BE A SECRET AGENT. IT'S FUCKING BOLLOCKS.
I'M NOT TALKING ABOUT THE COURSE. I'M ASKING WHY YOU GOT DRUNK AND STOLE MY BLOODY CAR.
2563 KX

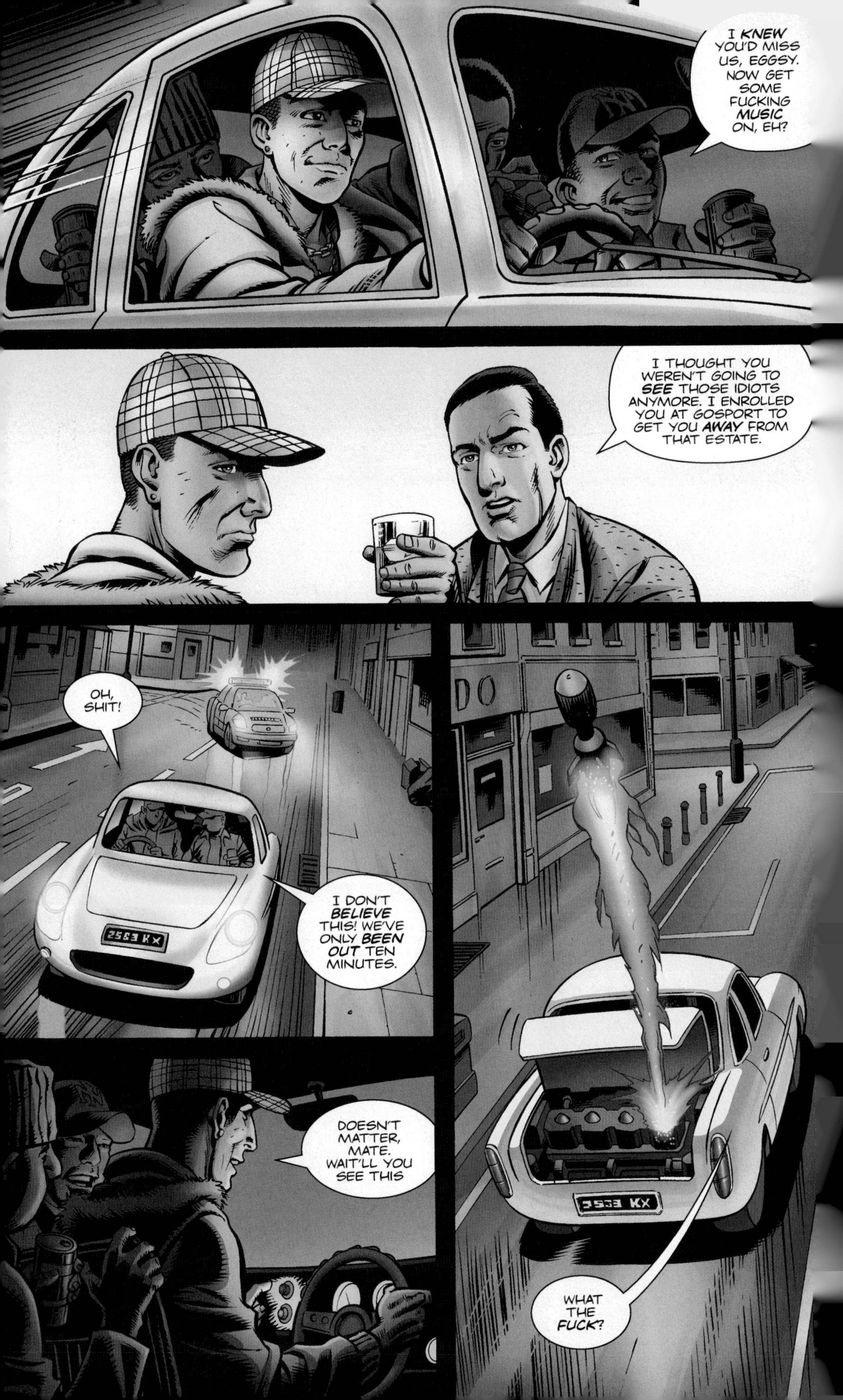
I KNEW YOU'D MISS US, EGGSY. NOW GET SOME FUCKING MUSIC ON, EH?
I THOUGHT YOU WEREN'T GOING TO SEE THOSE IDIOTS ANYMORE. I ENROLLED YOU AT GOSPORT TO GET YOU AWAY FROM THAT ESTATE.
OH, SHIT!
I DON'T BELIEVE THIS! WE'VE ONLY BEEN OUT TEN MINUTES.
2563 KX
DO
DOESN'T MATTER, MATE. WAIT'LL YOU SEE THIS
2563 KX
WHAT THE FUCK?

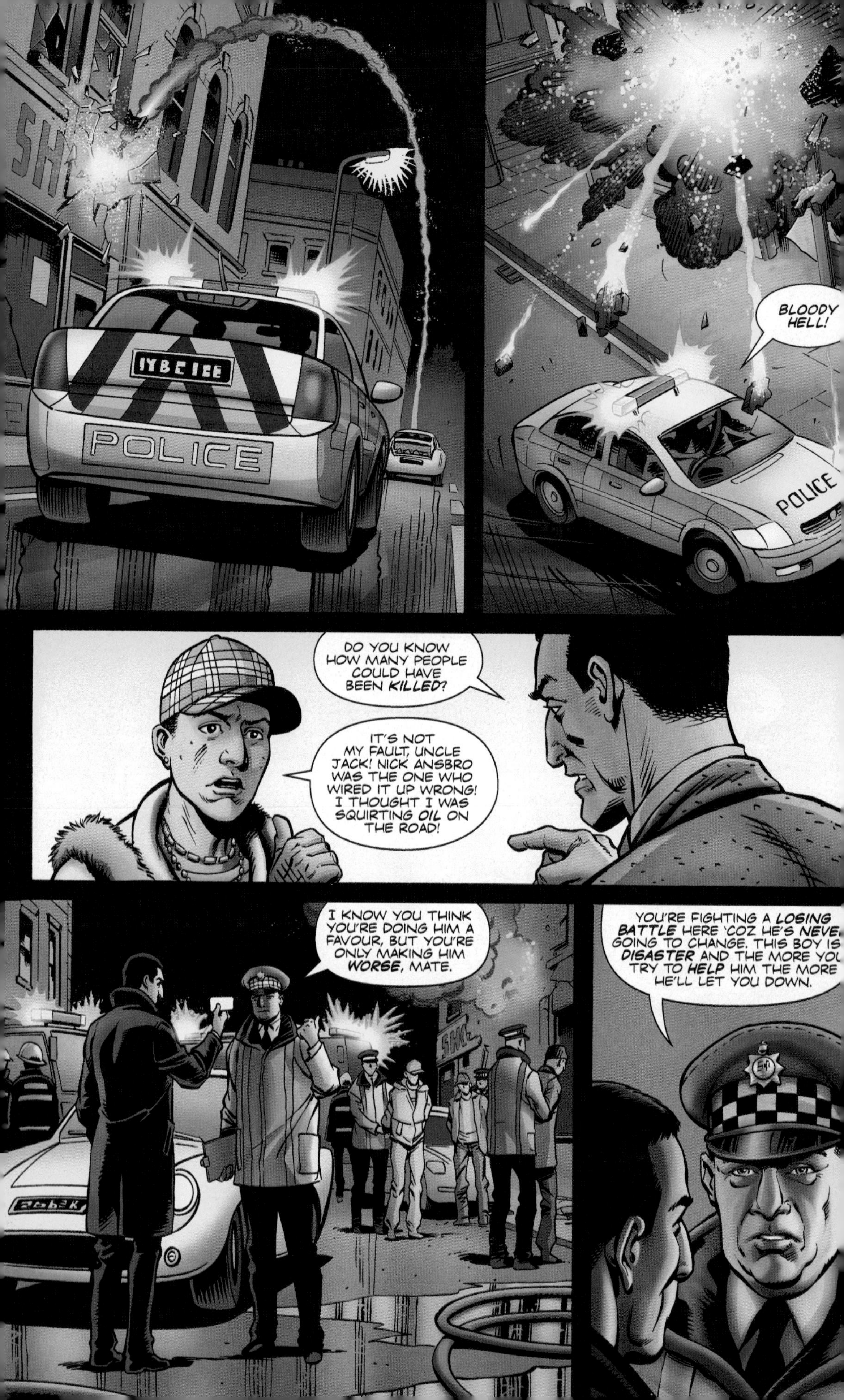
POLICE
BLOODY HELL!
POLICE
DO YOU KNOW HOW MANY PEOPLE COULD HAVE BEEN KILLED?
IT'S NOT MY FAULT, UNCLE JACK! NICK ANSBRO WAS THE ONE WHO WIRED IT UP WRONG! I THOUGHT I WAS SQUIRTING OIL ON THE ROAD!
I KNOW YOU THINK YOU'RE DOING HIM A FAVOUR, BUT YOU'RE ONLY MAKING HIM WORSE, MATE.
YOU'RE FIGHTING A LOSING BATTLE HERE 'COZ HE'S NEVE GOING TO CHANGE. THIS BOY IS DISASTER AND THE MORE YO TRY TO HELP HIM THE MORE HE'LL LET YOU DOWN.

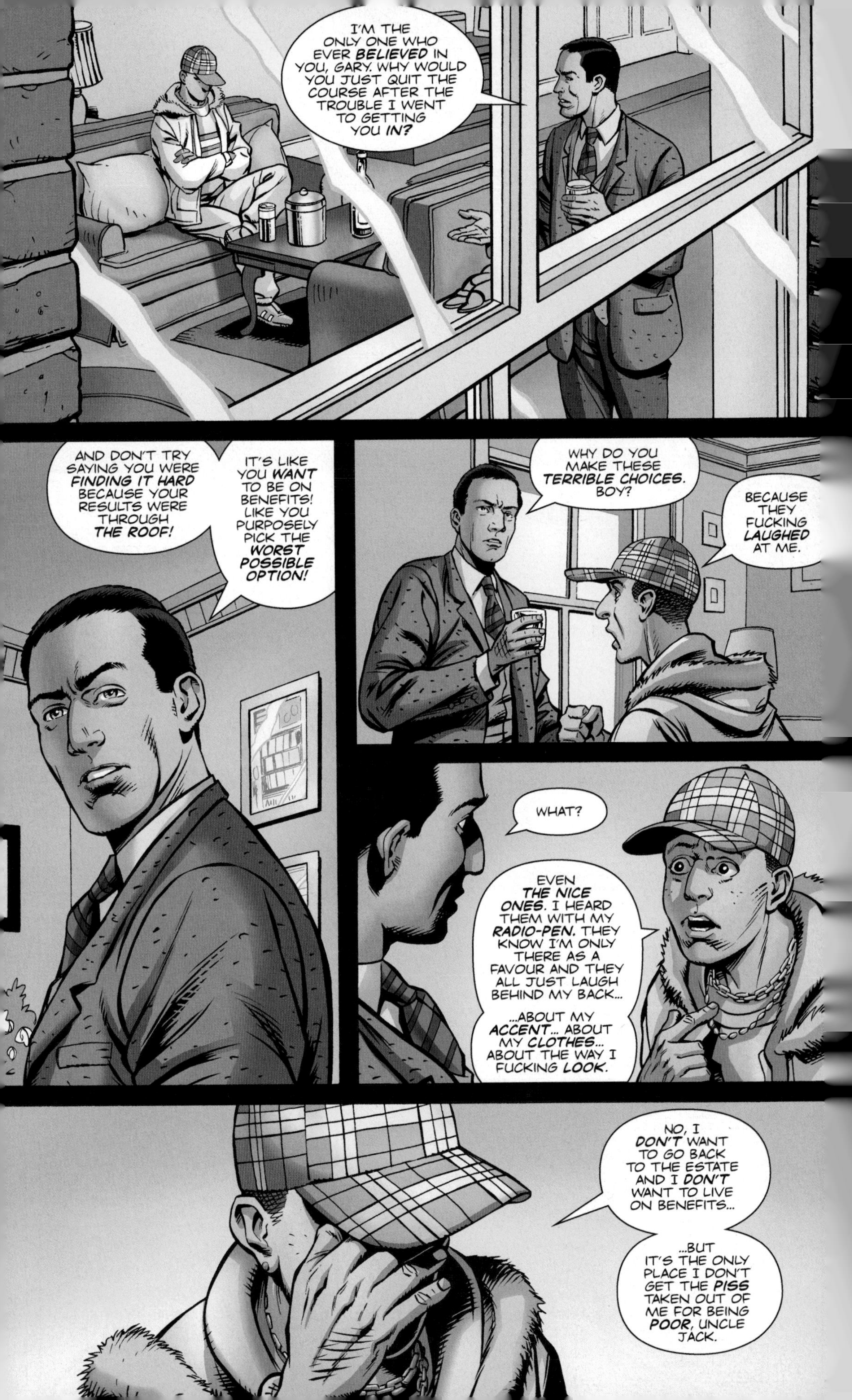

I'M THE ONLY ONE WHO EVER BELIEVED IN YOU, GARY. WHY WOULD YOU JUST QUIT THE COURSE AFTER THE TROUBLE I WENT TO GETTING YOU IN?
AND DON'T TRY SAYING YOU WERE FINDING IT HARD BECAUSE YOUR RESULTS WERE THROUGH THE ROOF!
IT'S LIKE YOU WANT TO BE ON BENEFITS! LIKE YOU PURPOSELY PICK THE WORST POSSIBLE OPTION!
WHY DO YOU MAKE THESE TERRIBLE CHOICES, BOY?
BECAUSE THEY FUCKING LAUGHED AT ME.
WHAT?
EVEN THE NICE ONES. I HEARD THEM WITH MY RADIO-PEN. THEY KNOW I'M ONLY THERE AS A FAVOUR AND THEY ALL JUST LAUGH BEHIND MY BACK...
...ABOUT MY ACCENT... ABOUT MY CLOTHES... ABOUT THE WAY I FUCKING LOOK.
NO, I DON'T WANT TO GO BACK TO THE ESTATE AND I DON'T WANT TO LIVE ON BENEFITS...
...BUT IT'S THE ONLY PLACE I DON'T GET THE PISS TAKEN OUT OF ME FOR BEING POOR, UNCLE JACK.

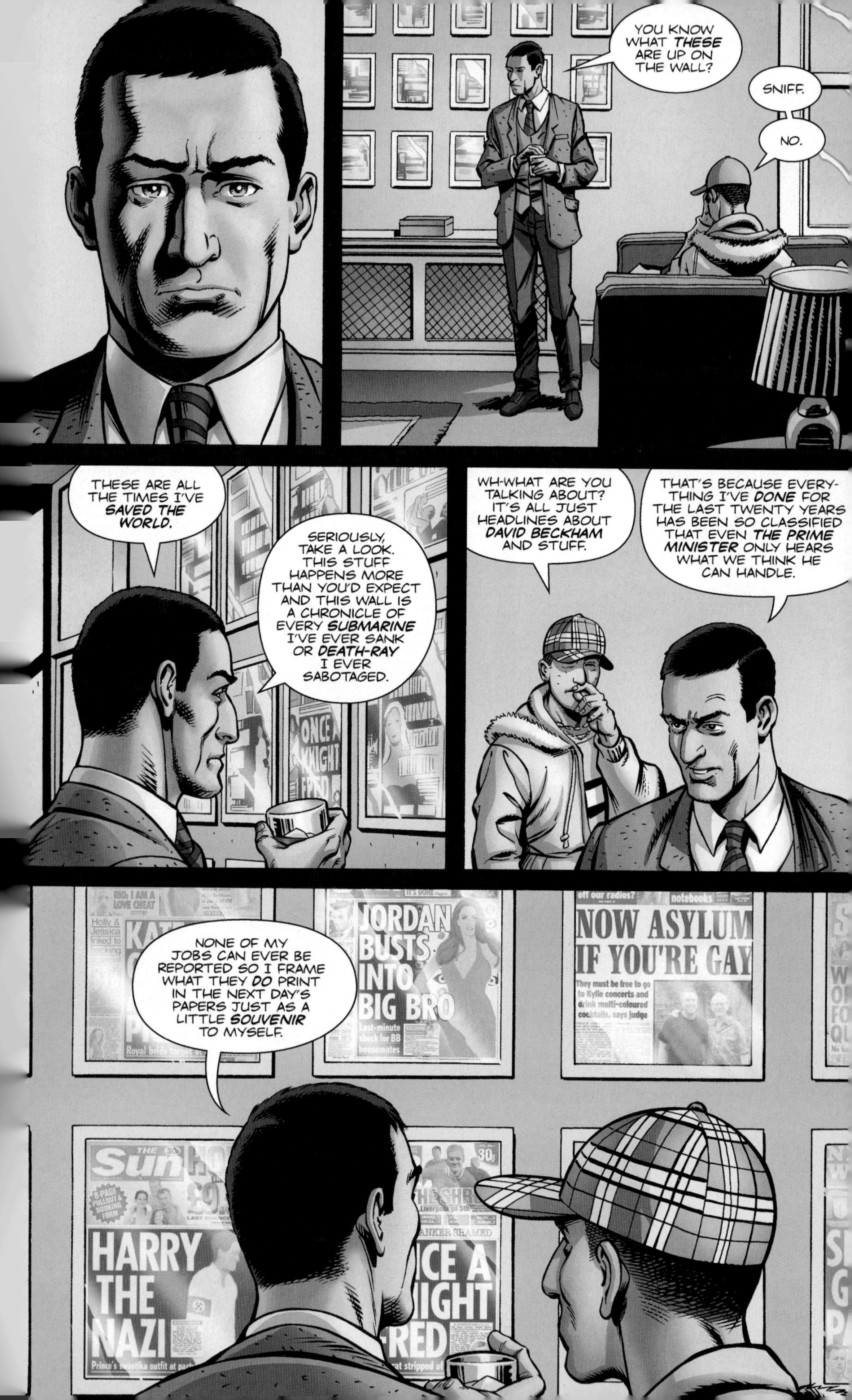
YOU KNOW WHAT THESE ARE UP ON THE WALL?
SNIFF.
NO.
THESE ARE ALL THE TIMES I'VE SAVED THE WORLD.
SERIOUSLY, TAKE A LOOK. THIS STUFF HAPPENS MORE THAN YOU'D EXPECT AND THIS WALL IS A CHRONICLE OF EVERY SUBMARINE I'VE EVER SANK OR DEATH-RAY I EVER SABOTAGED.
WH-WHAT ARE YOU TALKING ABOUT? IT'S ALL JUST HEADLINES ABOUT DAVID BECKHAM AND STUFF.
THAT'S BECAUSE EVERY-THING I'VE DONE FOR THE LAST TWENTY YEARS HAS BEEN SO CLASSIFIED THAT EVEN THE PRIME MINISTER ONLY HEARS WHAT WE THINK HE CAN HANDLE.
JORDAN BUSTS INTO BIG BRO
NOW ASYLUM IF YOU'RE GAY
They must be free to go to Kylie concerts and drink multi-coloured cocktails, says judge
NONE OF MY JOBS CAN EVER BE REPORTED SO I FRAME WHAT THEY DO PRINT IN THE NEXT DAY'S PAPERS JUST AS A LITTLE SOUVENIR TO MYSELF.
The Sun
HARRY THE NAZI
Prince's swastika outfit at party

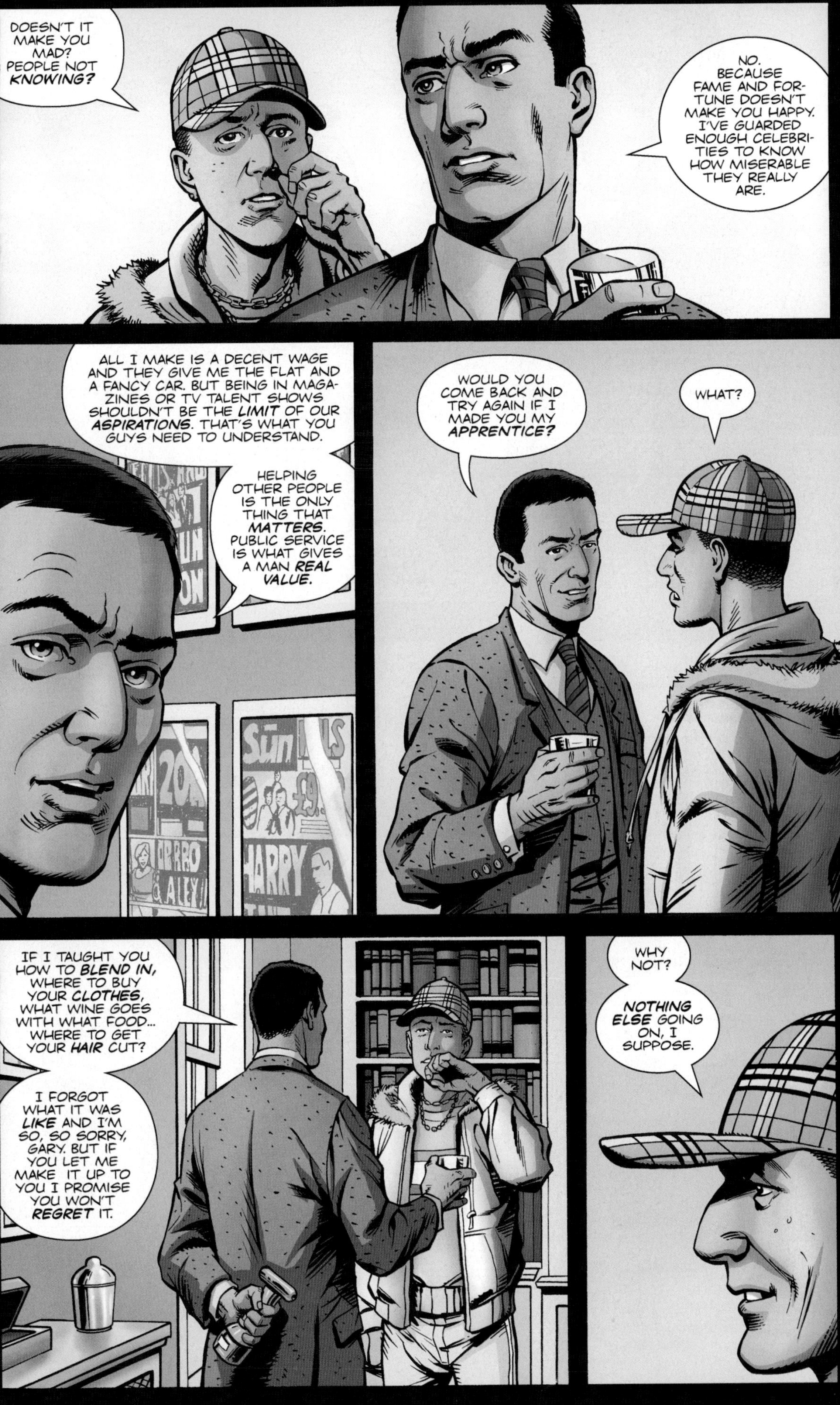
DOESN'T IT MAKE YOU MAD? PEOPLE NOT KNOWING?
NO. BECAUSE FAME AND FORTUNE DOESN'T MAKE YOU HAPPY. I'VE GUARDED ENOUGH CELEBRITIES TO KNOW HOW MISERABLE THEY REALLY ARE.
ALL I MAKE IS A DECENT WAGE AND THEY GIVE ME THE FLAT AND A FANCY CAR. BUT BEING IN MAGAZINES OR TV TALENT SHOWS SHOULDN'T BE THE LIMIT OF OUR ASPIRATIONS. THAT'S WHAT YOU GUYS NEED TO UNDERSTAND.
HELPING OTHER PEOPLE IS THE ONLY THING THAT MATTERS. PUBLIC SERVICE IS WHAT GIVES A MAN REAL VALUE.
WOULD YOU COME BACK AND TRY AGAIN IF I MADE YOU MY APPRENTICE?
WHAT?
IF I TAUGHT YOU HOW TO BLEND IN, WHERE TO BUY YOUR CLOTHES, WHAT WINE GOES WITH WHAT FOOD... WHERE TO GET YOUR HAIR CUT?
I FORGOT WHAT IT WAS LIKE AND I'M SO, SO SORRY, GARY. BUT IF YOU LET ME MAKE IT UP TO YOU I PROMISE YOU WON'T REGRET IT.
WHY NOT?
NOTHING ELSE GOING ON, I SUPPOSE.

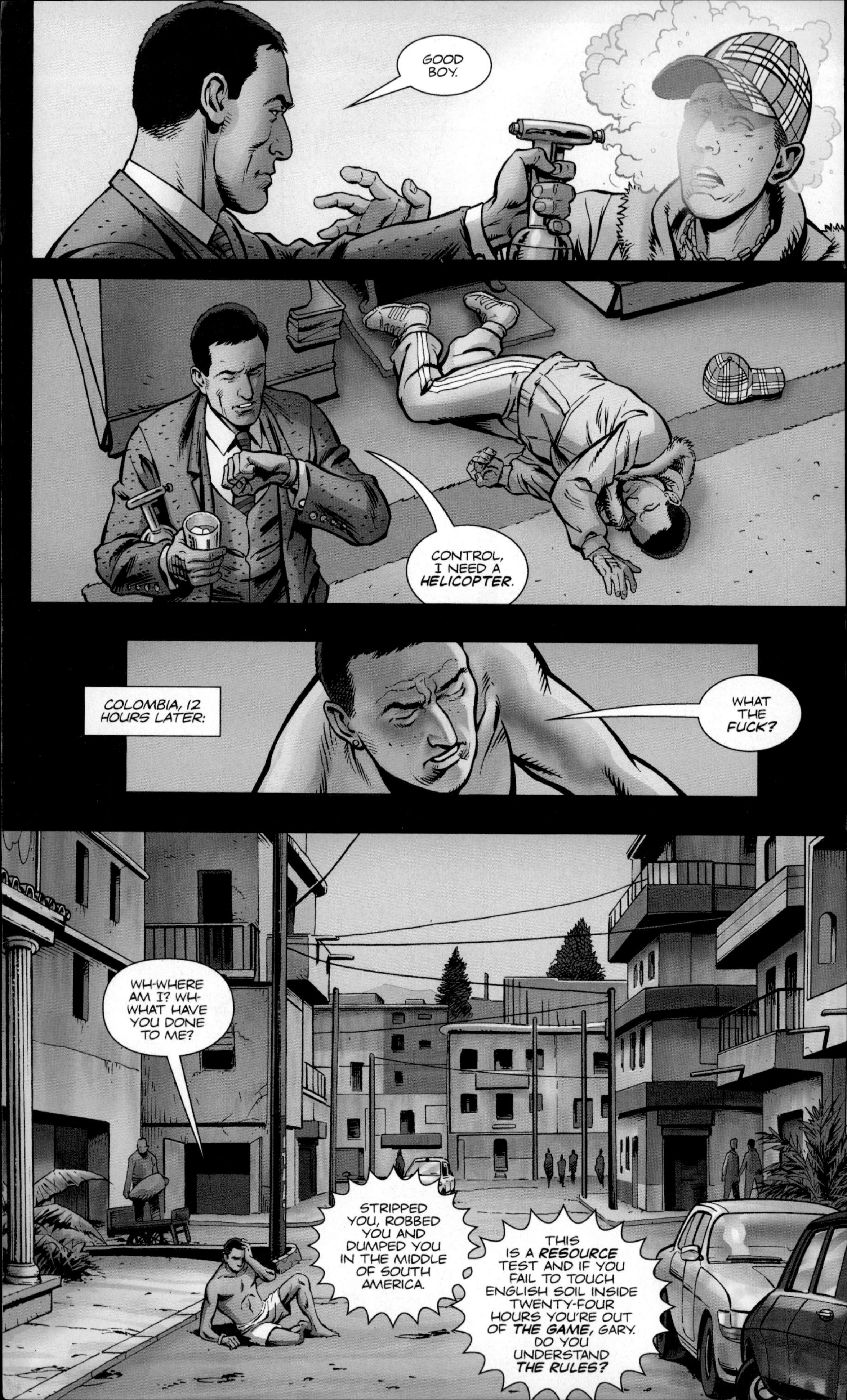
GOOD BOY.
CONTROL, I NEED A HELICOPTER.
COLOMBIA, 12 HOURS LATER:
WHAT THE FUCK?
WH-WHERE AM I? WH-WHAT HAVE YOU DONE TO ME?
STRIPPED YOU, ROBBED YOU AND DUMPED YOU IN THE MIDDLE OF SOUTH AMERICA.
THIS IS A RESOURCE TEST AND IF YOU FAIL TO TOUCH ENGLISH SOIL INSIDE TWENTY-FOUR HOURS YOU'RE OUT OF THE GAME, GARY. DO YOU UNDERSTAND THE RULES?

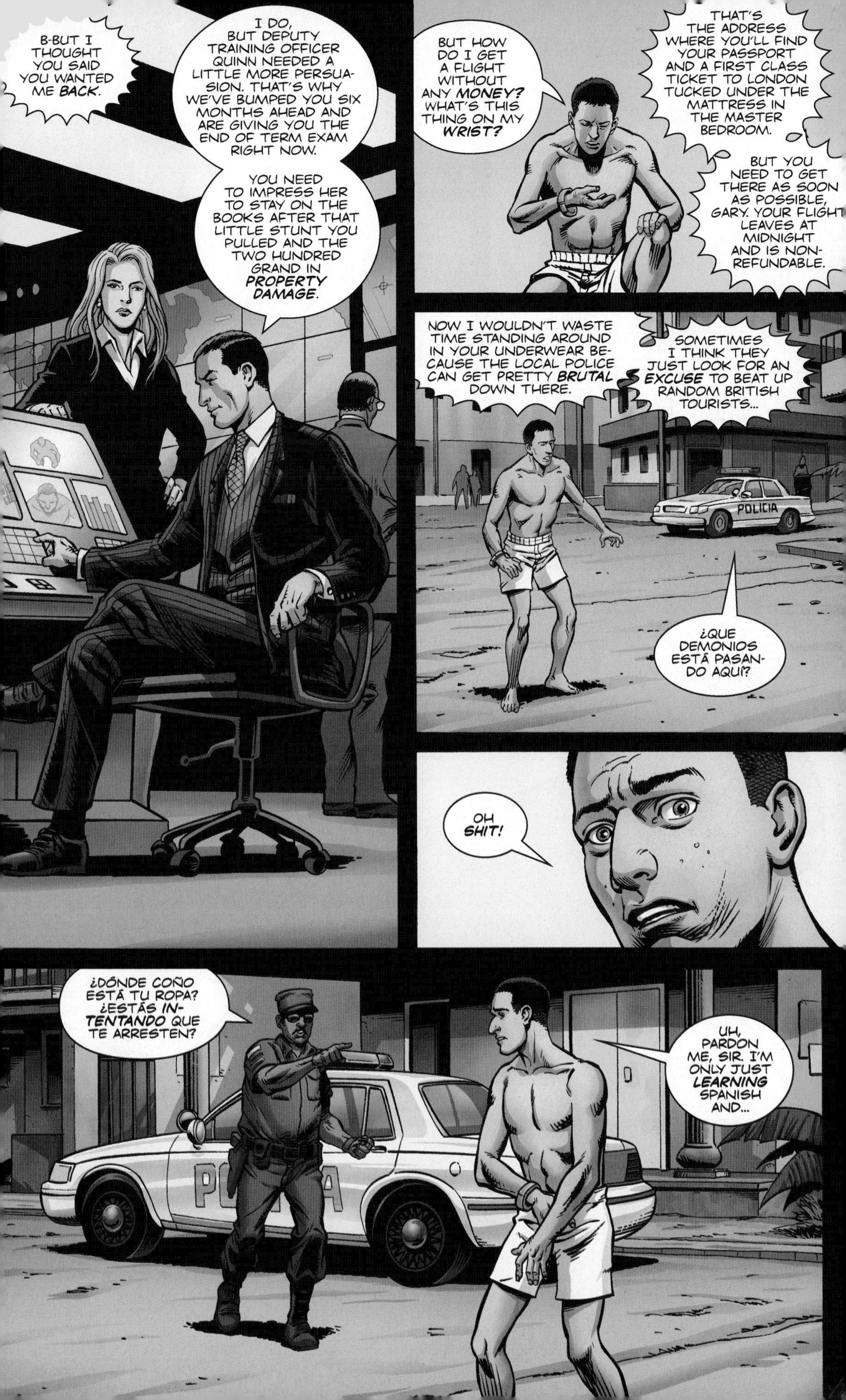
B-BUT I THOUGHT YOU SAID YOU WANTED ME BACK.
I DO, BUT DEPUTY TRAINING OFFICER QUINN NEEDED A LITTLE MORE PERSUASION. THAT'S WHY WE'VE BUMPED YOU SIX MONTHS AHEAD AND ARE GIVING YOU THE END OF TERM EXAM RIGHT NOW.
YOU NEED TO IMPRESS HER TO STAY ON THE BOOKS AFTER THAT LITTLE STUNT YOU PULLED AND THE TWO HUNDRED GRAND IN PROPERTY DAMAGE.
BUT HOW DO I GET A FLIGHT WITHOUT ANY MONEY? WHAT'S THIS THING ON MY WRIST?
THAT'S THE ADDRESS WHERE YOU'LL FIND YOUR PASSPORT AND A FIRST CLASS TICKET TO LONDON TUCKED UNDER THE MATTRESS IN THE MASTER BEDROOM.
BUT YOU NEED TO GET THERE AS SOON AS POSSIBLE, GARY. YOUR FLIGHT LEAVES AT MIDNIGHT AND IS NON-REFUNDABLE.
NOW I WOULDN'T WASTE TIME STANDING AROUND IN YOUR UNDERWEAR BECAUSE THE LOCAL POLICE CAN GET PRETTY BRUTAL DOWN THERE.
SOMETIMES I THINK THEY JUST LOOK FOR AN EXCUSE TO BEAT UP RANDOM BRITISH TOURISTS...
POLICIA
¿QUE DEMONIOS ESTÁ PASANDO AQUI?
OH SHIT!
¿DÓNDE COÑO ESTÁ TU ROPA? ¿ESTÁS INTENTANDO QUE TE ARRESTEN?
UH, PARDON ME, SIR. I'M ONLY JUST LEARNING SPANISH AND...

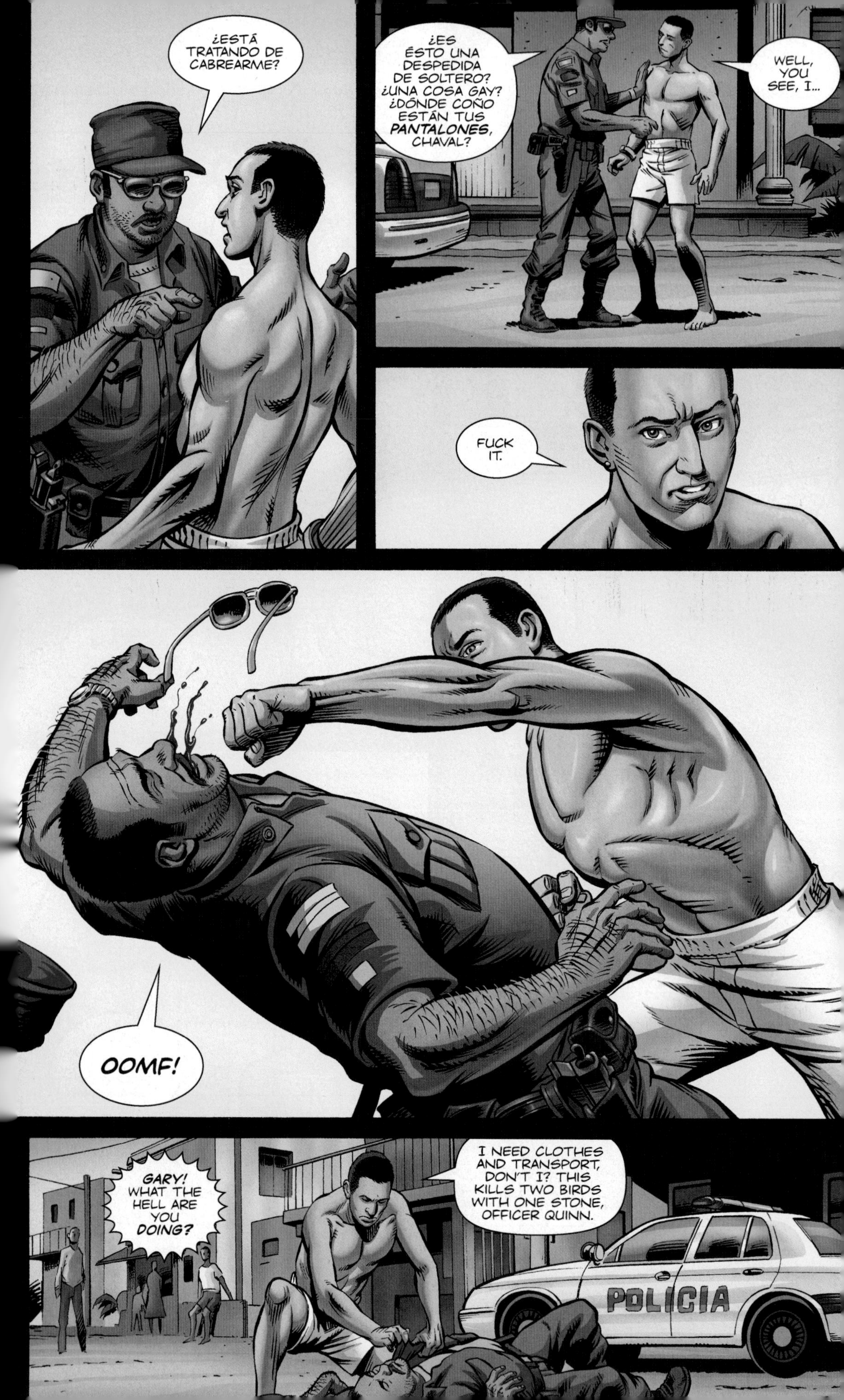
¿ESTÁ TRATANDO DE CABREARME?
¿ES ÉSTO UNA DESPEDIDA DE SOLTERO? ¿UNA COSA GAY? ¿DÓNDE COÑO ESTÁN TUS PANTALONES, CHAVAL?
WELL, YOU SEE, I...
FUCK IT.
OOMF!
GARY! WHAT THE HELL ARE YOU DOING?
I NEED CLOTHES AND TRANSPORT, DON'T I? THIS KILLS TWO BIRDS WITH ONE STONE, OFFICER QUINN.
POLICIA

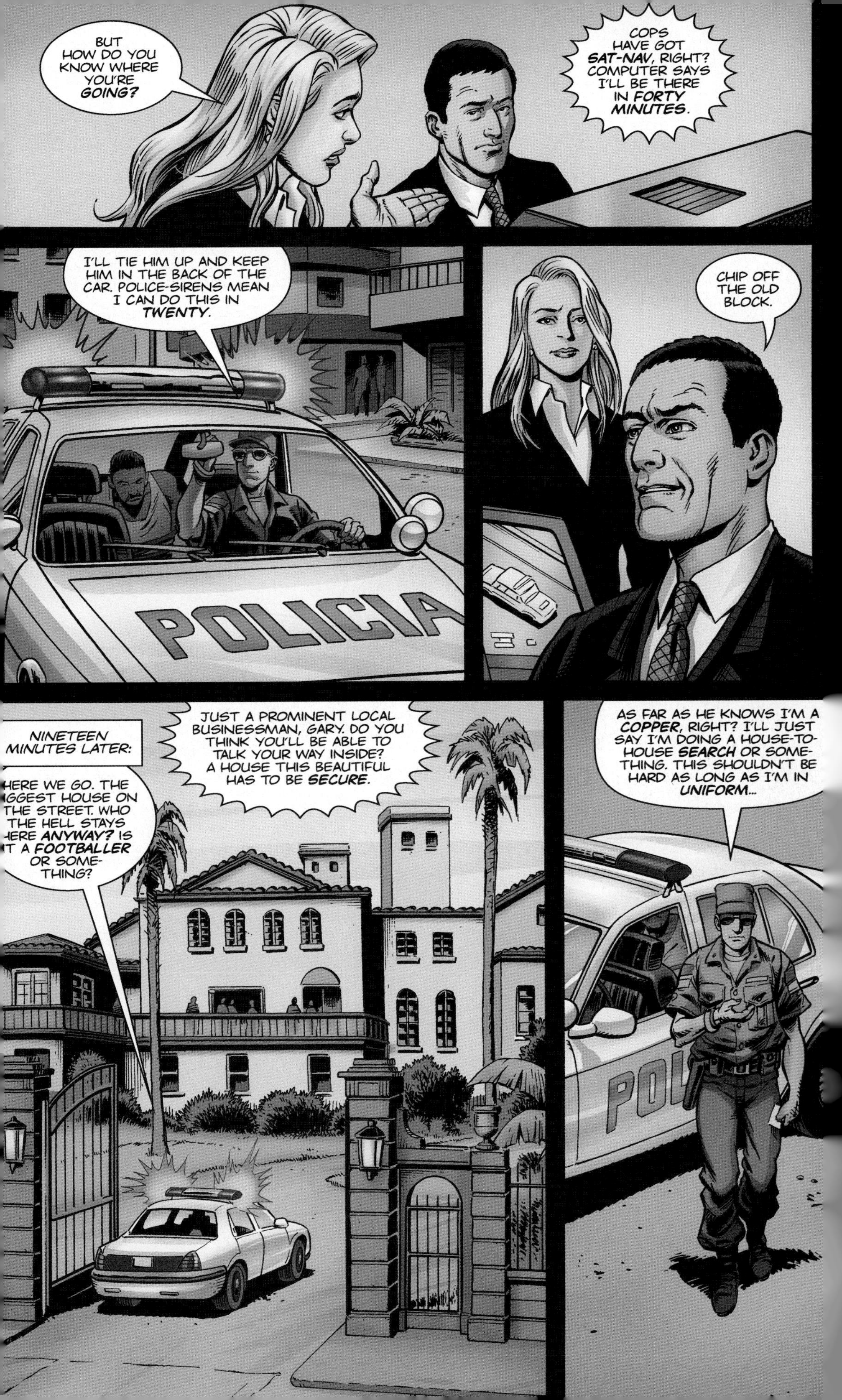
BUT HOW DO YOU KNOW WHERE YOU'RE GOING?
COPS HAVE GOT SAT-NAV, RIGHT? COMPUTER SAYS I'LL BE THERE IN FORTY MINUTES.
I'LL TIE HIM UP AND KEEP HIM IN THE BACK OF THE CAR. POLICE-SIRENS MEAN I CAN DO THIS IN TWENTY.
POLICIA
CHIP OFF THE OLD BLOCK.
NINETEEN MINUTES LATER:
HERE WE GO. THE BIGGEST HOUSE ON THE STREET. WHO THE HELL STAYS HERE ANYWAY? IS IT A FOOTBALLER OR SOMETHING?
JUST A PROMINENT LOCAL BUSINESSMAN, GARY. DO YOU THINK YOU'LL BE ABLE TO TALK YOUR WAY INSIDE? A HOUSE THIS BEAUTIFUL HAS TO BE SECURE.
AS FAR AS HE KNOWS I'M A COPPER, RIGHT? I'LL JUST SAY I'M DOING A HOUSE-TO-HOUSE SEARCH OR SOMETHING. THIS SHOULDN'T BE HARD AS LONG AS I'M IN UNIFORM...
POL

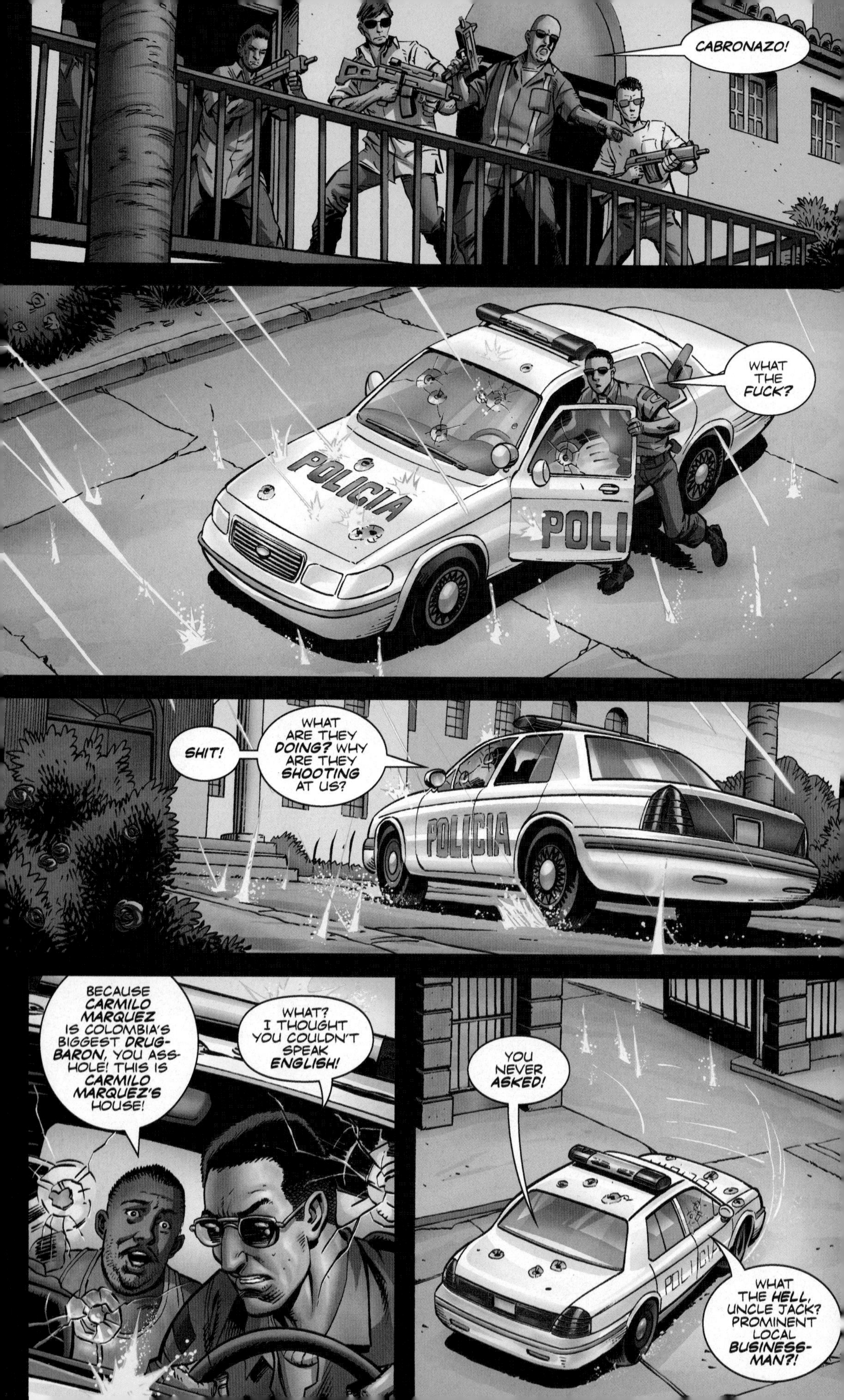
CABRONAZO!
WHAT THE FUCK?
SHIT!
WHAT ARE THEY DOING? WHY ARE THEY SHOOTING AT US?
BECAUSE CARMILO MARQUEZ IS COLOMBIA'S BIGGEST DRUG-BARON, YOU ASS-HOLE! THIS IS CARMILO MARQUEZ'S HOUSE!
WHAT? I THOUGHT YOU COULDN'T SPEAK ENGLISH!
YOU NEVER ASKED!
WHAT THE HELL, UNCLE JACK? PROMINENT LOCAL BUSINESS-MAN?!

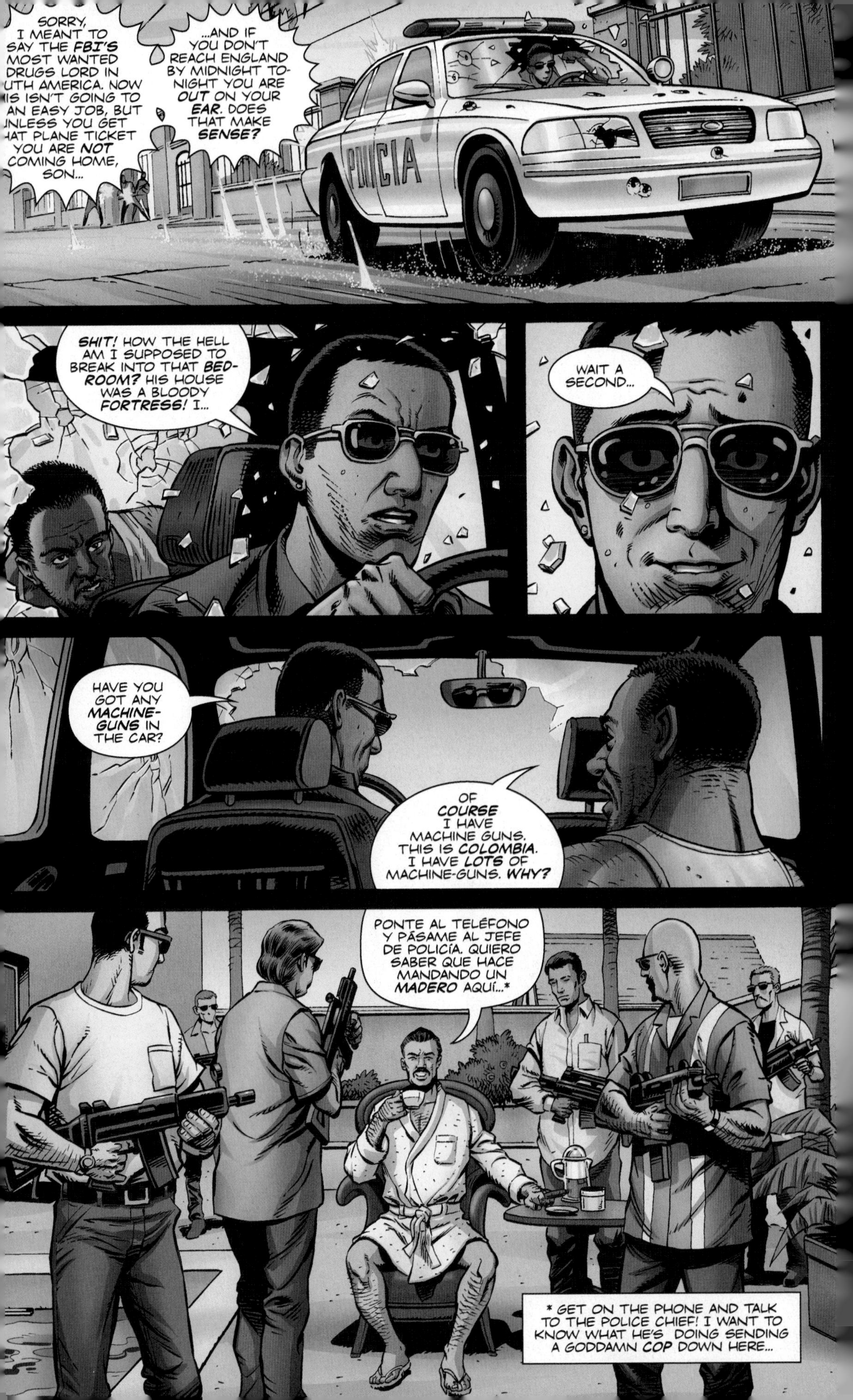
SORRY, I MEANT TO SAY THE FBI'S MOST WANTED DRUGS LORD IN UTH AMERICA. NOW IS ISN'T GOING TO AN EASY JOB, BUT NLESS YOU GET HAT PLANE TICKET YOU ARE NOT COMING HOME, SON...
...AND IF YOU DON'T REACH ENGLAND BY MIDNIGHT TO-NIGHT YOU ARE OUT ON YOUR EAR. DOES THAT MAKE SENSE?
POLICIA
SHIT! HOW THE HELL AM I SUPPOSED TO BREAK INTO THAT BED-ROOM? HIS HOUSE WAS A BLOODY FORTRESS! I...
WAIT A SECOND...
HAVE YOU GOT ANY MACHINE-GUNS IN THE CAR?
OF COURSE I HAVE MACHINE GUNS. THIS IS COLOMBIA. I HAVE LOTS OF MACHINE-GUNS. WHY?
PONTE AL TELÉFONO Y PÁSAME AL JEFE DE POLICÍA. QUIERO SABER QUE HACE MANDANDO UN MADERO AQUÍ...*
* GET ON THE PHONE AND TALK TO THE POLICE CHIEF! I WANT TO KNOW WHAT HE'S DOING SENDING A GODDAMN COP DOWN HERE...

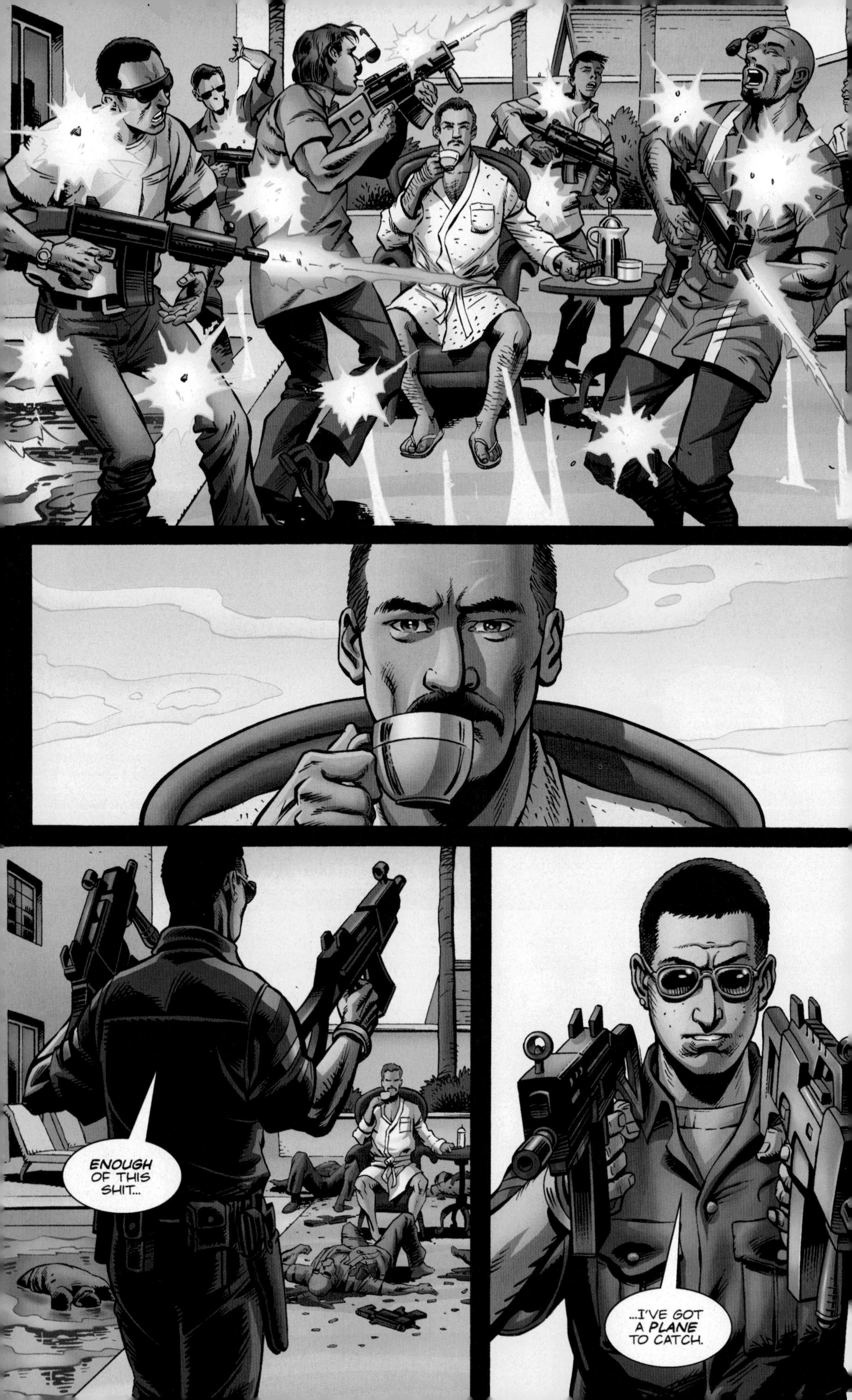
ENOUGH OF THIS SHIT...
...I'VE GOT A **PLANE** TO CATCH.

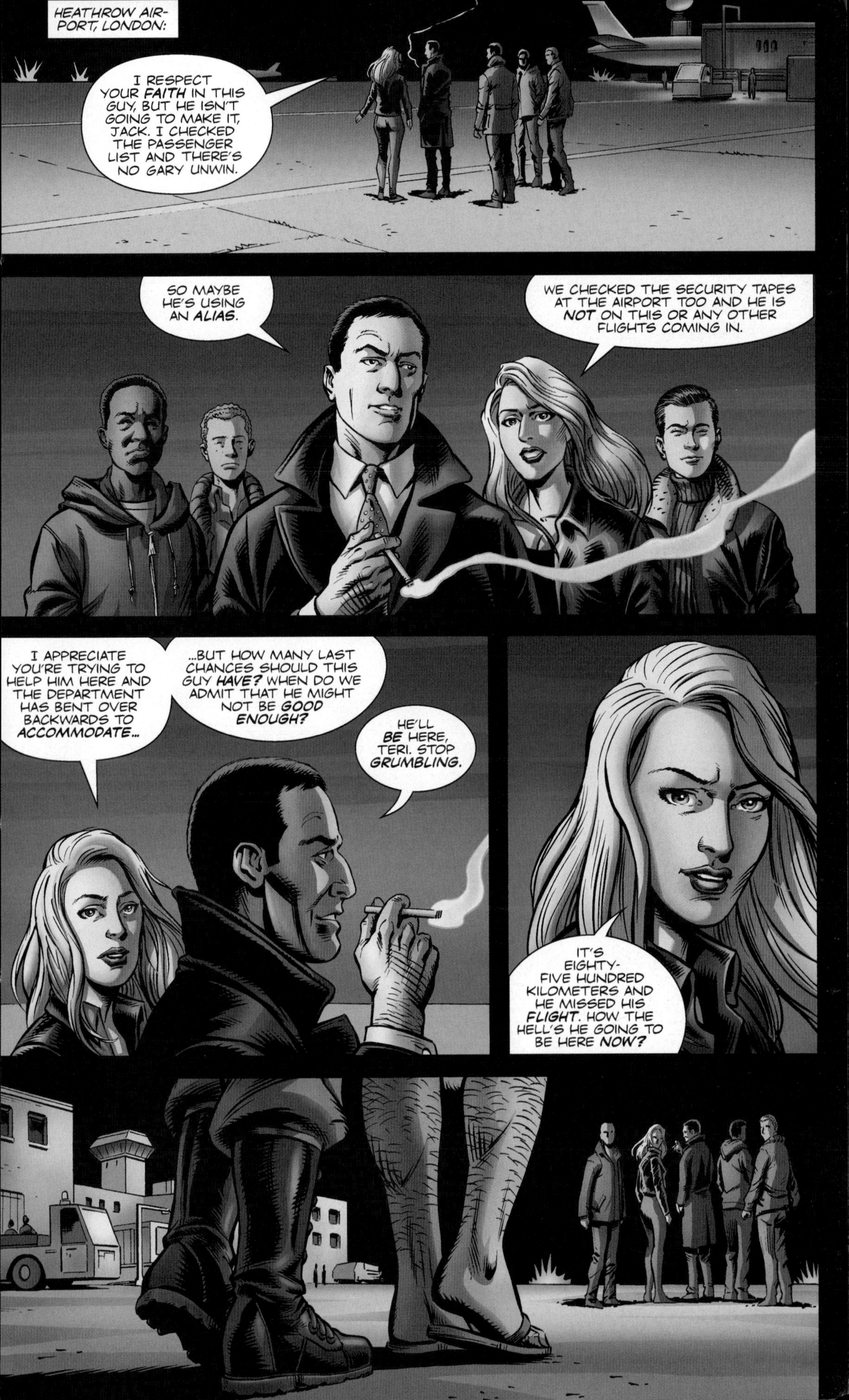
HEATHROW AIRPORT, LONDON:
I RESPECT YOUR FAITH IN THIS GUY, BUT HE ISN'T GOING TO MAKE IT, JACK. I CHECKED THE PASSENGER LIST AND THERE'S NO GARY UNWIN.
SO MAYBE HE'S USING AN ALIAS.
WE CHECKED THE SECURITY TAPES AT THE AIRPORT TOO AND HE IS NOT ON THIS OR ANY OTHER FLIGHTS COMING IN.
I APPRECIATE YOU'RE TRYING TO HELP HIM HERE AND THE DEPARTMENT HAS BENT OVER BACKWARDS TO ACCOMMODATE...
...BUT HOW MANY LAST CHANCES SHOULD THIS GUY HAVE? WHEN DO WE ADMIT THAT HE MIGHT NOT BE GOOD ENOUGH?
HE'LL BE HERE, TERI. STOP GRUMBLING.
IT'S EIGHTY-FIVE HUNDRED KILOMETERS AND HE MISSED HIS FLIGHT. HOW THE HELL'S HE GOING TO BE HERE NOW?

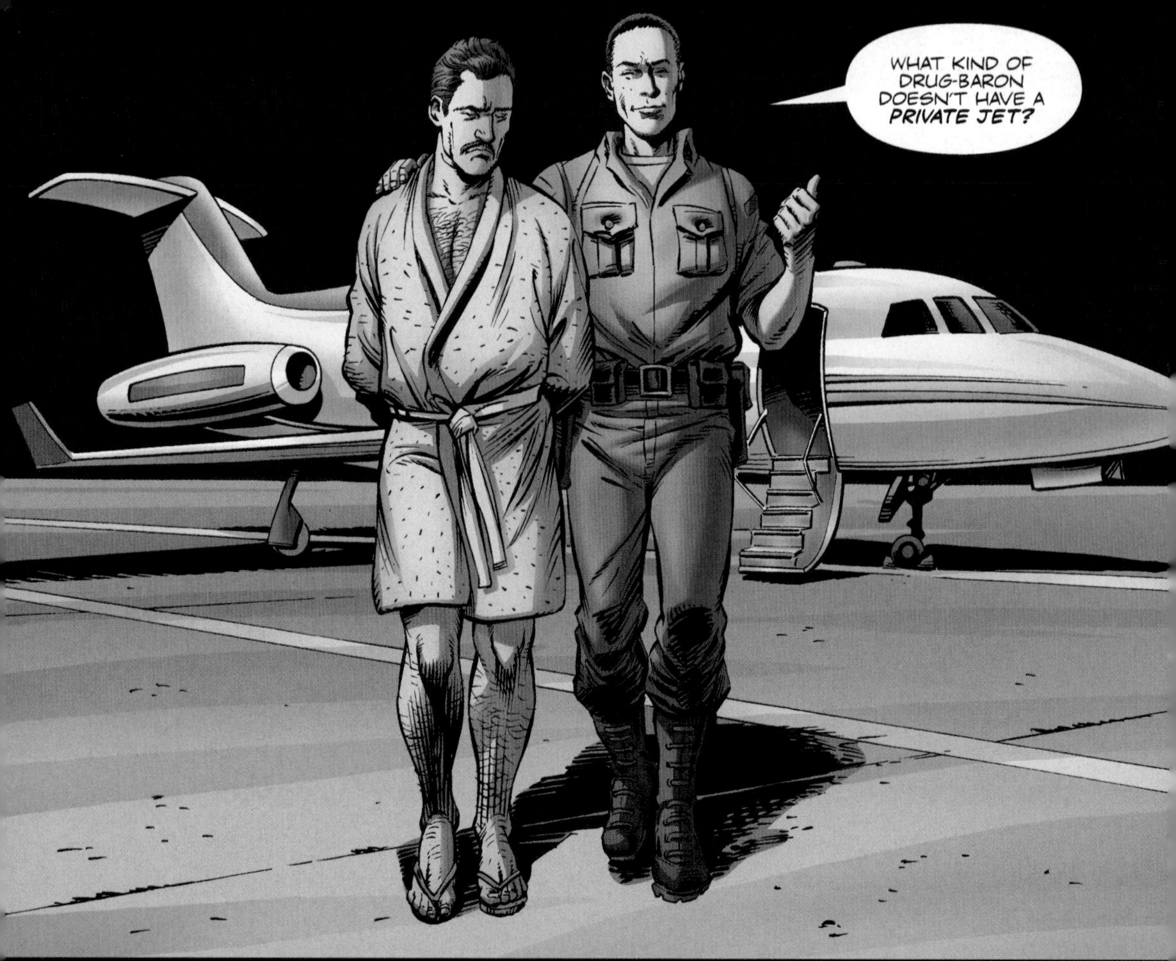
WHAT KIND OF DRUG-BARON DOESN'T HAVE A PRIVATE JET?

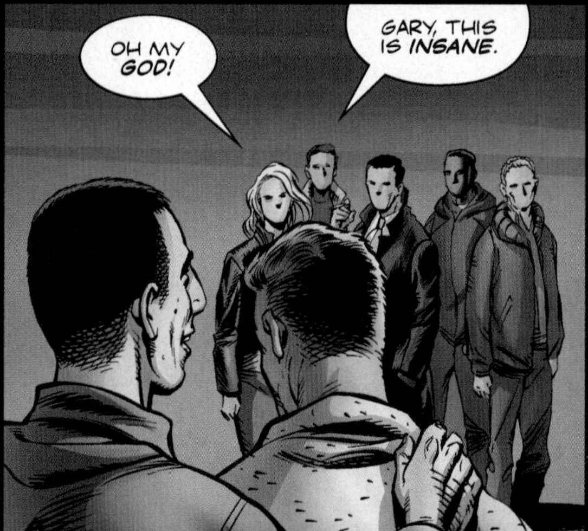
OH MY GOD!
GARY, THIS IS INSANE.

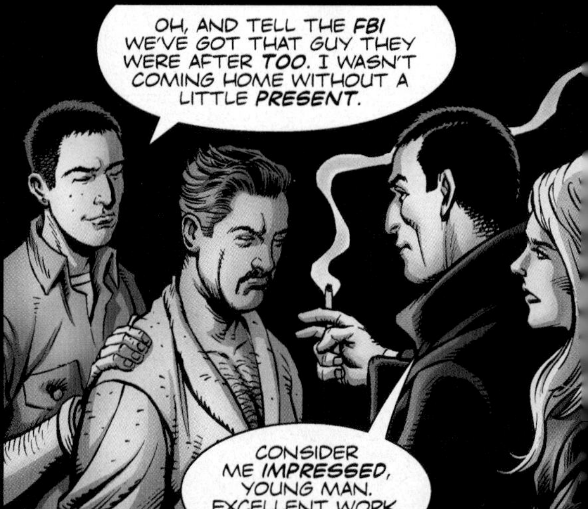
OH, AND TELL THE FBI WE'VE GOT THAT GUY THEY WERE AFTER TOO. I WASN'T COMING HOME WITHOUT A LITTLE PRESENT.
CONSIDER ME IMPRESSED, YOUNG MAN. EXCELLENT WORK.

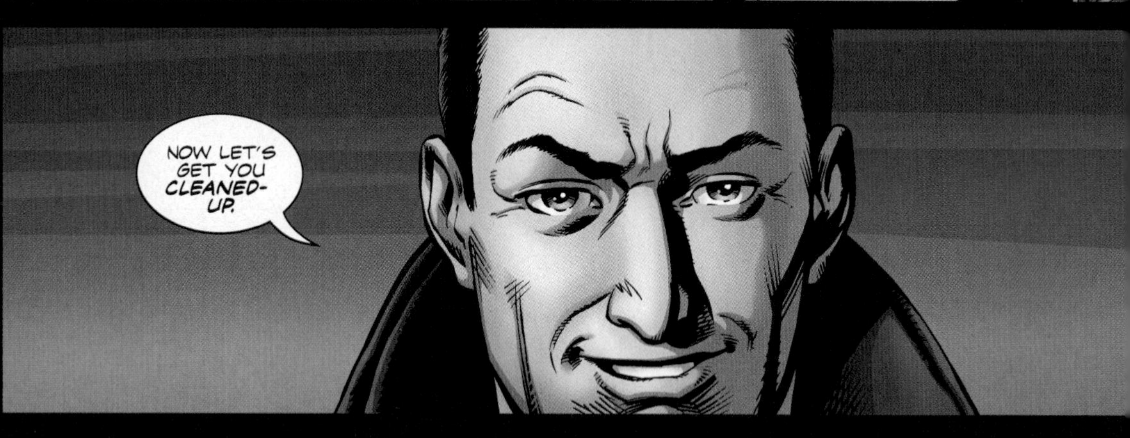
NOW LET'S GET YOU CLEANED-UP.

UNCLE JACK'S STYLE-TIPS:

OKAY, TO DRESS SMART YOU NEED TO START WITH YOUR FEET AND WORK YOUR WAY UP. A MAN IS ALWAYS JUDGED BY HIS SHOES AND FROM THIS MOMENT ON YOU WEAR **BROWN** OR **BLACK**.

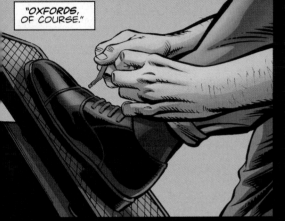

"OXFORDS, OF COURSE."

SELECT A HAIRCUT THAT DEMANDS **RESPECT**. THAT'S TIGHT ON THE SIDES AND A SHARP LEFT-PARTING. ANYTHING ELSE IS **NOT ACCEPT-ABLE**.

A CRISP WHITE SHIRT IS THE BACKBONE OF ANY WARDROBE. A LIGHT PATTERN CAN LIVEN THINGS UP, BUT STAY SIMPLE AND CLASSIC FOR THE TIME BEING.

"WE CAN GRADU-ATE TO COLOURS WHEN YOU'RE A LITTLE MORE **EXPERIENCED**."

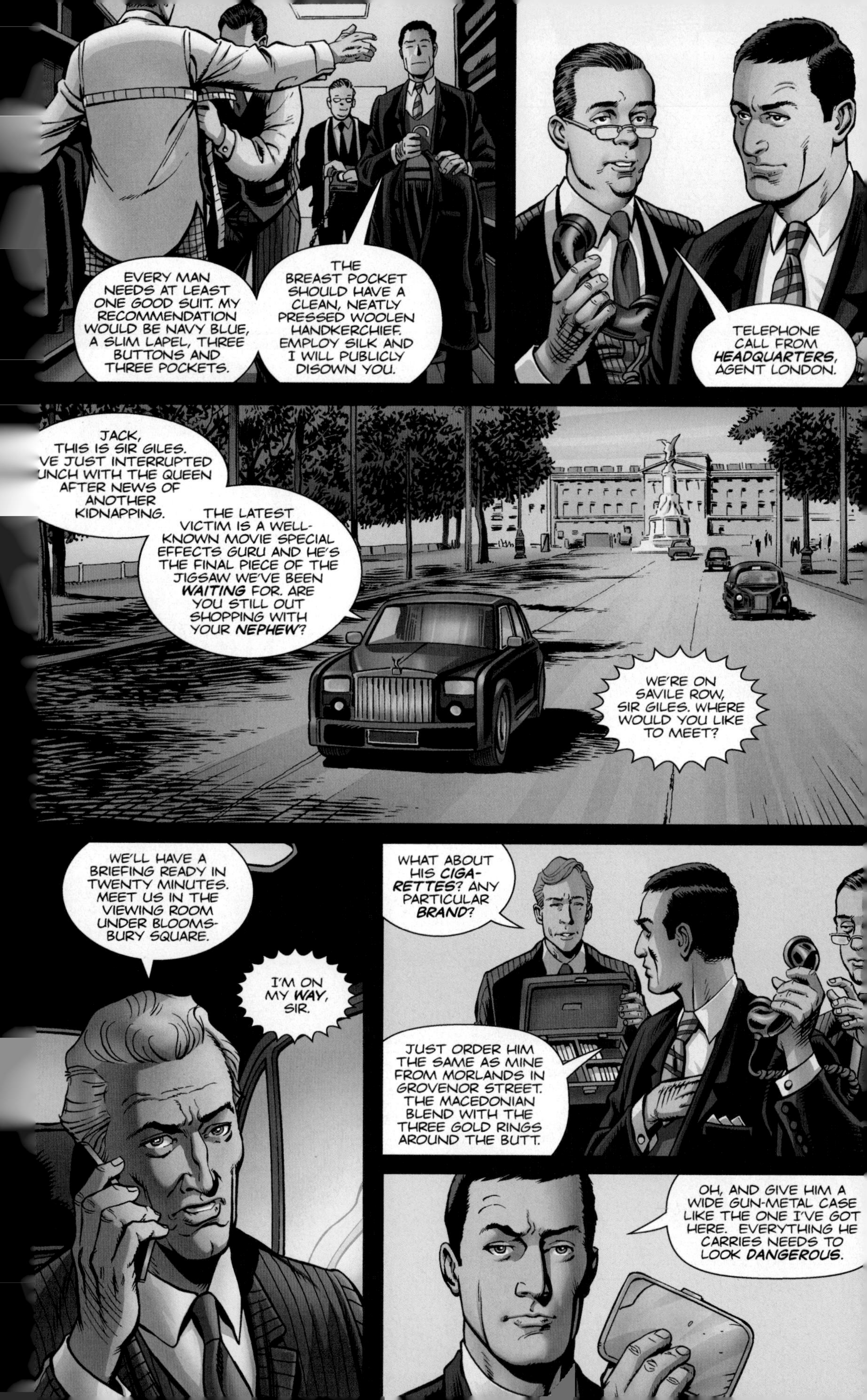
EVERY MAN NEEDS AT LEAST ONE GOOD SUIT. MY RECOMMENDATION WOULD BE NAVY BLUE, A SLIM LAPEL, THREE BUTTONS AND THREE POCKETS.
THE BREAST POCKET SHOULD HAVE A CLEAN, NEATLY PRESSED WOOLEN HANDKERCHIEF. EMPLOY SILK AND I WILL PUBLICLY DISOWN YOU.
TELEPHONE CALL FROM **HEADQUARTERS**, AGENT LONDON.
JACK, THIS IS SIR GILES. VE JUST INTERRUPTED UNCH WITH THE QUEEN AFTER NEWS OF ANOTHER KIDNAPPING.
THE LATEST VICTIM IS A WELL-KNOWN MOVIE SPECIAL EFFECTS GURU AND HE'S THE FINAL PIECE OF THE JIGSAW WE'VE BEEN **WAITING** FOR. ARE YOU STILL OUT SHOPPING WITH YOUR **NEPHEW**?
WE'RE ON SAVILE ROW, SIR GILES. WHERE WOULD YOU LIKE TO MEET?
WE'LL HAVE A BRIEFING READY IN TWENTY MINUTES. MEET US IN THE VIEWING ROOM UNDER BLOOMSBURY SQUARE.
I'M ON MY **WAY**, SIR.
WHAT ABOUT HIS **CIGARETTES**? ANY PARTICULAR **BRAND**?
JUST ORDER HIM THE SAME AS MINE FROM MORLANDS IN GROVENOR STREET. THE MACEDONIAN BLEND WITH THE THREE GOLD RINGS AROUND THE BUTT.
OH, AND GIVE HIM A WIDE GUN-METAL CASE LIKE THE ONE I'VE GOT HERE. EVERYTHING HE CARRIES NEEDS TO LOOK **DANGEROUS**.

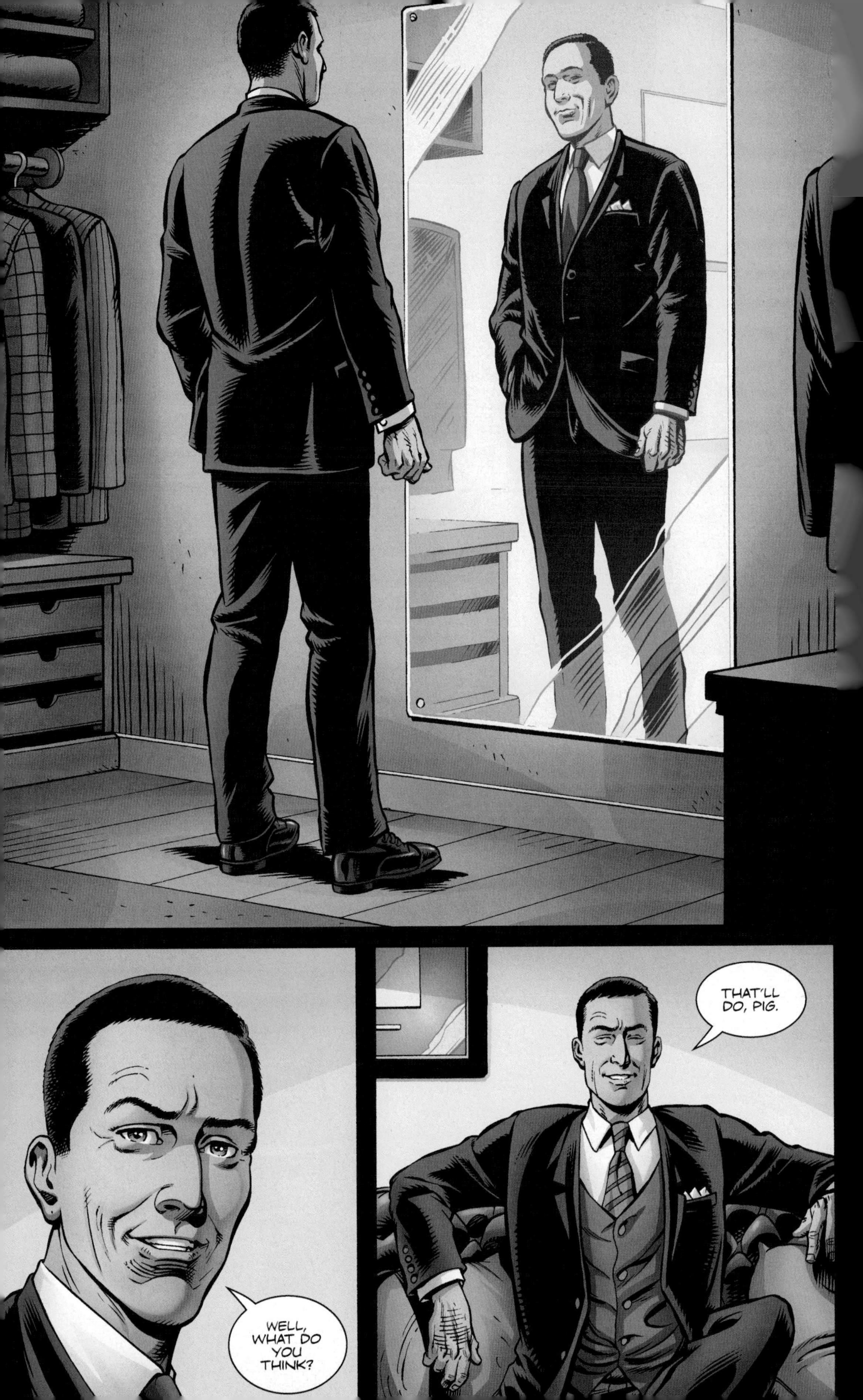
WELL, WHAT DO YOU THINK?
THAT'LL DO, PIG.

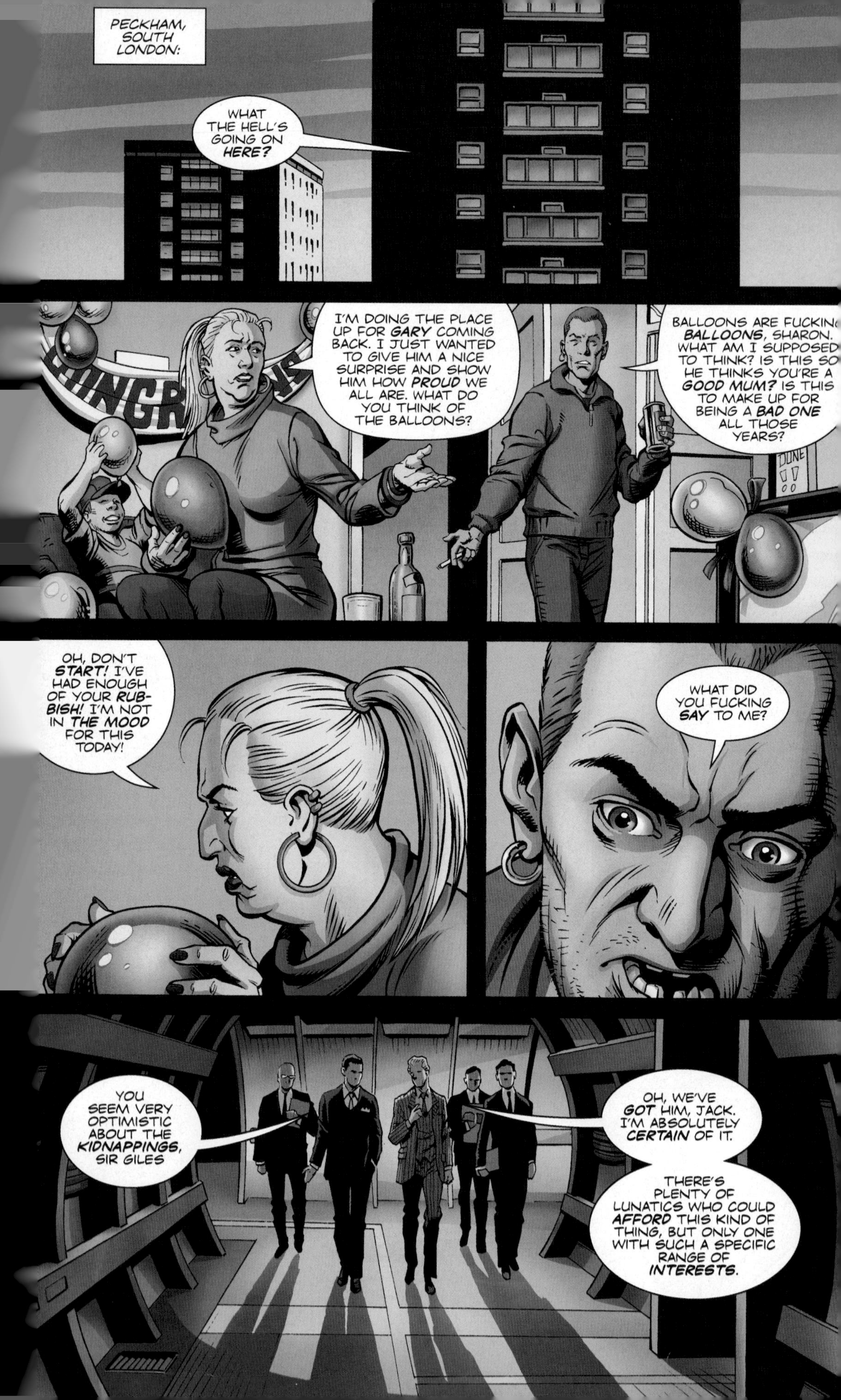
PECKHAM, SOUTH LONDON:
WHAT THE HELL'S GOING ON HERE?
I'M DOING THE PLACE UP FOR GARY COMING BACK. I JUST WANTED TO GIVE HIM A NICE SURPRISE AND SHOW HIM HOW PROUD WE ALL ARE. WHAT DO YOU THINK OF THE BALLOONS?
BALLOONS ARE FUCKING BALLOONS, SHARON. WHAT AM I SUPPOSED TO THINK? IS THIS SO HE THINKS YOU'RE A GOOD MUM? IS THIS TO MAKE UP FOR BEING A BAD ONE ALL THOSE YEARS?
OH, DON'T START! I'VE HAD ENOUGH OF YOUR RUB-BISH! I'M NOT IN THE MOOD FOR THIS TODAY!
WHAT DID YOU FUCKING SAY TO ME?
YOU SEEM VERY OPTIMISTIC ABOUT THE KIDNAPPINGS, SIR GILES
OH, WE'VE GOT HIM, JACK. I'M ABSOLUTELY CERTAIN OF IT.
THERE'S PLENTY OF LUNATICS WHO COULD AFFORD THIS KIND OF THING, BUT ONLY ONE WITH SUCH A SPECIFIC RANGE OF INTERESTS.

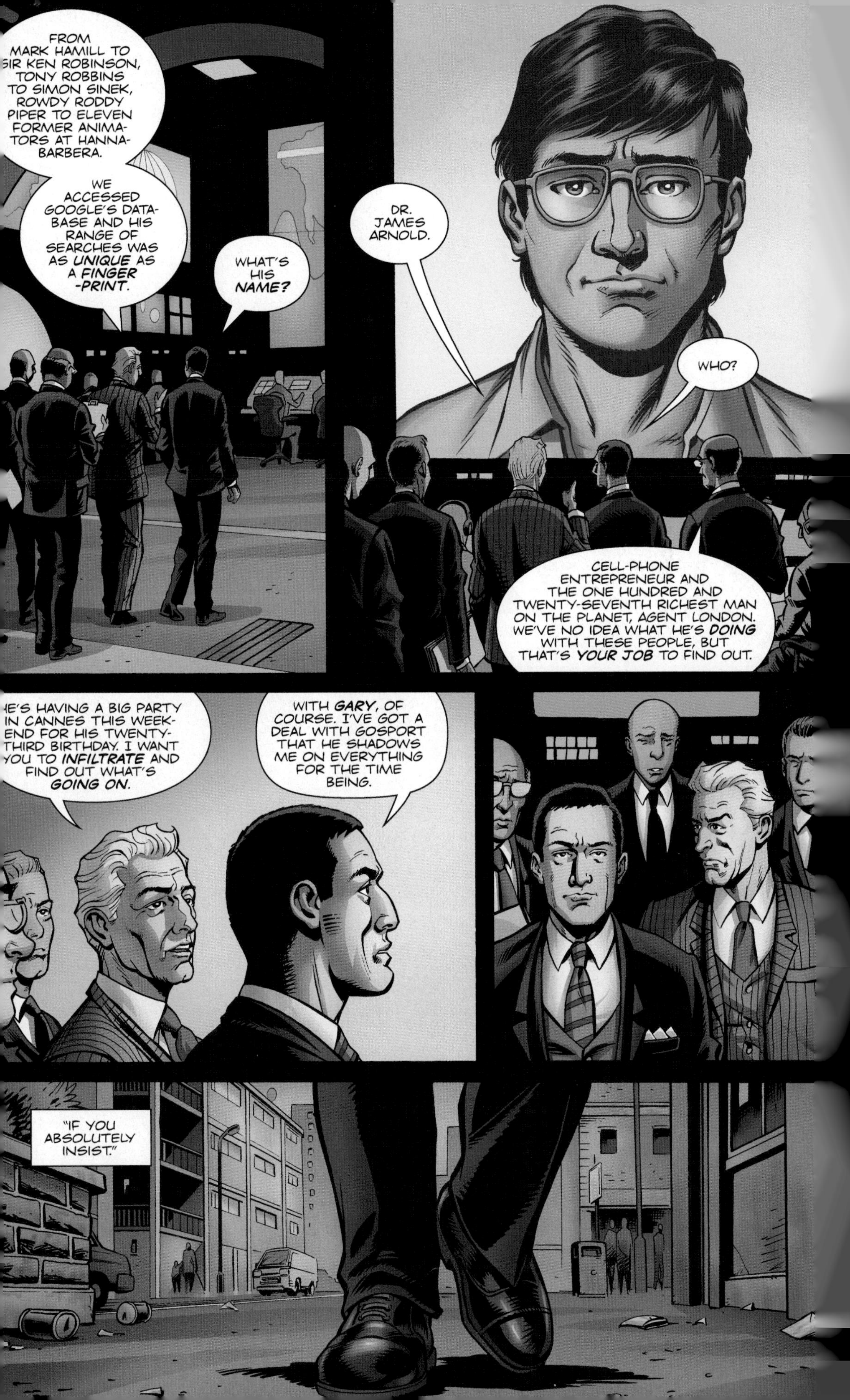
FROM MARK HAMILL TO SIR KEN ROBINSON, TONY ROBBINS TO SIMON SINEK, ROWDY RODDY PIPER TO ELEVEN FORMER ANIMATORS AT HANNA-BARBERA.
WE ACCESSED GOOGLE'S DATABASE AND HIS RANGE OF SEARCHES WAS AS UNIQUE AS A FINGER-PRINT.
WHAT'S HIS NAME?
DR. JAMES ARNOLD.
WHO?
CELL-PHONE ENTREPRENEUR AND THE ONE HUNDRED AND TWENTY-SEVENTH RICHEST MAN ON THE PLANET, AGENT LONDON. WE'VE NO IDEA WHAT HE'S DOING WITH THESE PEOPLE, BUT THAT'S YOUR JOB TO FIND OUT.
HE'S HAVING A BIG PARTY IN CANNES THIS WEEKEND FOR HIS TWENTY-THIRD BIRTHDAY. I WANT YOU TO INFILTRATE AND FIND OUT WHAT'S GOING ON.
WITH GARY, OF COURSE. I'VE GOT A DEAL WITH GOSPORT THAT HE SHADOWS ME ON EVERYTHING FOR THE TIME BEING.
"IF YOU ABSOLUTELY INSIST."

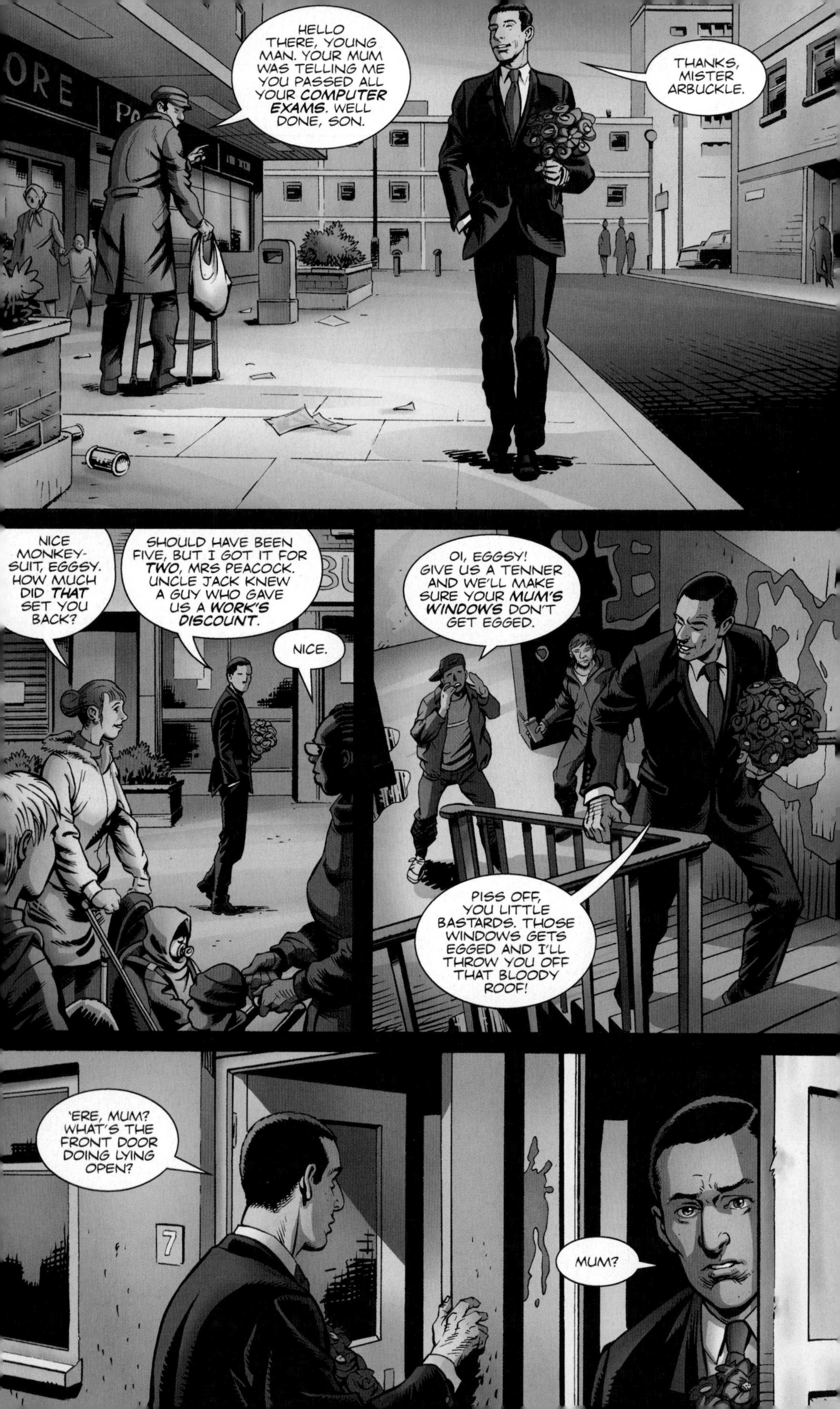
HELLO THERE, YOUNG MAN. YOUR MUM WAS TELLING ME YOU PASSED ALL YOUR COMPUTER EXAMS. WELL DONE, SON.
THANKS, MISTER ARBUCKLE.
NICE MONKEY-SUIT, EGGSY. HOW MUCH DID THAT SET YOU BACK?
SHOULD HAVE BEEN FIVE, BUT I GOT IT FOR TWO, MRS PEACOCK. UNCLE JACK KNEW A GUY WHO GAVE US A WORK'S DISCOUNT.
NICE.
OI, EGGSY! GIVE US A TENNER AND WE'LL MAKE SURE YOUR MUM'S WINDOWS DON'T GET EGGED.
PISS OFF, YOU LITTLE BASTARDS. THOSE WINDOWS GETS EGGED AND I'LL THROW YOU OFF THAT BLOODY ROOF!
'ERE, MUM? WHAT'S THE FRONT DOOR DOING LYING OPEN?
7
MUM?

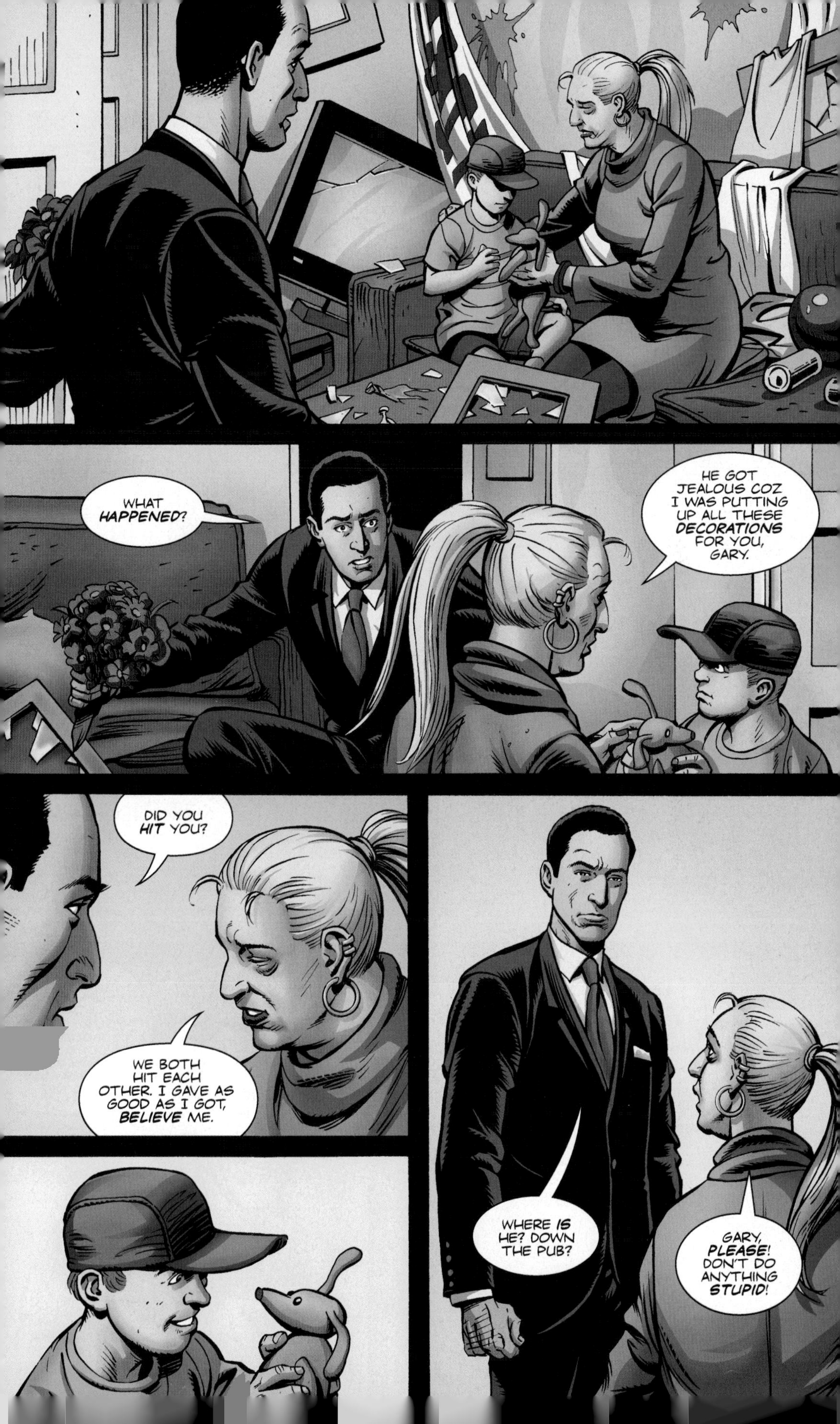
WHAT HAPPENED?
HE GOT JEALOUS COZ I WAS PUTTING UP ALL THESE DECORATIONS FOR YOU, GARY.
DID YOU HIT YOU?
WE BOTH HIT EACH OTHER. I GAVE AS GOOD AS I GOT, BELIEVE ME.
WHERE IS HE? DOWN THE PUB?
GARY, PLEASE! DON'T DO ANYTHING STUPID!

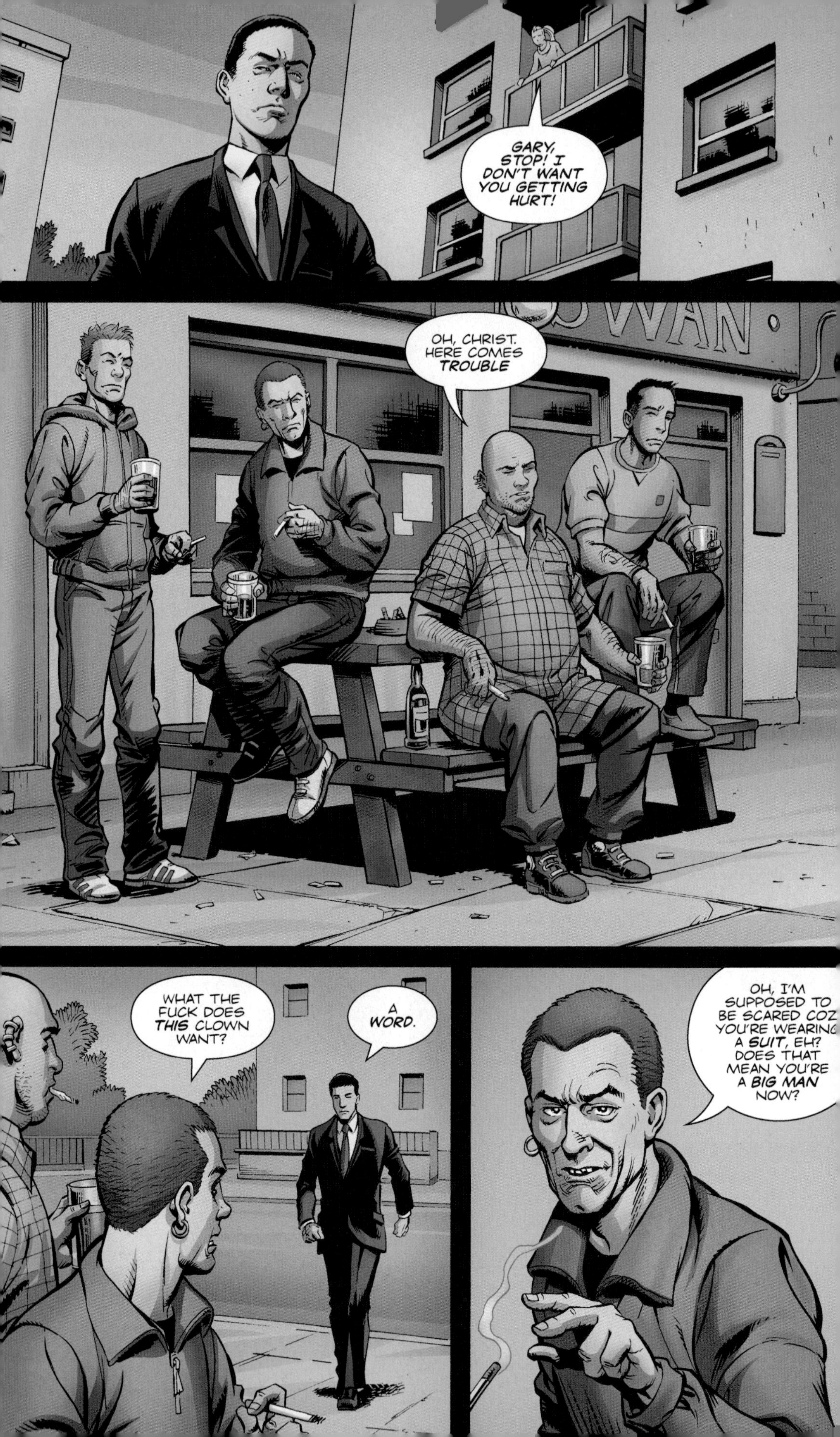
GARY, STOP! I DON'T WANT YOU GETTING HURT!
WAN
OH, CHRIST. HERE COMES TROUBLE
WHAT THE FUCK DOES THIS CLOWN WANT?
A WORD.
OH, I'M SUPPOSED TO BE SCARED COZ YOU'RE WEARING A SUIT, EH? DOES THAT MEAN YOU'RE A BIG MAN NOW?

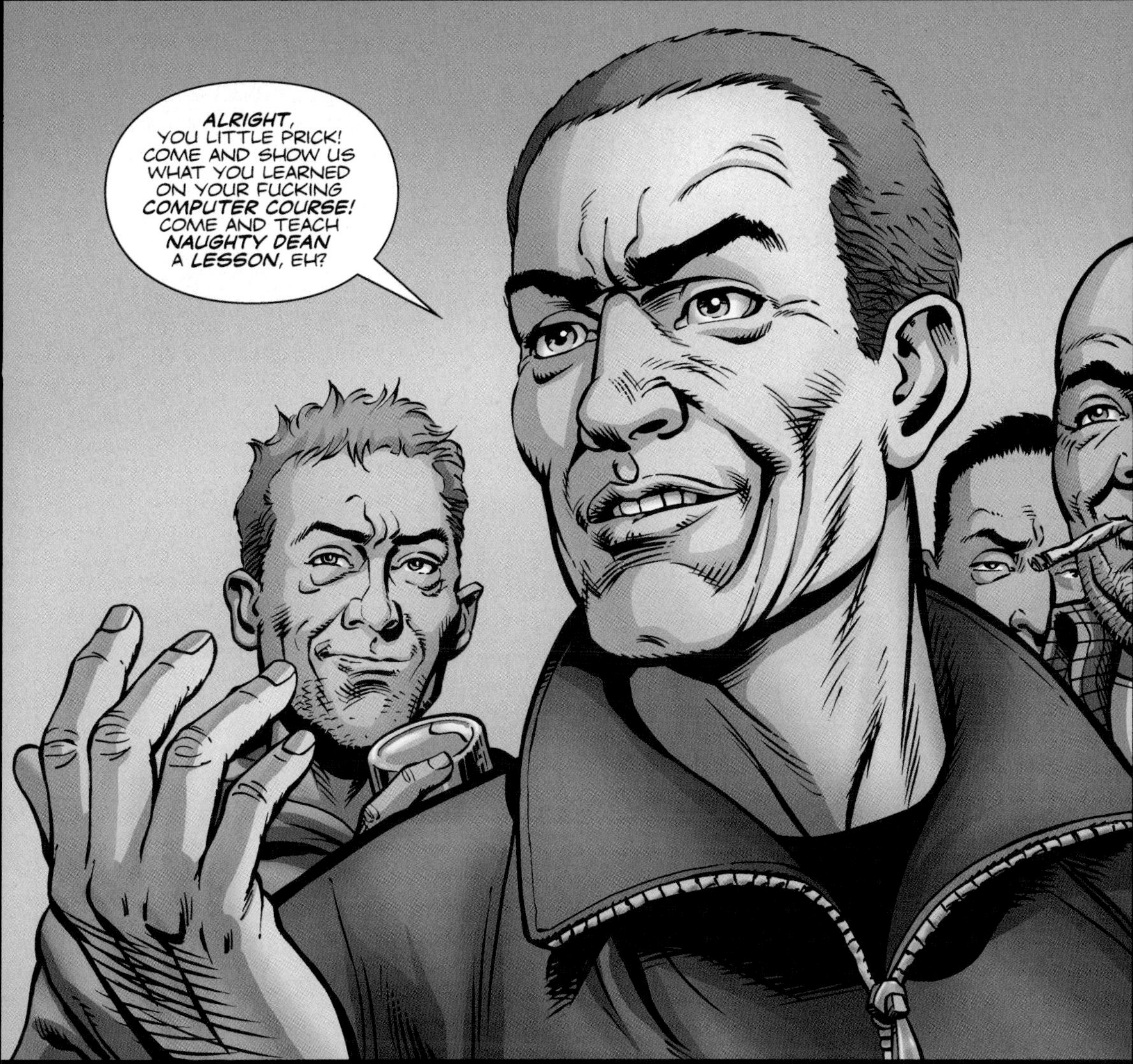
ALRIGHT, YOU LITTLE PRICK! COME AND SHOW US WHAT YOU LEARNED ON YOUR FUCKING COMPUTER COURSE! COME AND TEACH NAUGHTY DEAN A LESSON, EH?

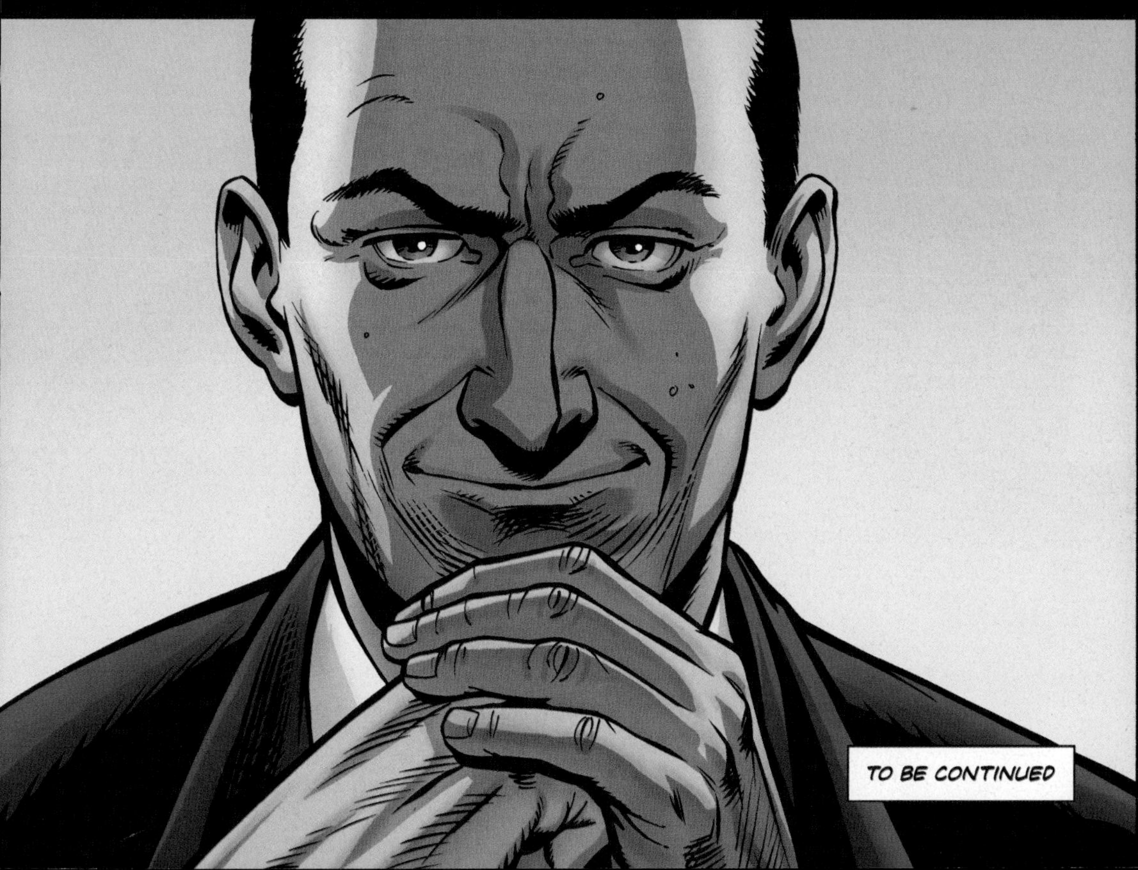
TO BE CONTINUED

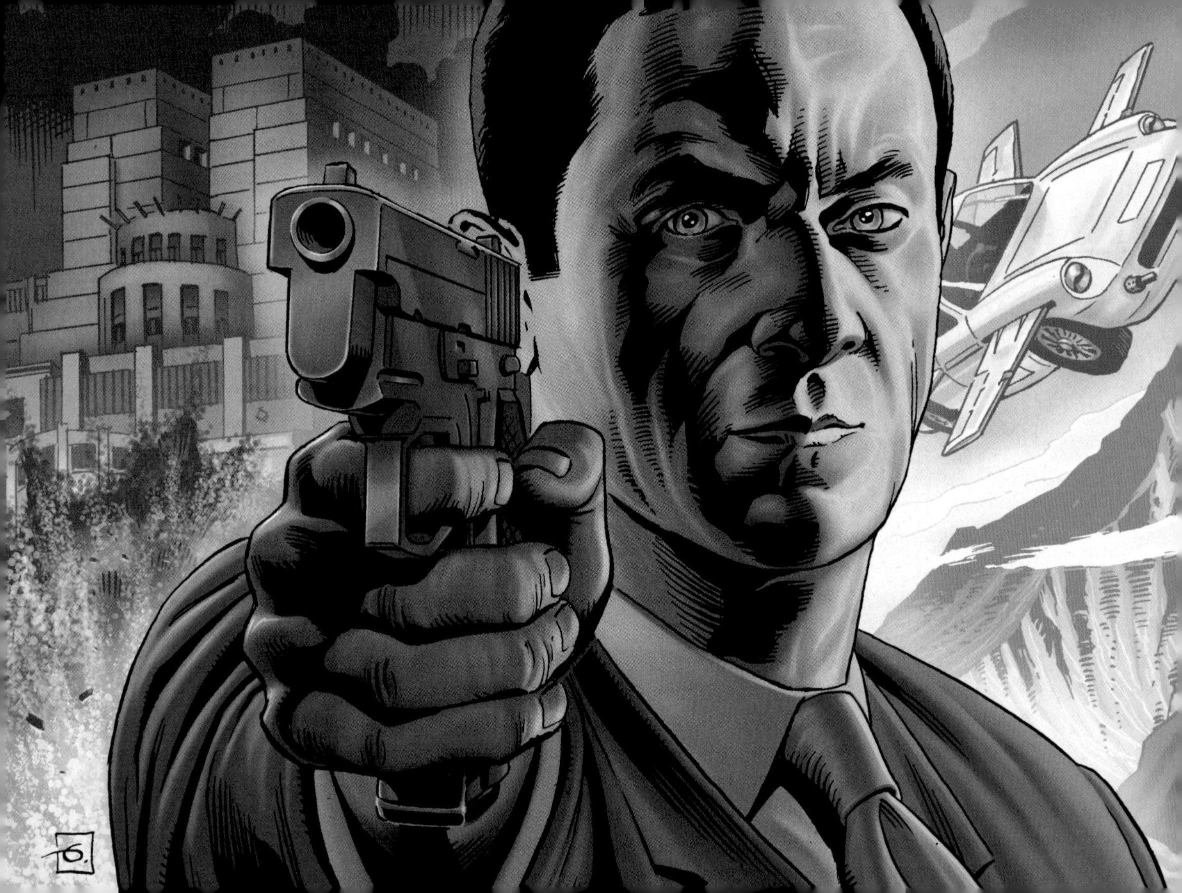

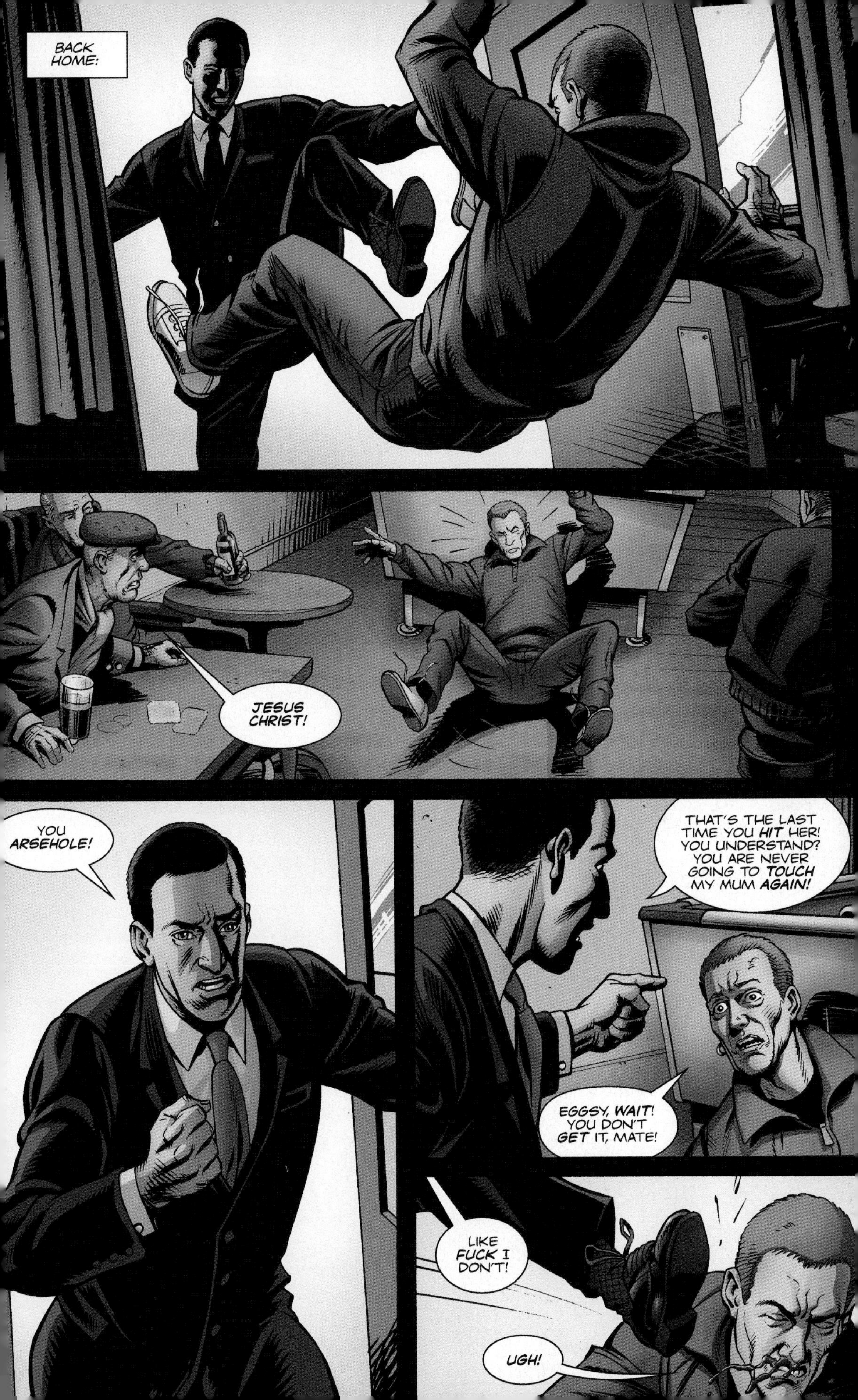
BACK HOME:
JESUS CHRIST!
YOU ARSEHOLE!
THAT'S THE LAST TIME YOU HIT HER! YOU UNDERSTAND? YOU ARE NEVER GOING TO TOUCH MY MUM AGAIN!
EGGSY, WAIT! YOU DON'T GET IT, MATE!
LIKE FUCK I DON'T!
UGH!

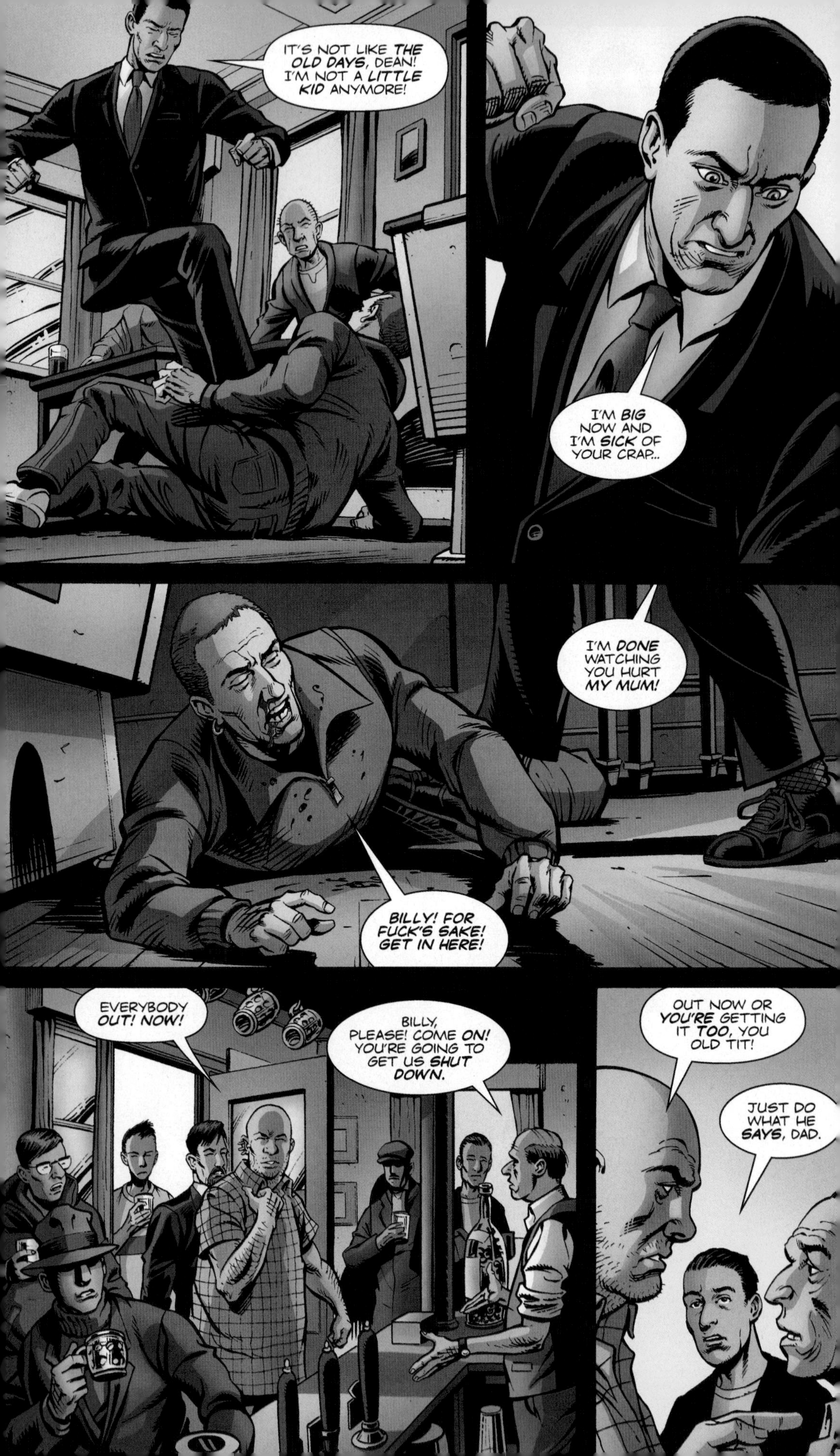
IT'S NOT LIKE THE OLD DAYS, DEAN! I'M NOT A LITTLE KID ANYMORE!
I'M BIG NOW AND I'M SICK OF YOUR CRAP...
I'M DONE WATCHING YOU HURT MY MUM!
BILLY! FOR FUCK'S SAKE! GET IN HERE!
EVERYBODY OUT! NOW!
BILLY, PLEASE! COME ON! YOU'RE GOING TO GET US SHUT DOWN.
OUT NOW OR YOU'RE GETTING IT TOO, YOU OLD TIT!
JUST DO WHAT HE SAYS, DAD.

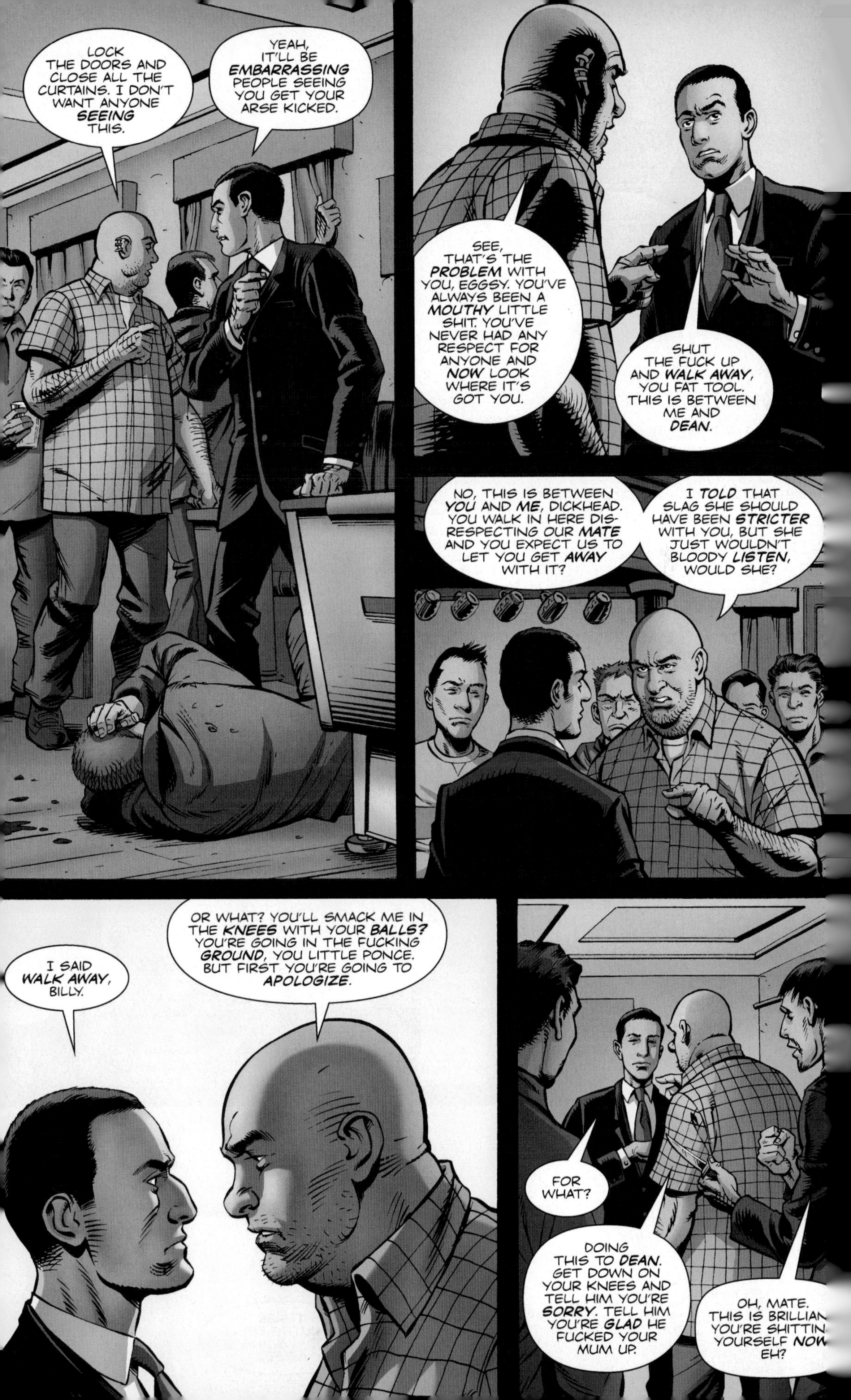

LOCK THE DOORS AND CLOSE ALL THE CURTAINS. I DON'T WANT ANYONE **SEEING** THIS.
YEAH, IT'LL BE **EMBARRASSING** PEOPLE SEEING YOU GET YOUR ARSE KICKED.
SEE, THAT'S THE **PROBLEM** WITH YOU, EGGSY. YOU'VE ALWAYS BEEN A **MOUTHY** LITTLE SHIT. YOU'VE NEVER HAD ANY RESPECT FOR ANYONE AND **NOW** LOOK WHERE IT'S GOT YOU.
SHUT THE FUCK UP AND **WALK AWAY**, YOU FAT TOOL. THIS IS BETWEEN ME AND **DEAN**.
NO, THIS IS BETWEEN **YOU** AND **ME**, DICKHEAD. YOU WALK IN HERE DIS-RESPECTING OUR **MATE** AND YOU EXPECT US TO LET YOU GET **AWAY** WITH IT?
I **TOLD** THAT SLAG SHE SHOULD HAVE BEEN **STRICTER** WITH YOU, BUT SHE JUST WOULDN'T BLOODY **LISTEN**, WOULD SHE?
I SAID **WALK AWAY**, BILLY.
OR WHAT? YOU'LL SMACK ME IN THE **KNEES** WITH YOUR **BALLS?** YOU'RE GOING IN THE FUCKING **GROUND**, YOU LITTLE PONCE. BUT FIRST YOU'RE GOING TO **APOLOGIZE**.
FOR WHAT?
DOING THIS TO **DEAN**. GET DOWN ON YOUR KNEES AND TELL HIM YOU'RE **SORRY**. TELL HIM YOU'RE **GLAD** HE FUCKED YOUR MUM UP.
OH, MATE. THIS IS BRILLIAN YOU'RE SHITTIN YOURSELF **NOW** EH?

MAN, DID I REALLY USED TO BE **SCARED** OF YOU IDIOTS?

OW!

WHAT THE HELL

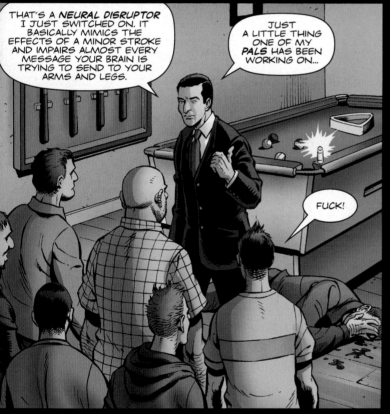

THAT'S A **NEURAL DISRUPTOR** I JUST SWITCHED ON. IT BASICALLY MIMICS THE EFFECTS OF A MINOR STROKE AND IMPAIRS ALMOST EVERY MESSAGE YOUR BRAIN IS TRYING TO SEND TO YOUR ARMS AND LEGS.

JUST A LITTLE THING ONE OF MY **PALS** HAS BEEN WORKING ON...

FUCK!

THE EFFECTS ARE **TEMPORARY,** YOU'LL BE HAPPY TO HEAR, BUT FOR THE NEXT THREE MINUTES YOU'VE PRETTY MUCH BEEN IM-**MOBILIZED.**

WH-WHAT

THREE MINUTES BEING ALL I'M GOING TO **NEED...**

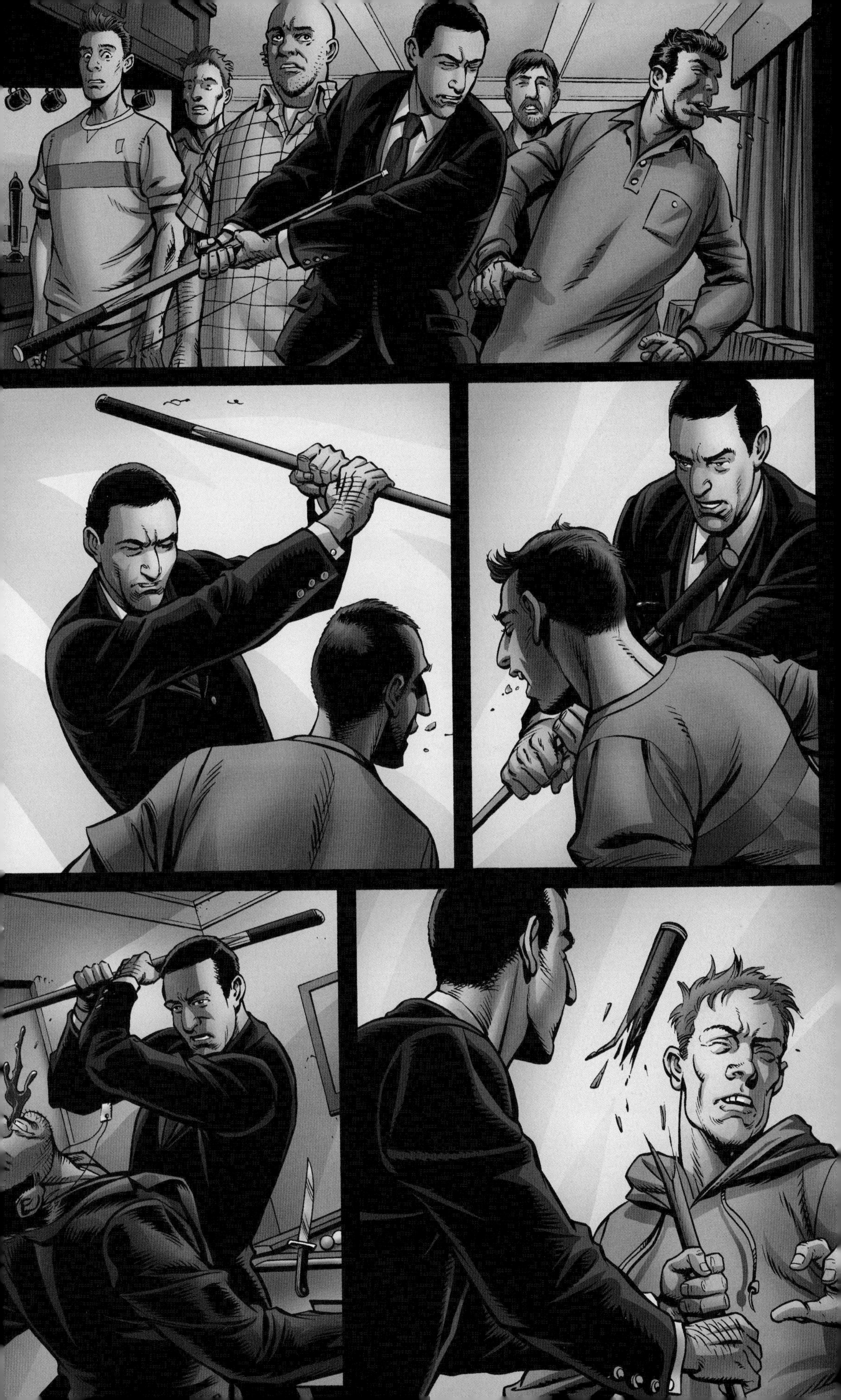

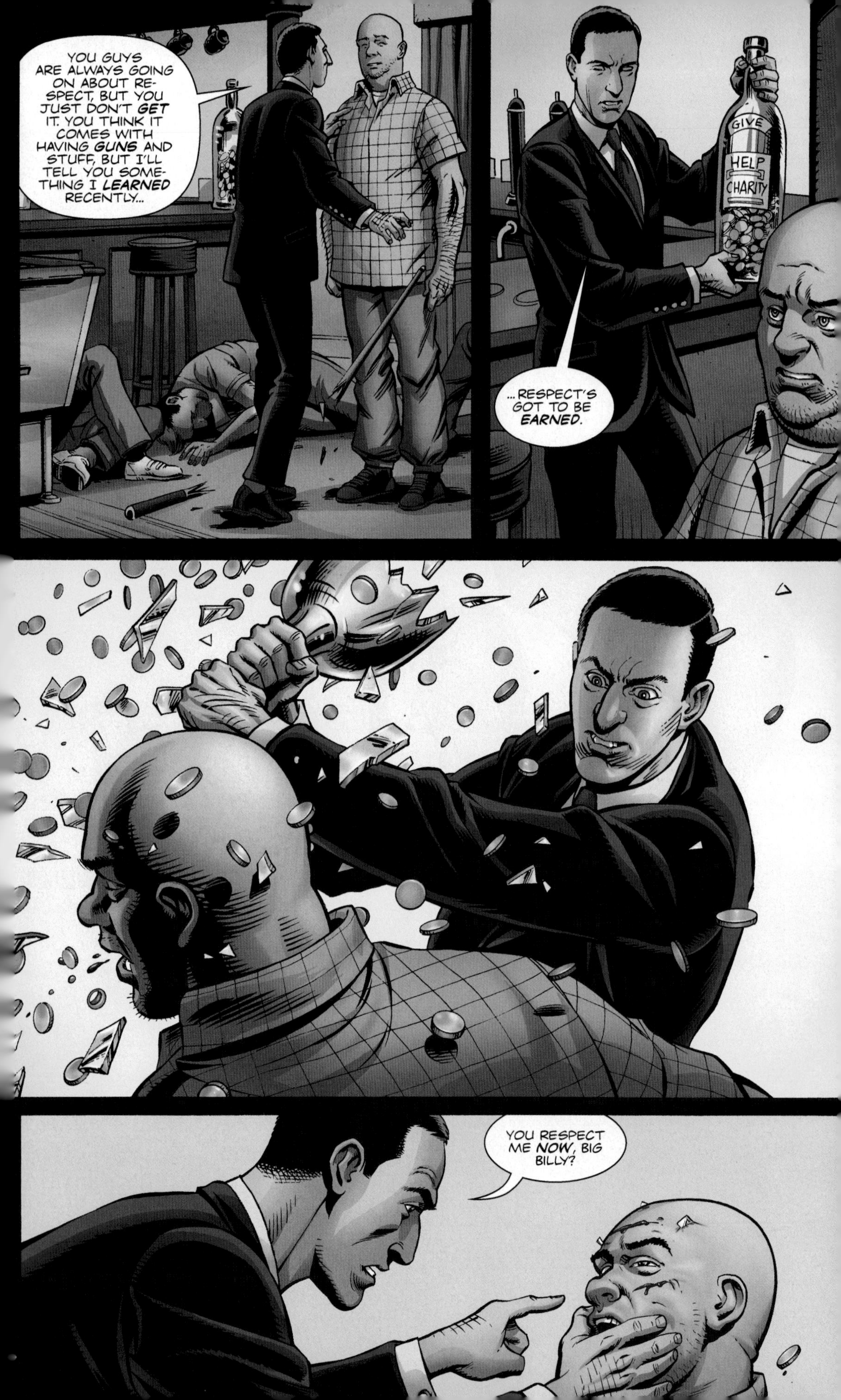
YOU GUYS ARE ALWAYS GOING ON ABOUT RESPECT, BUT YOU JUST DON'T GET IT. YOU THINK IT COMES WITH HAVING GUNS AND STUFF, BUT I'LL TELL YOU SOMETHING I LEARNED RECENTLY...
...RESPECT'S GOT TO BE EARNED.
GIVE
HELP
CHARITY
YOU RESPECT ME NOW, BIG BILLY?

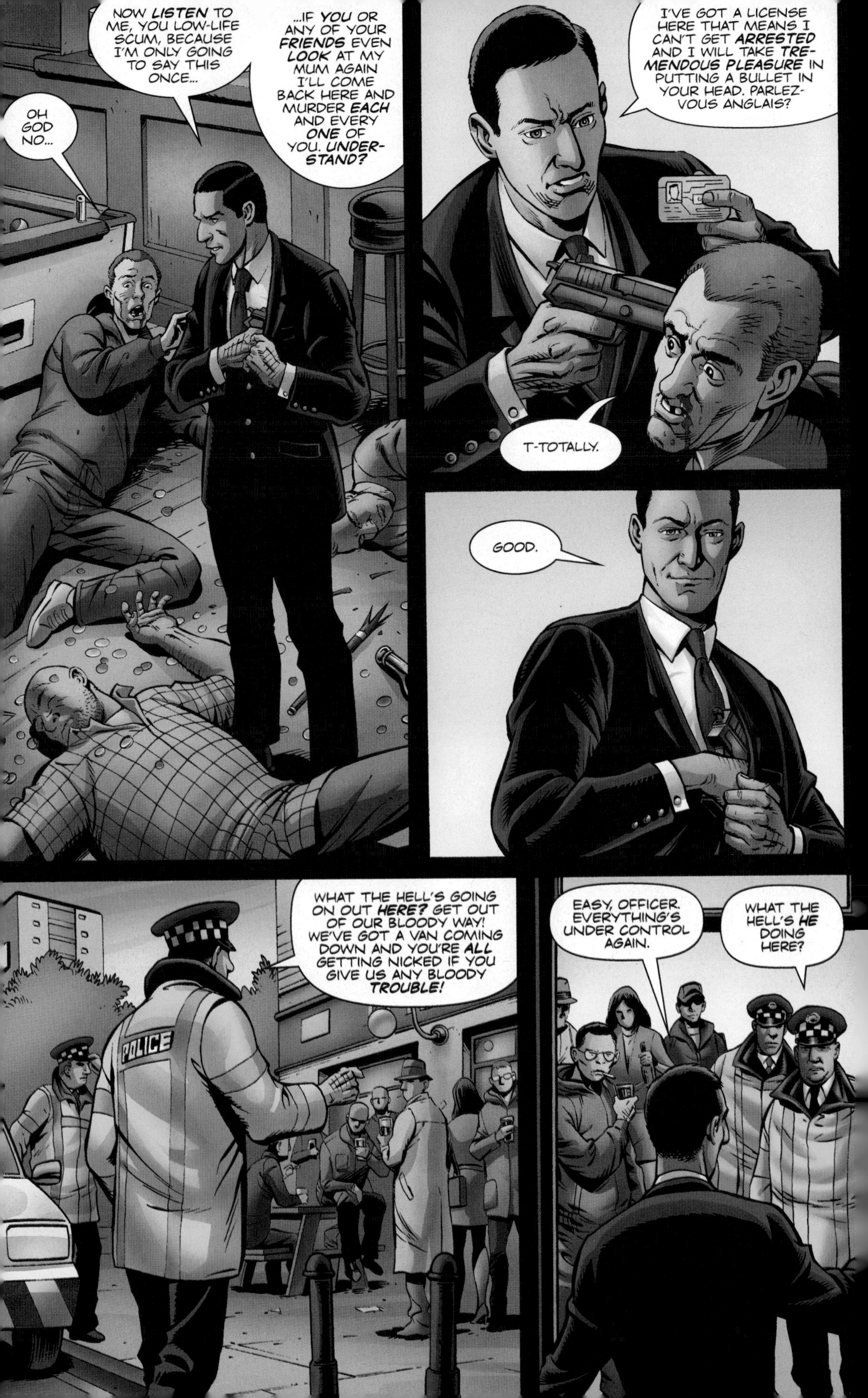
NOW LISTEN TO ME, YOU LOW-LIFE SCUM, BECAUSE I'M ONLY GOING TO SAY THIS ONCE...
OH GOD NO...
...IF YOU OR ANY OF YOUR FRIENDS EVEN LOOK AT MY MUM AGAIN I'LL COME BACK HERE AND MURDER EACH AND EVERY ONE OF YOU. UNDERSTAND?
I'VE GOT A LICENSE HERE THAT MEANS I CAN'T GET ARRESTED AND I WILL TAKE TREMENDOUS PLEASURE IN PUTTING A BULLET IN YOUR HEAD. PARLEZ-VOUS ANGLAIS?
T-TOTALLY.
GOOD.
WHAT THE HELL'S GOING ON OUT HERE? GET OUT OF OUR BLOODY WAY! WE'VE GOT A VAN COMING DOWN AND YOU'RE ALL GETTING NICKED IF YOU GIVE US ANY BLOODY TROUBLE!
POLICE
EASY, OFFICER. EVERYTHING'S UNDER CONTROL AGAIN.
WHAT THE HELL'S HE DOING HERE?

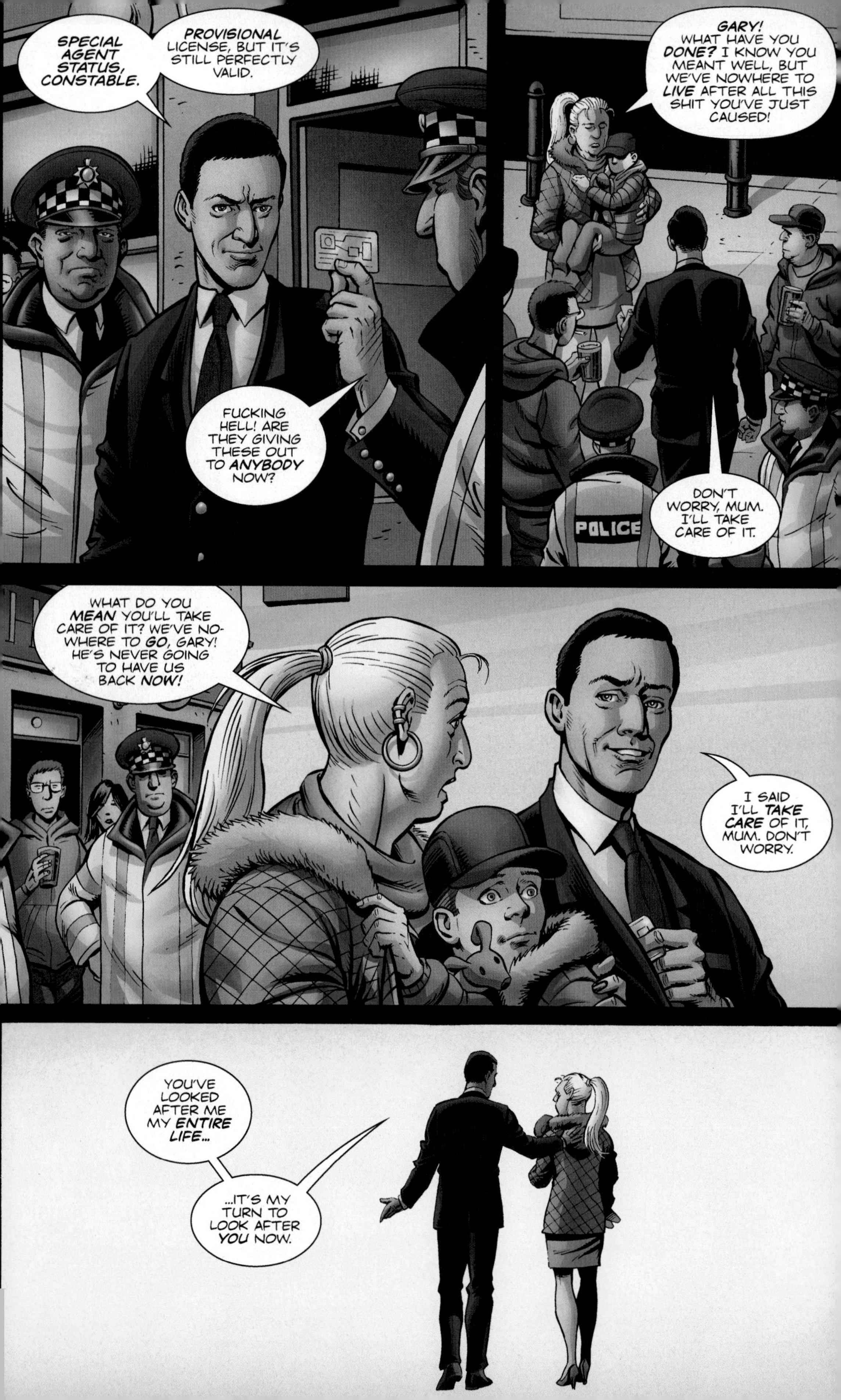
SPECIAL AGENT STATUS, CONSTABLE.
PROVISIONAL LICENSE, BUT IT'S STILL PERFECTLY VALID.
FUCKING HELL! ARE THEY GIVING THESE OUT TO ANYBODY NOW?
GARY! WHAT HAVE YOU DONE? I KNOW YOU MEANT WELL, BUT WE'VE NOWHERE TO LIVE AFTER ALL THIS SHIT YOU'VE JUST CAUSED!
DON'T WORRY, MUM. I'LL TAKE CARE OF IT.
POLICE
WHAT DO YOU MEAN YOU'LL TAKE CARE OF IT? WE'VE NO-WHERE TO GO, GARY! HE'S NEVER GOING TO HAVE US BACK NOW!
I SAID I'LL TAKE CARE OF IT, MUM. DON'T WORRY.
YOU'VE LOOKED AFTER ME MY ENTIRE LIFE...
...IT'S MY TURN TO LOOK AFTER YOU NOW.

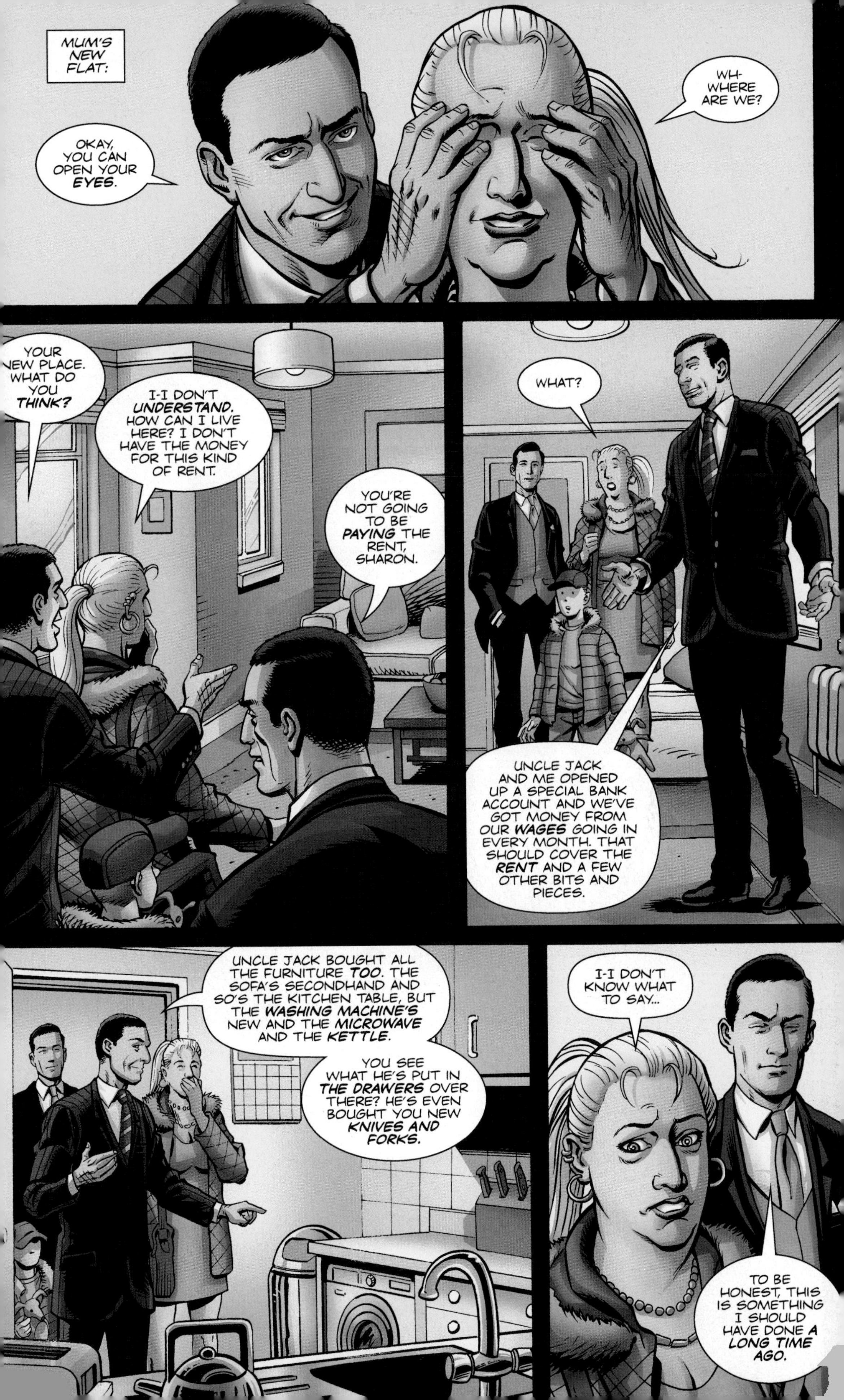
MUM'S NEW FLAT:
OKAY, YOU CAN OPEN YOUR EYES.
WH- WHERE ARE WE?
YOUR NEW PLACE. WHAT DO YOU THINK?
I-I DON'T UNDERSTAND. HOW CAN I LIVE HERE? I DON'T HAVE THE MONEY FOR THIS KIND OF RENT.
YOU'RE NOT GOING TO BE PAYING THE RENT, SHARON.
WHAT?
UNCLE JACK AND ME OPENED UP A SPECIAL BANK ACCOUNT AND WE'VE GOT MONEY FROM OUR WAGES GOING IN EVERY MONTH. THAT SHOULD COVER THE RENT AND A FEW OTHER BITS AND PIECES.
UNCLE JACK BOUGHT ALL THE FURNITURE TOO. THE SOFA'S SECONDHAND AND SO'S THE KITCHEN TABLE, BUT THE WASHING MACHINE'S NEW AND THE MICROWAVE AND THE KETTLE.
YOU SEE WHAT HE'S PUT IN THE DRAWERS OVER THERE? HE'S EVEN BOUGHT YOU NEW KNIVES AND FORKS.
I-I DON'T KNOW WHAT TO SAY...
TO BE HONEST, THIS IS SOMETHING I SHOULD HAVE DONE A LONG TIME AGO.

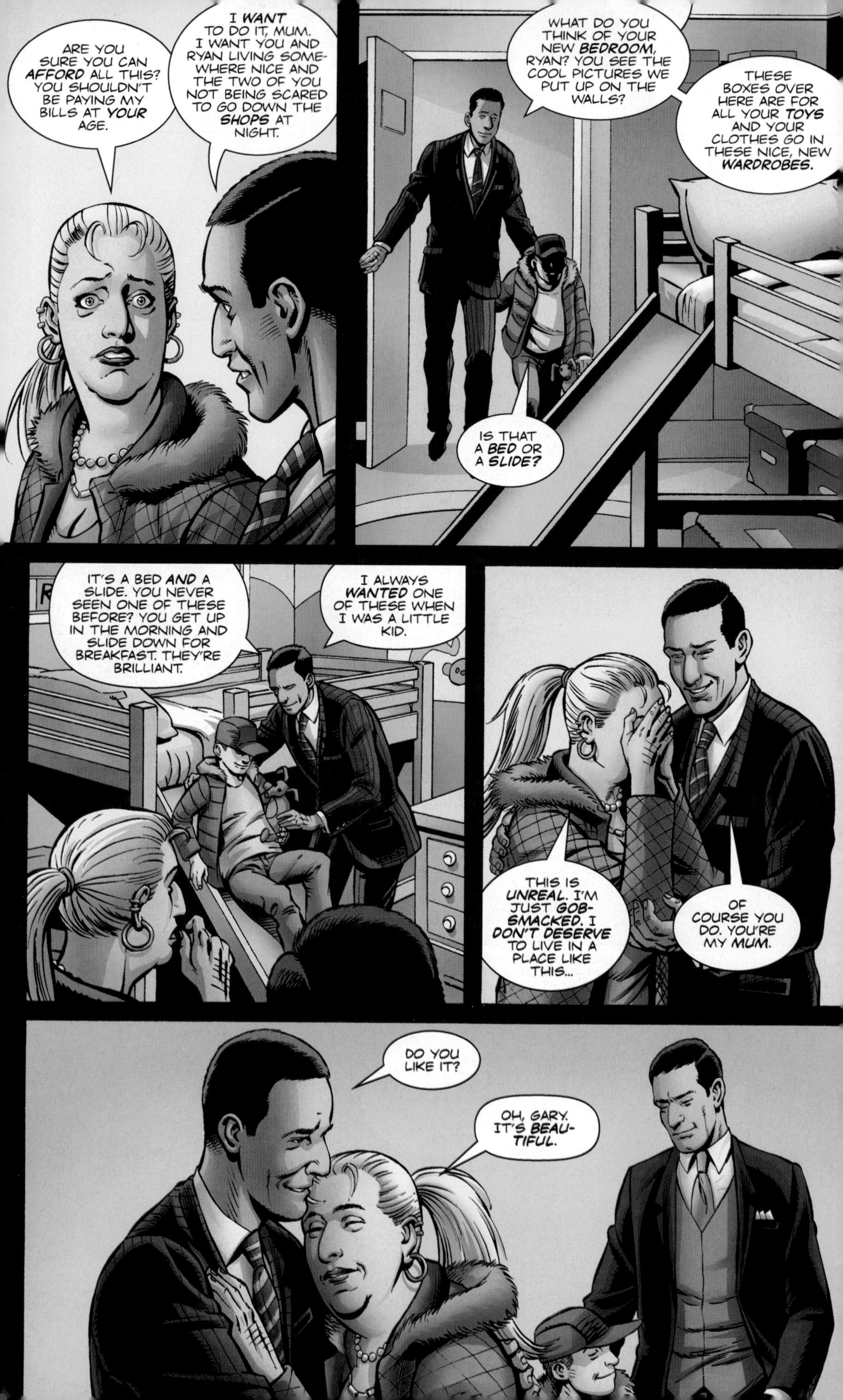

ARE YOU SURE YOU CAN AFFORD ALL THIS? YOU SHOULDN'T BE PAYING MY BILLS AT YOUR AGE.
I WANT TO DO IT, MUM. I WANT YOU AND RYAN LIVING SOMEWHERE NICE AND THE TWO OF YOU NOT BEING SCARED TO GO DOWN THE SHOPS AT NIGHT.
WHAT DO YOU THINK OF YOUR NEW BEDROOM, RYAN? YOU SEE THE COOL PICTURES WE PUT UP ON THE WALLS?
THESE BOXES OVER HERE ARE FOR ALL YOUR TOYS AND YOUR CLOTHES GO IN THESE NICE, NEW WARDROBES.
IS THAT A BED OR A SLIDE?
IT'S A BED AND A SLIDE. YOU NEVER SEEN ONE OF THESE BEFORE? YOU GET UP IN THE MORNING AND SLIDE DOWN FOR BREAKFAST. THEY'RE BRILLIANT.
I ALWAYS WANTED ONE OF THESE WHEN I WAS A LITTLE KID.
THIS IS UNREAL. I'M JUST GOBSMACKED. I DON'T DESERVE TO LIVE IN A PLACE LIKE THIS...
OF COURSE YOU DO. YOU'RE MY MUM.
DO YOU LIKE IT?
OH, GARY. IT'S BEAUTIFUL.

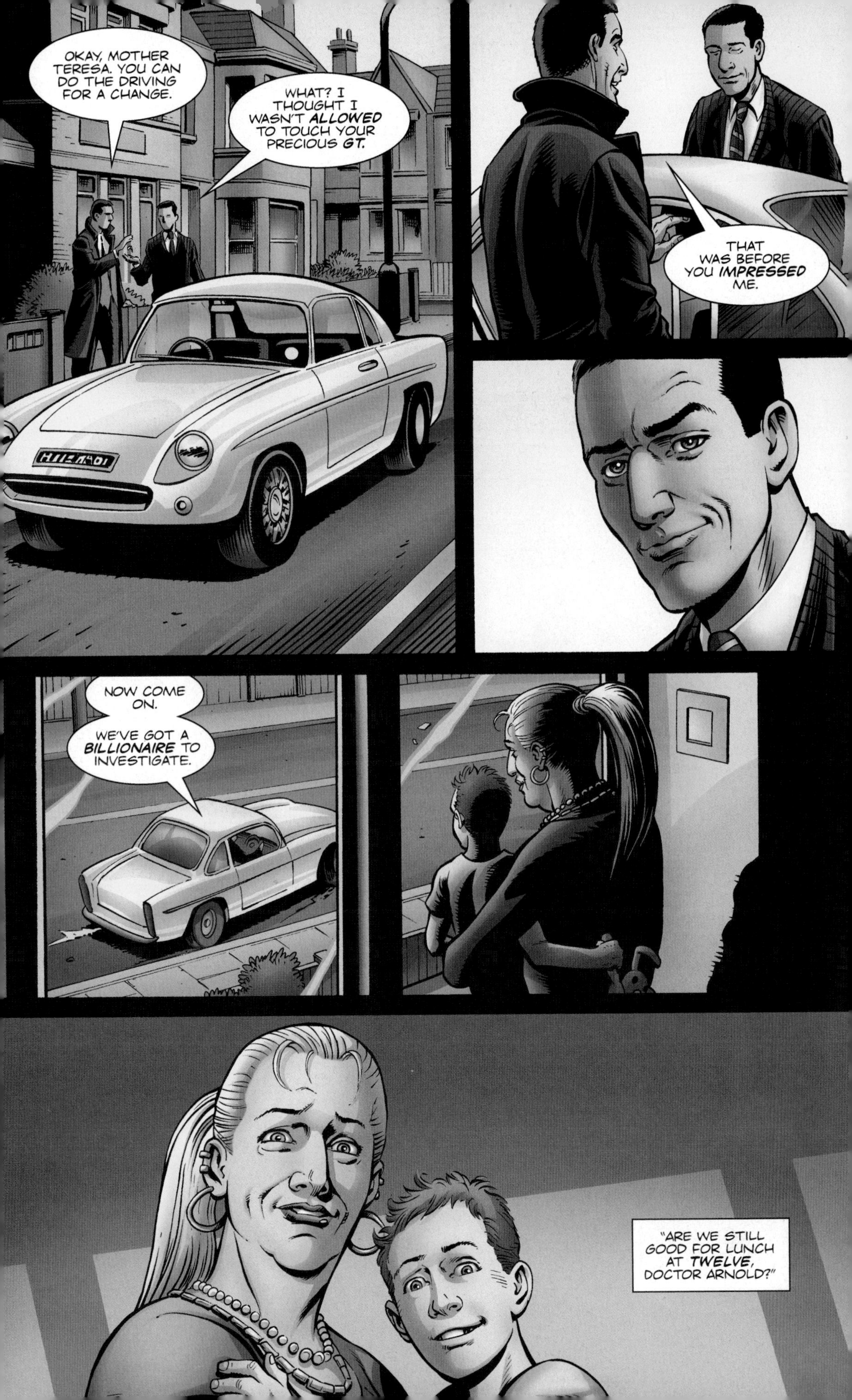
OKAY, MOTHER TERESA. YOU CAN DO THE DRIVING FOR A CHANGE.
WHAT? I THOUGHT I WASN'T ALLOWED TO TOUCH YOUR PRECIOUS GT.
THAT WAS BEFORE YOU IMPRESSED ME.
NOW COME ON.
WE'VE GOT A BILLIONAIRE TO INVESTIGATE.
"ARE WE STILL GOOD FOR LUNCH AT TWELVE, DOCTOR ARNOLD?"

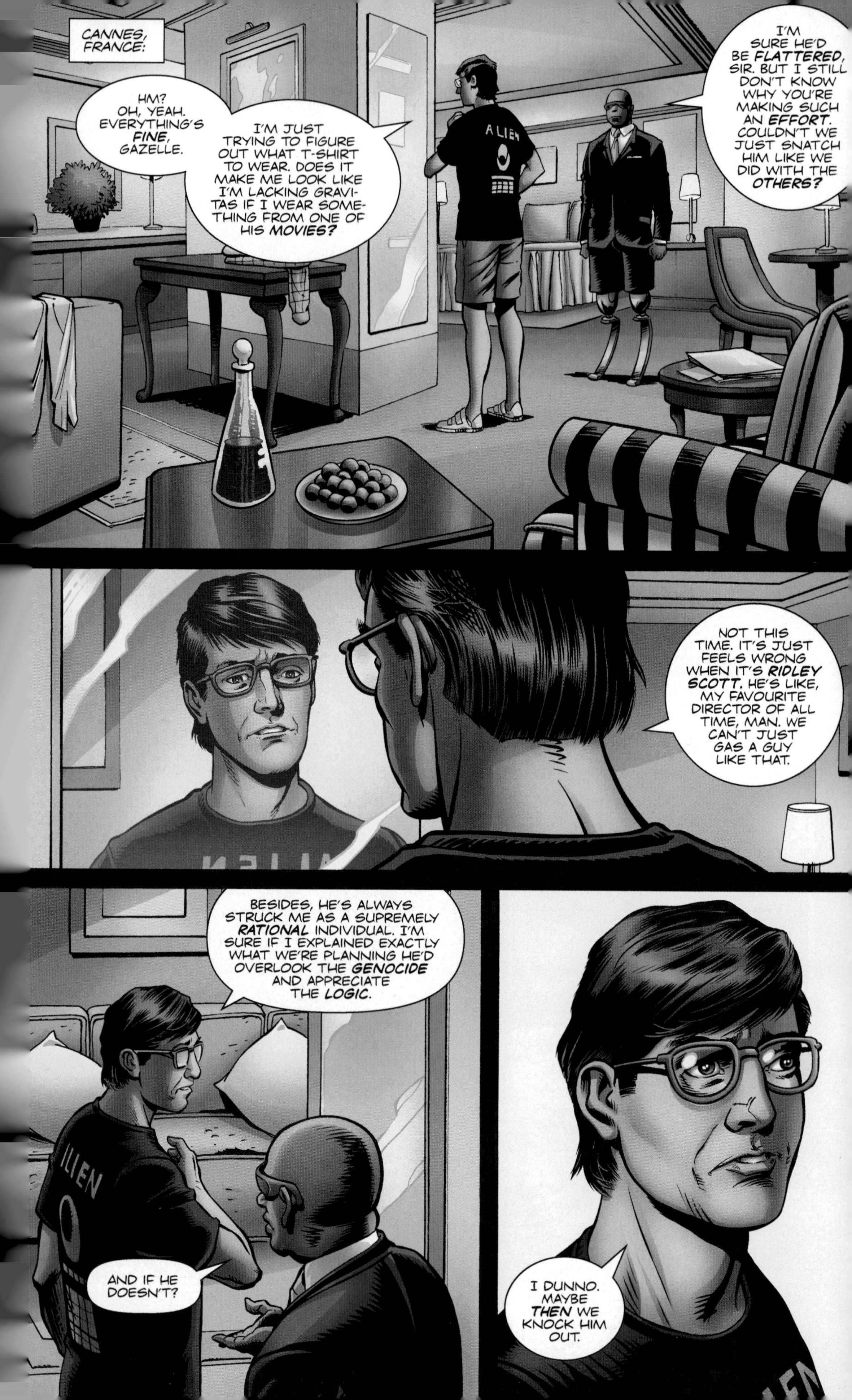
CANNES, FRANCE:
HM? OH, YEAH. EVERYTHING'S **FINE**, GAZELLE.
I'M JUST TRYING TO FIGURE OUT WHAT T-SHIRT TO WEAR. DOES IT MAKE ME LOOK LIKE I'M LACKING GRAVITAS IF I WEAR SOMETHING FROM ONE OF HIS **MOVIES?**
ALIEN
I'M SURE HE'D BE **FLATTERED**, SIR. BUT I STILL DON'T KNOW WHY YOU'RE MAKING SUCH AN **EFFORT**. COULDN'T WE JUST SNATCH HIM LIKE WE DID WITH THE **OTHERS?**
NOT THIS TIME. IT'S JUST FEELS WRONG WHEN IT'S **RIDLEY SCOTT.** HE'S LIKE, MY FAVOURITE DIRECTOR OF ALL TIME, MAN. WE CAN'T JUST GAS A GUY LIKE THAT.
BESIDES, HE'S ALWAYS STRUCK ME AS A SUPREMELY **RATIONAL** INDIVIDUAL. I'M SURE IF I EXPLAINED EXACTLY WHAT WE'RE PLANNING HE'D OVERLOOK THE **GENOCIDE** AND APPRECIATE THE **LOGIC**.
AND IF HE DOESN'T?
I DUNNO. MAYBE **THEN** WE KNOCK HIM OUT.

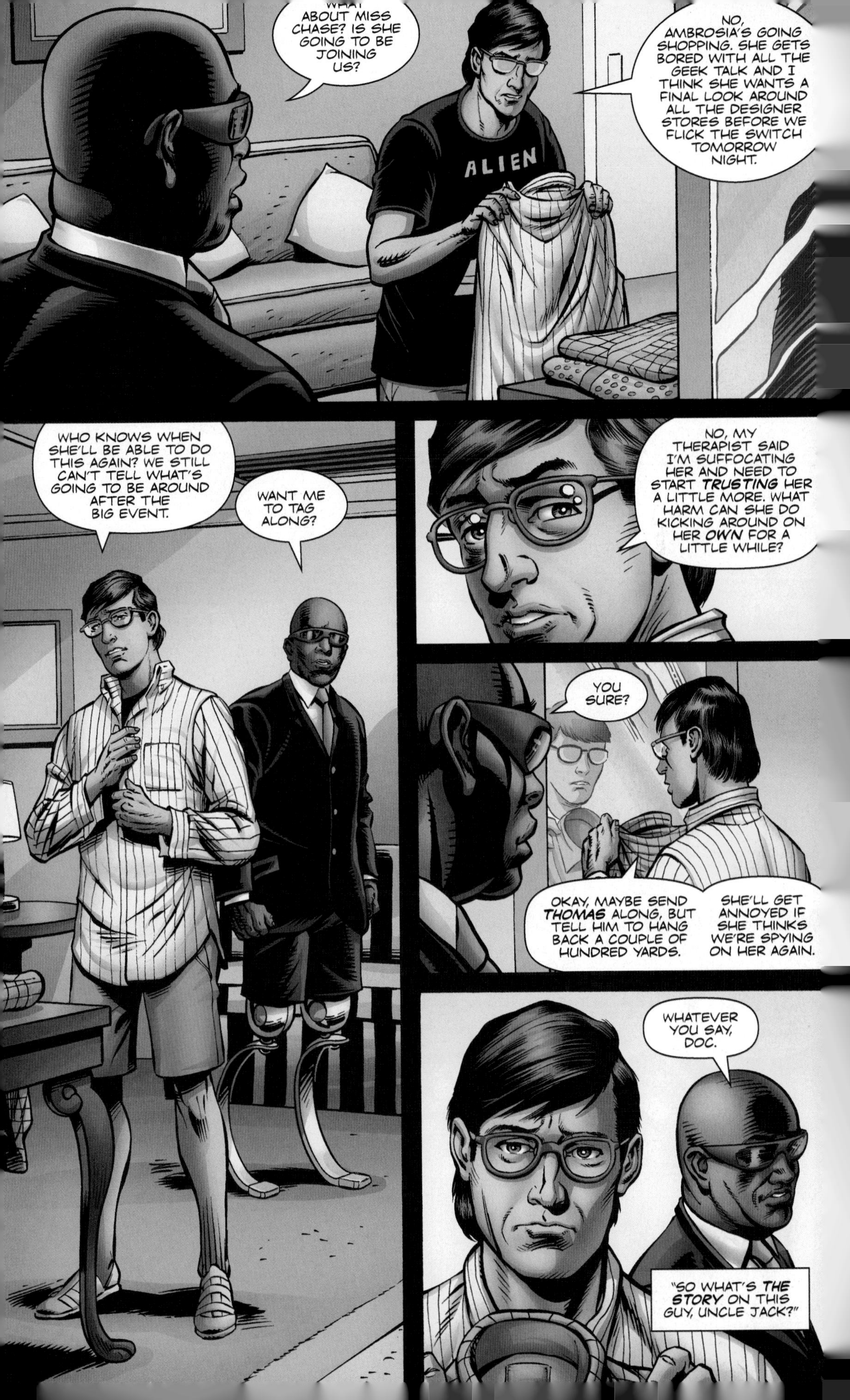

WHAT ABOUT MISS CHASE? IS SHE GOING TO BE JOINING US?
NO, AMBROSIA'S GOING SHOPPING. SHE GETS BORED WITH ALL THE GEEK TALK AND I THINK SHE WANTS A FINAL LOOK AROUND ALL THE DESIGNER STORES BEFORE WE FLICK THE SWITCH TOMORROW NIGHT.
ALIEN
WHO KNOWS WHEN SHE'LL BE ABLE TO DO THIS AGAIN? WE STILL CAN'T TELL WHAT'S GOING TO BE AROUND AFTER THE BIG EVENT.
WANT ME TO TAG ALONG?
NO, MY THERAPIST SAID I'M SUFFOCATING HER AND NEED TO START **TRUSTING** HER A LITTLE MORE. WHAT HARM CAN SHE DO KICKING AROUND ON HER ***OWN*** FOR A LITTLE WHILE?
YOU SURE?
OKAY, MAYBE SEND **THOMAS** ALONG, BUT TELL HIM TO HANG BACK A COUPLE OF HUNDRED YARDS.
SHE'LL GET ANNOYED IF SHE THINKS WE'RE SPYING ON HER AGAIN.
WHATEVER YOU SAY, DOC.
"SO WHAT'S ***THE STORY*** ON THIS GUY, UNCLE JACK?"

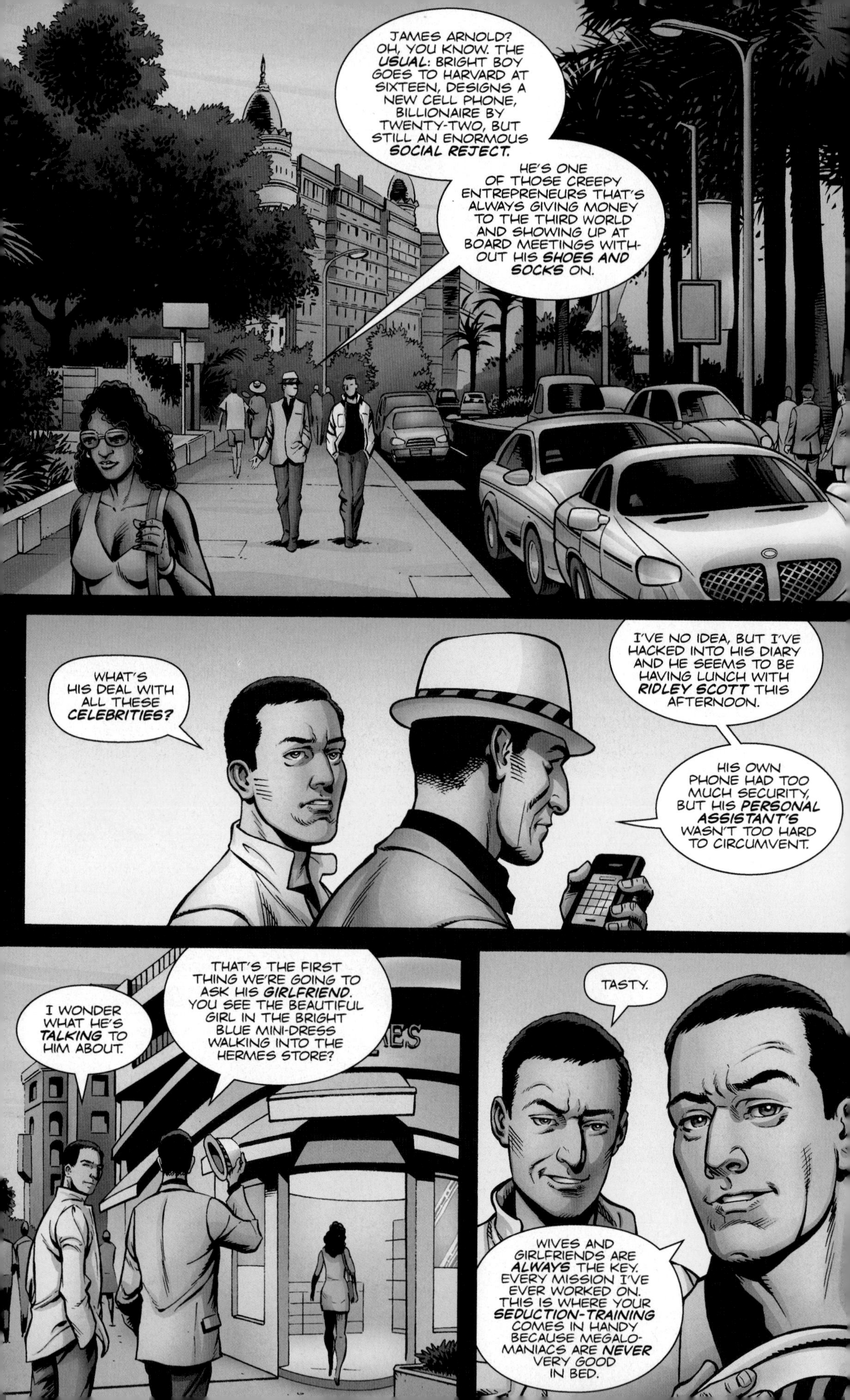
JAMES ARNOLD? OH, YOU KNOW. THE USUAL: BRIGHT BOY GOES TO HARVARD AT SIXTEEN, DESIGNS A NEW CELL PHONE, BILLIONAIRE BY TWENTY-TWO, BUT STILL AN ENORMOUS SOCIAL REJECT.
HE'S ONE OF THOSE CREEPY ENTREPRENEURS THAT'S ALWAYS GIVING MONEY TO THE THIRD WORLD AND SHOWING UP AT BOARD MEETINGS WITH-OUT HIS SHOES AND SOCKS ON.
WHAT'S HIS DEAL WITH ALL THESE CELEBRITIES?
I'VE NO IDEA, BUT I'VE HACKED INTO HIS DIARY AND HE SEEMS TO BE HAVING LUNCH WITH RIDLEY SCOTT THIS AFTERNOON.
HIS OWN PHONE HAD TOO MUCH SECURITY, BUT HIS PERSONAL ASSISTANT'S WASN'T TOO HARD TO CIRCUMVENT.
I WONDER WHAT HE'S TALKING TO HIM ABOUT.
THAT'S THE FIRST THING WE'RE GOING TO ASK HIS GIRLFRIEND. YOU SEE THE BEAUTIFUL GIRL IN THE BRIGHT BLUE MINI-DRESS WALKING INTO THE HERMES STORE?
TASTY.
WIVES AND GIRLFRIENDS ARE ALWAYS THE KEY. EVERY MISSION I'VE EVER WORKED ON. THIS IS WHERE YOUR SEDUCTION-TRAINING COMES IN HANDY BECAUSE MEGALO-MANIACS ARE NEVER VERY GOOD IN BED.

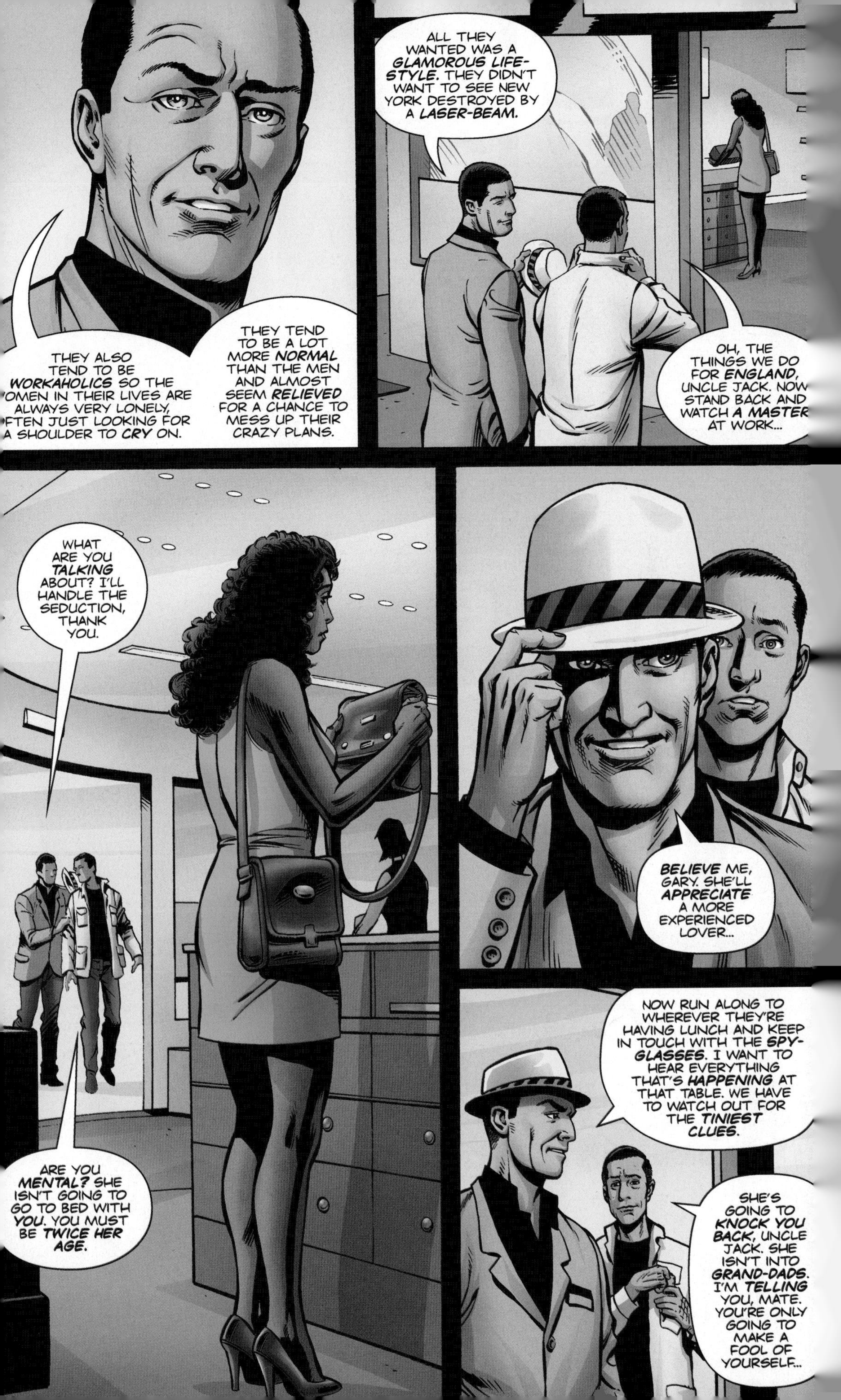
THEY ALSO TEND TO BE WORKAHOLICS SO THE OMEN IN THEIR LIVES ARE ALWAYS VERY LONELY, FTEN JUST LOOKING FOR A SHOULDER TO CRY ON.
THEY TEND TO BE A LOT MORE NORMAL THAN THE MEN AND ALMOST SEEM RELIEVED FOR A CHANCE TO MESS UP THEIR CRAZY PLANS.
ALL THEY WANTED WAS A GLAMOROUS LIFE-STYLE. THEY DIDN'T WANT TO SEE NEW YORK DESTROYED BY A LASER-BEAM.
OH, THE THINGS WE DO FOR ENGLAND, UNCLE JACK. NOW STAND BACK AND WATCH A MASTER AT WORK...
WHAT ARE YOU TALKING ABOUT? I'LL HANDLE THE SEDUCTION, THANK YOU.
ARE YOU MENTAL? SHE ISN'T GOING TO GO TO BED WITH YOU. YOU MUST BE TWICE HER AGE.
BELIEVE ME, GARY. SHE'LL APPRECIATE A MORE EXPERIENCED LOVER...
NOW RUN ALONG TO WHEREVER THEY'RE HAVING LUNCH AND KEEP IN TOUCH WITH THE SPY-GLASSES. I WANT TO HEAR EVERYTHING THAT'S HAPPENING AT THAT TABLE. WE HAVE TO WATCH OUT FOR THE TINIEST CLUES.
SHE'S GOING TO KNOCK YOU BACK, UNCLE JACK. SHE ISN'T INTO GRAND-DADS. I'M TELLING YOU, MATE. YOU'RE ONLY GOING TO MAKE A FOOL OF YOURSELF...

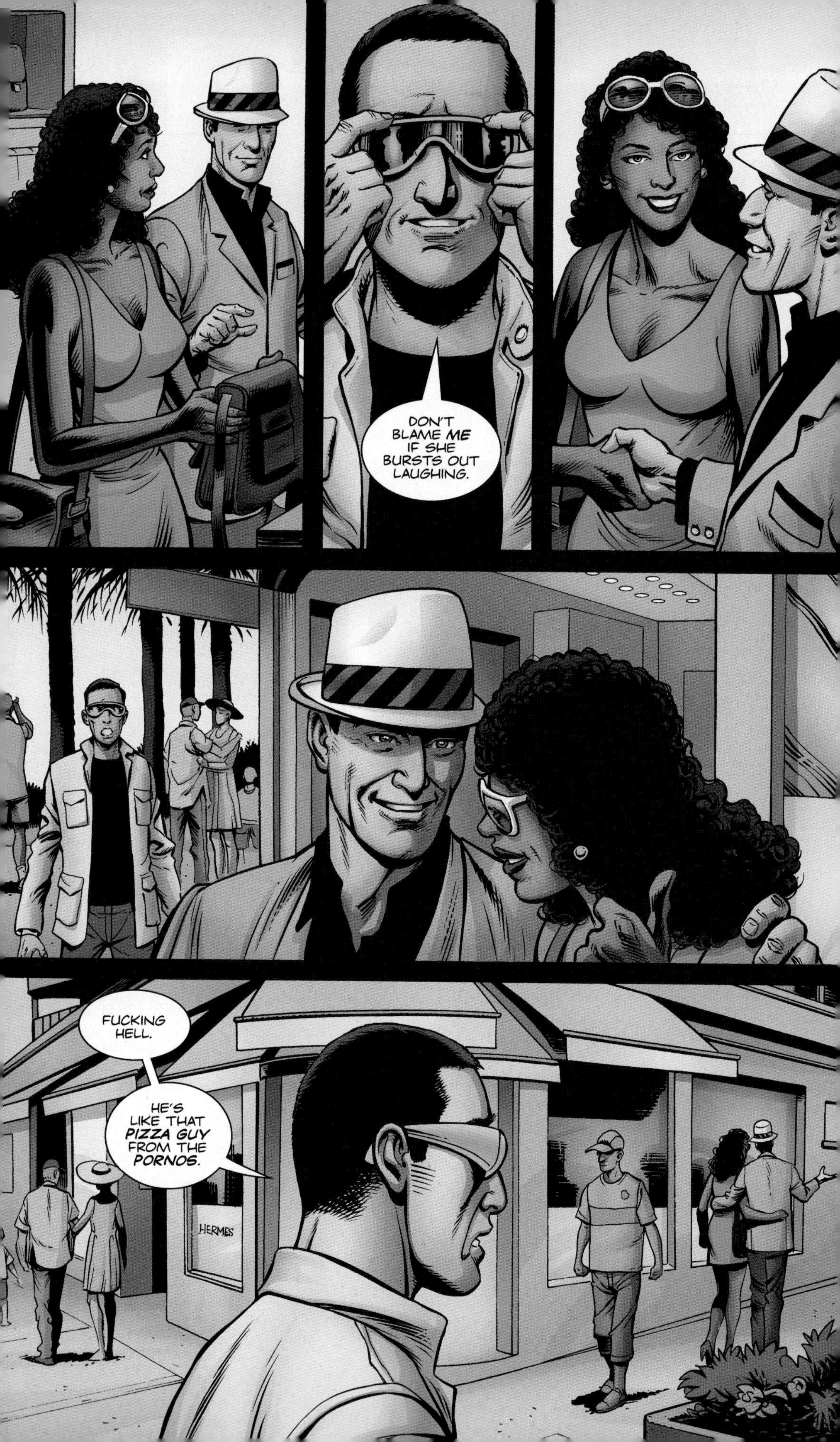
DON'T BLAME ME IF SHE BURSTS OUT LAUGHING.
FUCKING HELL.
HE'S LIKE THAT PIZZA GUY FROM THE PORNOS.
HERMES

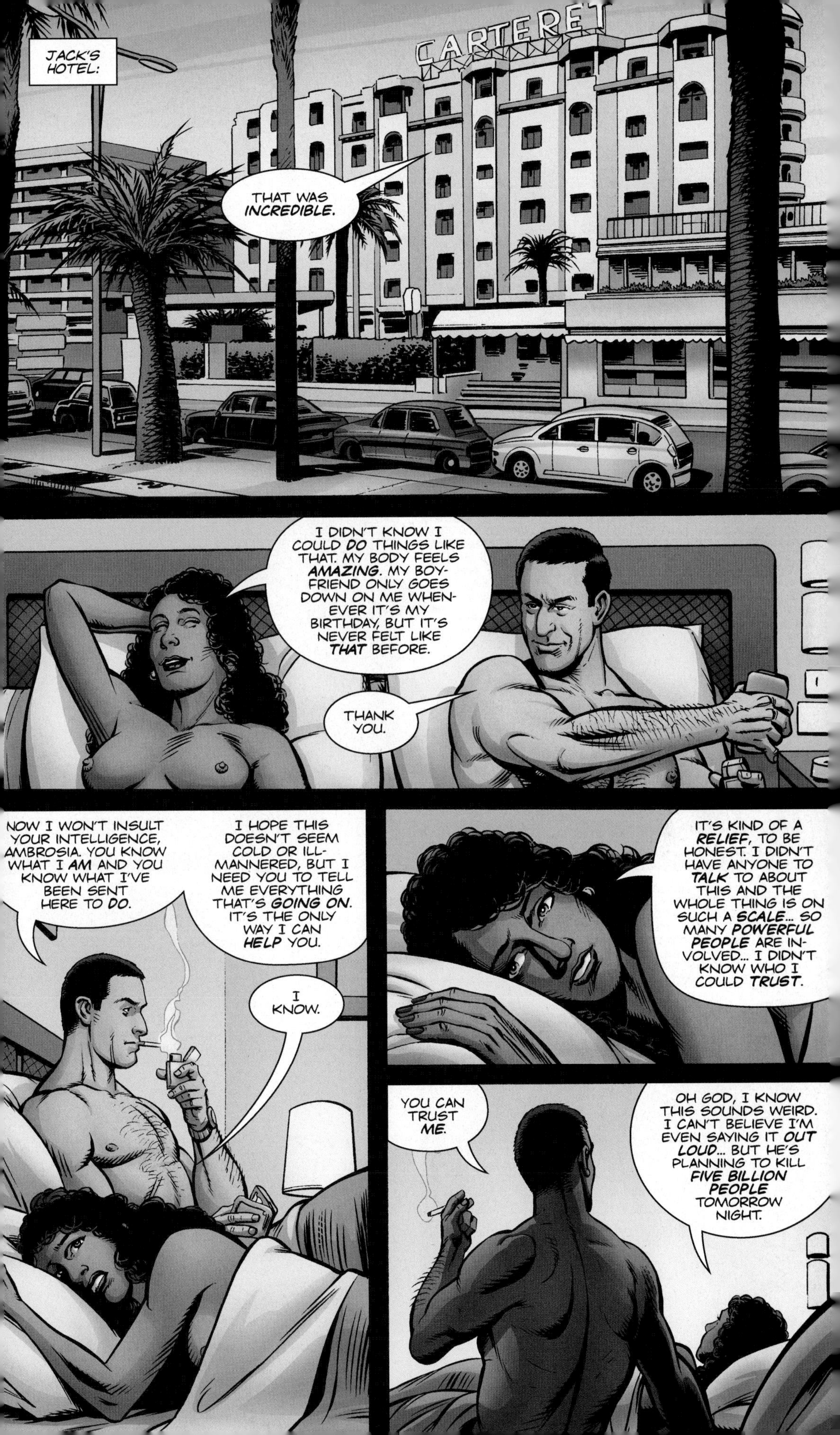
JACK'S HOTEL:
CARTERET
THAT WAS *INCREDIBLE*.
I DIDN'T KNOW I COULD *DO* THINGS LIKE THAT. MY BODY FEELS *AMAZING*. MY BOY-FRIEND ONLY GOES DOWN ON ME WHEN-EVER IT'S MY BIRTHDAY, BUT IT'S NEVER FELT LIKE *THAT* BEFORE.
THANK YOU.
NOW I WON'T INSULT YOUR INTELLIGENCE, AMBROSIA. YOU KNOW WHAT I *AM* AND YOU KNOW WHAT I'VE BEEN SENT HERE TO *DO*.
I HOPE THIS DOESN'T SEEM COLD OR ILL-MANNERED, BUT I NEED YOU TO TELL ME EVERYTHING THAT'S *GOING ON*. IT'S THE ONLY WAY I CAN *HELP* YOU.
I KNOW.
IT'S KIND OF A *RELIEF*, TO BE HONEST. I DIDN'T HAVE ANYONE TO *TALK* TO ABOUT THIS AND THE WHOLE THING IS ON SUCH A *SCALE*... SO MANY *POWERFUL PEOPLE* ARE IN-VOLVED... I DIDN'T KNOW WHO I COULD *TRUST*.
YOU CAN TRUST *ME*.
OH GOD, I KNOW THIS SOUNDS WEIRD. I CAN'T BELIEVE I'M EVEN SAYING IT *OUT LOUD*... BUT HE'S PLANNING TO KILL *FIVE BILLION PEOPLE* TOMORROW NIGHT.

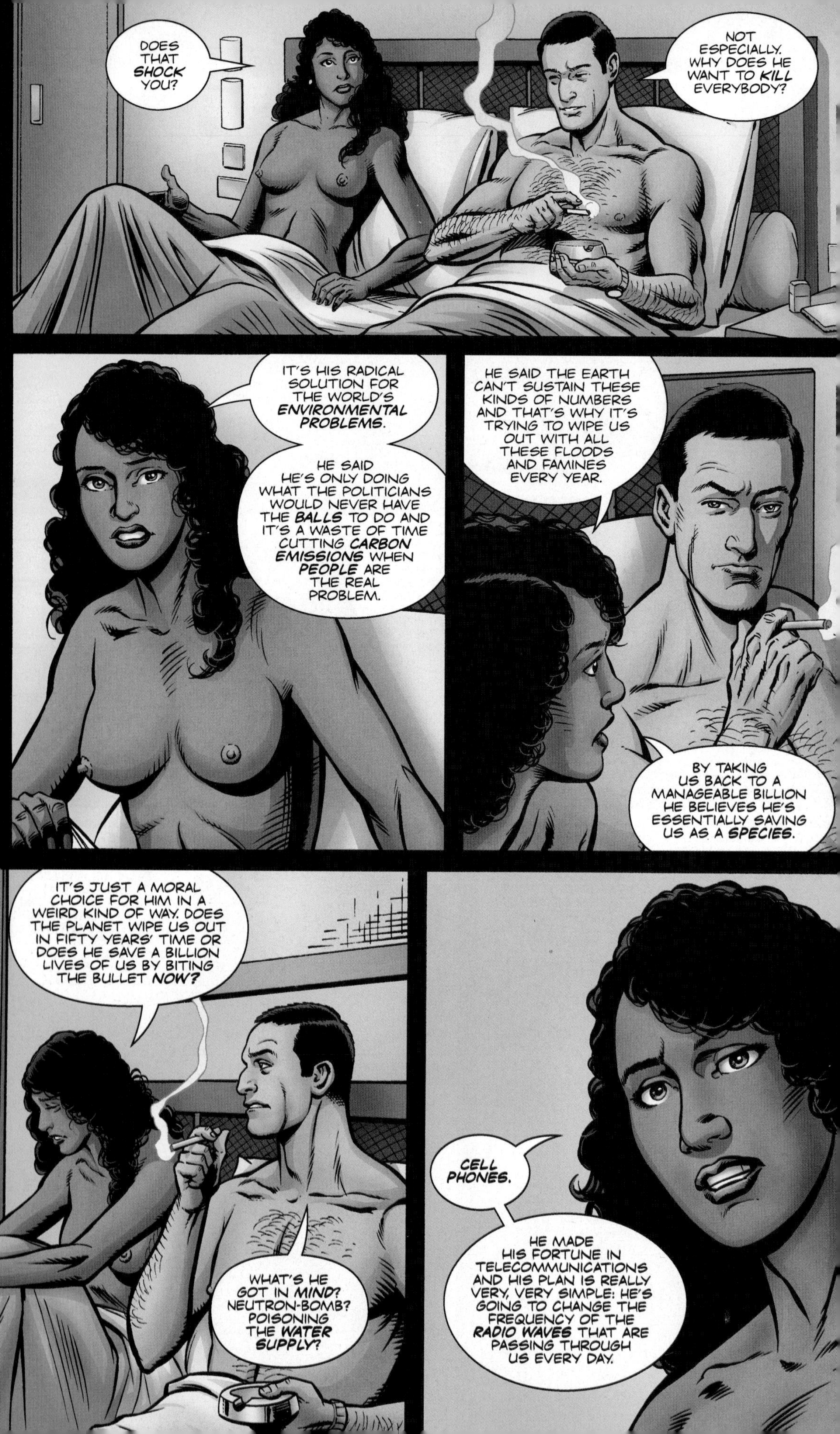
DOES THAT SHOCK YOU?
NOT ESPECIALLY. WHY DOES HE WANT TO KILL EVERYBODY?
IT'S HIS RADICAL SOLUTION FOR THE WORLD'S ENVIRONMENTAL PROBLEMS.
HE SAID HE'S ONLY DOING WHAT THE POLITICIANS WOULD NEVER HAVE THE BALLS TO DO AND IT'S A WASTE OF TIME CUTTING CARBON EMISSIONS WHEN PEOPLE ARE THE REAL PROBLEM.
HE SAID THE EARTH CAN'T SUSTAIN THESE KINDS OF NUMBERS AND THAT'S WHY IT'S TRYING TO WIPE US OUT WITH ALL THESE FLOODS AND FAMINES EVERY YEAR.
BY TAKING US BACK TO A MANAGEABLE BILLION HE BELIEVES HE'S ESSENTIALLY SAVING US AS A SPECIES.
IT'S JUST A MORAL CHOICE FOR HIM IN A WEIRD KIND OF WAY. DOES THE PLANET WIPE US OUT IN FIFTY YEARS' TIME OR DOES HE SAVE A BILLION LIVES OF US BY BITING THE BULLET NOW?
WHAT'S HE GOT IN MIND? NEUTRON-BOMB? POISONING THE WATER SUPPLY?
CELL PHONES.
HE MADE HIS FORTUNE IN TELECOMMUNICATIONS AND HIS PLAN IS REALLY VERY, VERY SIMPLE: HE'S GOING TO CHANGE THE FREQUENCY OF THE RADIO WAVES THAT ARE PASSING THROUGH US EVERY DAY.

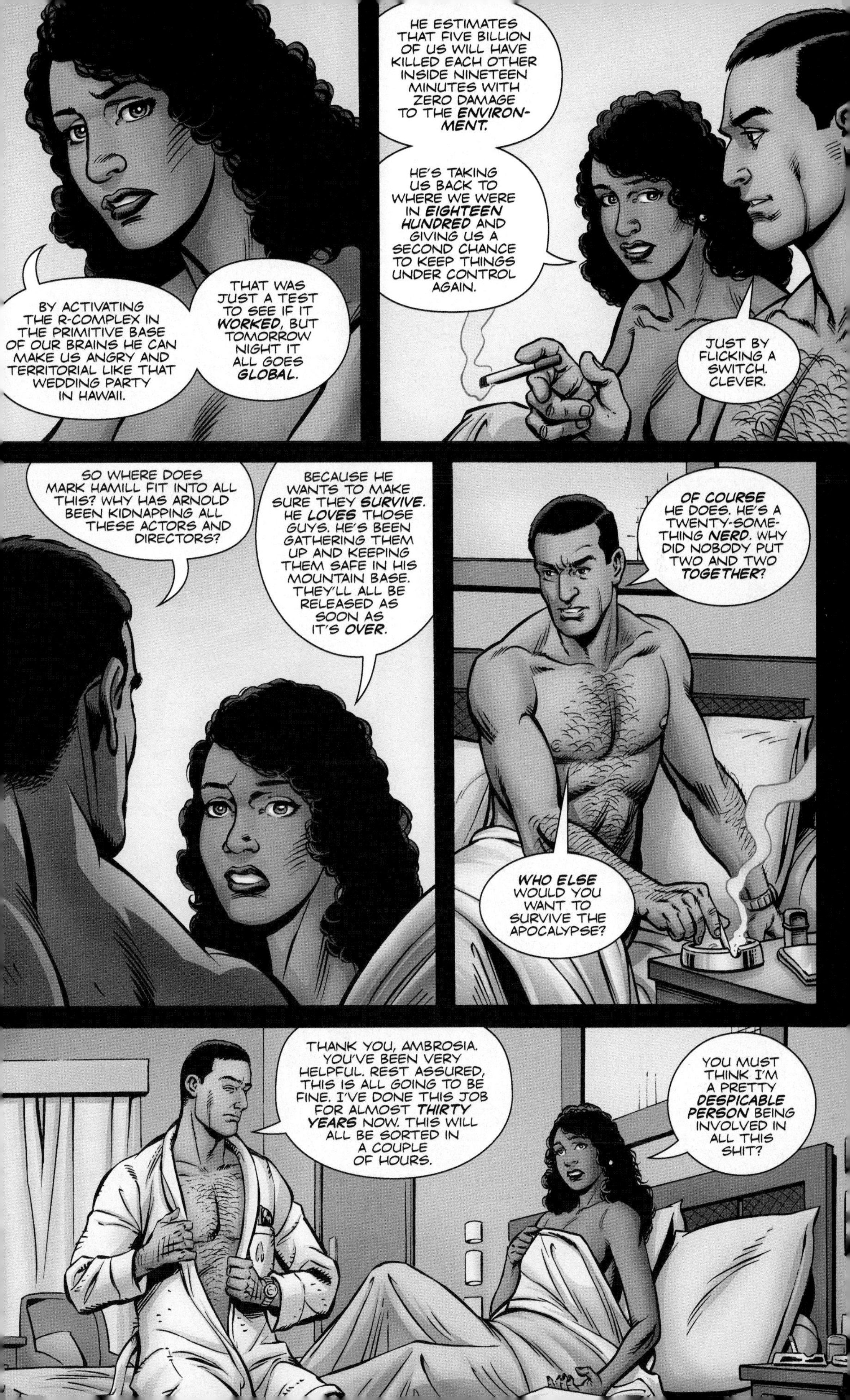
BY ACTIVATING THE R-COMPLEX IN THE PRIMITIVE BASE OF OUR BRAINS HE CAN MAKE US ANGRY AND TERRITORIAL LIKE THAT WEDDING PARTY IN HAWAII.
THAT WAS JUST A TEST TO SEE IF IT WORKED, BUT TOMORROW NIGHT IT ALL GOES GLOBAL.
HE ESTIMATES THAT FIVE BILLION OF US WILL HAVE KILLED EACH OTHER INSIDE NINETEEN MINUTES WITH ZERO DAMAGE TO THE ENVIRONMENT.
HE'S TAKING US BACK TO WHERE WE WERE IN EIGHTEEN HUNDRED AND GIVING US A SECOND CHANCE TO KEEP THINGS UNDER CONTROL AGAIN.
JUST BY FLICKING A SWITCH. CLEVER.
SO WHERE DOES MARK HAMILL FIT INTO ALL THIS? WHY HAS ARNOLD BEEN KIDNAPPING ALL THESE ACTORS AND DIRECTORS?
BECAUSE HE WANTS TO MAKE SURE THEY SURVIVE. HE LOVES THOSE GUYS. HE'S BEEN GATHERING THEM UP AND KEEPING THEM SAFE IN HIS MOUNTAIN BASE. THEY'LL ALL BE RELEASED AS SOON AS IT'S OVER.
OF COURSE HE DOES. HE'S A TWENTY-SOMETHING NERD. WHY DID NOBODY PUT TWO AND TWO TOGETHER?
WHO ELSE WOULD YOU WANT TO SURVIVE THE APOCALYPSE?
THANK YOU, AMBROSIA. YOU'VE BEEN VERY HELPFUL. REST ASSURED, THIS IS ALL GOING TO BE FINE. I'VE DONE THIS JOB FOR ALMOST THIRTY YEARS NOW. THIS WILL ALL BE SORTED IN A COUPLE OF HOURS.
YOU MUST THINK I'M A PRETTY DESPICABLE PERSON BEING INVOLVED IN ALL THIS SHIT?

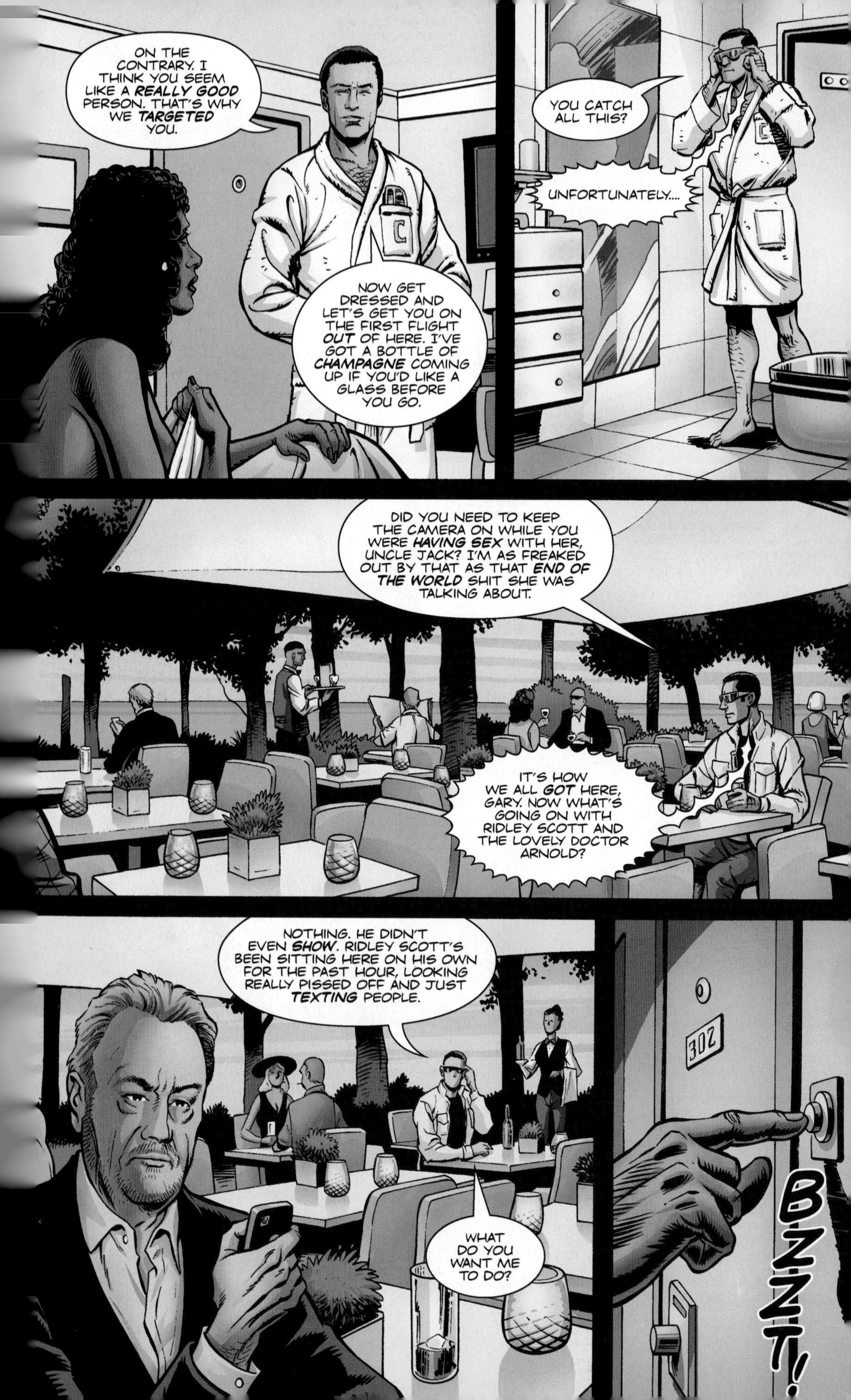
ON THE CONTRARY. I THINK YOU SEEM LIKE A REALLY GOOD PERSON. THAT'S WHY WE TARGETED YOU.
NOW GET DRESSED AND LET'S GET YOU ON THE FIRST FLIGHT OUT OF HERE. I'VE GOT A BOTTLE OF CHAMPAGNE COMING UP IF YOU'D LIKE A GLASS BEFORE YOU GO.
YOU CATCH ALL THIS?
UNFORTUNATELY....
DID YOU NEED TO KEEP THE CAMERA ON WHILE YOU WERE HAVING SEX WITH HER, UNCLE JACK? I'M AS FREAKED OUT BY THAT AS THAT END OF THE WORLD SHIT SHE WAS TALKING ABOUT.
IT'S HOW WE ALL GOT HERE, GARY. NOW WHAT'S GOING ON WITH RIDLEY SCOTT AND THE LOVELY DOCTOR ARNOLD?
NOTHING. HE DIDN'T EVEN SHOW. RIDLEY SCOTT'S BEEN SITTING HERE ON HIS OWN FOR THE PAST HOUR, LOOKING REALLY PISSED OFF AND JUST TEXTING PEOPLE.
WHAT DO YOU WANT ME TO DO?
302
B-Z-Z-T!

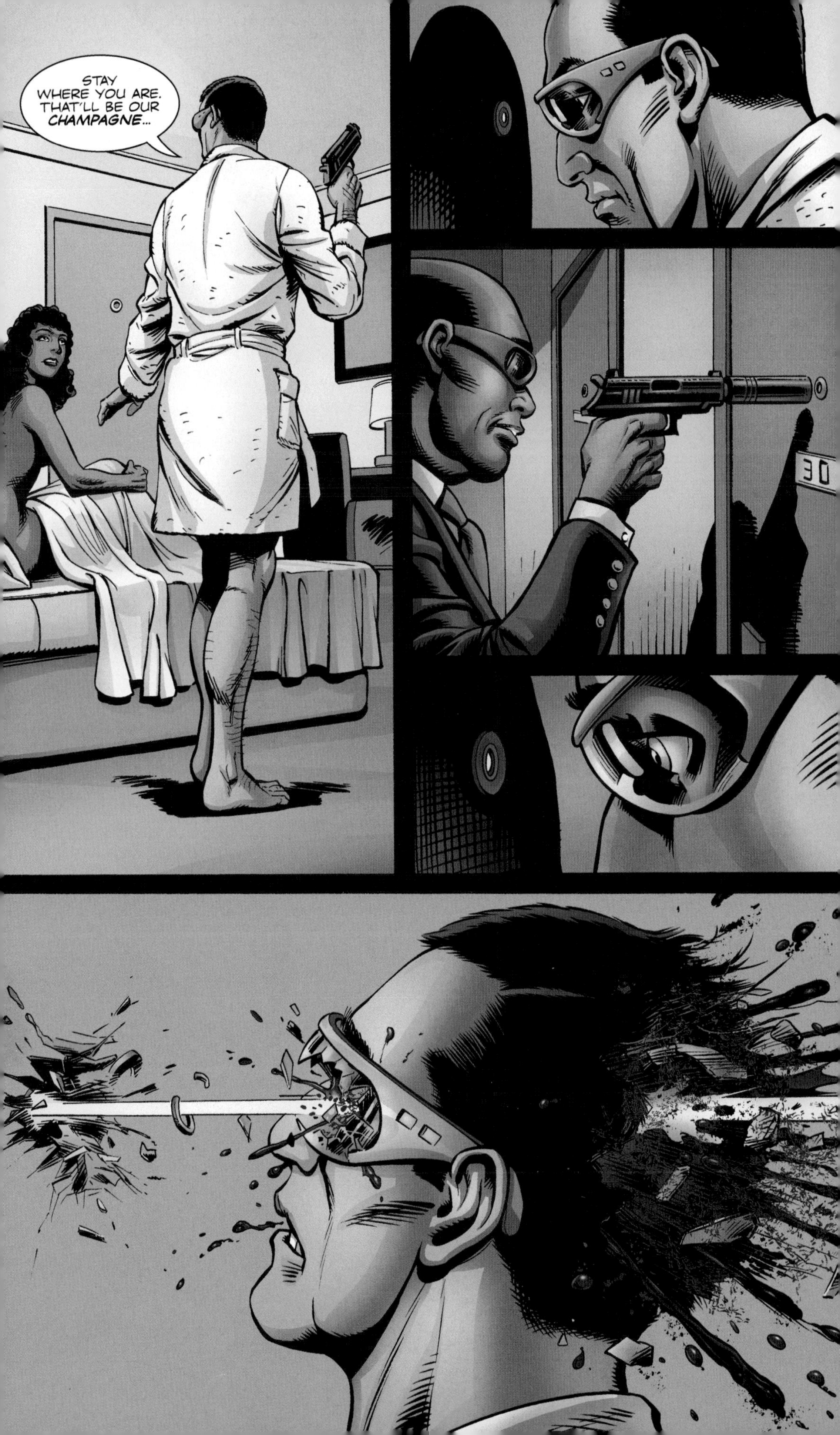
STAY WHERE YOU ARE. THAT'LL BE OUR *CHAMPAGNE*...
30

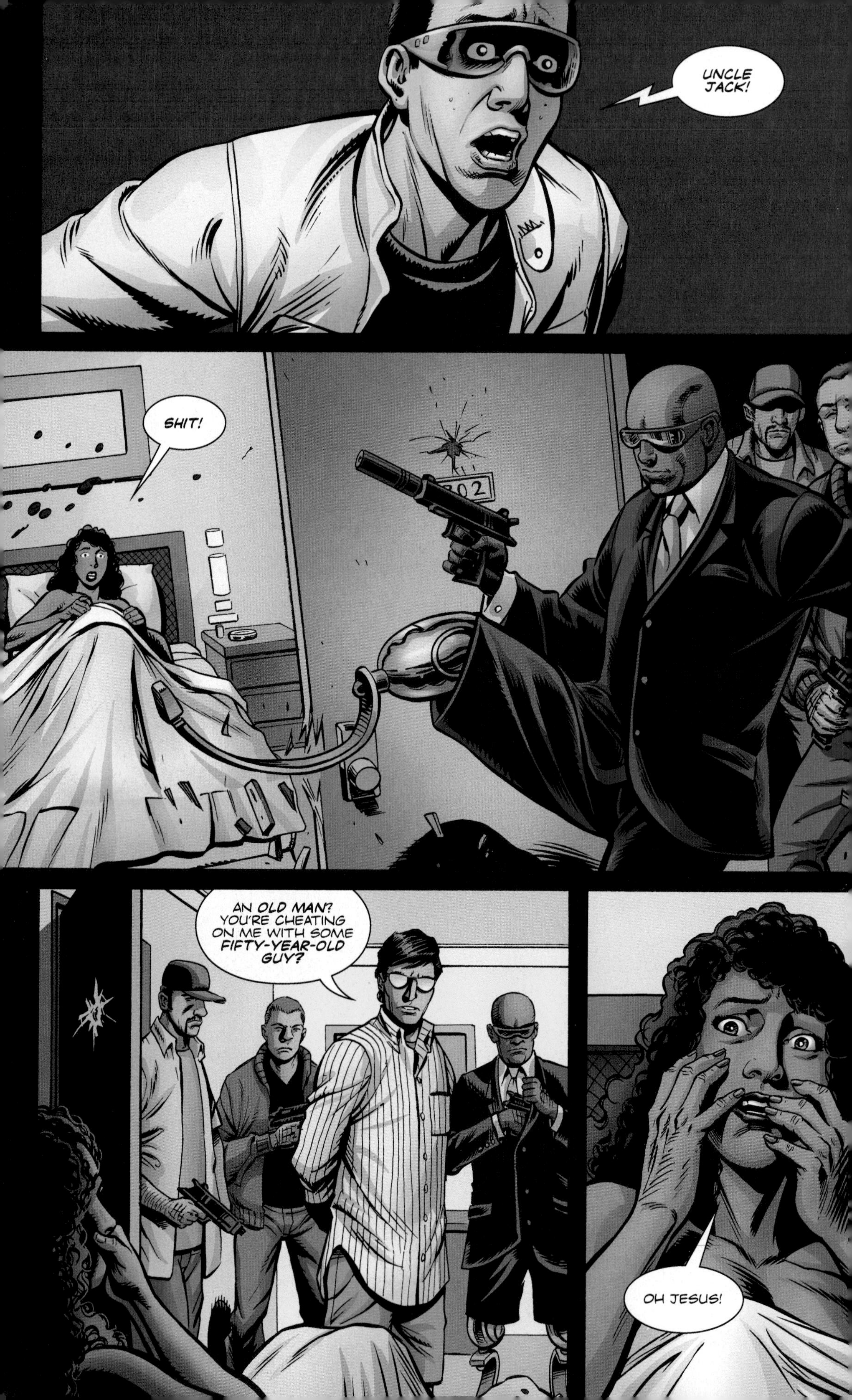
UNCLE JACK!
SHIT!
302
AN OLD MAN? YOU'RE CHEATING ON ME WITH SOME FIFTY-YEAR-OLD GUY?
OH JESUS!

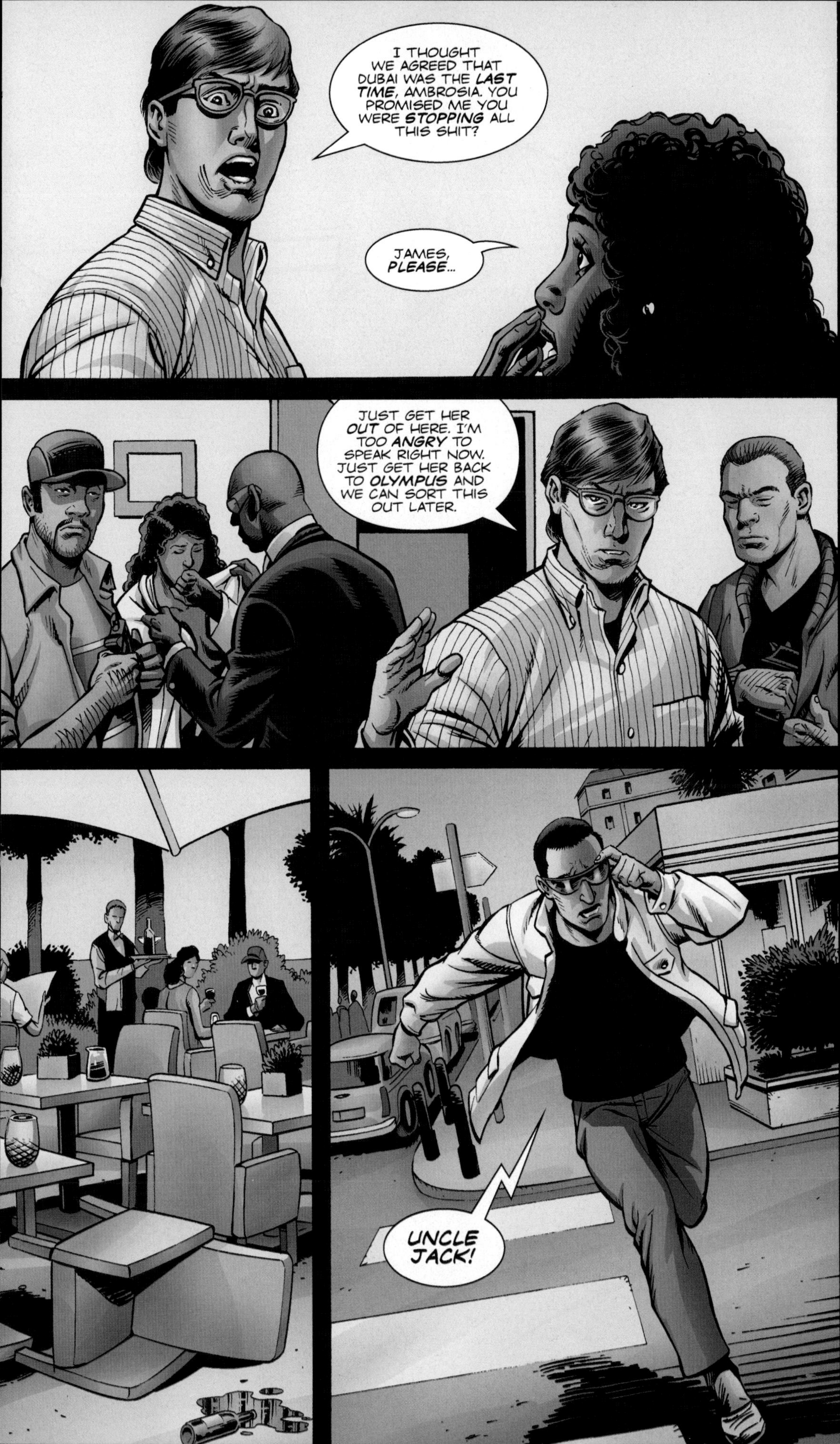
I THOUGHT WE AGREED THAT DUBAI WAS THE **LAST TIME**, AMBROSIA. YOU PROMISED ME YOU WERE **STOPPING** ALL THIS SHIT?
JAMES, **PLEASE**...
JUST GET HER **OUT** OF HERE. I'M TOO **ANGRY** TO SPEAK RIGHT NOW. JUST GET HER BACK TO **OLYMPUS** AND WE CAN SORT THIS OUT LATER.
UNCLE JACK!

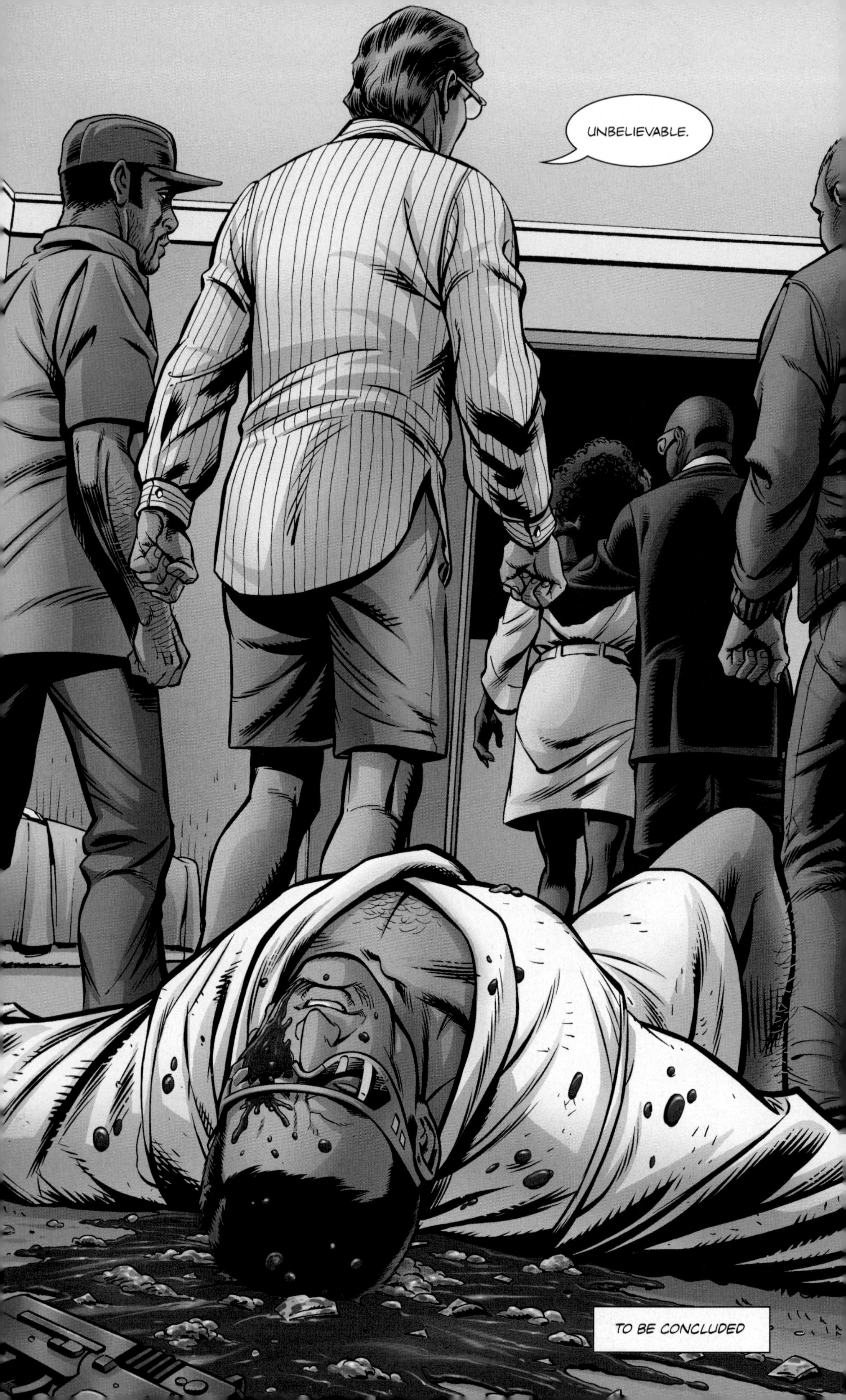
UNBELIEVABLE.
TO BE CONCLUDED

SIX

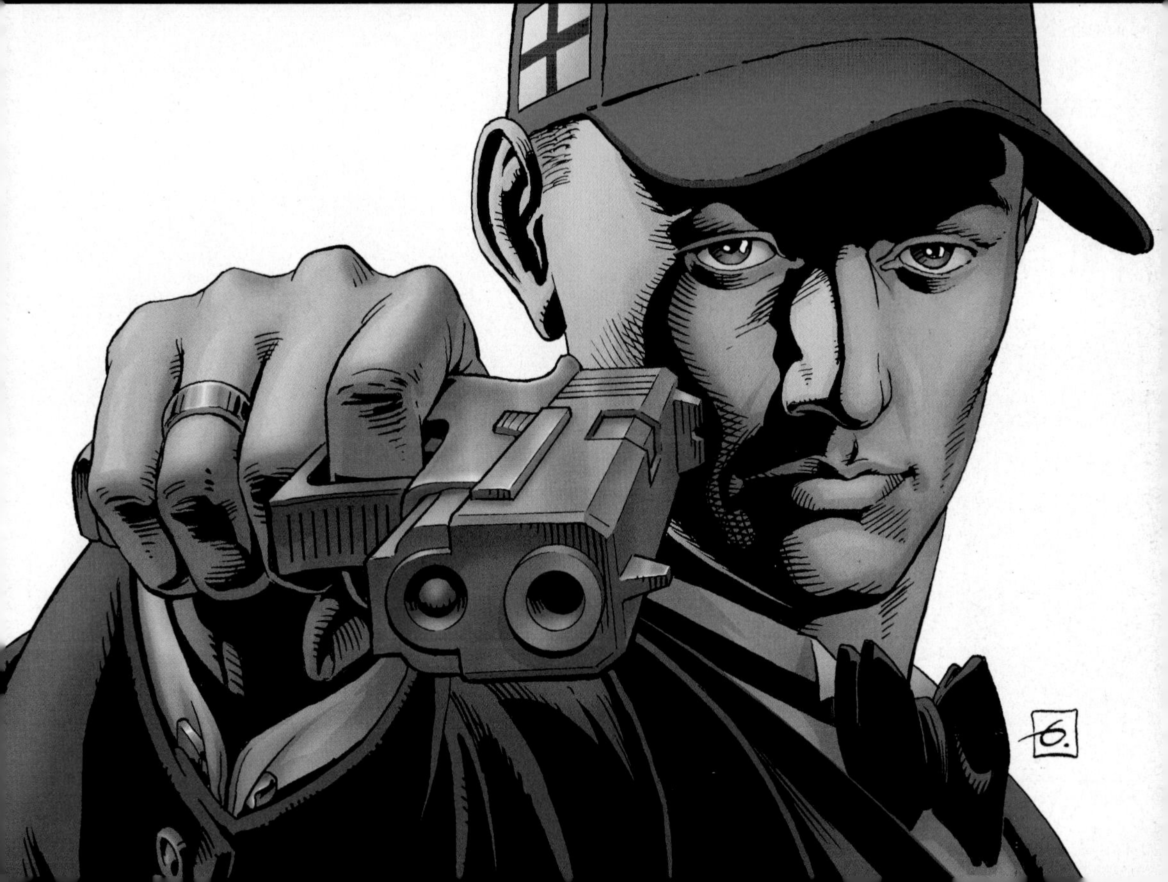

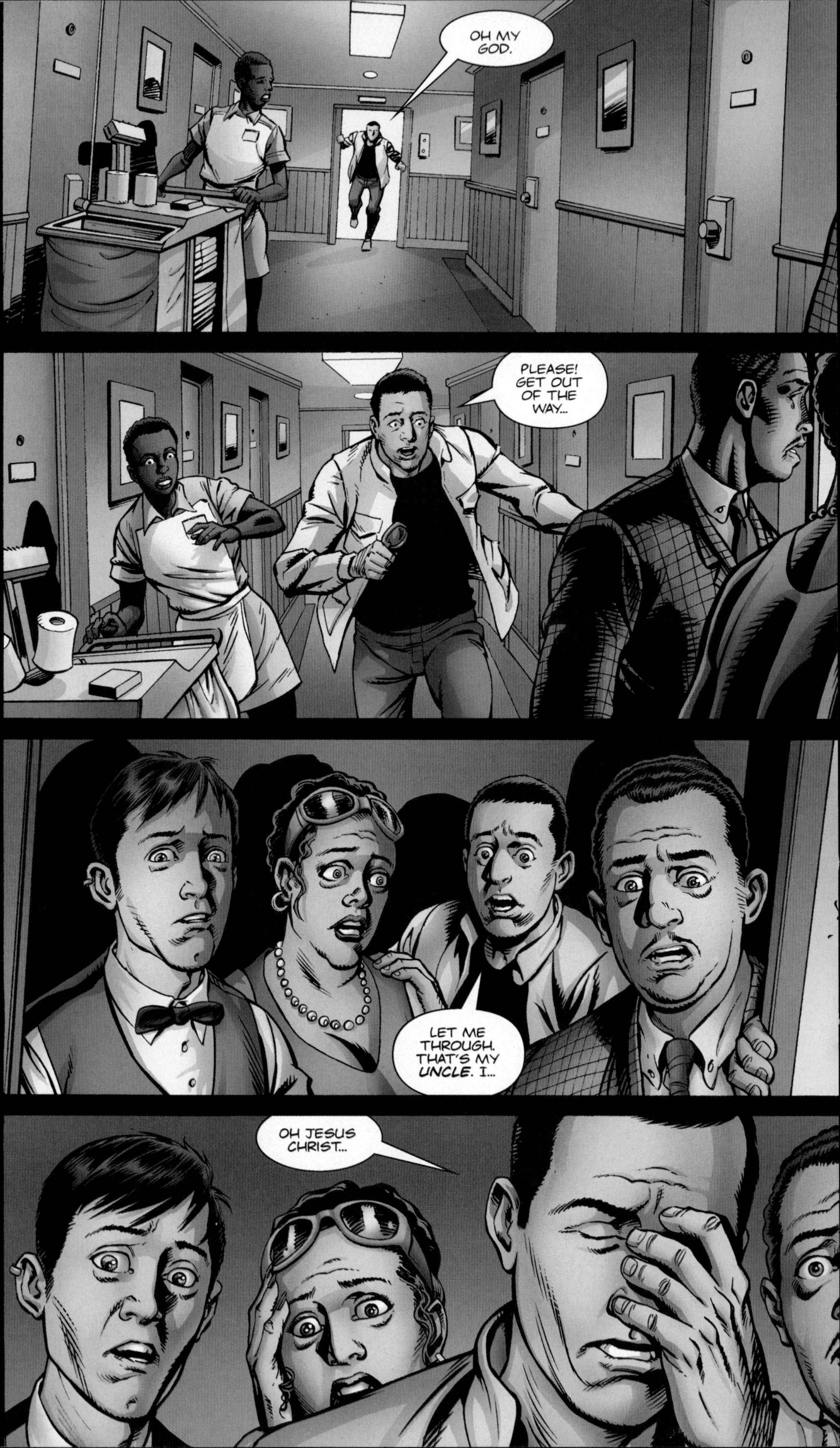
OH MY GOD.
PLEASE! GET OUT OF THE WAY...
LET ME THROUGH. THAT'S MY UNCLE. I...
OH JESUS CHRIST...

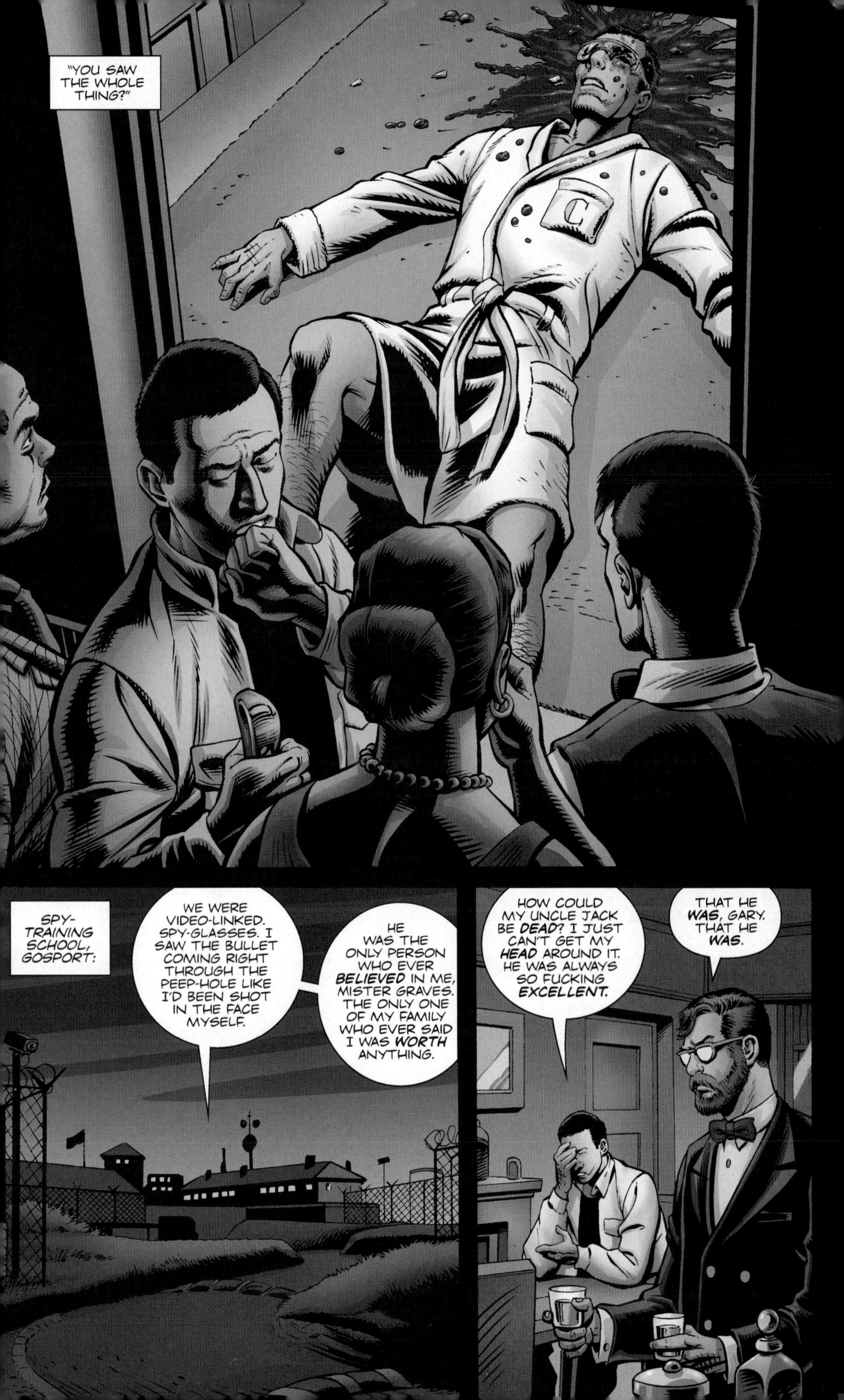
"YOU SAW THE WHOLE THING?"
SPY-TRAINING SCHOOL, GOSPORT:
WE WERE VIDEO-LINKED. SPY-GLASSES. I SAW THE BULLET COMING RIGHT THROUGH THE PEEP-HOLE LIKE I'D BEEN SHOT IN THE FACE MYSELF.
HE WAS THE ONLY PERSON WHO EVER **BELIEVED** IN ME, MISTER GRAVES. THE ONLY ONE OF MY FAMILY WHO EVER SAID I WAS **WORTH** ANYTHING.
HOW COULD MY UNCLE JACK BE **DEAD**? I JUST CAN'T GET MY **HEAD** AROUND IT. HE WAS ALWAYS SO FUCKING **EXCELLENT**.
THAT HE **WAS**, GARY. THAT HE **WAS**.

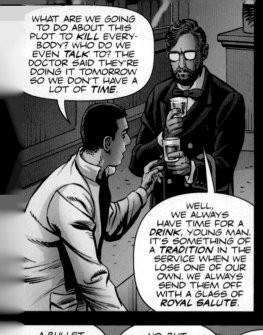

WHAT ARE WE GOING TO DO ABOUT THIS PLOT TO **KILL** EVERY-BODY? WHO DO WE EVEN **TALK** TO? THE DOCTOR SAID THEY'RE DOING IT TOMORROW SO WE DON'T HAVE A LOT OF **TIME.**

WELL, WE ALWAYS HAVE TIME FOR A **DRINK,** YOUNG MAN. IT'S SOMETHING OF A **TRADITION** IN THE SERVICE WHEN WE LOSE ONE OF OUR OWN. WE ALWAYS SEND THEM OFF WITH A GLASS OF **ROYAL SALUTE.**

YOUR UNCLE AND I TOASTED **A LOT** OF OLD PALS OVER THE YEARS.... STEED, GAMBIT, EVEN SOME OF THE OLD-TIMERS LIKE DRAKE AND TEMPLAR ONCE UPON A TIME.

WE ALWAYS ASSUME WE'LL GO OUT IN A **BLAZE OF GLORY,** BUT IT'S USUALLY JUST **ILLNESS** OR AN **ACCIDENT** LIKE JACK'S.

A BULLET IN THE HEAD ISN'T REALLY AN **ACCIDENT,** MATE.

NO, BUT **THIS** TIME IT WAS. POOR DOCTOR ARNOLD JUST THOUGHT JACK WAS ANOTHER MAN HIS GIRLFRIEND HAD PICKED UP IN THE CITY.

THEY'VE BEEN GOING THROUGH A **ROUGH PATCH** LATELY AND HAVING A LOT OF COUNSEL-LING ABOUT HER APPETITE FOR SEX WITH **STRANGERS.**

H-HOW DO YOU **KNOW** ALL THIS?

BECAUSE I'M **WORKING** FOR ARNOLD, OF COURSE. RE-CRUITING OUR PEOPLE TO HIS WONDERFUL PLAN. I ACTUALLY HOPED WE MIGHT RECRUIT **JACK,** BUT THERE'S NO CHANCE OF THAT **NOW,** IS THERE?

IT WAS ME WHO BROUGHT IN **GAZELLE** AND **THE OTHERS.** I PICKED **MOST** OF HIS GUARDS FROM OUR WOUNDED SOLDIERS.

B-BUT **WHY?** I DON'T UN-DERSTAND...

WHY **WOULDN'T I?** WE'RE SUPPOSED TO BE **SAVING THE WORLD** IN THIS GAME, BUT LOOK AT THE BLOODY **MESS** IT'S ALWAYS IN.

I'VE BEEN SERVING THIS DEPARTMENT FOR THIRTY-EIGHT YEARS AND, BELIEVE ME, WE'RE FIGHTING A **LOSING BATTLE** OUT THERE.

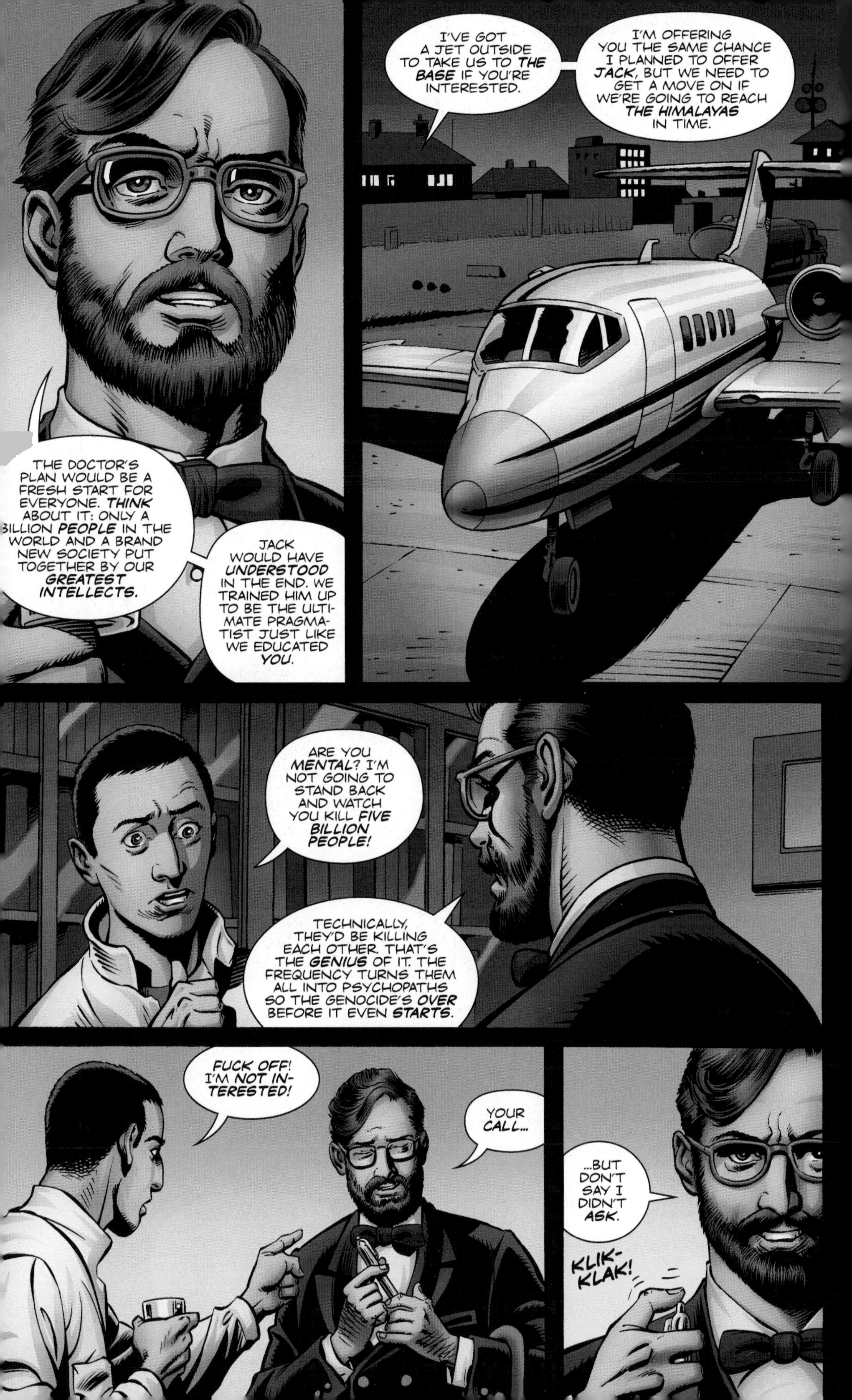
THE DOCTOR'S PLAN WOULD BE A FRESH START FOR EVERYONE. THINK ABOUT IT: ONLY A BILLION PEOPLE IN THE WORLD AND A BRAND NEW SOCIETY PUT TOGETHER BY OUR GREATEST INTELLECTS.
JACK WOULD HAVE UNDERSTOOD IN THE END. WE TRAINED HIM UP TO BE THE ULTIMATE PRAGMATIST JUST LIKE WE EDUCATED YOU.
I'VE GOT A JET OUTSIDE TO TAKE US TO THE BASE IF YOU'RE INTERESTED.
I'M OFFERING YOU THE SAME CHANCE I PLANNED TO OFFER JACK, BUT WE NEED TO GET A MOVE ON IF WE'RE GOING TO REACH THE HIMALAYAS IN TIME.
ARE YOU MENTAL? I'M NOT GOING TO STAND BACK AND WATCH YOU KILL FIVE BILLION PEOPLE!
TECHNICALLY, THEY'D BE KILLING EACH OTHER. THAT'S THE GENIUS OF IT. THE FREQUENCY TURNS THEM ALL INTO PSYCHOPATHS SO THE GENOCIDE'S OVER BEFORE IT EVEN STARTS.
FUCK OFF! I'M NOT INTERESTED!
YOUR CALL...
...BUT DON'T SAY I DIDN'T ASK.
KLIK-KLAK!

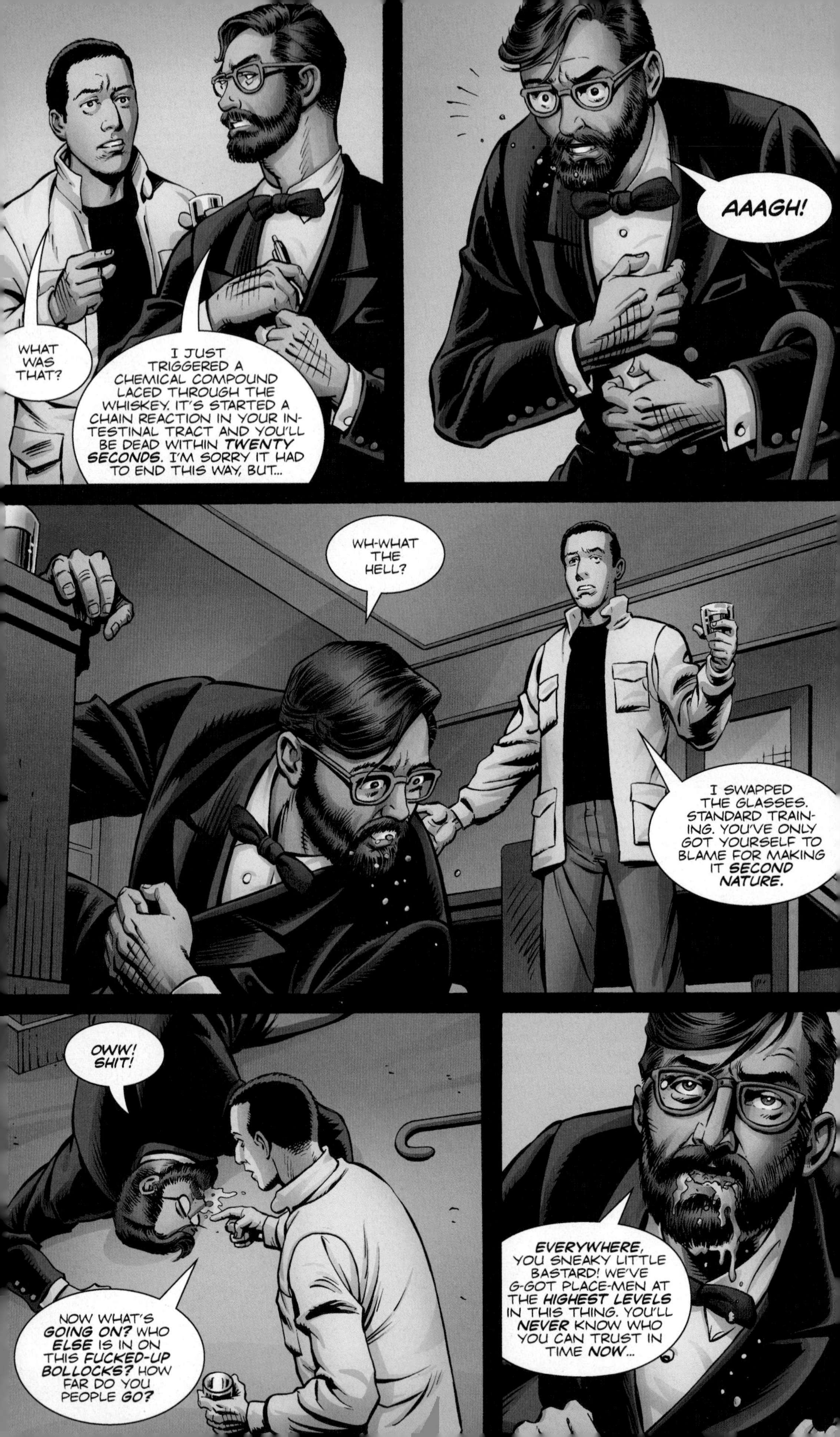
WHAT WAS THAT?
I JUST TRIGGERED A CHEMICAL COMPOUND LACED THROUGH THE WHISKEY. IT'S STARTED A CHAIN REACTION IN YOUR INTESTINAL TRACT AND YOU'LL BE DEAD WITHIN TWENTY SECONDS. I'M SORRY IT HAD TO END THIS WAY, BUT...
AAAGH!
WH-WHAT THE HELL?
I SWAPPED THE GLASSES. STANDARD TRAINING. YOU'VE ONLY GOT YOURSELF TO BLAME FOR MAKING IT SECOND NATURE.
OWW! SHIT!
NOW WHAT'S GOING ON? WHO ELSE IS IN ON THIS FUCKED-UP BOLLOCKS? HOW FAR DO YOU PEOPLE GO?
EVERYWHERE, YOU SNEAKY LITTLE BASTARD! WE'VE G-GOT PLACE-MEN AT THE HIGHEST LEVELS IN THIS THING. YOU'LL NEVER KNOW WHO YOU CAN TRUST IN TIME NOW...

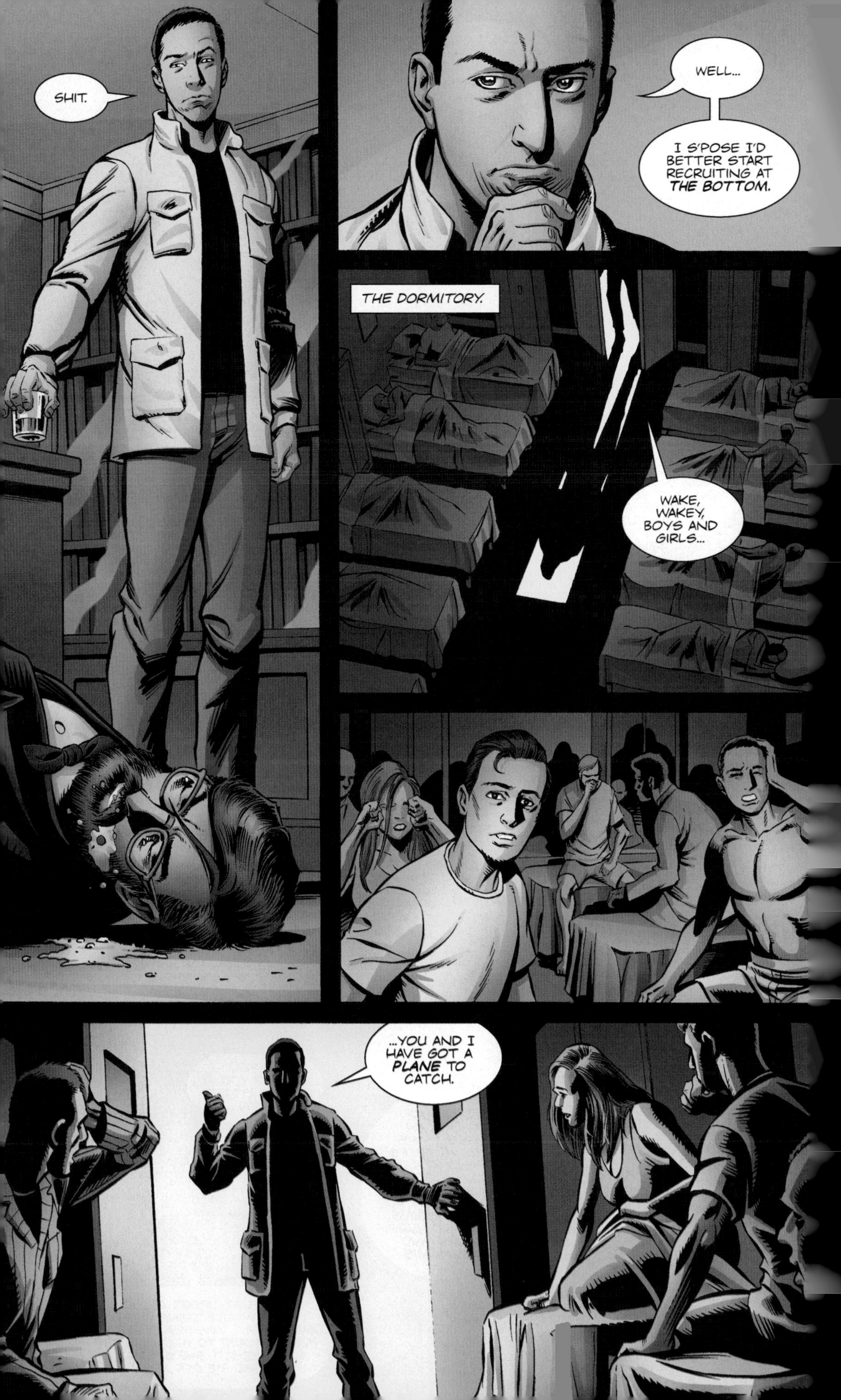
SHIT.
WELL...
I S'POSE I'D BETTER START RECRUITING AT THE BOTTOM.
THE DORMITORY.
WAKE, WAKEY, BOYS AND GIRLS...
...YOU AND I HAVE GOT A PLANE TO CATCH.

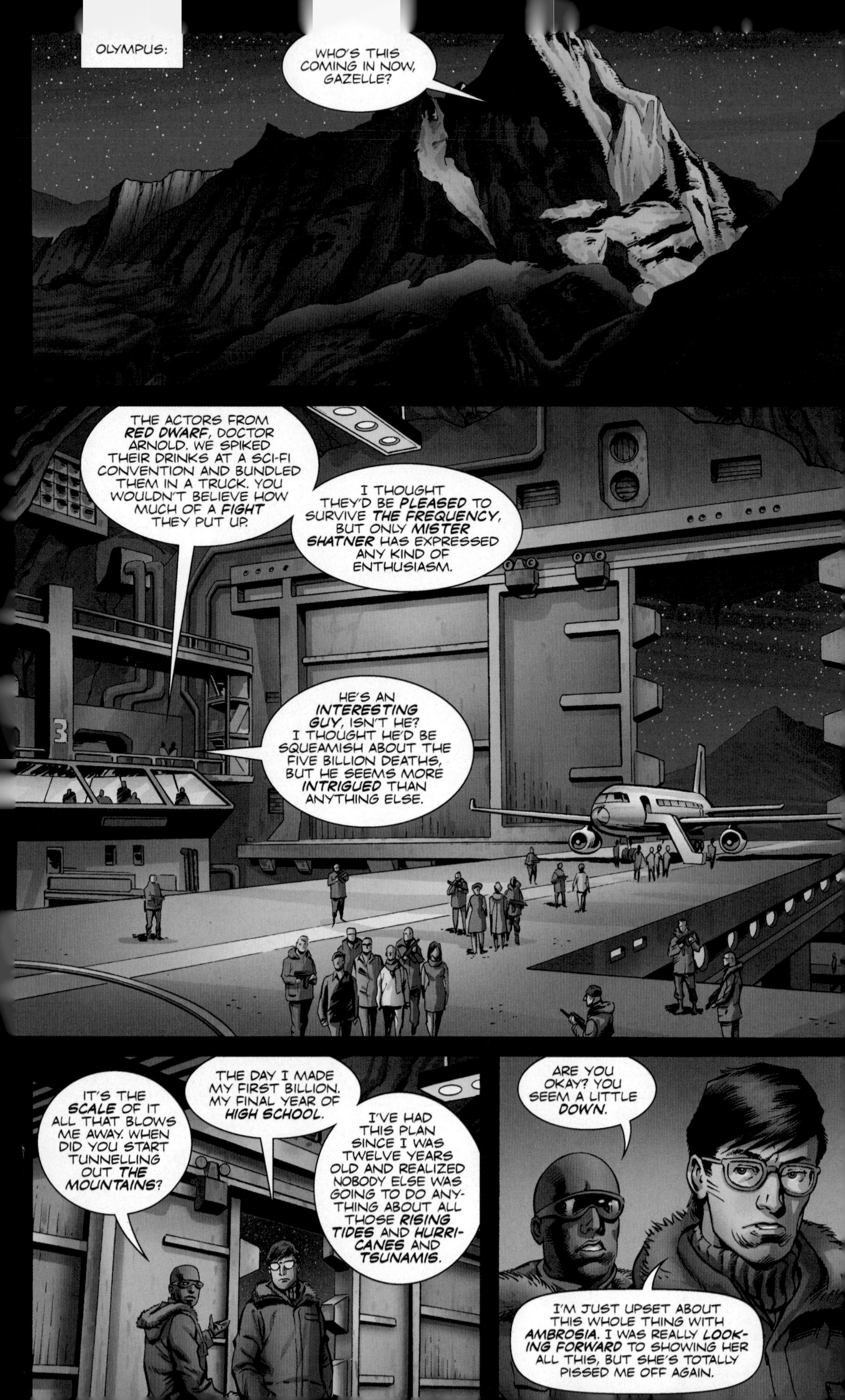
OLYMPUS:
WHO'S THIS COMING IN NOW, GAZELLE?
THE ACTORS FROM RED DWARF, DOCTOR ARNOLD. WE SPIKED THEIR DRINKS AT A SCI-FI CONVENTION AND BUNDLED THEM IN A TRUCK. YOU WOULDN'T BELIEVE HOW MUCH OF A FIGHT THEY PUT UP.
I THOUGHT THEY'D BE PLEASED TO SURVIVE THE FREQUENCY, BUT ONLY MISTER SHATNER HAS EXPRESSED ANY KIND OF ENTHUSIASM.
HE'S AN INTERESTING GUY, ISN'T HE? I THOUGHT HE'D BE SQUEAMISH ABOUT THE FIVE BILLION DEATHS, BUT HE SEEMS MORE INTRIGUED THAN ANYTHING ELSE.
3
IT'S THE SCALE OF IT ALL THAT BLOWS ME AWAY. WHEN DID YOU START TUNNELLING OUT THE MOUNTAINS?
THE DAY I MADE MY FIRST BILLION. MY FINAL YEAR OF HIGH SCHOOL.
I'VE HAD THIS PLAN SINCE I WAS TWELVE YEARS OLD AND REALIZED NOBODY ELSE WAS GOING TO DO ANYTHING ABOUT ALL THOSE RISING TIDES AND HURRICANES AND TSUNAMIS.
ARE YOU OKAY? YOU SEEM A LITTLE DOWN.
I'M JUST UPSET ABOUT THIS WHOLE THING WITH AMBROSIA. I WAS REALLY LOOKING FORWARD TO SHOWING HER ALL THIS, BUT SHE'S TOTALLY PISSED ME OFF AGAIN.

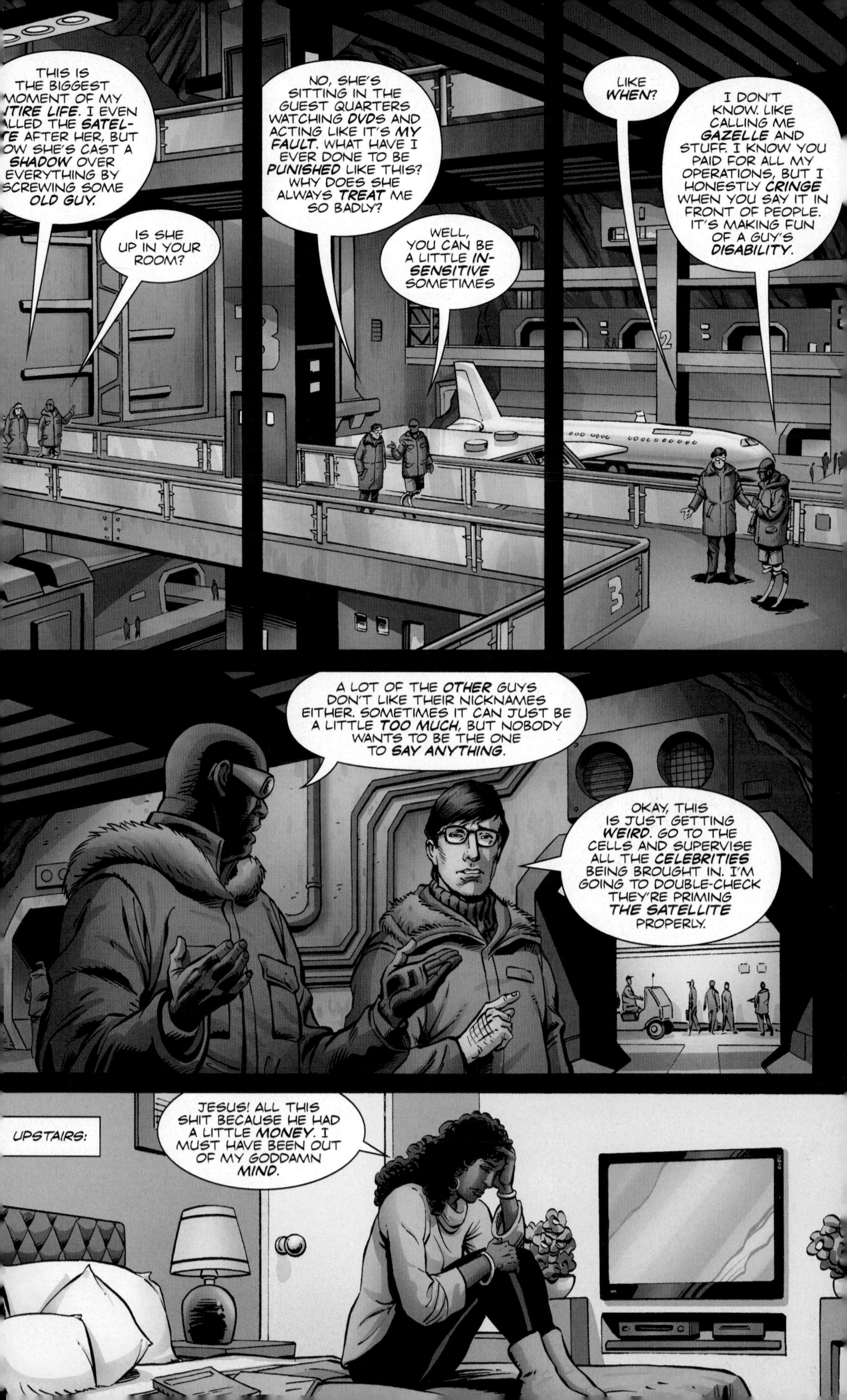
THIS IS THE BIGGEST MOMENT OF MY ENTIRE LIFE. I EVEN CALLED THE SATELLITE AFTER HER, BUT NOW SHE'S CAST A SHADOW OVER EVERYTHING BY SCREWING SOME OLD GUY.
IS SHE UP IN YOUR ROOM?
NO, SHE'S SITTING IN THE GUEST QUARTERS WATCHING DVDS AND ACTING LIKE IT'S MY FAULT. WHAT HAVE I EVER DONE TO BE PUNISHED LIKE THIS? WHY DOES SHE ALWAYS TREAT ME SO BADLY?
WELL, YOU CAN BE A LITTLE IN-SENSITIVE SOMETIMES
LIKE WHEN?
I DON'T KNOW. LIKE CALLING ME GAZELLE AND STUFF. I KNOW YOU PAID FOR ALL MY OPERATIONS, BUT I HONESTLY CRINGE WHEN YOU SAY IT IN FRONT OF PEOPLE. IT'S MAKING FUN OF A GUY'S DISABILITY.
A LOT OF THE OTHER GUYS DON'T LIKE THEIR NICKNAMES EITHER. SOMETIMES IT CAN JUST BE A LITTLE TOO MUCH, BUT NOBODY WANTS TO BE THE ONE TO SAY ANYTHING.
OKAY, THIS IS JUST GETTING WEIRD. GO TO THE CELLS AND SUPERVISE ALL THE CELEBRITIES BEING BROUGHT IN. I'M GOING TO DOUBLE-CHECK THEY'RE PRIMING THE SATELLITE PROPERLY.
UPSTAIRS:
JESUS! ALL THIS SHIT BECAUSE HE HAD A LITTLE MONEY. I MUST HAVE BEEN OUT OF MY GODDAMN MIND.

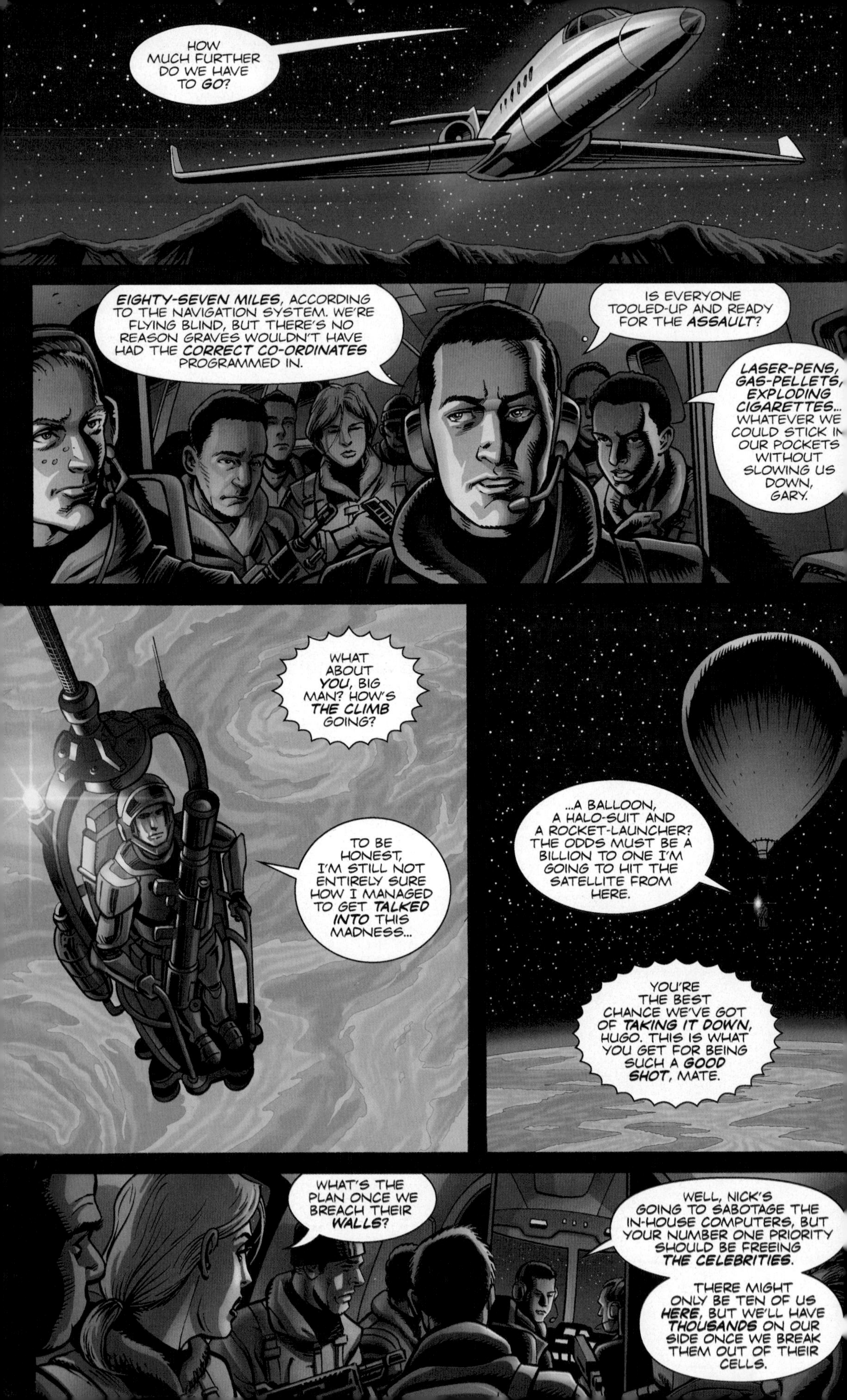
HOW MUCH FURTHER DO WE HAVE TO GO?
EIGHTY-SEVEN MILES, ACCORDING TO THE NAVIGATION SYSTEM. WE'RE FLYING BLIND, BUT THERE'S NO REASON GRAVES WOULDN'T HAVE HAD THE CORRECT CO-ORDINATES PROGRAMMED IN.
IS EVERYONE TOOLED-UP AND READY FOR THE ASSAULT?
LASER-PENS, GAS-PELLETS, EXPLODING CIGARETTES... WHATEVER WE COULD STICK IN OUR POCKETS WITHOUT SLOWING US DOWN, GARY.
WHAT ABOUT YOU, BIG MAN? HOW'S THE CLIMB GOING?
TO BE HONEST, I'M STILL NOT ENTIRELY SURE HOW I MANAGED TO GET TALKED INTO THIS MADNESS...
...A BALLOON, A HALO-SUIT AND A ROCKET-LAUNCHER? THE ODDS MUST BE A BILLION TO ONE I'M GOING TO HIT THE SATELLITE FROM HERE.
YOU'RE THE BEST CHANCE WE'VE GOT OF TAKING IT DOWN, HUGO. THIS IS WHAT YOU GET FOR BEING SUCH A GOOD SHOT, MATE.
WHAT'S THE PLAN ONCE WE BREACH THEIR WALLS?
WELL, NICK'S GOING TO SABOTAGE THE IN-HOUSE COMPUTERS, BUT YOUR NUMBER ONE PRIORITY SHOULD BE FREEING THE CELEBRITIES.
THERE MIGHT ONLY BE TEN OF US HERE, BUT WE'LL HAVE THOUSANDS ON OUR SIDE ONCE WE BREAK THEM OUT OF THEIR CELLS.

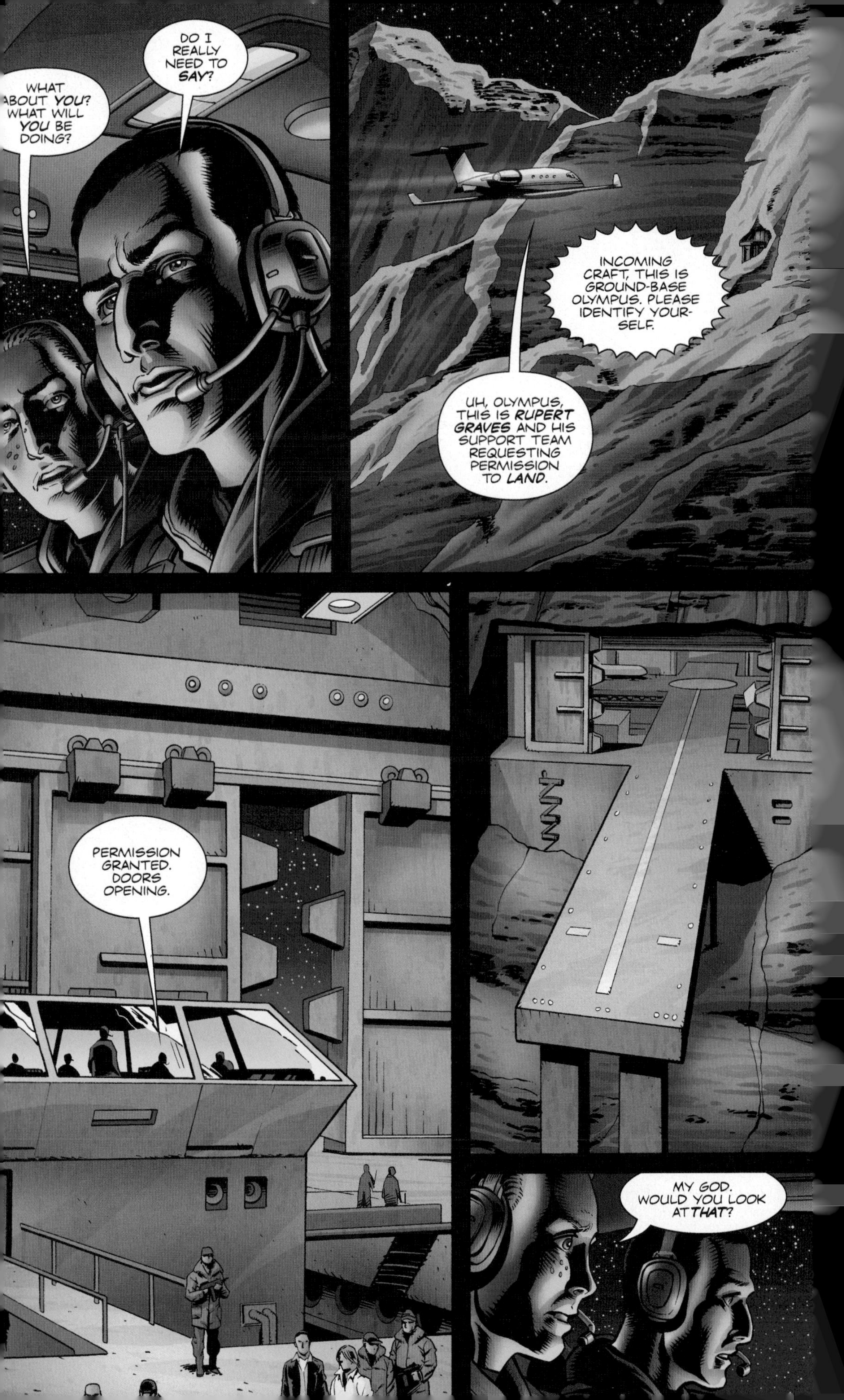
WHAT ABOUT YOU? WHAT WILL YOU BE DOING?
DO I REALLY NEED TO SAY?
INCOMING CRAFT, THIS IS GROUND-BASE OLYMPUS. PLEASE IDENTIFY YOUR-SELF.
UH, OLYMPUS, THIS IS RUPERT GRAVES AND HIS SUPPORT TEAM REQUESTING PERMISSION TO LAND.
PERMISSION GRANTED. DOORS OPENING.
MY GOD. WOULD YOU LOOK AT THAT?

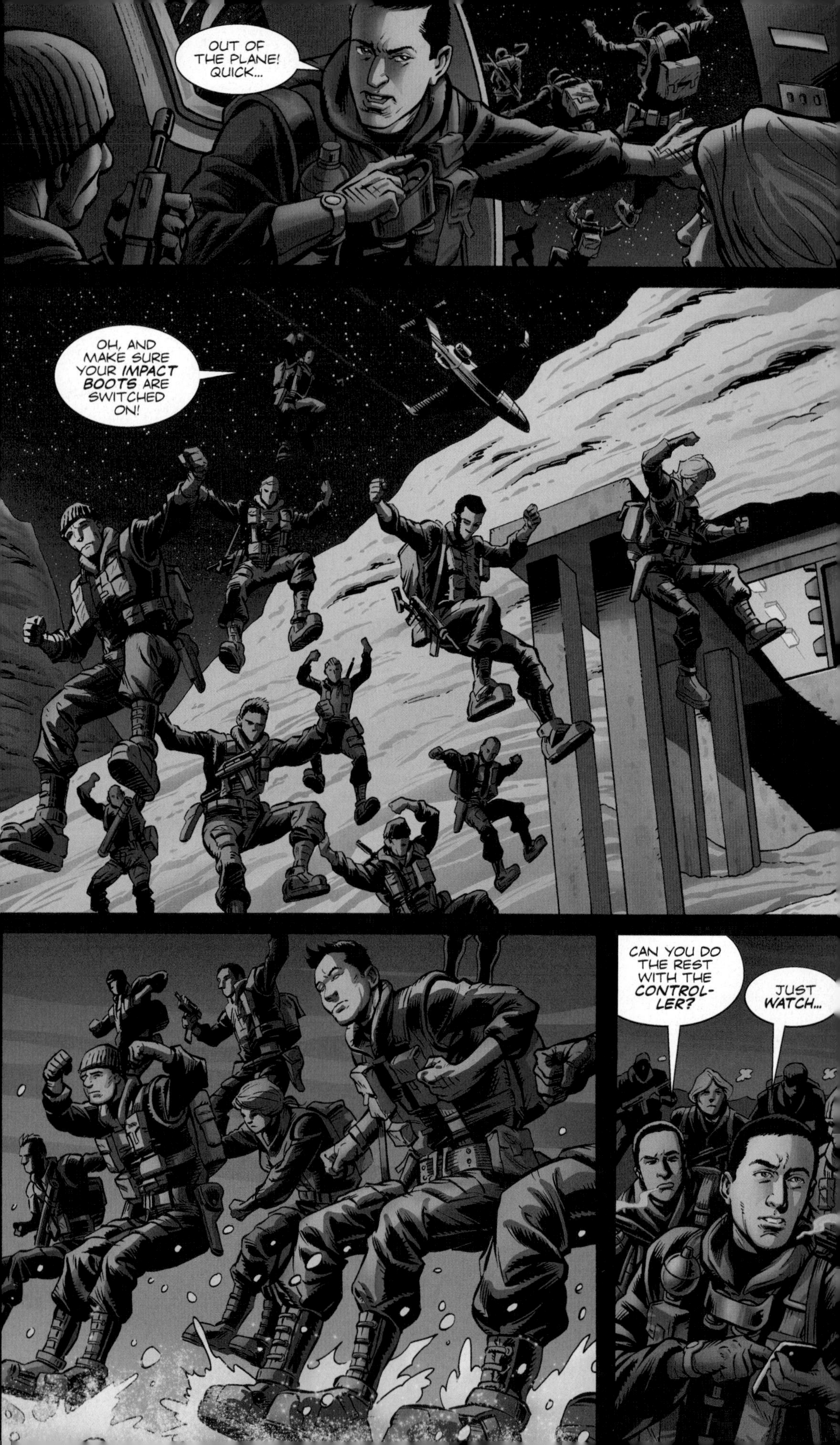
OUT OF THE PLANE! QUICK...
OH, AND MAKE SURE YOUR IMPACT BOOTS ARE SWITCHED ON!
CAN YOU DO THE REST WITH THE CONTROL-LER?
JUST WATCH...

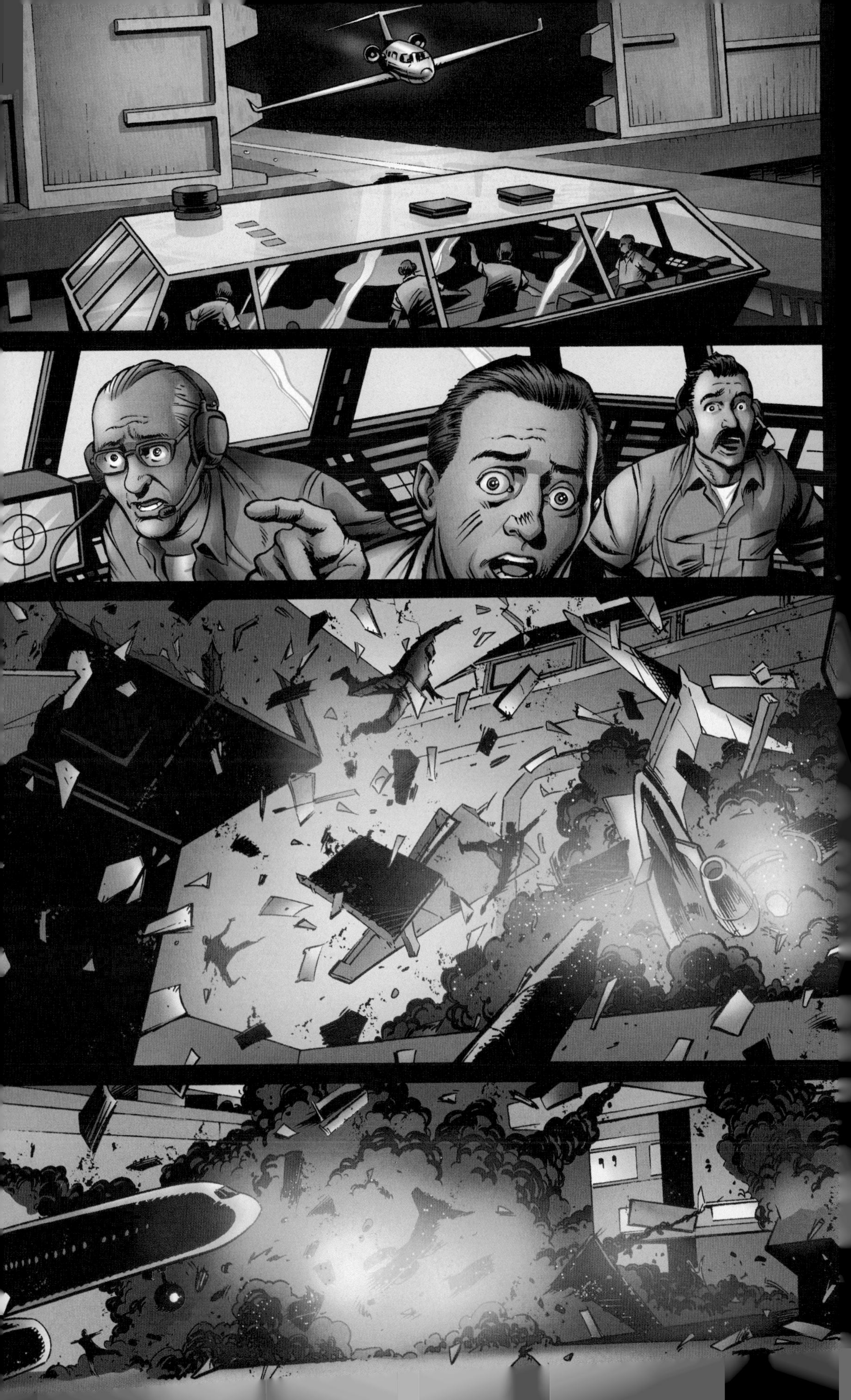

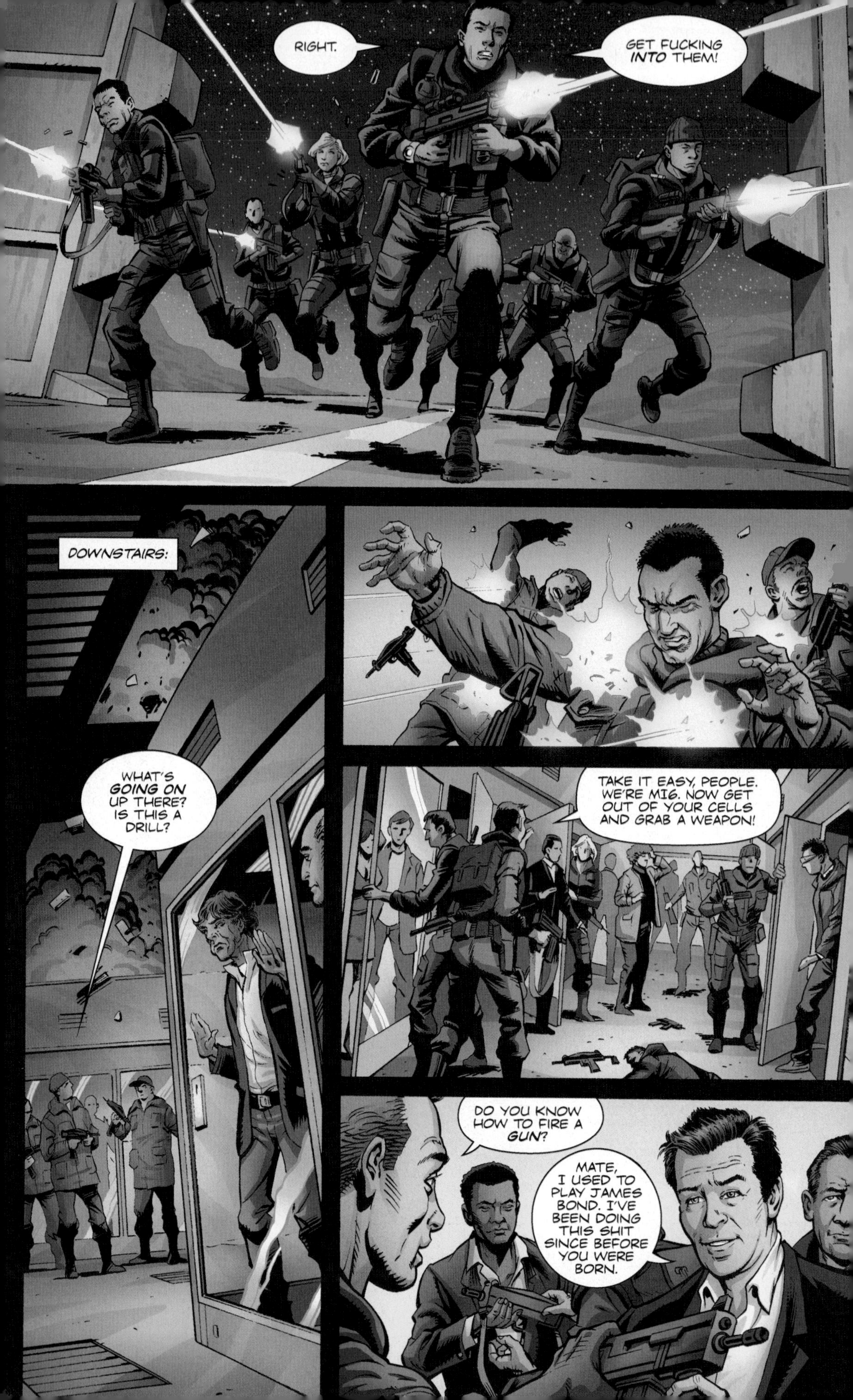
RIGHT.
GET FUCKING INTO THEM!
DOWNSTAIRS:
WHAT'S GOING ON UP THERE? IS THIS A DRILL?
TAKE IT EASY, PEOPLE. WE'RE MI6. NOW GET OUT OF YOUR CELLS AND GRAB A WEAPON!
DO YOU KNOW HOW TO FIRE A GUN?
MATE, I USED TO PLAY JAMES BOND. I'VE BEEN DOING THIS SHIT SINCE BEFORE YOU WERE BORN.

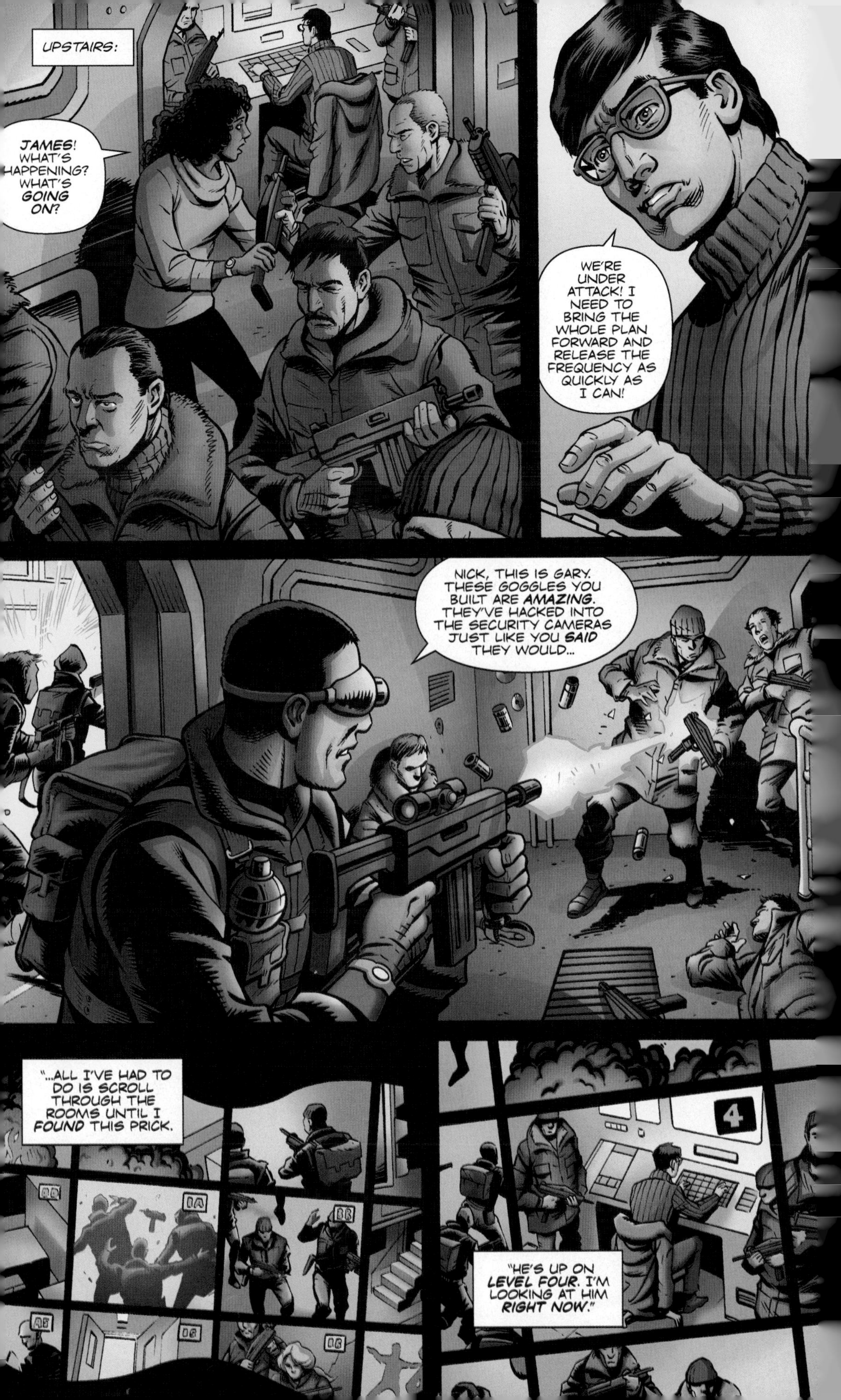
UPSTAIRS:
JAMES! WHAT'S HAPPENING? WHAT'S GOING ON?
WE'RE UNDER ATTACK! I NEED TO BRING THE WHOLE PLAN FORWARD AND RELEASE THE FREQUENCY AS QUICKLY AS I CAN!
NICK, THIS IS GARY. THESE GOGGLES YOU BUILT ARE AMAZING. THEY'VE HACKED INTO THE SECURITY CAMERAS JUST LIKE YOU SAID THEY WOULD...
"...ALL I'VE HAD TO DO IS SCROLL THROUGH THE ROOMS UNTIL I FOUND THIS PRICK.
4
"HE'S UP ON LEVEL FOUR. I'M LOOKING AT HIM RIGHT NOW."

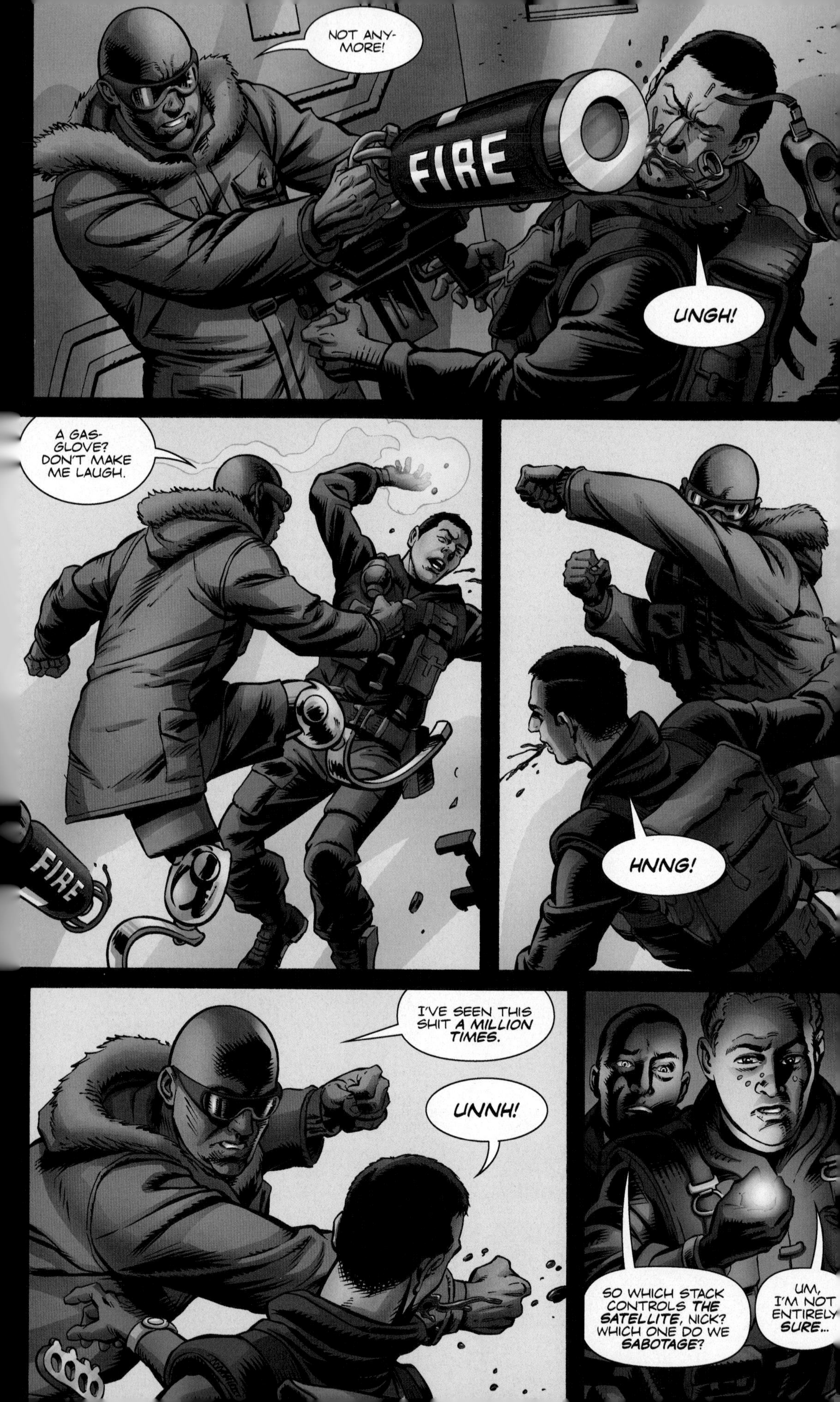
NOT ANY-MORE!
FIRE
UNGH!
A GAS-GLOVE? DON'T MAKE ME LAUGH.
FIRE
HNNG!
I'VE SEEN THIS SHIT A MILLION TIMES.
UNNH!
SO WHICH STACK CONTROLS THE SATELLITE, NICK? WHICH ONE DO WE SABOTAGE?
UM, I'M NOT ENTIRELY SURE...

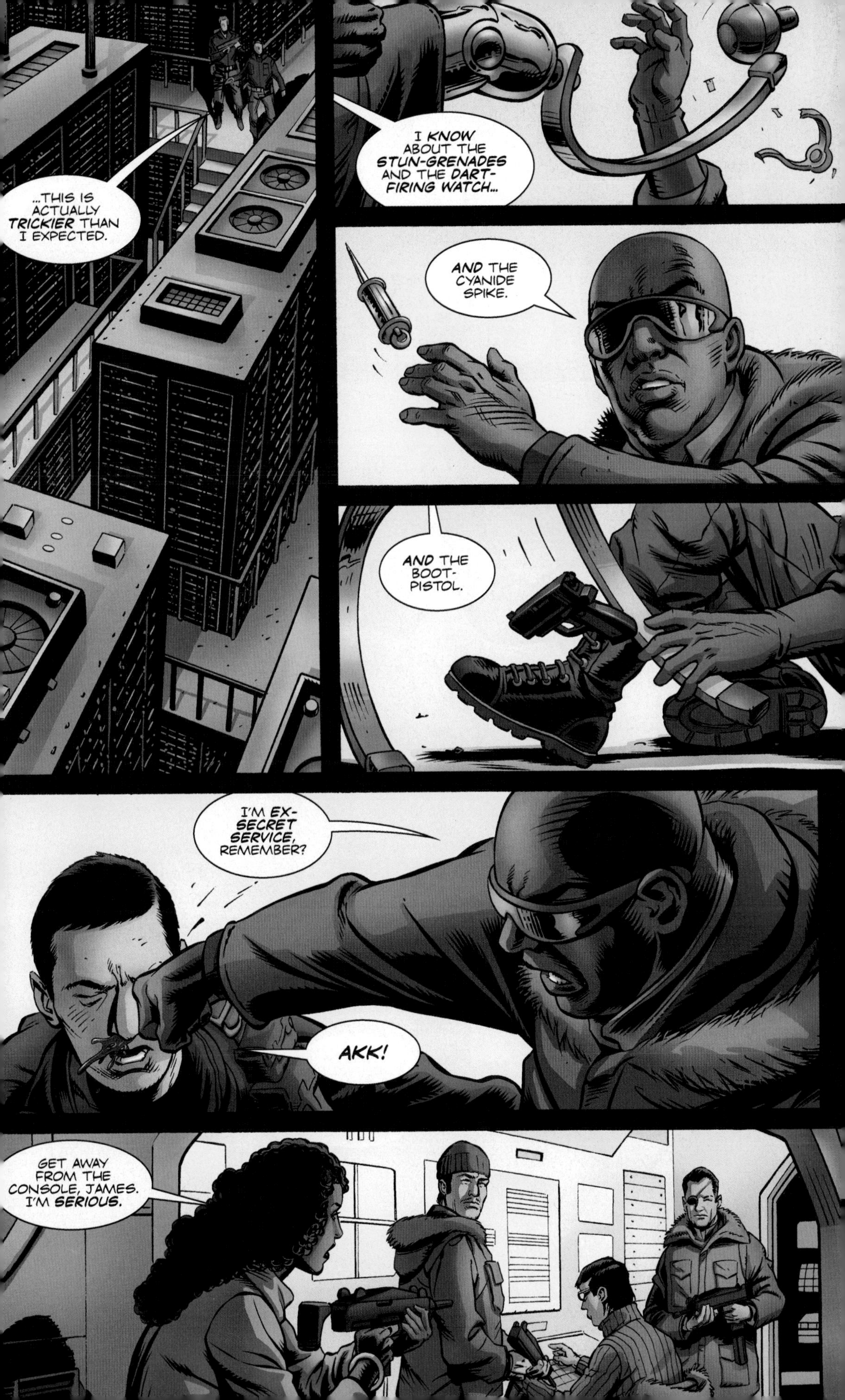
...THIS IS ACTUALLY TRICKIER THAN I EXPECTED.
I KNOW ABOUT THE STUN-GRENADES AND THE DART-FIRING WATCH...
AND THE CYANIDE SPIKE.
AND THE BOOT-PISTOL.
I'M EX-SECRET SERVICE, REMEMBER?
AKK!
GET AWAY FROM THE CONSOLE, JAMES. I'M SERIOUS.

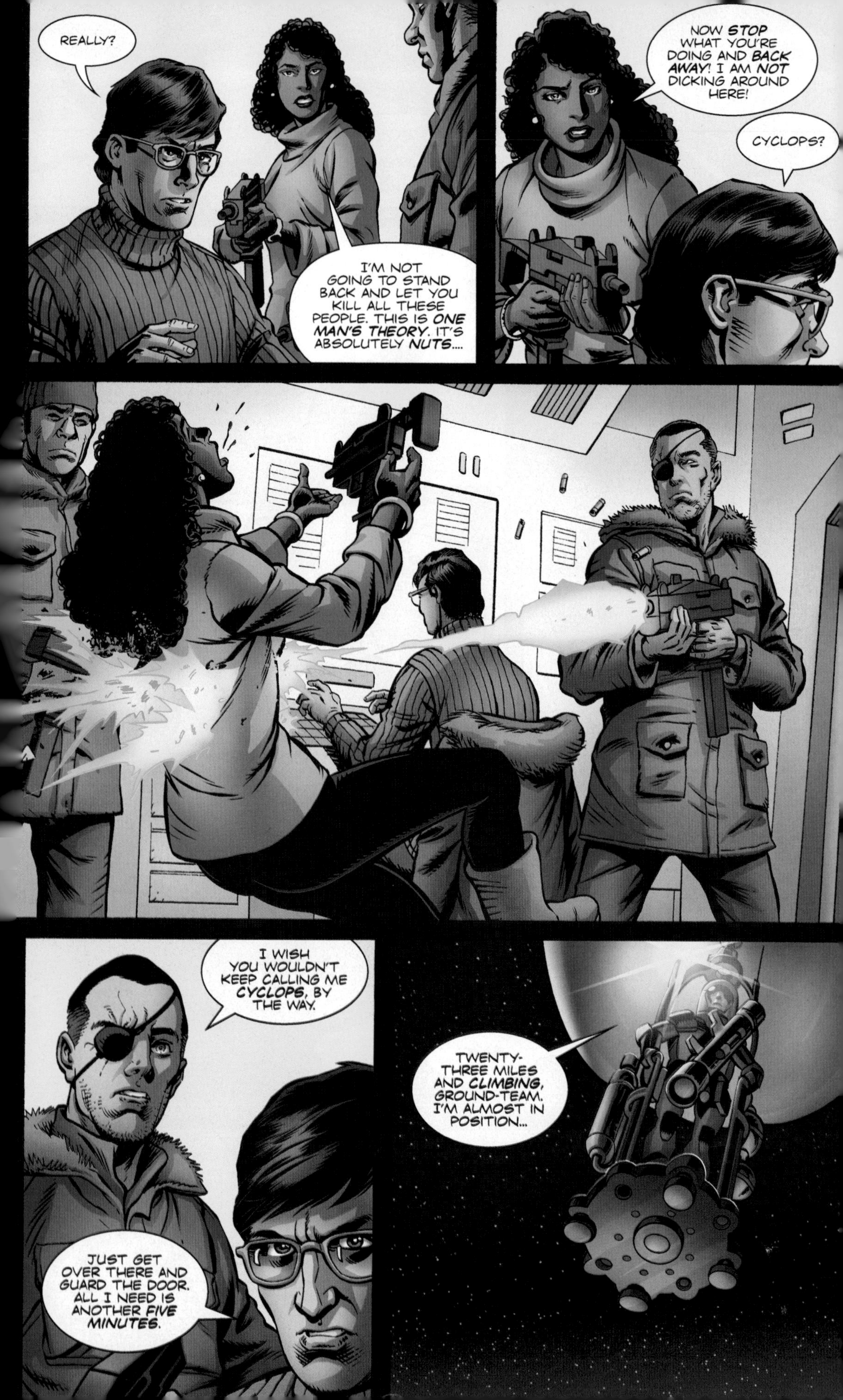
REALLY?
I'M NOT GOING TO STAND BACK AND LET YOU KILL ALL THESE PEOPLE. THIS IS ONE MAN'S THEORY. IT'S ABSOLUTELY NUTS....
NOW STOP WHAT YOU'RE DOING AND BACK AWAY! I AM NOT DICKING AROUND HERE!
CYCLOPS?
I WISH YOU WOULDN'T KEEP CALLING ME CYCLOPS, BY THE WAY.
JUST GET OVER THERE AND GUARD THE DOOR. ALL I NEED IS ANOTHER FIVE MINUTES.
TWENTY-THREE MILES AND CLIMBING, GROUND-TEAM. I'M ALMOST IN POSITION...

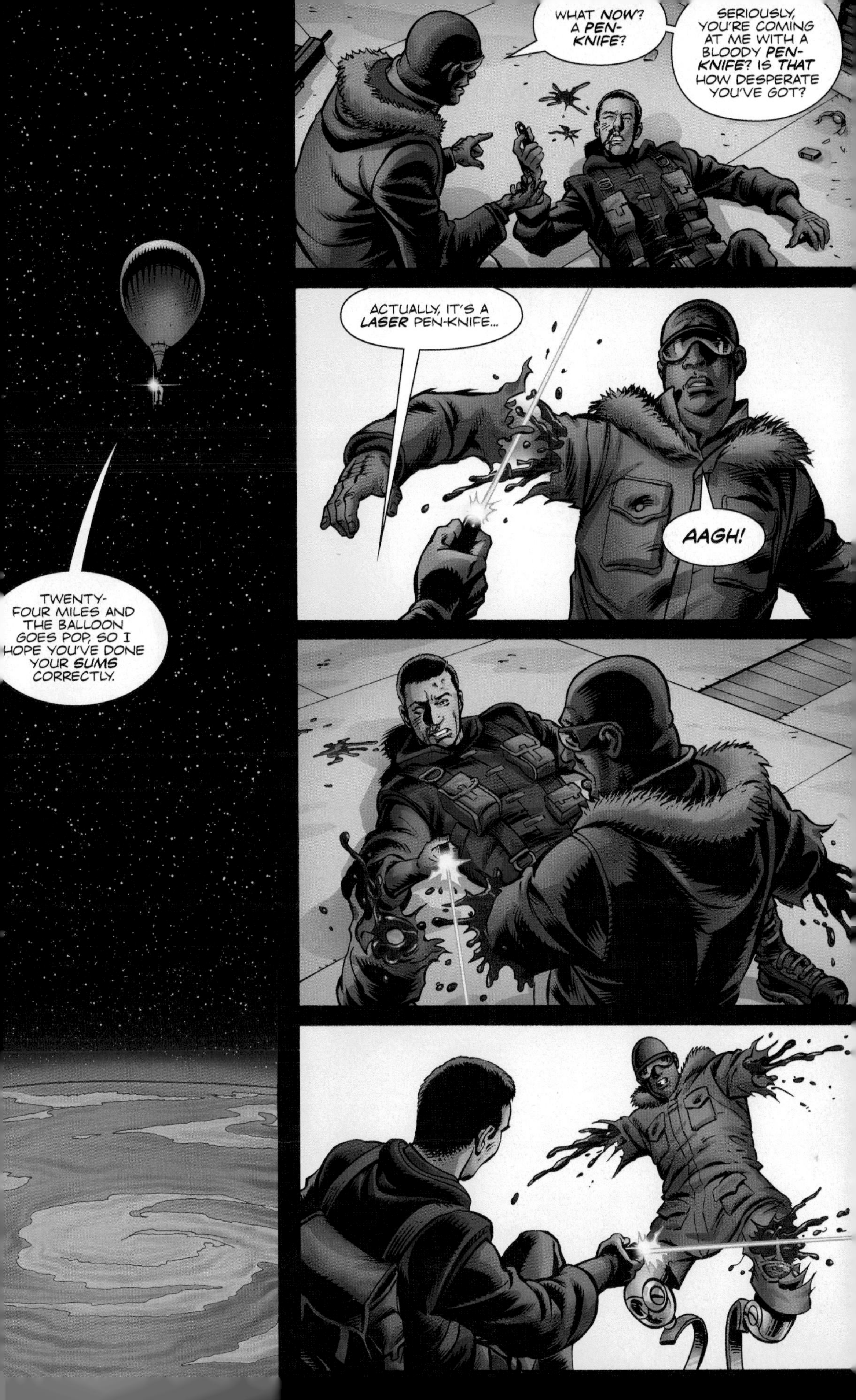
WHAT NOW? A PEN-KNIFE?
SERIOUSLY, YOU'RE COMING AT ME WITH A BLOODY PEN-KNIFE? IS THAT HOW DESPERATE YOU'VE GOT?
ACTUALLY, IT'S A LASER PEN-KNIFE...
AAGH!
TWENTY-FOUR MILES AND THE BALLOON GOES POP, SO I HOPE YOU'VE DONE YOUR SUMS CORRECTLY.

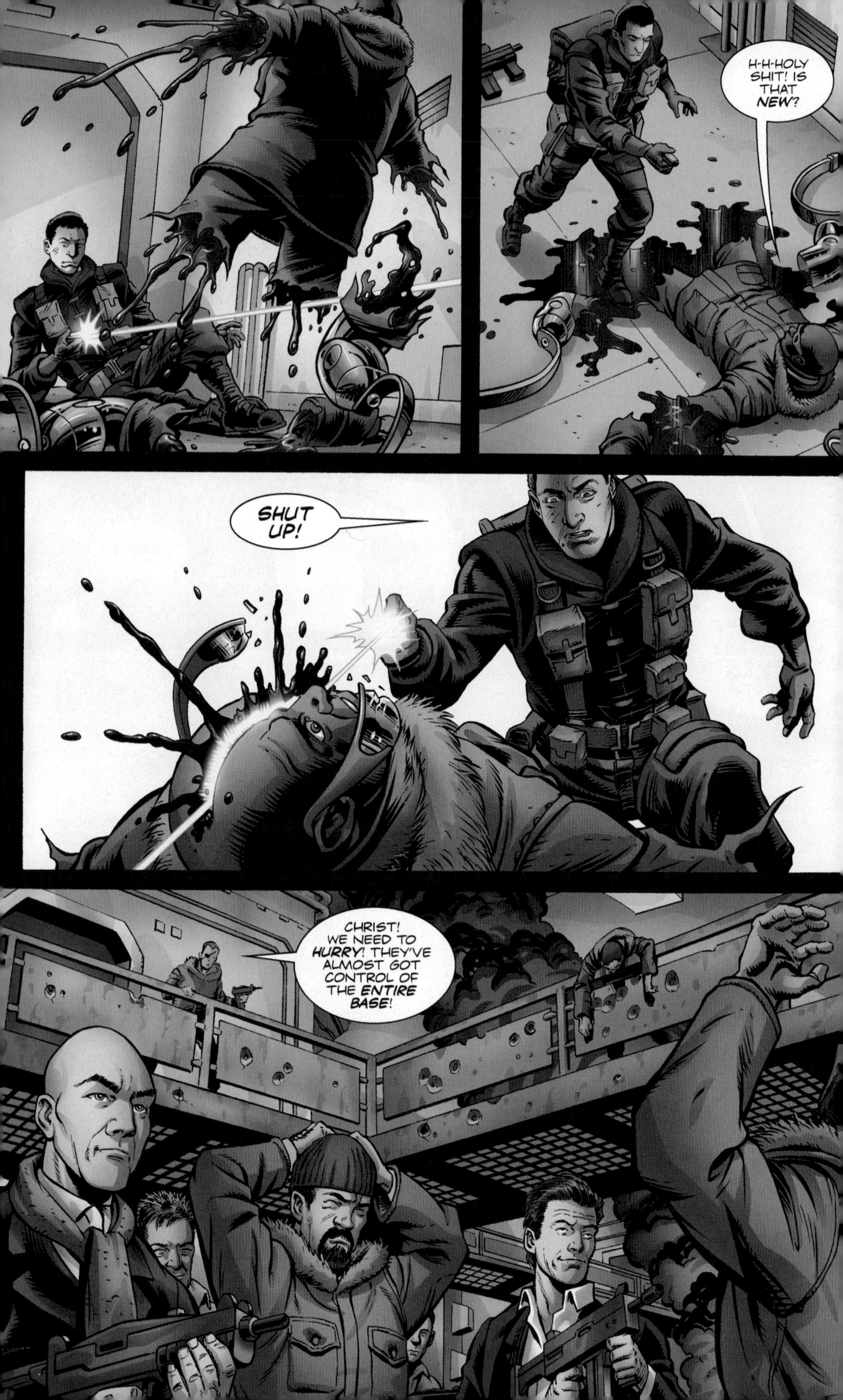
H-H-HOLY SHIT! IS THAT NEW?
SHUT UP!
CHRIST! WE NEED TO HURRY! THEY'VE ALMOST GOT CONTROL OF THE ENTIRE BASE!

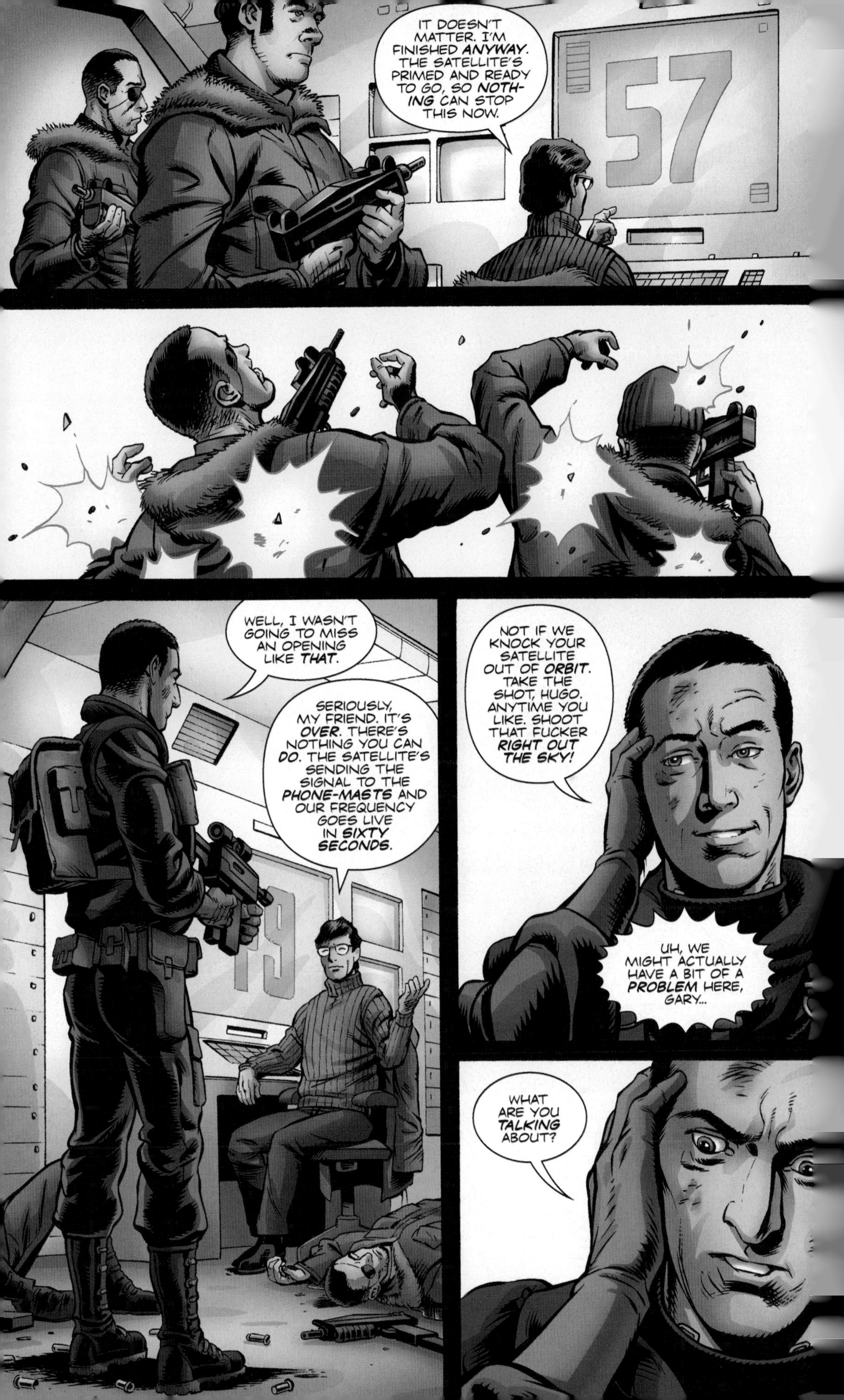
IT DOESN'T MATTER. I'M FINISHED ANYWAY. THE SATELLITE'S PRIMED AND READY TO GO, SO NOTHING CAN STOP THIS NOW.
WELL, I WASN'T GOING TO MISS AN OPENING LIKE THAT.
SERIOUSLY, MY FRIEND. IT'S OVER. THERE'S NOTHING YOU CAN DO. THE SATELLITE'S SENDING THE SIGNAL TO THE PHONE-MASTS AND OUR FREQUENCY GOES LIVE IN SIXTY SECONDS.
NOT IF WE KNOCK YOUR SATELLITE OUT OF ORBIT. TAKE THE SHOT, HUGO. ANYTIME YOU LIKE. SHOOT THAT FUCKER RIGHT OUT THE SKY!
UH, WE MIGHT ACTUALLY HAVE A BIT OF A PROBLEM HERE, GARY...
WHAT ARE YOU TALKING ABOUT?

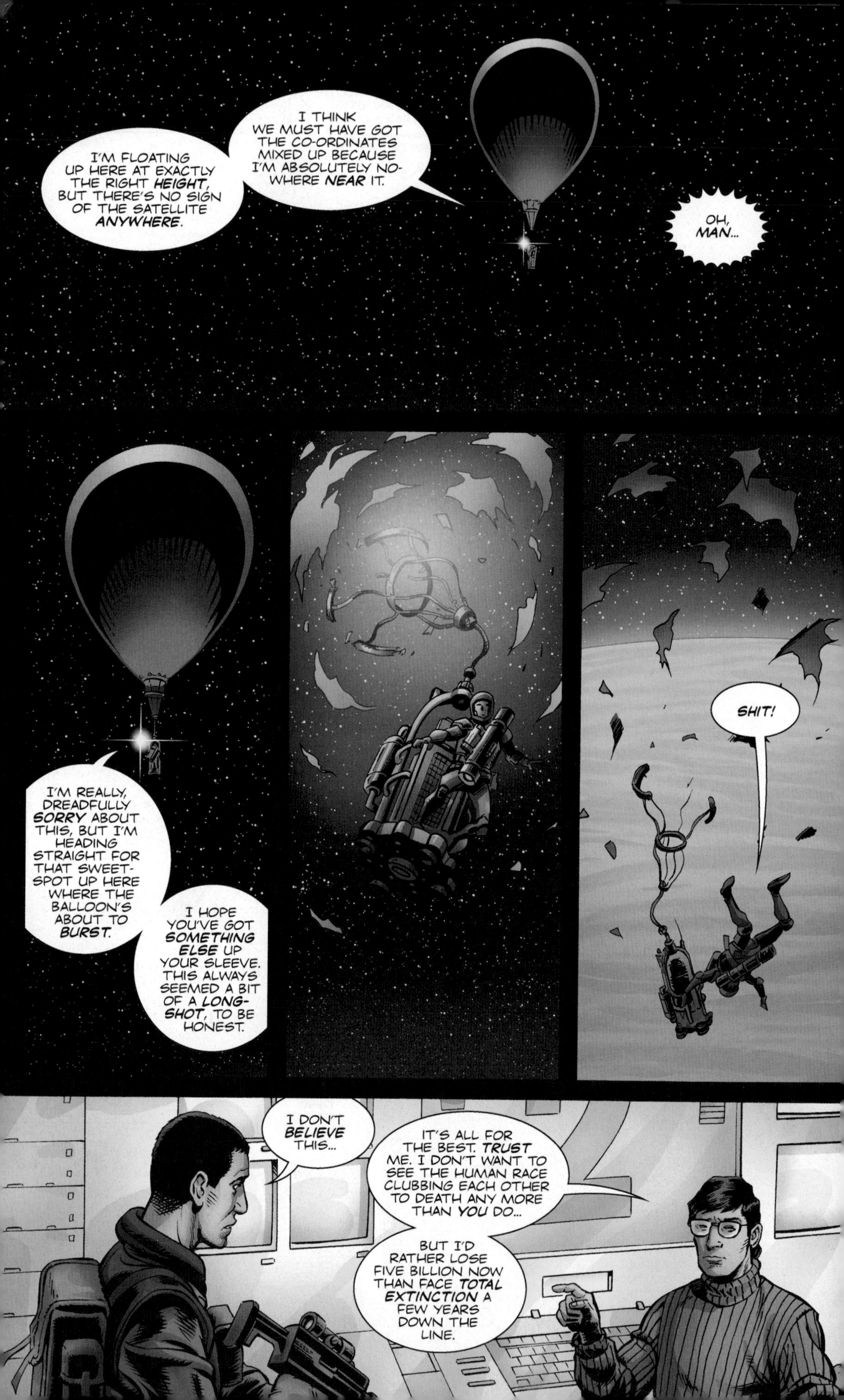
I'M FLOATING UP HERE AT EXACTLY THE RIGHT HEIGHT, BUT THERE'S NO SIGN OF THE SATELLITE ANYWHERE.
I THINK WE MUST HAVE GOT THE CO-ORDINATES MIXED UP BECAUSE I'M ABSOLUTELY NO-WHERE NEAR IT.
OH, MAN...
I'M REALLY, DREADFULLY SORRY ABOUT THIS, BUT I'M HEADING STRAIGHT FOR THAT SWEET-SPOT UP HERE WHERE THE BALLOON'S ABOUT TO BURST.
I HOPE YOU'VE GOT SOMETHING ELSE UP YOUR SLEEVE. THIS ALWAYS SEEMED A BIT OF A LONG-SHOT, TO BE HONEST.
SHIT!
I DON'T BELIEVE THIS...
IT'S ALL FOR THE BEST. TRUST ME. I DON'T WANT TO SEE THE HUMAN RACE CLUBBING EACH OTHER TO DEATH ANY MORE THAN YOU DO...
BUT I'D RATHER LOSE FIVE BILLION NOW THAN FACE TOTAL EXTINCTION A FEW YEARS DOWN THE LINE.

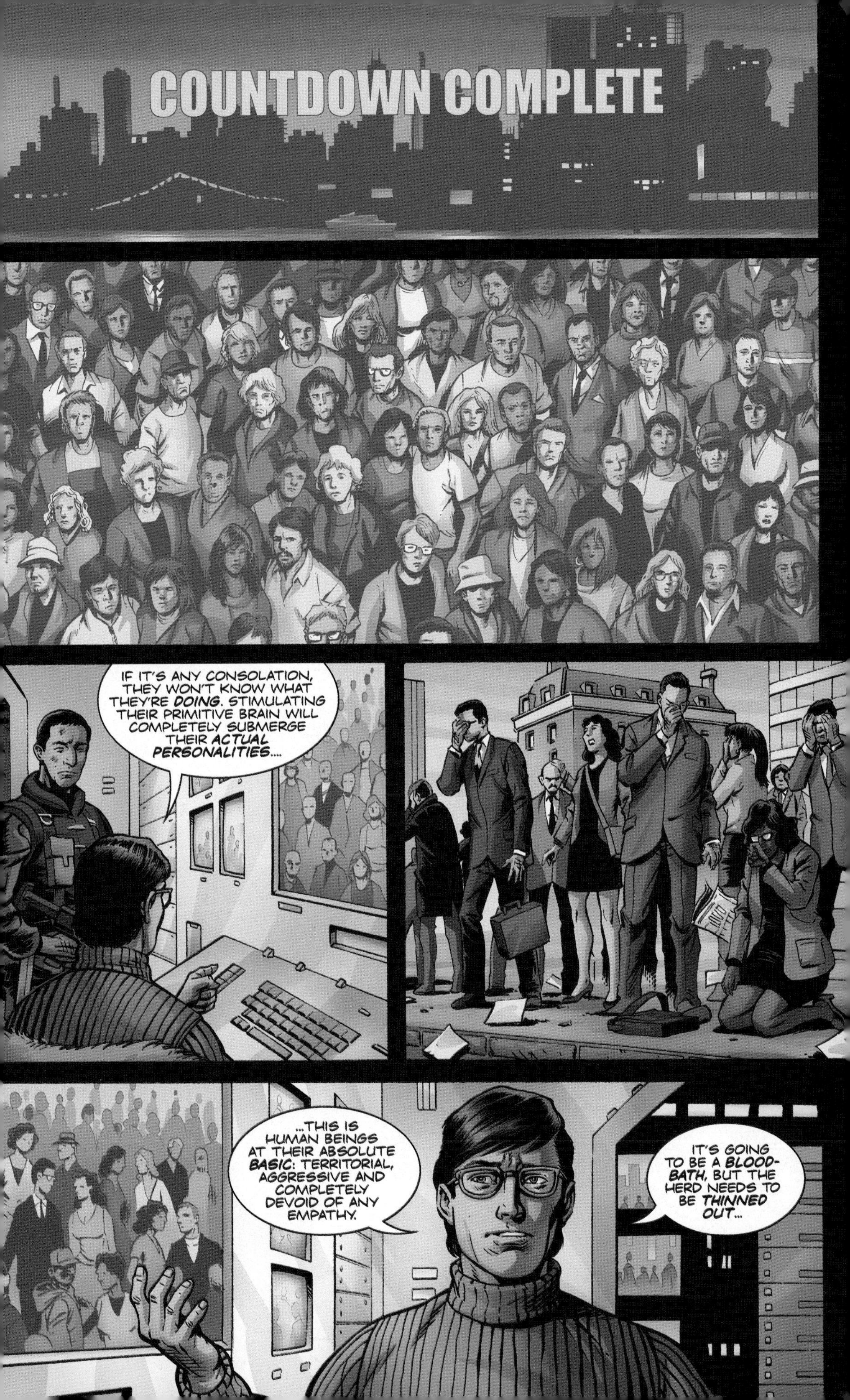
COUNTDOWN COMPLETE
IF IT'S ANY CONSOLATION, THEY WON'T KNOW WHAT THEY'RE DOING. STIMULATING THEIR PRIMITIVE BRAIN WILL COMPLETELY SUBMERGE THEIR ACTUAL PERSONALITIES....
...THIS IS HUMAN BEINGS AT THEIR ABSOLUTE BASIC: TERRITORIAL, AGGRESSIVE AND COMPLETELY DEVOID OF ANY EMPATHY.
IT'S GOING TO BE A BLOOD-BATH, BUT THE HERD NEEDS TO BE THINNED OUT...

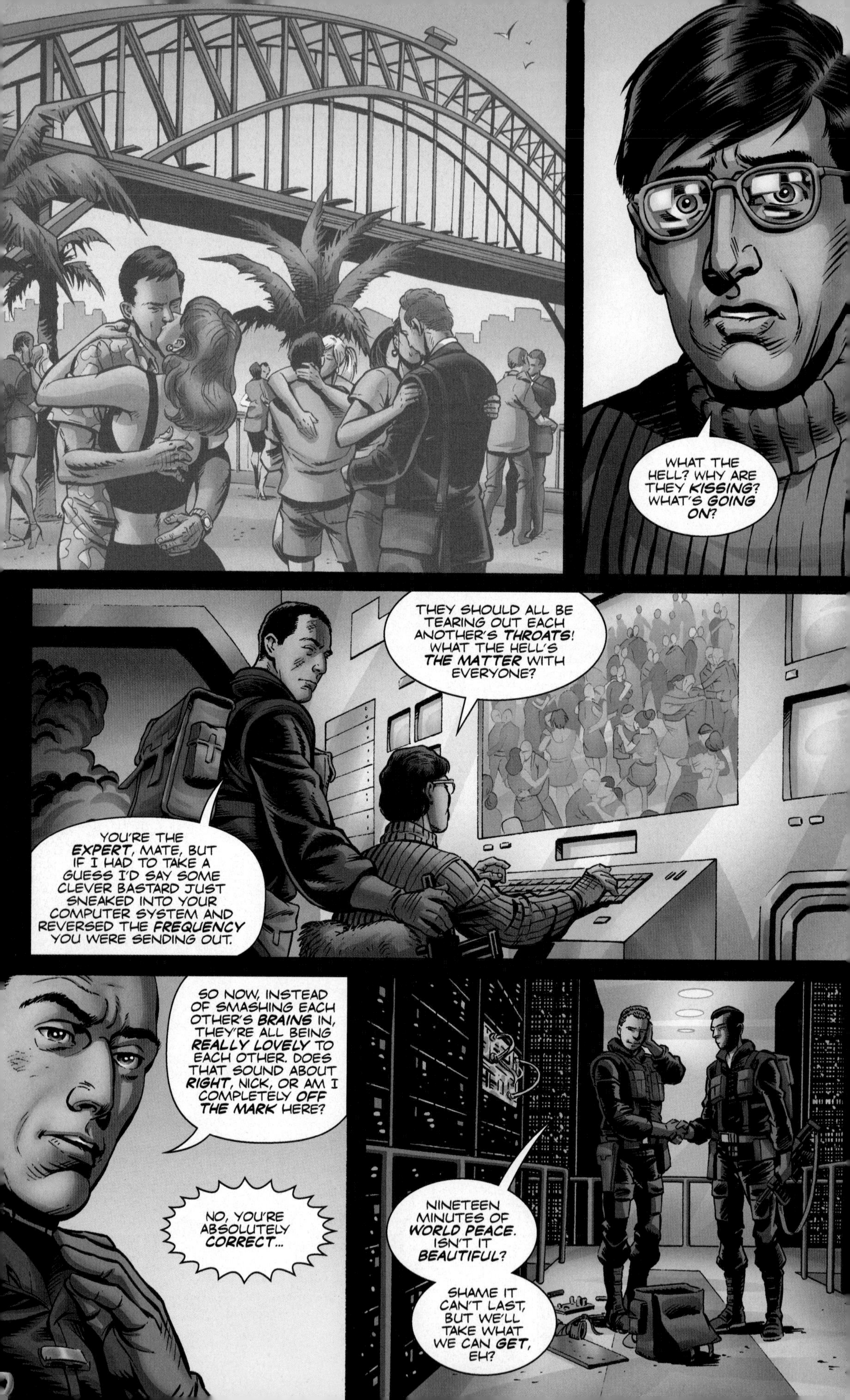
WHAT THE HELL? WHY ARE THEY KISSING? WHAT'S GOING ON?
THEY SHOULD ALL BE TEARING OUT EACH ANOTHER'S THROATS! WHAT THE HELL'S THE MATTER WITH EVERYONE?
YOU'RE THE EXPERT, MATE, BUT IF I HAD TO TAKE A GUESS I'D SAY SOME CLEVER BASTARD JUST SNEAKED INTO YOUR COMPUTER SYSTEM AND REVERSED THE FREQUENCY YOU WERE SENDING OUT.
SO NOW, INSTEAD OF SMASHING EACH OTHER'S BRAINS IN, THEY'RE ALL BEING REALLY LOVELY TO EACH OTHER. DOES THAT SOUND ABOUT RIGHT, NICK, OR AM I COMPLETELY OFF THE MARK HERE?
NO, YOU'RE ABSOLUTELY CORRECT...
NINETEEN MINUTES OF WORLD PEACE. ISN'T IT BEAUTIFUL?
SHAME IT CAN'T LAST, BUT WE'LL TAKE WHAT WE CAN GET, EH?

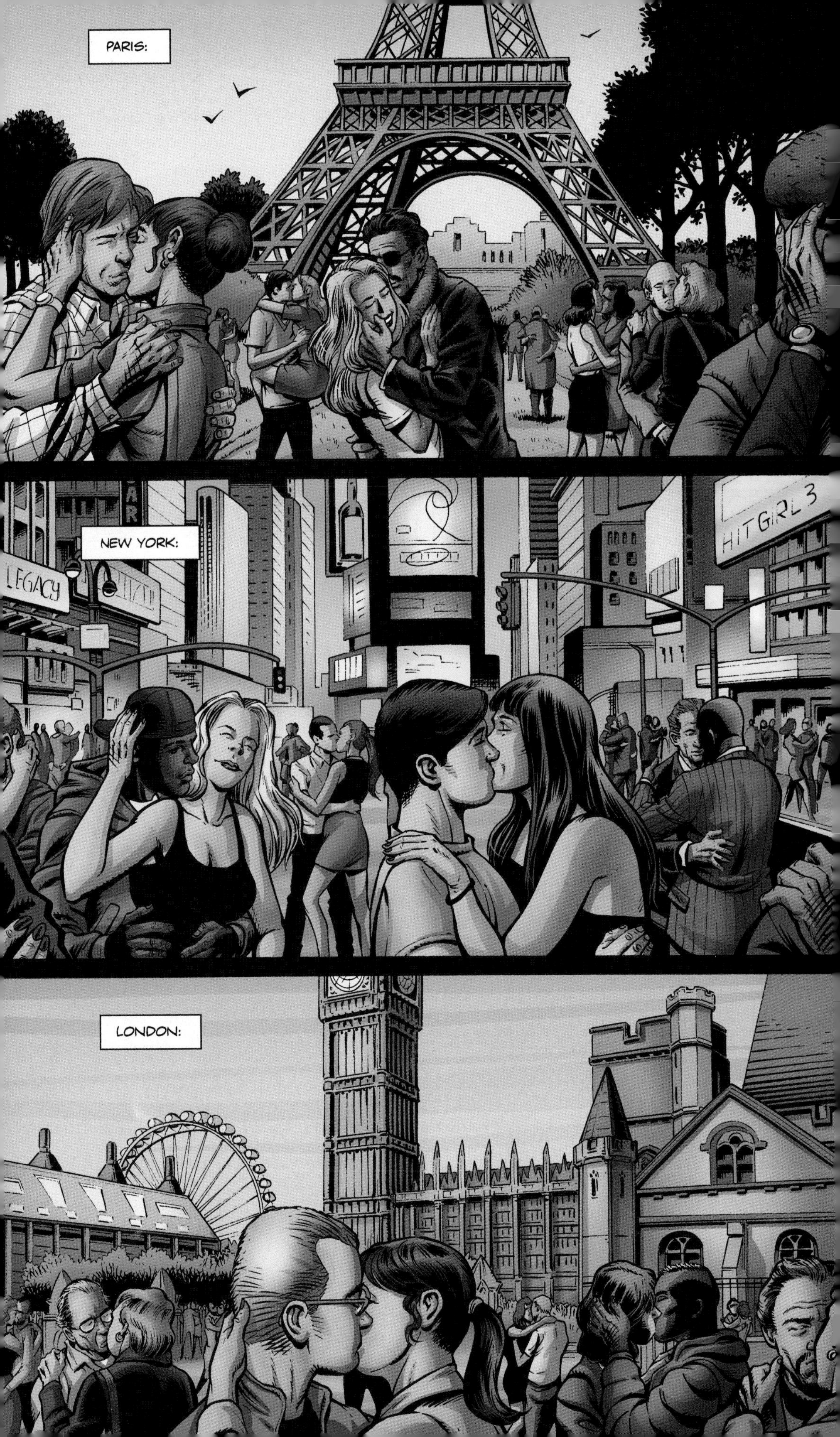
PARIS:
NEW YORK:
LEGACY
HITGIRL 3
LONDON:

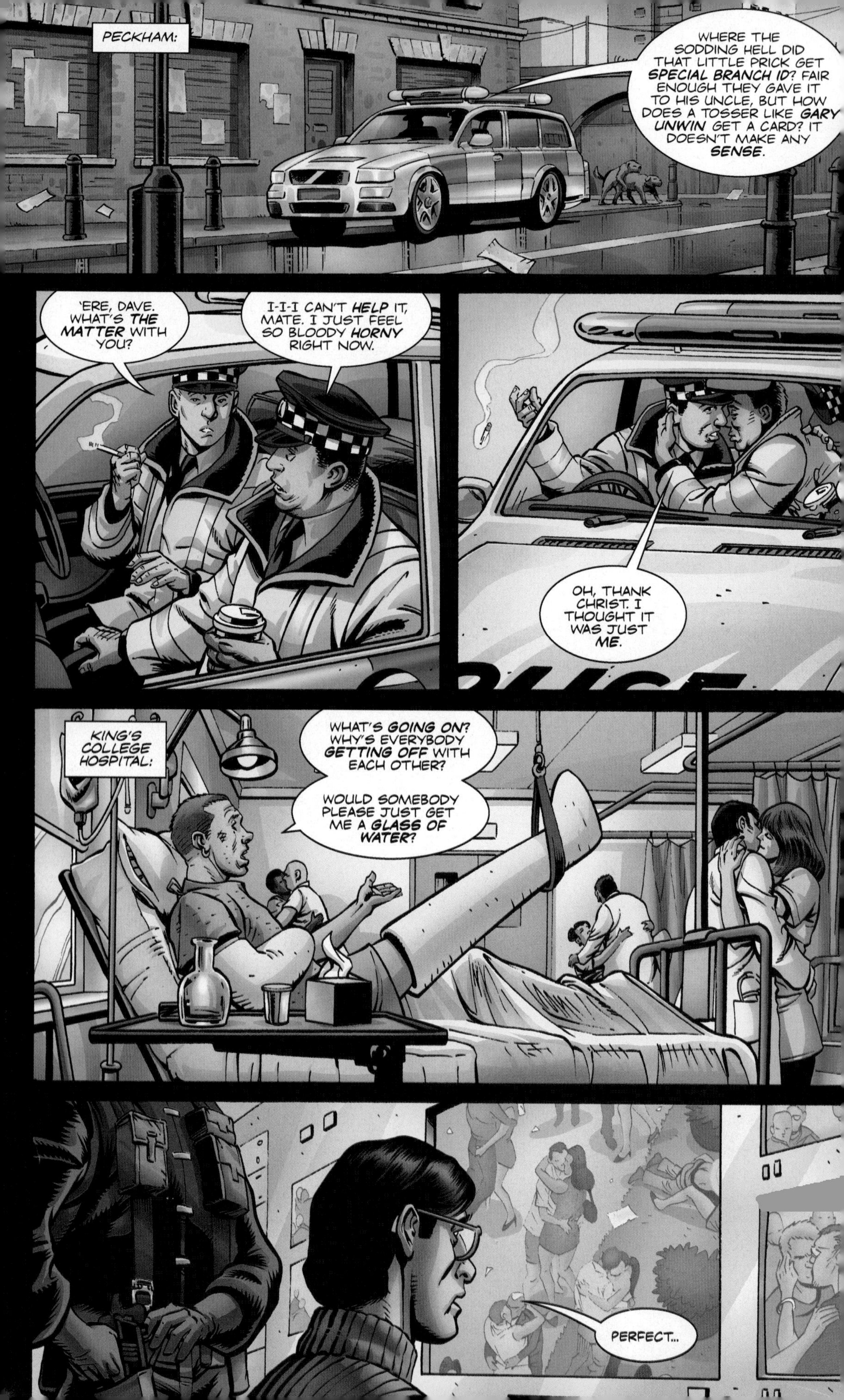
PECKHAM:
WHERE THE SODDING HELL DID THAT LITTLE PRICK GET SPECIAL BRANCH ID? FAIR ENOUGH THEY GAVE IT TO HIS UNCLE, BUT HOW DOES A TOSSER LIKE GARY UNWIN GET A CARD? IT DOESN'T MAKE ANY SENSE.
'ERE, DAVE. WHAT'S THE MATTER WITH YOU?
I-I-I CAN'T HELP IT, MATE. I JUST FEEL SO BLOODY HORNY RIGHT NOW.
OH, THANK CHRIST. I THOUGHT IT WAS JUST ME.
KING'S COLLEGE HOSPITAL:
WHAT'S GOING ON? WHY'S EVERYBODY GETTING OFF WITH EACH OTHER?
WOULD SOMEBODY PLEASE JUST GET ME A GLASS OF WATER?
PERFECT...

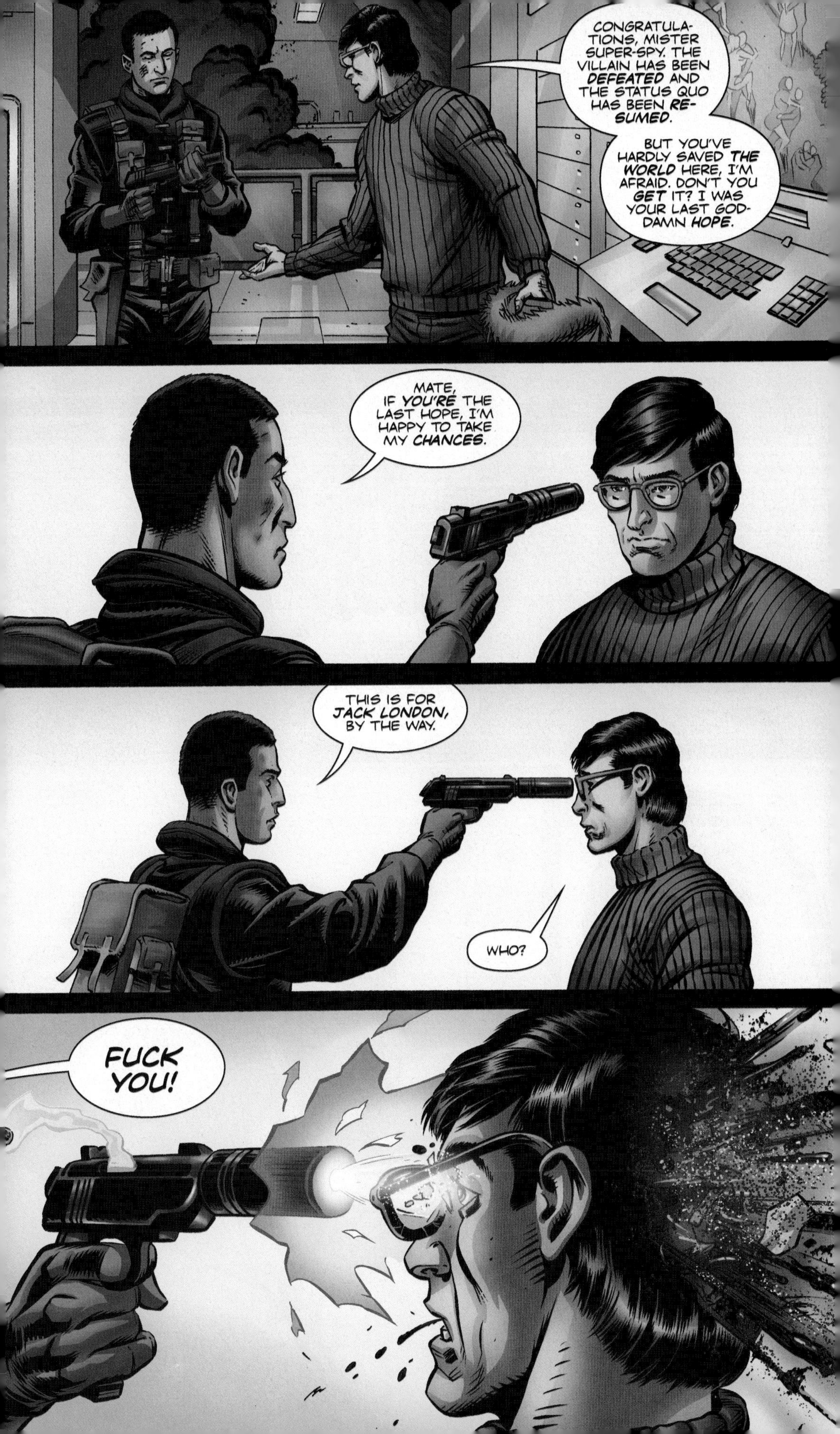
CONGRATULATIONS, MISTER SUPER-SPY. THE VILLAIN HAS BEEN DEFEATED AND THE STATUS QUO HAS BEEN RESUMED.
BUT YOU'VE HARDLY SAVED THE WORLD HERE, I'M AFRAID. DON'T YOU GET IT? I WAS YOUR LAST GOD-DAMN HOPE.
MATE, IF YOU'RE THE LAST HOPE, I'M HAPPY TO TAKE MY CHANCES.
THIS IS FOR JACK LONDON, BY THE WAY.
WHO?
FUCK YOU!

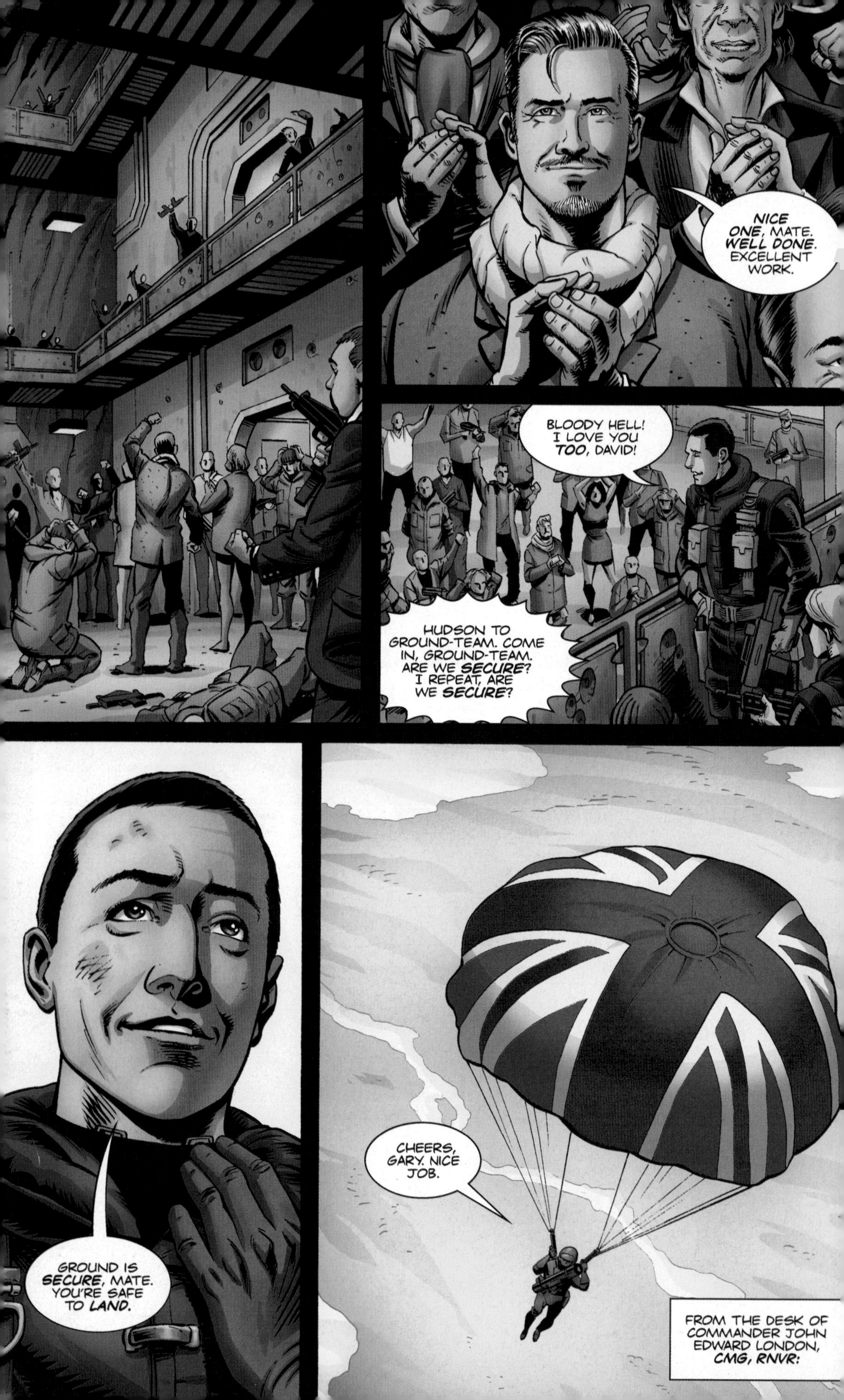
NICE ONE, MATE. WELL DONE. EXCELLENT WORK.
BLOODY HELL! I LOVE YOU TOO, DAVID!
HUDSON TO GROUND-TEAM. COME IN, GROUND-TEAM. ARE WE SECURE? I REPEAT, ARE WE SECURE?
GROUND IS SECURE, MATE. YOU'RE SAFE TO LAND.
CHEERS, GARY. NICE JOB.
FROM THE DESK OF COMMANDER JOHN EDWARD LONDON, CMG, RNVR:

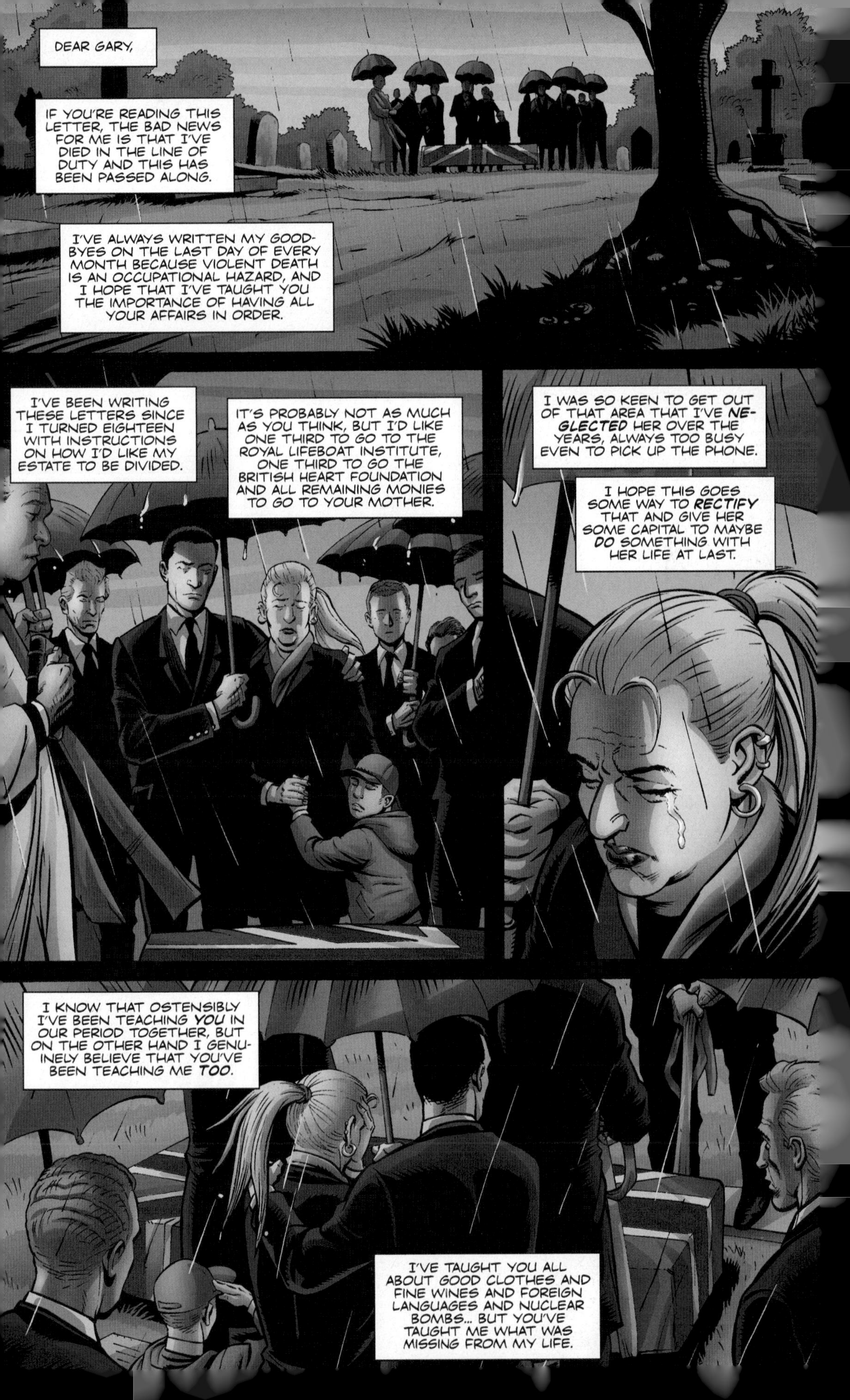
DEAR GARY,
IF YOU'RE READING THIS LETTER, THE BAD NEWS FOR ME IS THAT I'VE DIED IN THE LINE OF DUTY AND THIS HAS BEEN PASSED ALONG.
I'VE ALWAYS WRITTEN MY GOOD-BYES ON THE LAST DAY OF EVERY MONTH BECAUSE VIOLENT DEATH IS AN OCCUPATIONAL HAZARD, AND I HOPE THAT I'VE TAUGHT YOU THE IMPORTANCE OF HAVING ALL YOUR AFFAIRS IN ORDER.
I'VE BEEN WRITING THESE LETTERS SINCE I TURNED EIGHTEEN WITH INSTRUCTIONS ON HOW I'D LIKE MY ESTATE TO BE DIVIDED.
IT'S PROBABLY NOT AS MUCH AS YOU THINK, BUT I'D LIKE ONE THIRD TO GO TO THE ROYAL LIFEBOAT INSTITUTE, ONE THIRD TO GO THE BRITISH HEART FOUNDATION AND ALL REMAINING MONIES TO GO TO YOUR MOTHER.
I WAS SO KEEN TO GET OUT OF THAT AREA THAT I'VE *NEGLECTED* HER OVER THE YEARS, ALWAYS TOO BUSY EVEN TO PICK UP THE PHONE.
I HOPE THIS GOES SOME WAY TO ***RECTIFY*** THAT AND GIVE HER SOME CAPITAL TO MAYBE ***DO*** SOMETHING WITH HER LIFE AT LAST.
I KNOW THAT OSTENSIBLY I'VE BEEN TEACHING ***YOU*** IN OUR PERIOD TOGETHER, BUT ON THE OTHER HAND I GENUINELY BELIEVE THAT YOU'VE BEEN TEACHING ME ***TOO***.
I'VE TAUGHT YOU ALL ABOUT GOOD CLOTHES AND FINE WINES AND FOREIGN LANGUAGES AND NUCLEAR BOMBS... BUT YOU'VE TAUGHT ME WHAT WAS MISSING FROM MY LIFE.

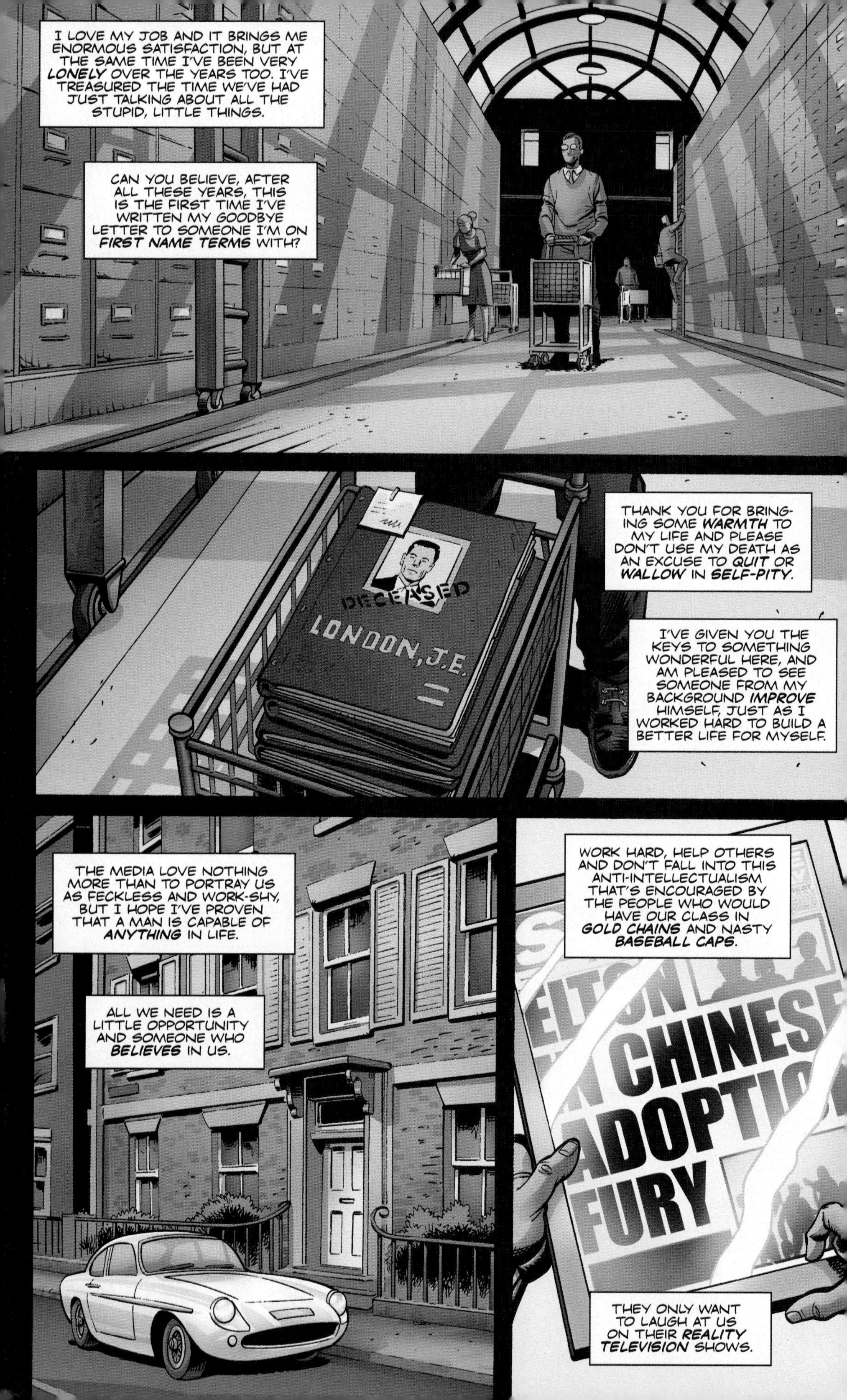
I LOVE MY JOB AND IT BRINGS ME ENORMOUS SATISFACTION, BUT AT THE SAME TIME I'VE BEEN VERY LONELY OVER THE YEARS TOO. I'VE TREASURED THE TIME WE'VE HAD JUST TALKING ABOUT ALL THE STUPID, LITTLE THINGS.
CAN YOU BELIEVE, AFTER ALL THESE YEARS, THIS IS THE FIRST TIME I'VE WRITTEN MY GOODBYE LETTER TO SOMEONE I'M ON FIRST NAME TERMS WITH?
THANK YOU FOR BRINGING SOME WARMTH TO MY LIFE AND PLEASE DON'T USE MY DEATH AS AN EXCUSE TO QUIT OR WALLOW IN SELF-PITY.
LONDON, J.E.
I'VE GIVEN YOU THE KEYS TO SOMETHING WONDERFUL HERE, AND AM PLEASED TO SEE SOMEONE FROM MY BACKGROUND IMPROVE HIMSELF, JUST AS I WORKED HARD TO BUILD A BETTER LIFE FOR MYSELF.
THE MEDIA LOVE NOTHING MORE THAN TO PORTRAY US AS FECKLESS AND WORK-SHY, BUT I HOPE I'VE PROVEN THAT A MAN IS CAPABLE OF ANYTHING IN LIFE.
ALL WE NEED IS A LITTLE OPPORTUNITY AND SOMEONE WHO BELIEVES IN US.
WORK HARD, HELP OTHERS AND DON'T FALL INTO THIS ANTI-INTELLECTUALISM THAT'S ENCOURAGED BY THE PEOPLE WHO WOULD HAVE OUR CLASS IN GOLD CHAINS AND NASTY BASEBALL CAPS.
FURY
THEY ONLY WANT TO LAUGH AT US ON THEIR REALITY TELEVISION SHOWS.

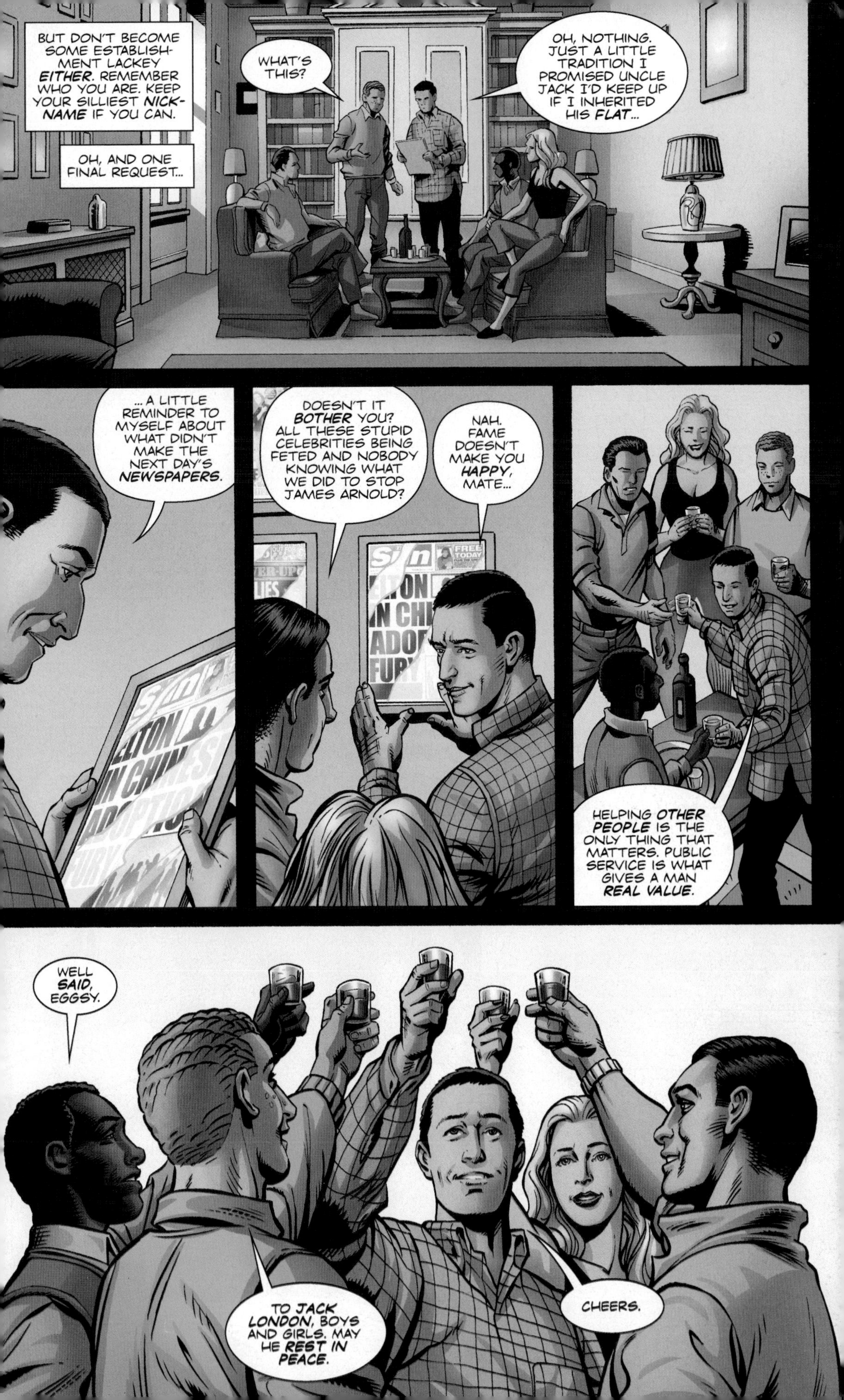
BUT DON'T BECOME SOME ESTABLISHMENT LACKEY EITHER. REMEMBER WHO YOU ARE. KEEP YOUR SILLIEST NICKNAME IF YOU CAN.
OH, AND ONE FINAL REQUEST...
WHAT'S THIS?
OH, NOTHING. JUST A LITTLE TRADITION I PROMISED UNCLE JACK I'D KEEP UP IF I INHERITED HIS FLAT...
... A LITTLE REMINDER TO MYSELF ABOUT WHAT DIDN'T MAKE THE NEXT DAY'S NEWSPAPERS.
DOESN'T IT BOTHER YOU? ALL THESE STUPID CELEBRITIES BEING FETED AND NOBODY KNOWING WHAT WE DID TO STOP JAMES ARNOLD?
NAH. FAME DOESN'T MAKE YOU HAPPY, MATE...
HELPING OTHER PEOPLE IS THE ONLY THING THAT MATTERS. PUBLIC SERVICE IS WHAT GIVES A MAN REAL VALUE.
WELL SAID, EGGSY.
TO JACK LONDON, BOYS AND GIRLS. MAY HE REST IN PEACE.
CHEERS.

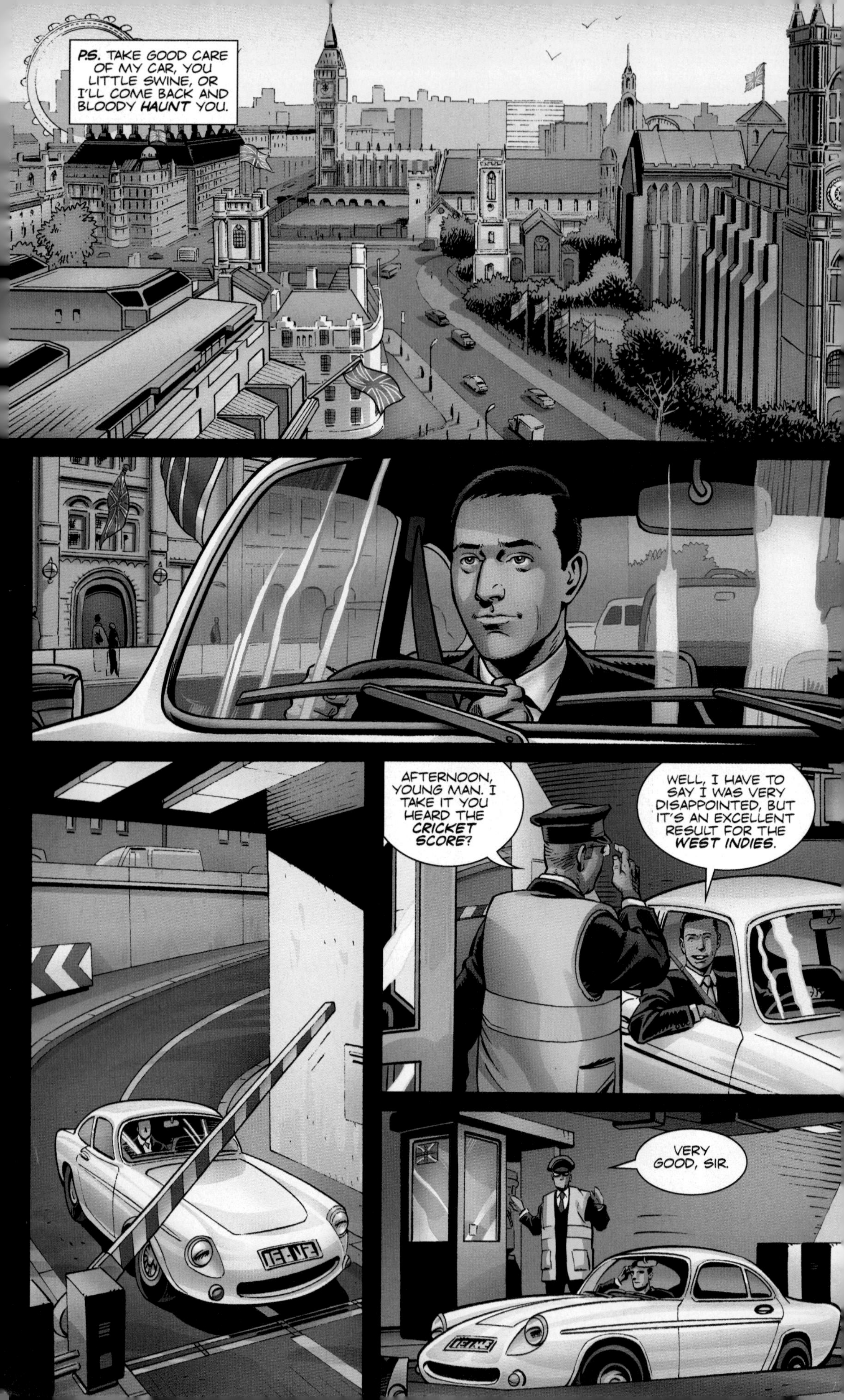
P.S. TAKE GOOD CARE OF MY CAR, YOU LITTLE SWINE, OR I'LL COME BACK AND BLOODY HAUNT YOU.
AFTERNOON, YOUNG MAN. I TAKE IT YOU HEARD THE CRICKET SCORE?
WELL, I HAVE TO SAY I WAS VERY DISAPPOINTED, BUT IT'S AN EXCELLENT RESULT FOR THE WEST INDIES.
VERY GOOD, SIR.

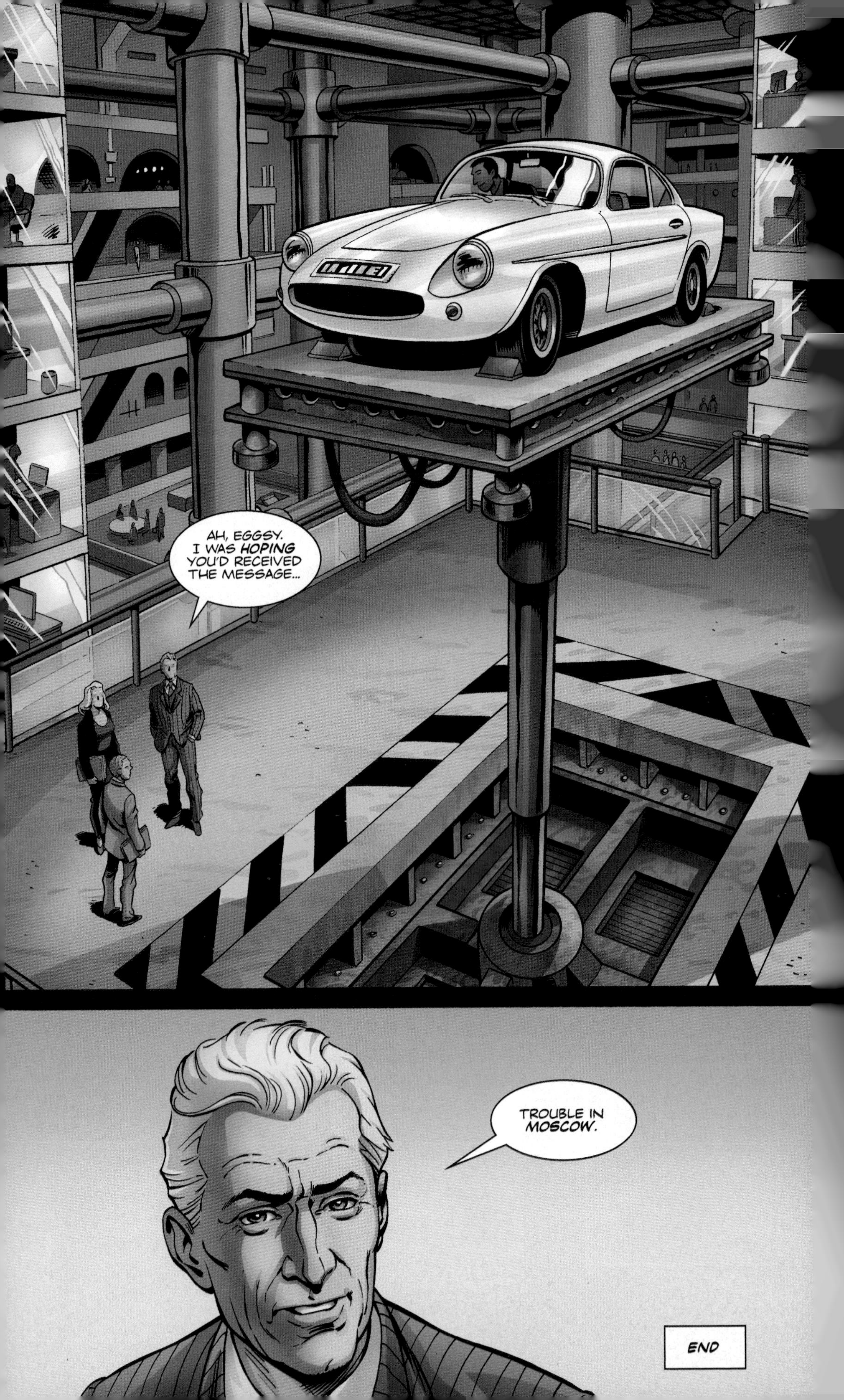
AH, EGGSY. I WAS HOPING YOU'D RECEIVED THE MESSAGE...
TROUBLE IN MOSCOW.
END

MILLAR

KICK ASS
MARK MILLAR
JOHN ROMITA JR.

HIT-GIRL
MARK MILLAR
JOHN ROMITA JR.
TOM PALMER and DEAN WHITE

KICK-ASS 2
MARK MILLAR
JOHN ROMITA JR.

MARK MILLAR DUNCAN FEGREDO
MPH
NUMBER ONE
$2.99

WANTED
MARK MILLAR • JG JONES • PAUL MOUNTS
NOW A MAJOR MOTION PICTURE FROM
UNIVERSAL PICTURES

MARK MILLAR & LEINIL YU
SUPERIOR
FROM THE WRITER OF KICK-ASS

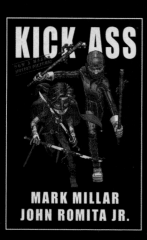

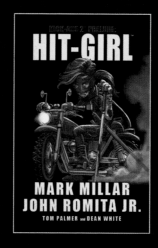

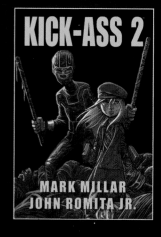

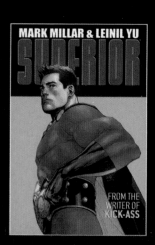

WORLD THE COLLECTION

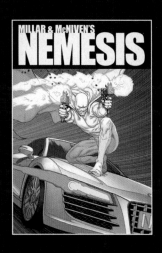

MILLAR & McNIVEN'S
NEMESIS

MARK MILLAR • GORAN PARLOV
STARLIGHT

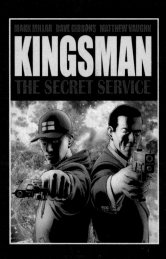

MARK MILLAR   DAVE GIBBONS   MATTHEW VAUGHN
KINGSMAN
THE SECRET SERVICE

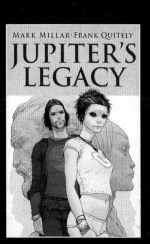

MARK MILLAR • FRANK QUITELY
JUPITER'S LEGACY

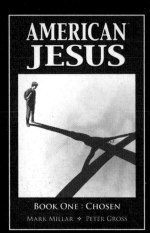

AMERICAN JESUS

BOOK ONE : CHOSEN
MARK MILLAR ✦ PETER GROSS

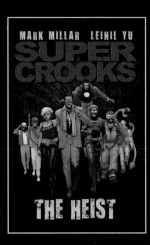

MARK MILLAR   LEINIL YU
SUPER CROOKS

THE HEIST

THE CREATORS

Mark Millar is the *New York Times* best-selling writer of *Wanted*, the *Kick-Ass* series, *The Secret Service*, *Jupiter's Legacy*, *Nemesis*, *Superior*, *Super Crooks*, *American Jesus*, *MPH*, and *Starlight*. *Wanted*, *Kick-Ass*, *Kick-Ass 2*, and *The Secret Service* (as *Kingsman: The Secret Service*) have been adapted into feature films, and *Nemesis*, *Superior*, *Starlight*, and *War Heroes* are in development at major studios. His DC Comics work includes the seminal *Superman: Red Son*, and at Marvel Comics he created *The Ultimates* — selected by *Time* magazine as the comic book of the decade — *Wolverine: Old Man Logan*, and *Civil War* — the industry's biggest-selling series in almost two decades. Mark was a producer on the past adaptations of his works and is an Executive Producer on the feature-film and television projects currently in development. He is CEO of Millarworld Productions, an advisor on motion pictures to the Scottish government, and Creative Consultant to Fox Studios.

Dave Gibbons began his career in British comics working on *2000AD* and *Dr. Who* before being recruited to America by DC Comics. His collaboration with Alan Moore, the Hugo Award-winning *Watchmen*, is the best-selling graphic novel of all time. With writer Frank Miller he created the acclaimed *Martha Washington/Give Me Liberty* series. Also a writer, his work for Marvel includes *Captain America*, *Dr. Strange,* and *The Hulk*. He is currently consulting on new storytelling technologies with a number of companies.

Matthew Vaughn produced such films as *Lock, Stock and Two Smoking Barrels* and *Snatch* in his native England before taking the director's chair for crime thriller *Layer Cake* in 2004 and fantasy epic *Stardust* in 2007. In his first collaboration with Mark Millar, Vaughn directed the film adaptation of *Kick-Ass,* before helming *X-Men: First Class* in 2011. He produced *Kick-Ass 2,* wrote and produced *X-Men: Days of Future Past,* and produced, wrote, and directed *Kingsman: The Secret Service*, the feature motion-picture adaptation of *The Secret Service*. He's a producer of the upcoming *The Fantastic Four* and *Superior*.